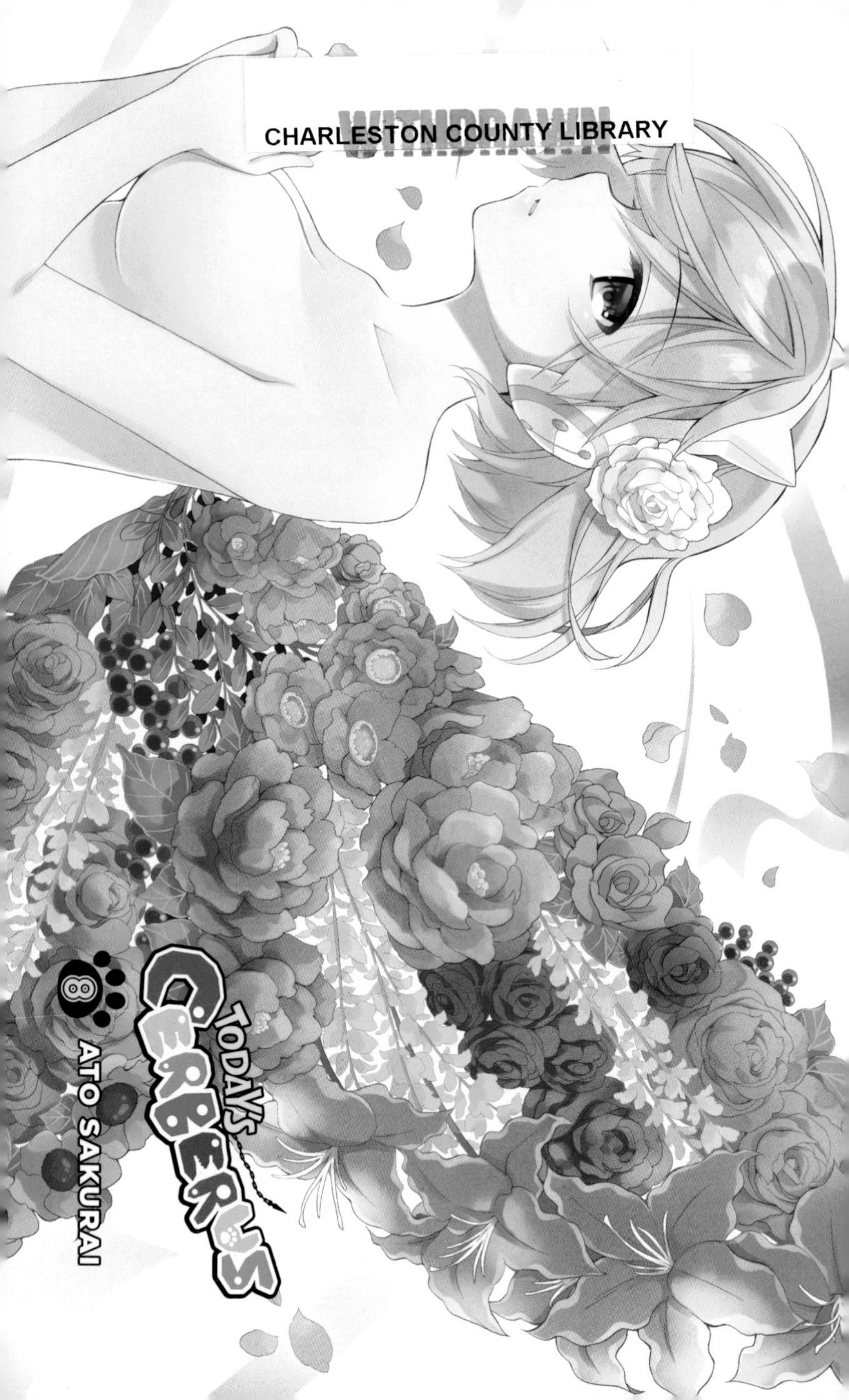

TODAY'S CERBERUS
8
ATO SAKURAI

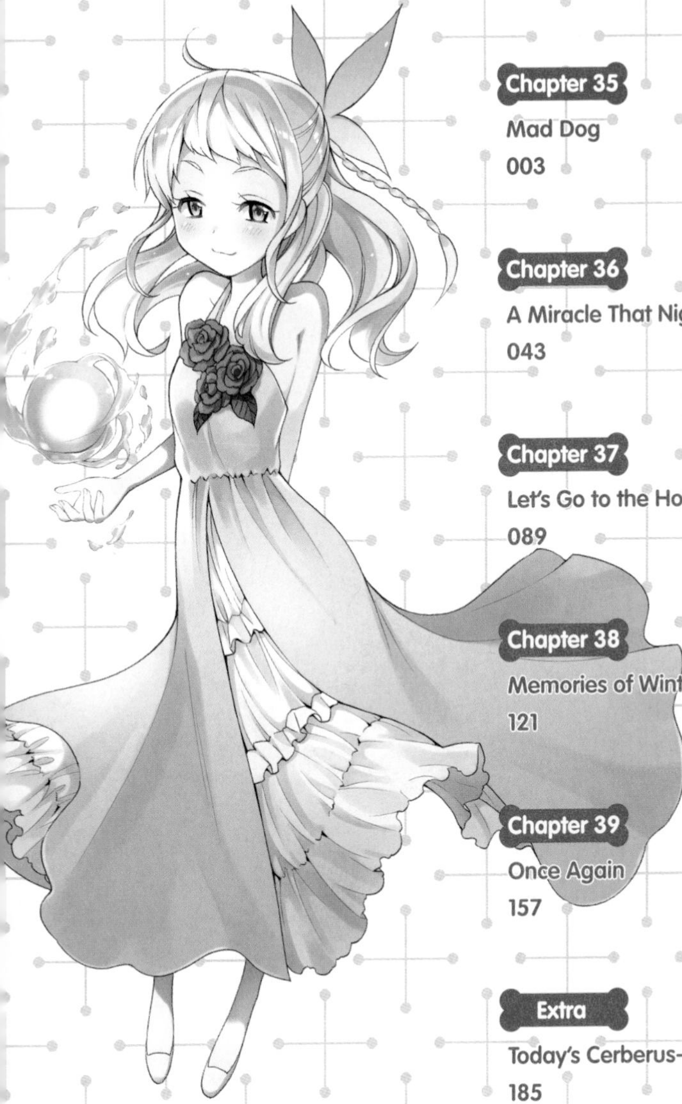

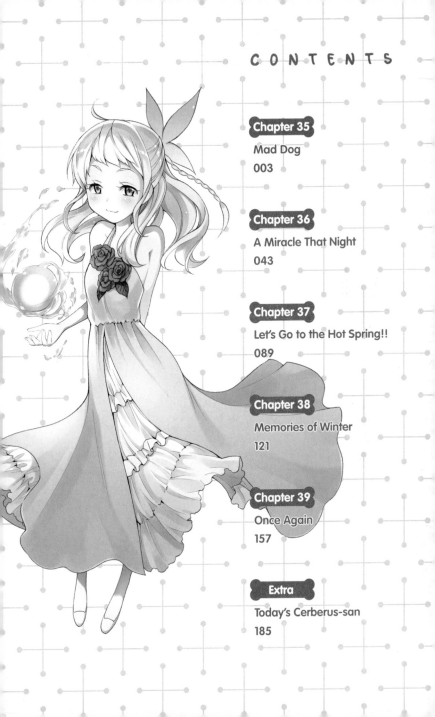

CONTENTS

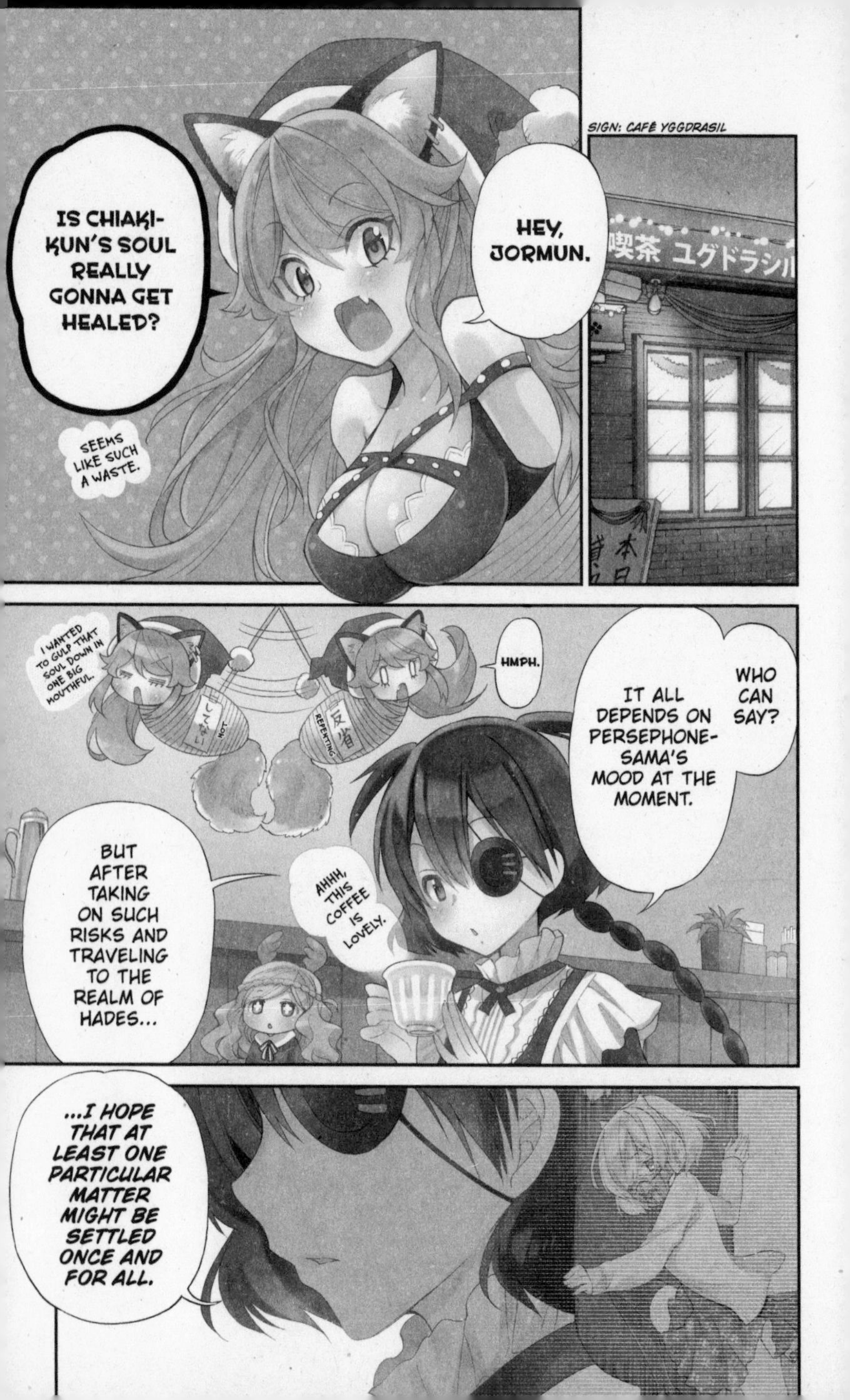
SIGN: CAFÉ YGGDRASIL
喫茶 ユグドラシル
HEY, JORMUN.
IS CHIAKI-KUN'S SOUL REALLY GONNA GET HEALED?
SEEMS LIKE SUCH A WASTE.
WHO CAN SAY?
IT ALL DEPENDS ON PERSEPHONE-SAMA'S MOOD AT THE MOMENT.
HMPH.
反省
REPENTING
してない
NOT
I WANTED TO GULP THAT SOUL DOWN IN ONE BIG MOUTHFUL.
BUT AFTER TAKING ON SUCH RISKS AND TRAVELING TO THE REALM OF HADES...
AHHH, THIS COFFEE IS LOVELY.
...I HOPE THAT AT LEAST ONE PARTICULAR MATTER MIGHT BE SETTLED ONCE AND FOR ALL.

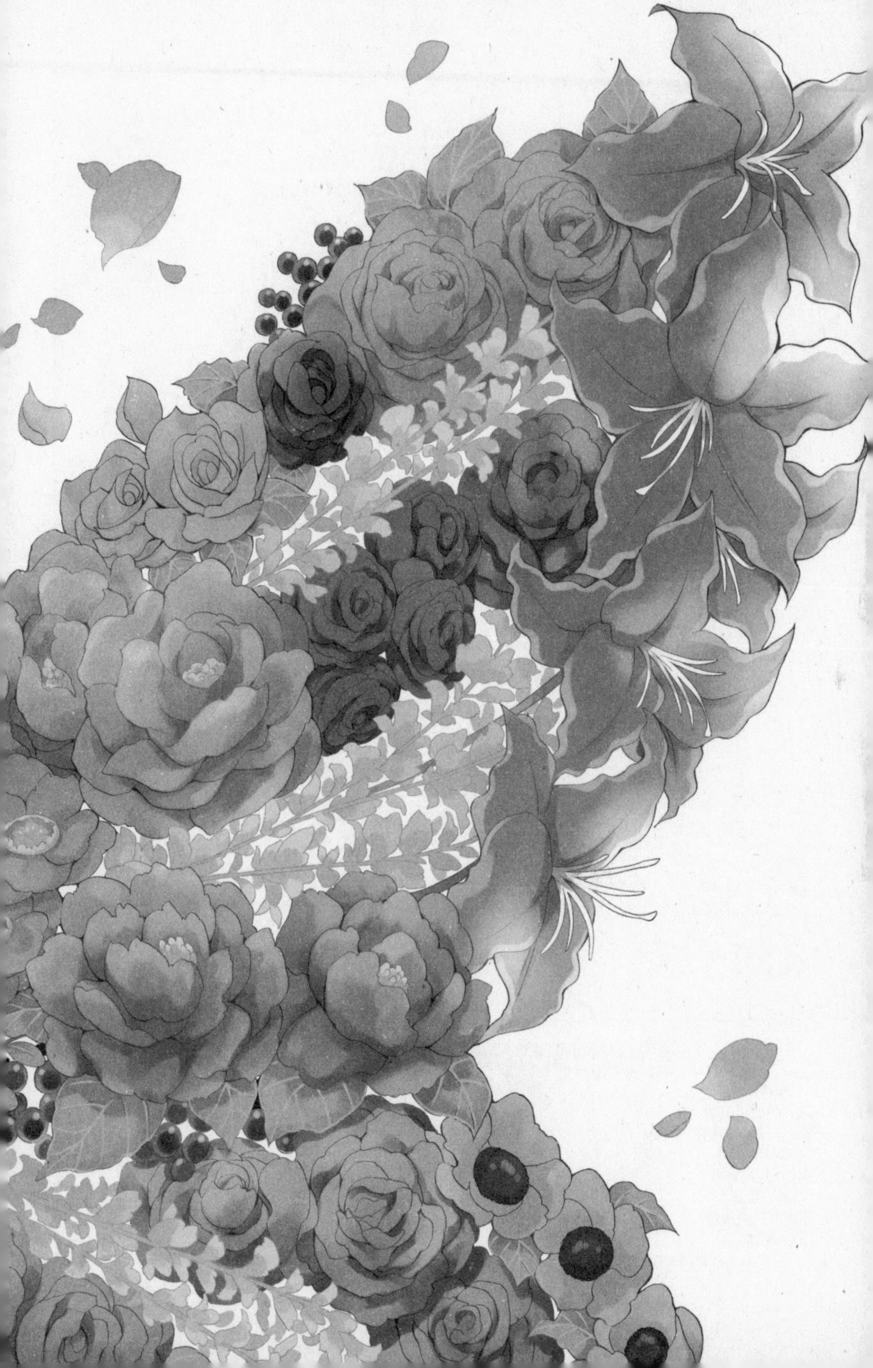

CHAPTER 35
MAD DOG

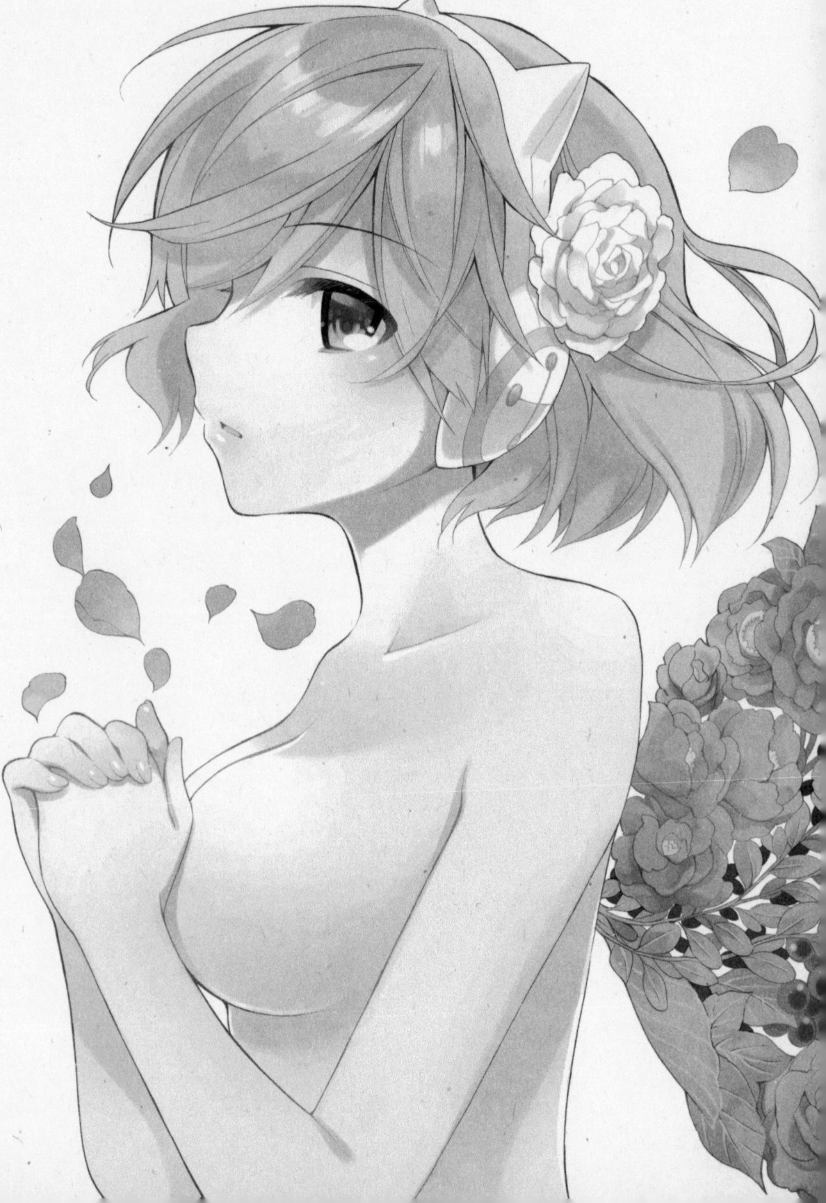

TODAY'S CERBERUS

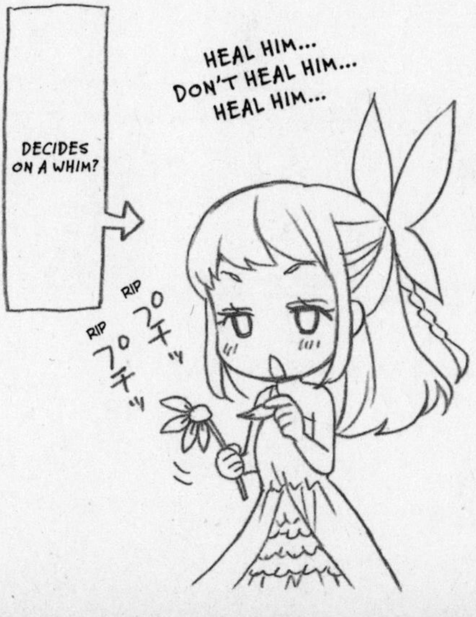
HEAL HIM...
DON'T HEAL HIM...
HEAL HIM...
DECIDES ON A WHIM?
RIP
プチッ
RIP
プチッ

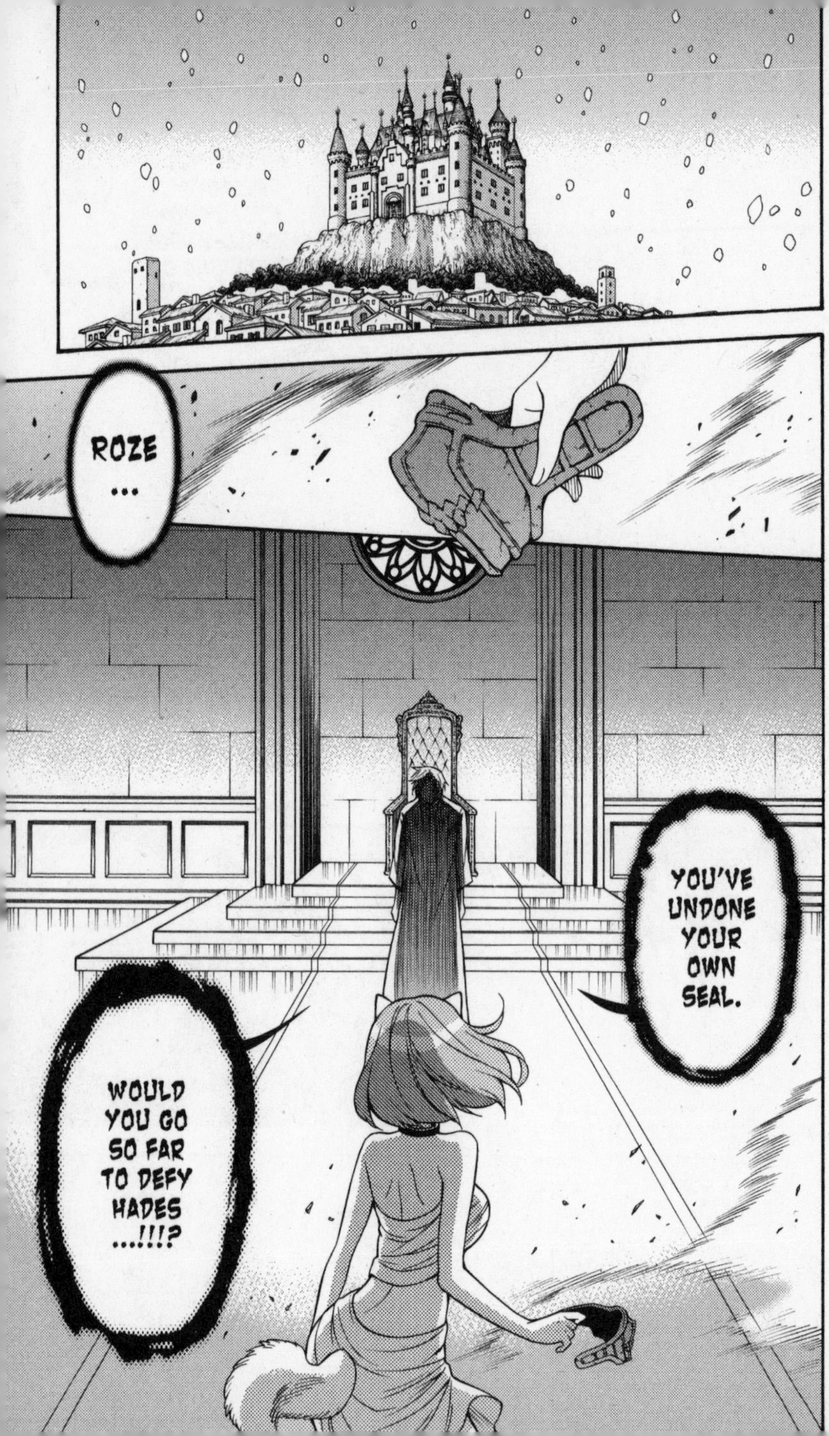
ROZE ...
YOU'VE UNDONE YOUR OWN SEAL.
WOULD YOU GO SO FAR TO DEFY HADES ...!!!?

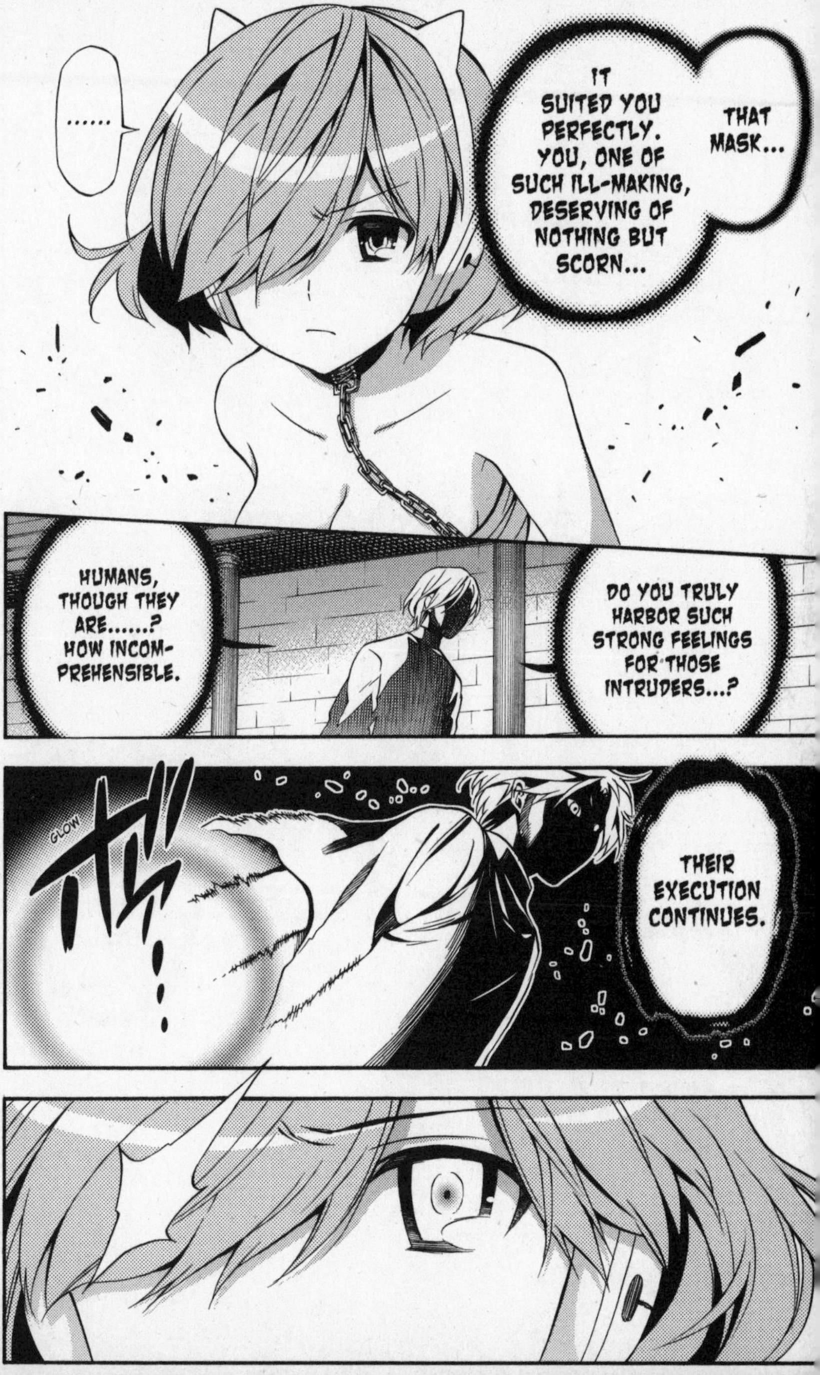
THAT MASK...
IT SUITED YOU PERFECTLY. YOU, ONE OF SUCH ILL-MAKING, DESERVING OF NOTHING BUT SCORN...
......
DO YOU TRULY HARBOR SUCH STRONG FEELINGS FOR THOSE INTRUDERS...?
HUMANS, THOUGH THEY ARE......? HOW INCOMPREHENSIBLE.
THEIR EXECUTION CONTINUES.
GLOW

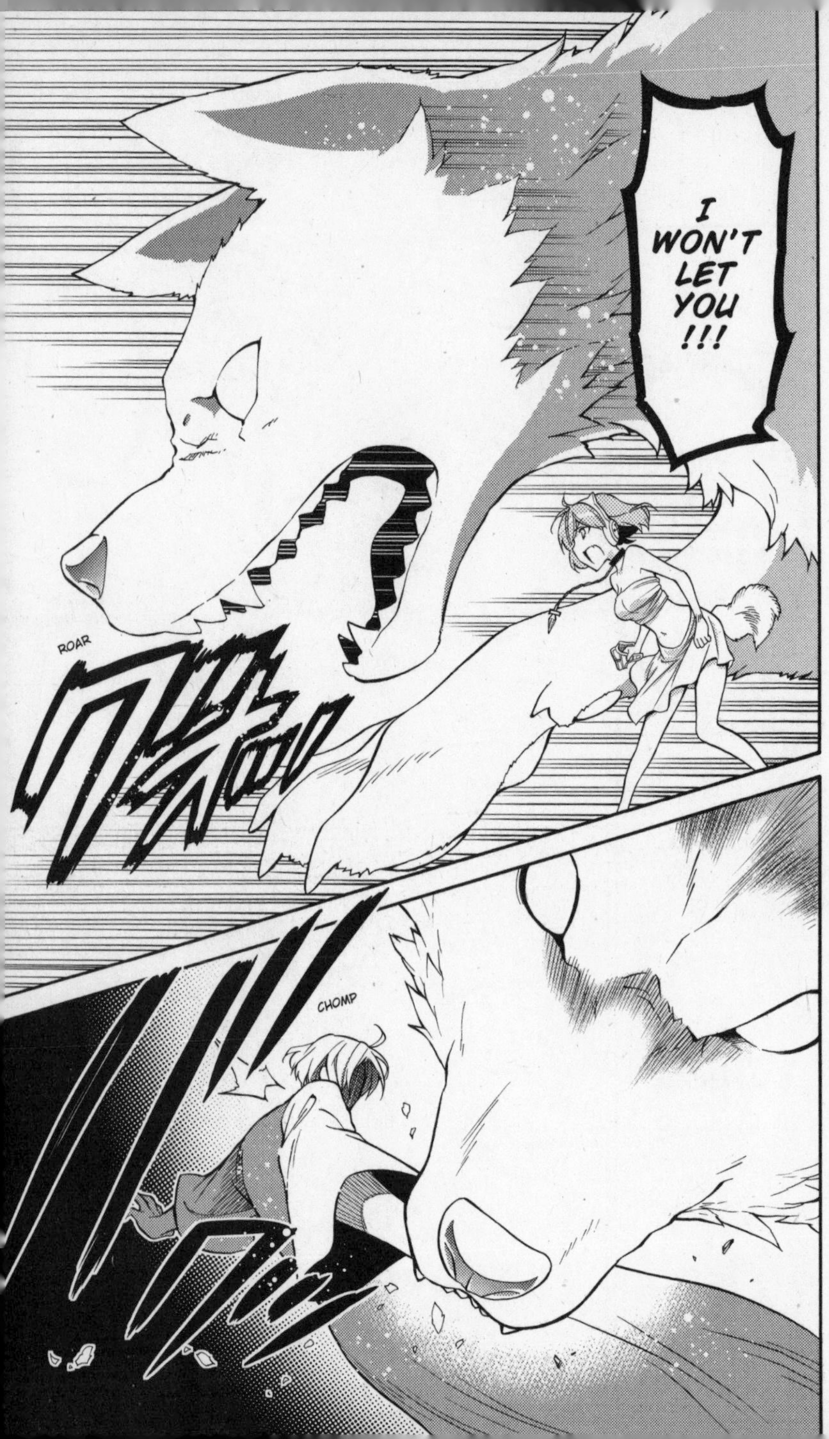
I WON'T LET YOU!!!
ROAR
CHOMP

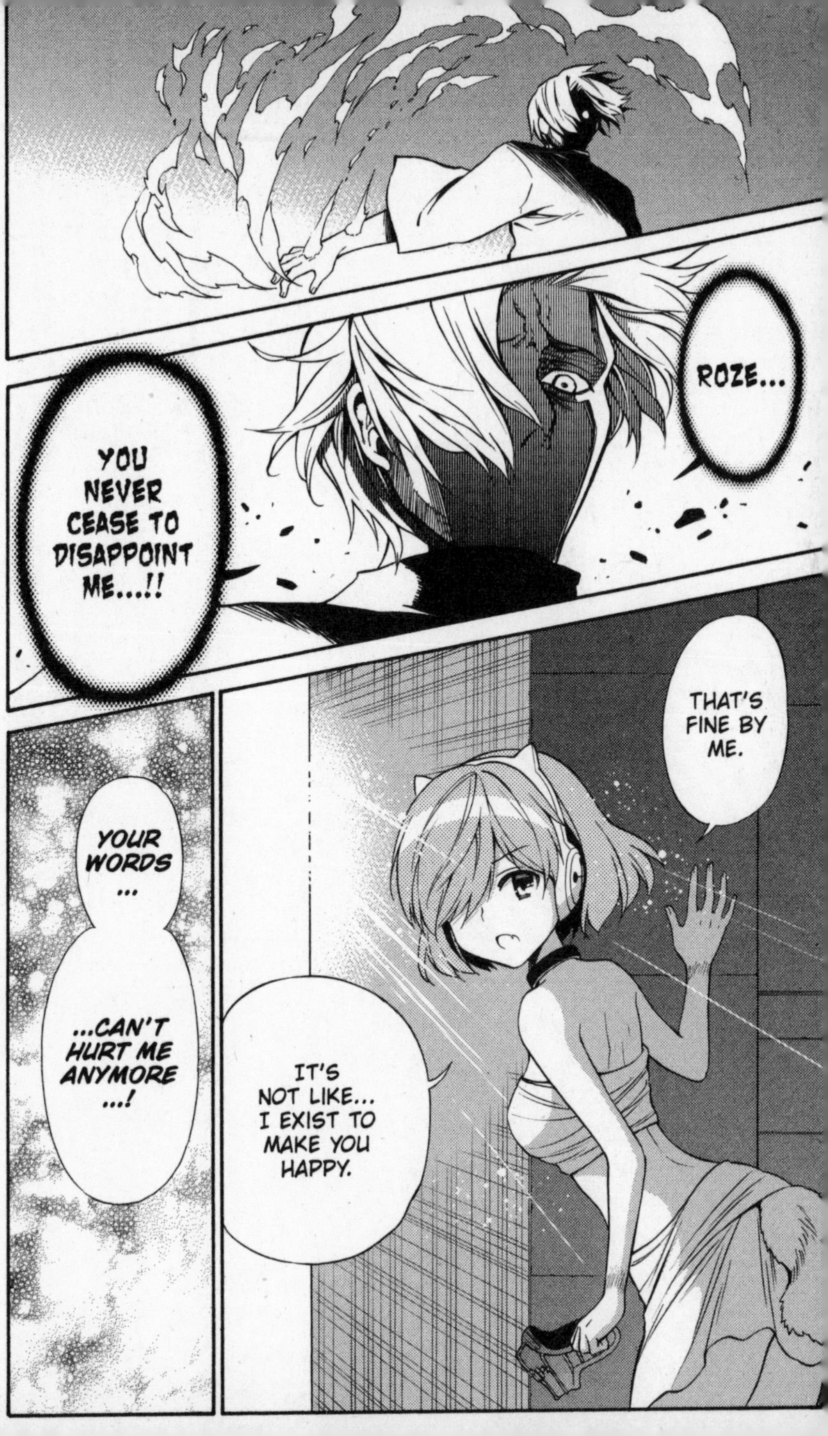
ROZE...
YOU NEVER CEASE TO DISAPPOINT ME...!!
THAT'S FINE BY ME.
IT'S NOT LIKE... I EXIST TO MAKE YOU HAPPY.
YOUR WORDS...
...CAN'T HURT ME ANYMORE...!

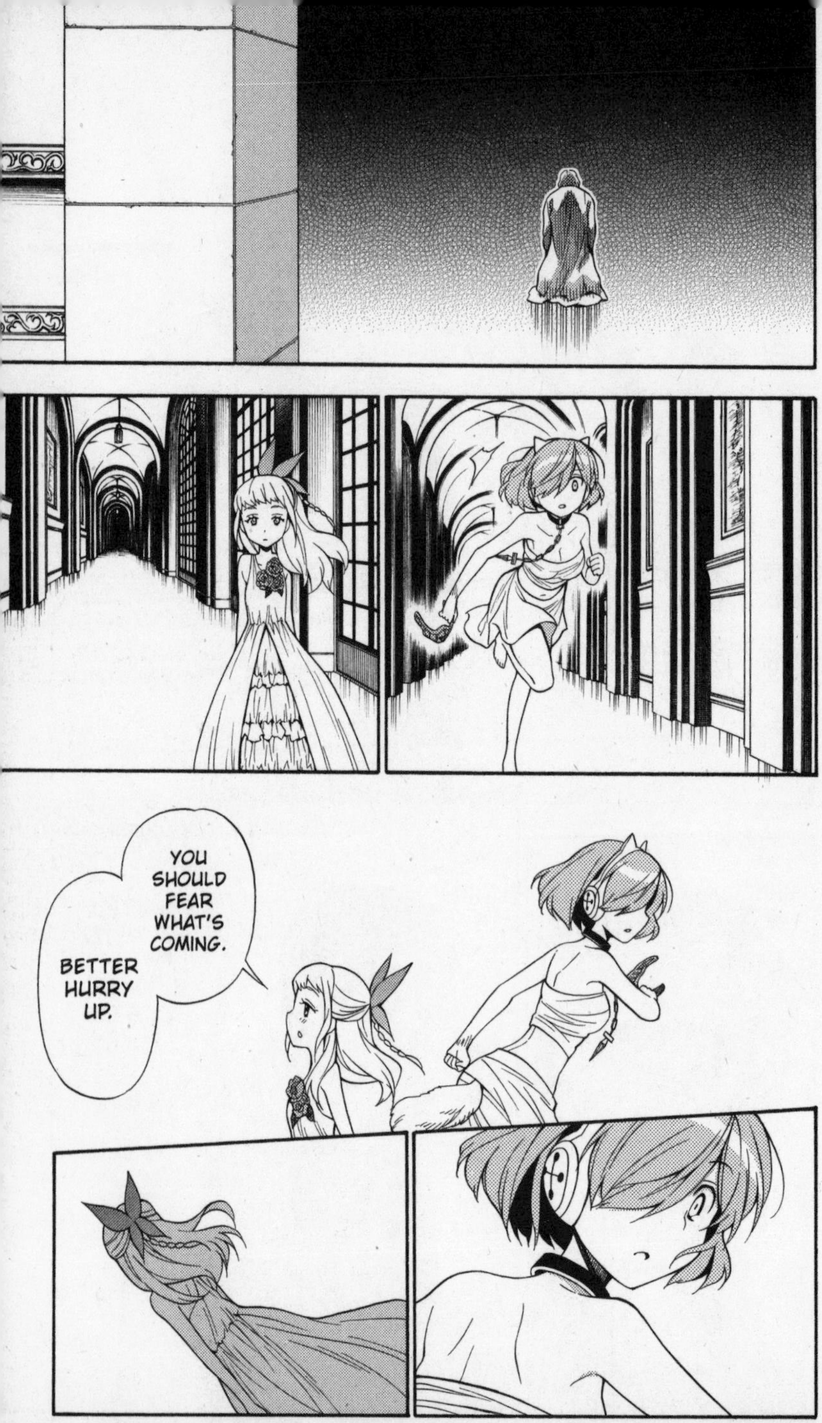
YOU SHOULD FEAR WHAT'S COMING.
BETTER HURRY UP.

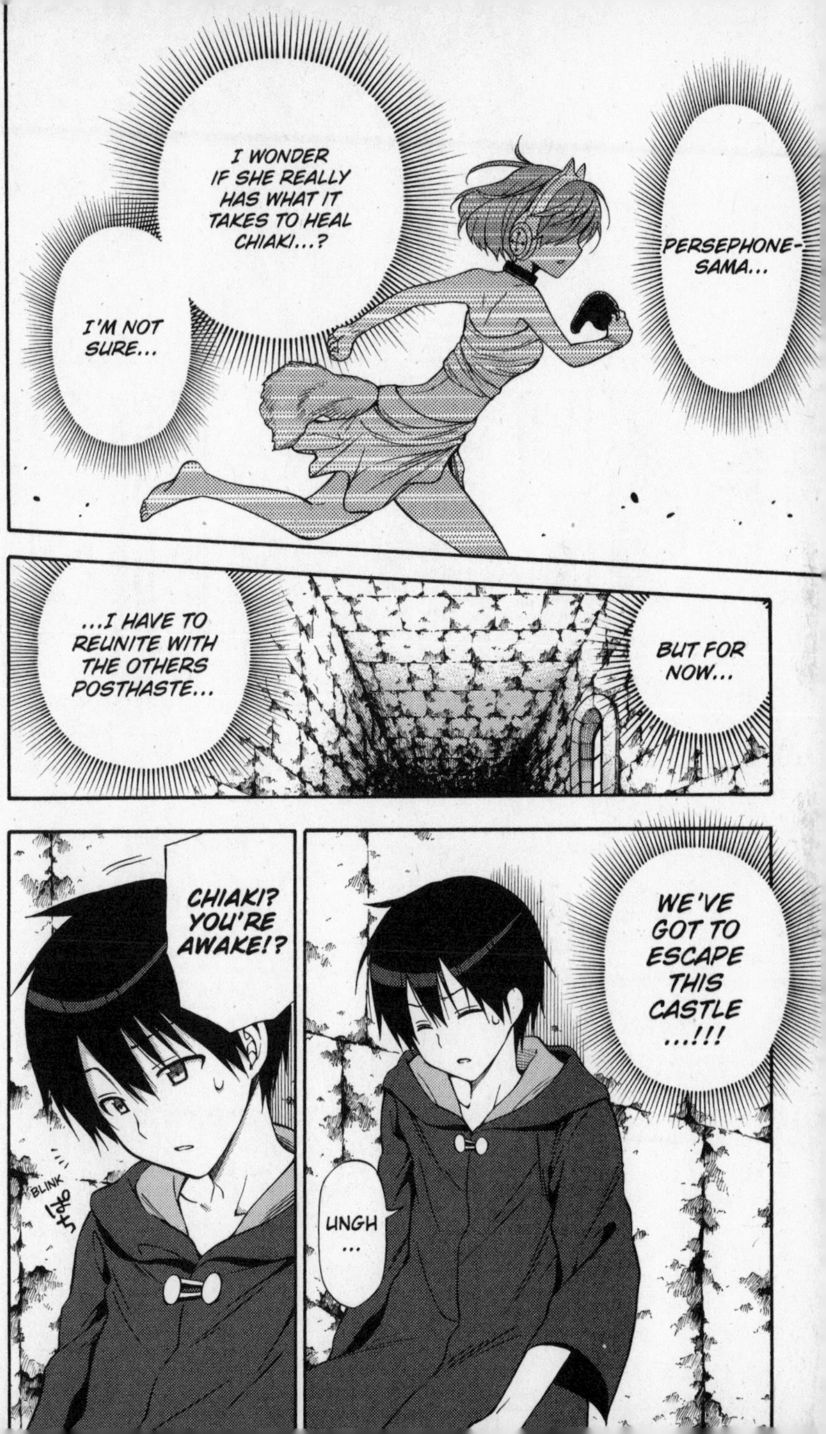
PERSEPHONE-SAMA...
I WONDER IF SHE REALLY HAS WHAT IT TAKES TO HEAL CHIAKI...?
I'M NOT SURE...
BUT FOR NOW...
...I HAVE TO REUNITE WITH THE OTHERS POSTHASTE...
WE'VE GOT TO ESCAPE THIS CASTLE ...!!!
UNGH ...
CHIAKI? YOU'RE AWAKE!?
BLINK

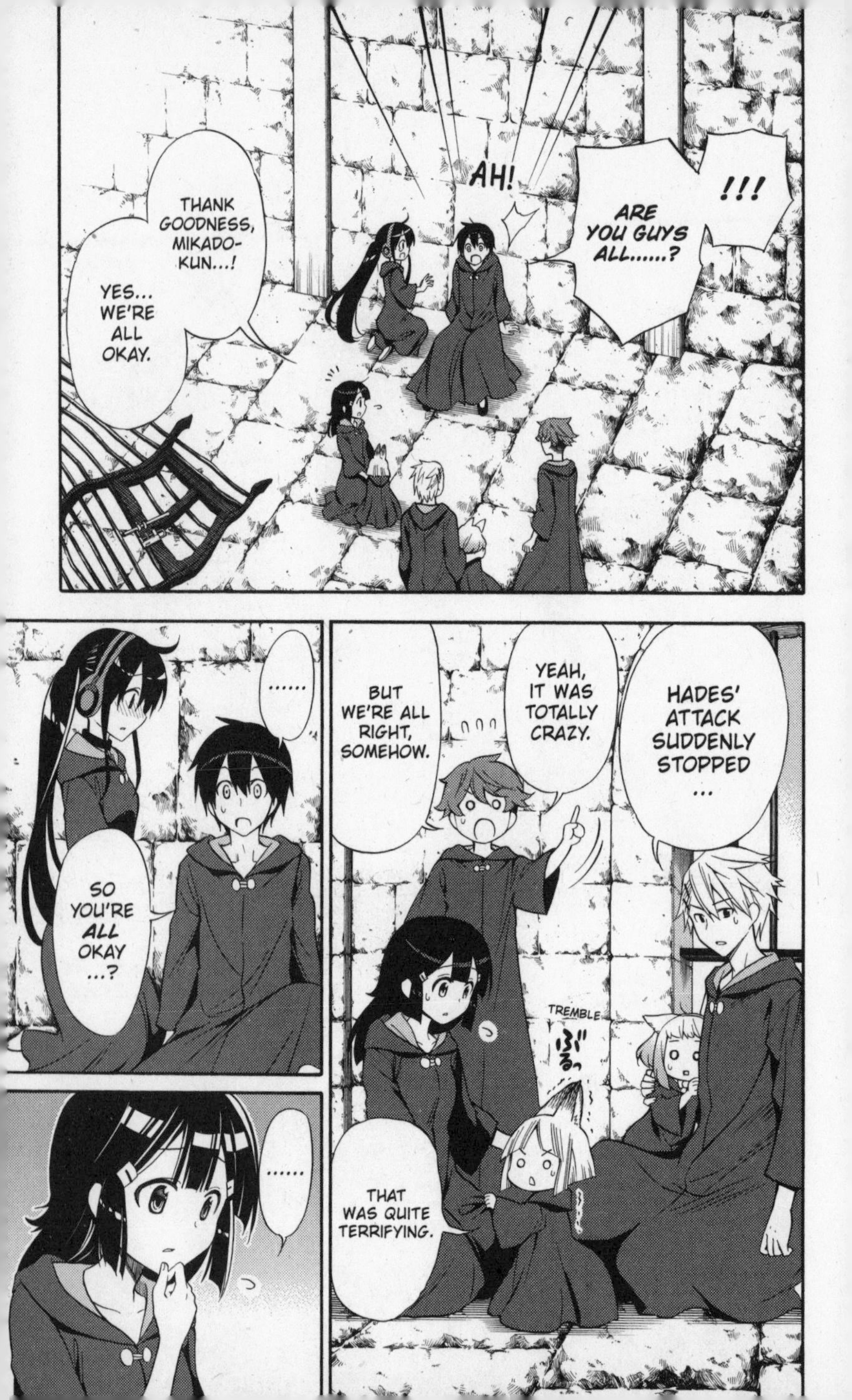
!!!
ARE YOU GUYS ALL......?
AH!
THANK GOODNESS, MIKADO-KUN...!
YES... WE'RE ALL OKAY.
HADES' ATTACK SUDDENLY STOPPED...
YEAH, IT WAS TOTALLY CRAZY.
BUT WE'RE ALL RIGHT, SOMEHOW.
TREMBLE
THAT WAS QUITE TERRIFYING.
......
SO YOU'RE ALL OKAY...?
......

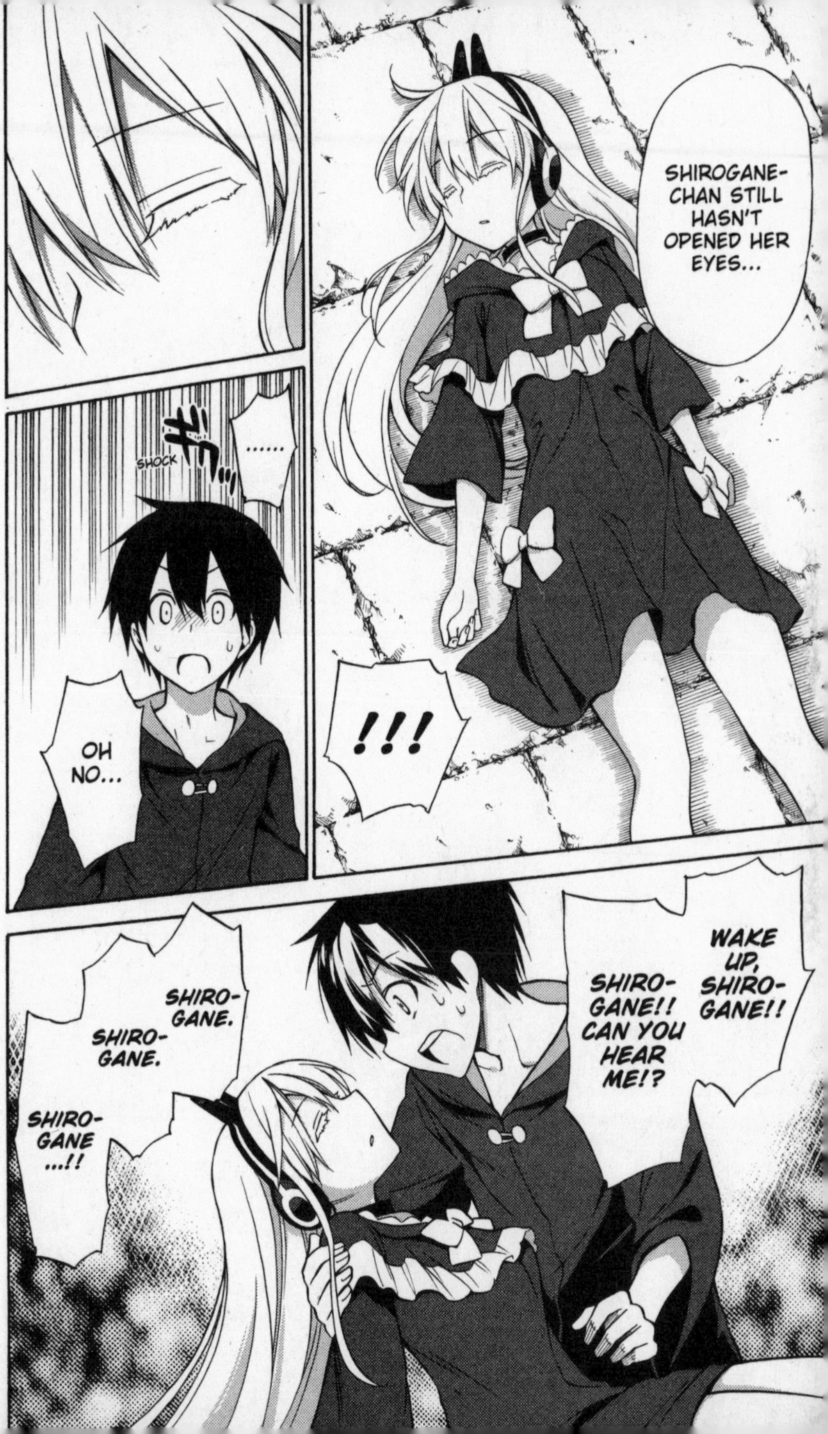
SHIROGANE-CHAN STILL HASN'T OPENED HER EYES...
!!!
......
SHOCK
OH NO...
WAKE UP, SHIRO-GANE!!
SHIRO-GANE!! CAN YOU HEAR ME!?
SHIRO-GANE.
SHIRO-GANE.
SHIRO-GANE ...!!

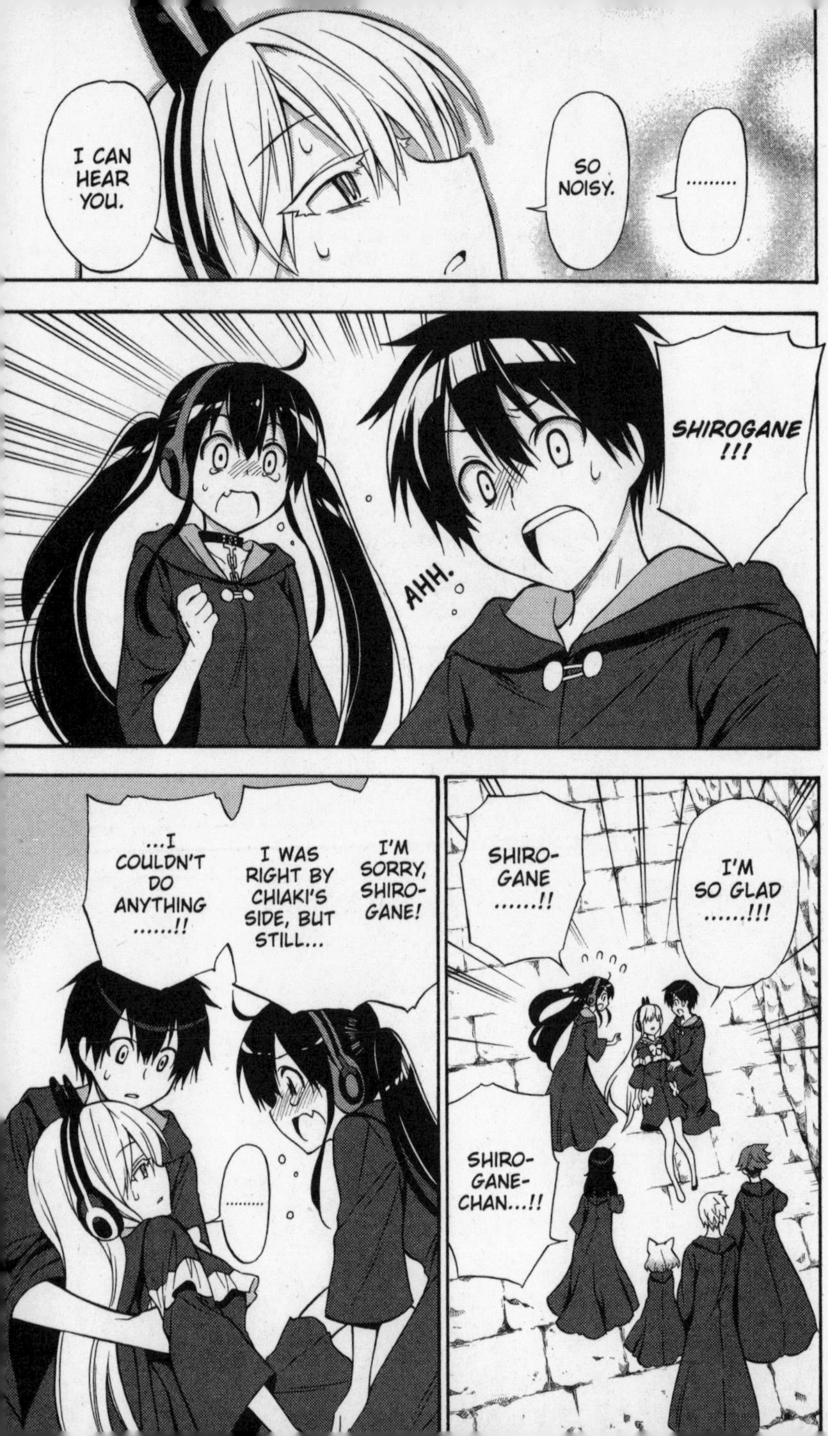
....
SO NOISY.
I CAN HEAR YOU.
SHIROGANE !!!
AHH.
I'M SO GLAD ......!!!
SHIRO-GANE ......!!
SHIRO-GANE-CHAN...!!
I'M SORRY, SHIRO-GANE!
I WAS RIGHT BY CHIAKI'S SIDE, BUT STILL...
...I COULDN'T DO ANYTHING ......!!
....

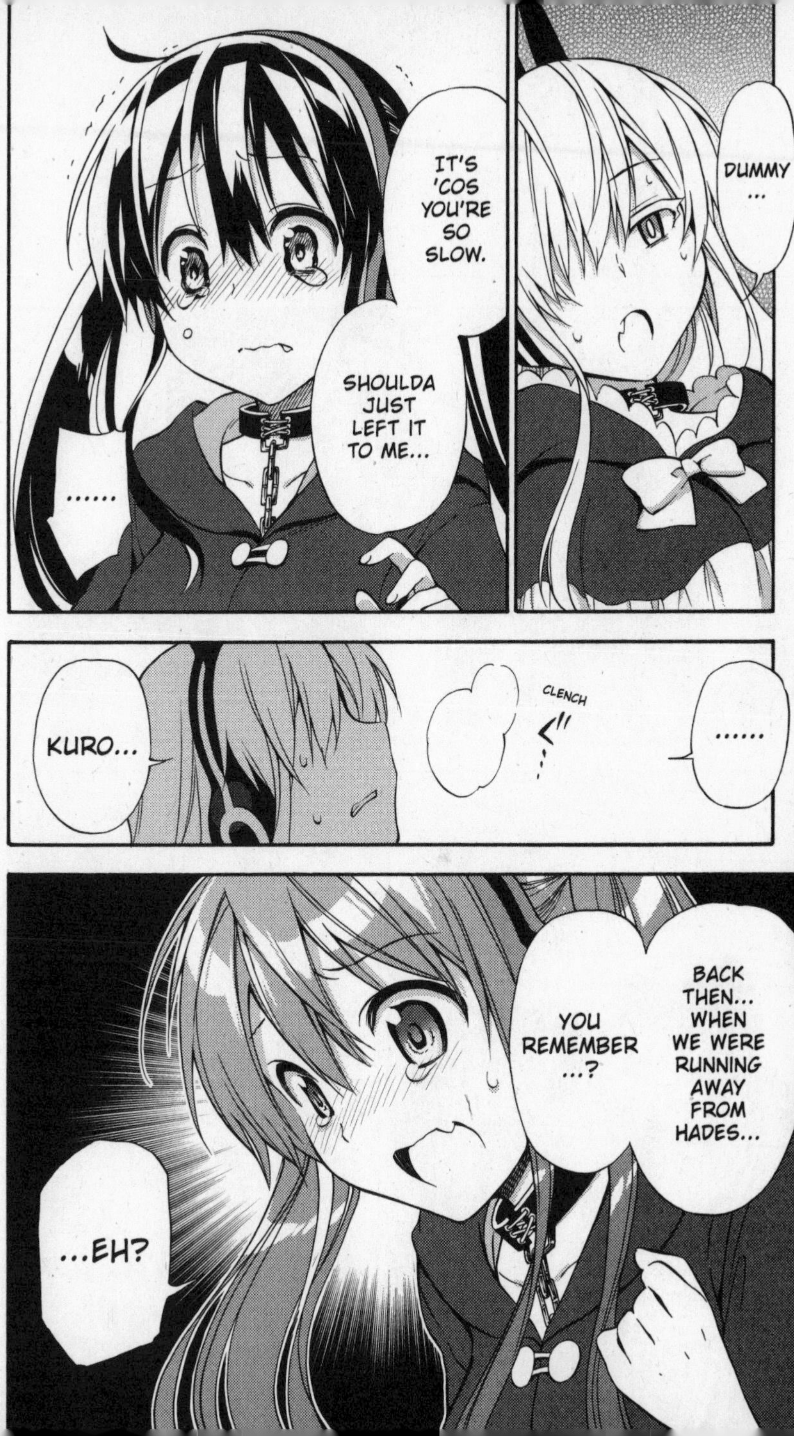

DUMMY ...
IT'S 'COS YOU'RE SO SLOW.
SHOULDA JUST LEFT IT TO ME...
......
......
CLENCH
KURO...
BACK THEN... WHEN WE WERE RUNNING AWAY FROM HADES...
YOU REMEMBER ...?
...EH?

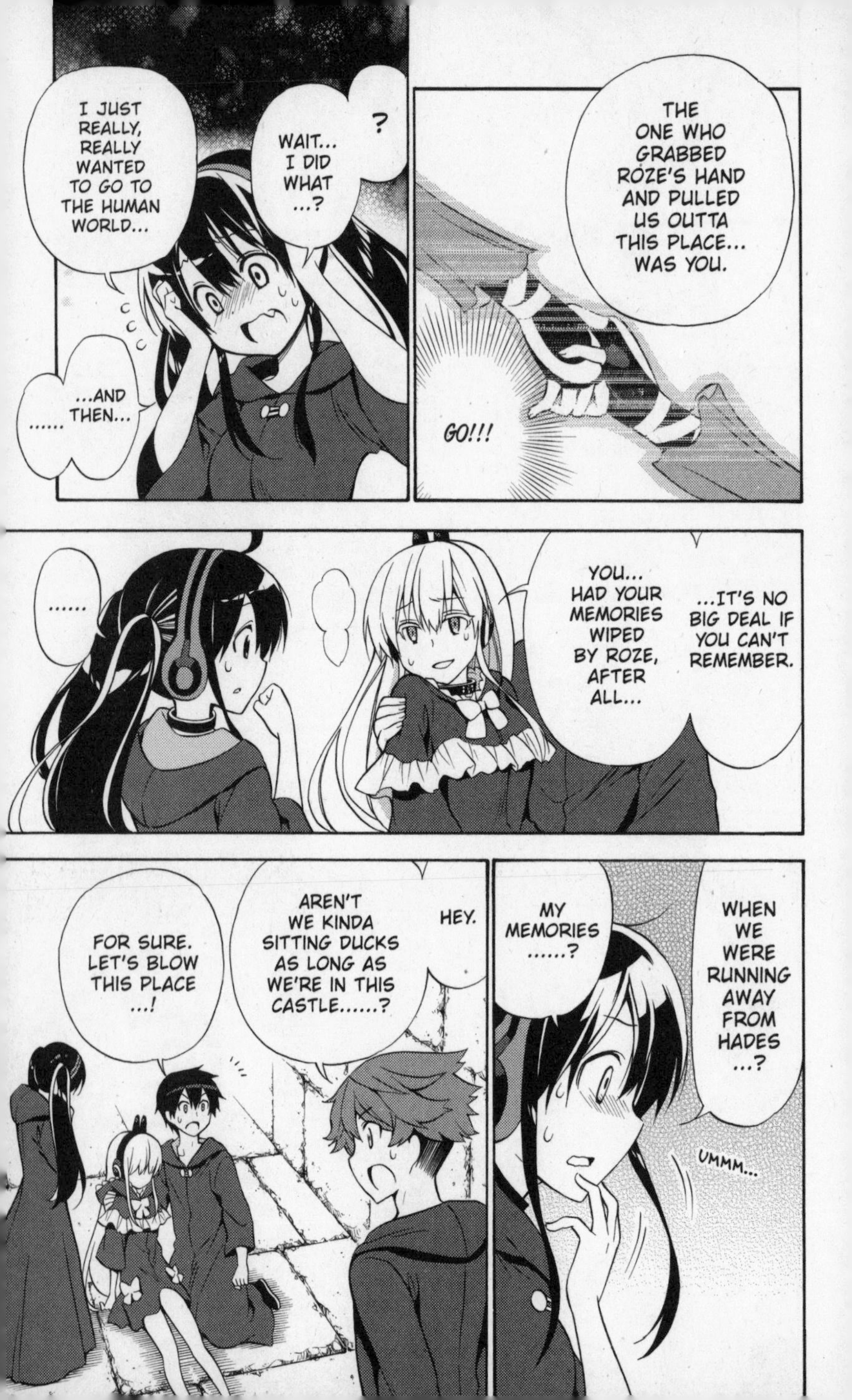
THE ONE WHO GRABBED ROZE'S HAND AND PULLED US OUTTA THIS PLACE... WAS YOU.
GO!!!
?
WAIT... I DID WHAT ...?
I JUST REALLY, REALLY WANTED TO GO TO THE HUMAN WORLD...
...AND THEN...
......
...IT'S NO BIG DEAL IF YOU CAN'T REMEMBER.
YOU... HAD YOUR MEMORIES WIPED BY ROZE, AFTER ALL...
......
WHEN WE WERE RUNNING AWAY FROM HADES ...?
MY MEMORIES ......?
UMMM...
HEY.
AREN'T WE KINDA SITTING DUCKS AS LONG AS WE'RE IN THIS CASTLE......?
FOR SURE. LET'S BLOW THIS PLACE ...!

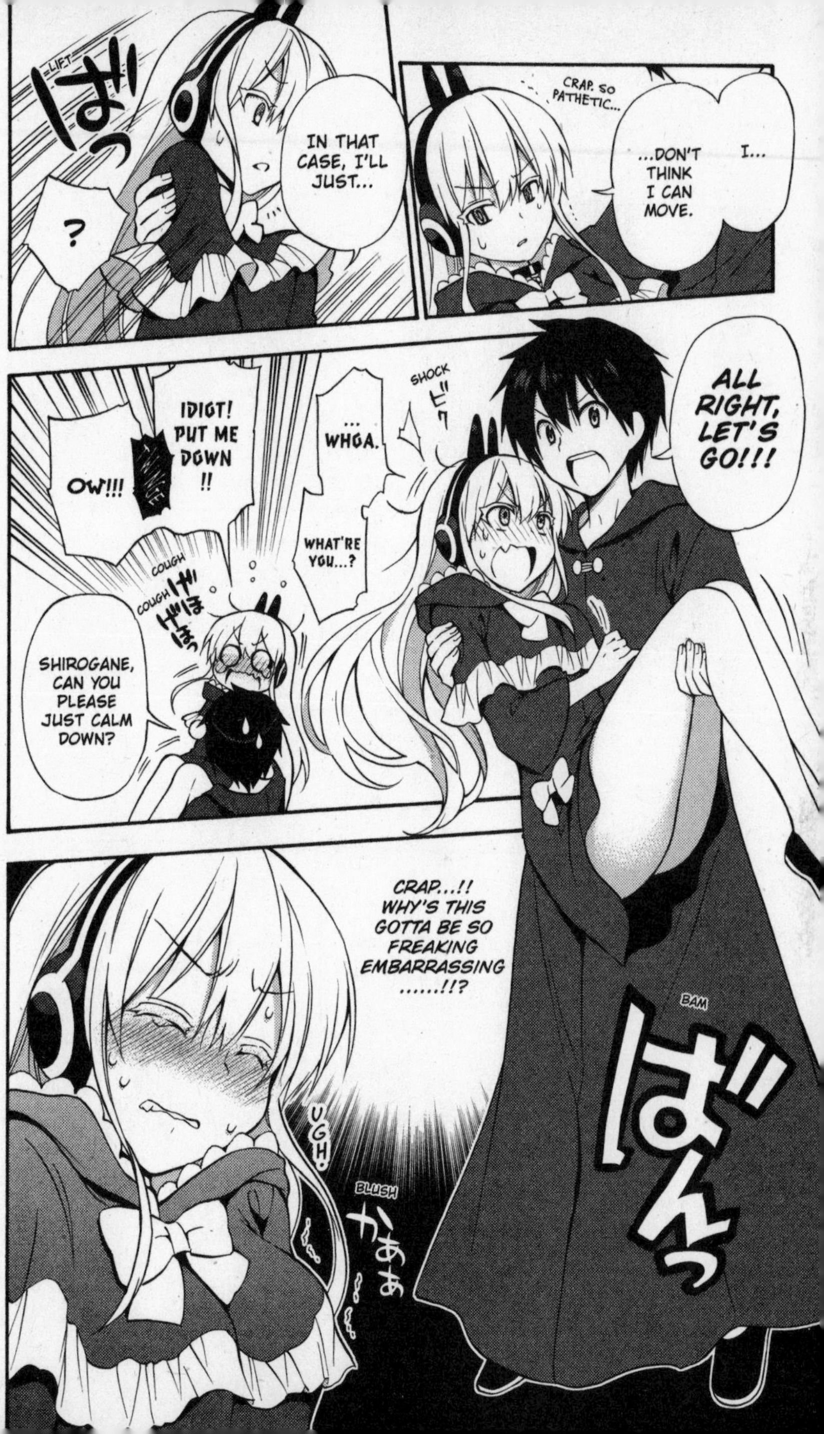
CRAP. SO PATHETIC...
I...
...DON'T THINK I CAN MOVE.
LIFT
IN THAT CASE, I'LL JUST...
?
ALL RIGHT, LET'S GO!!!
SHOCK
... WHOA.
WHAT'RE YOU...?
IDIOT! PUT ME DOWN!!
OW!!!
COUGH
COUGH
SHIROGANE, CAN YOU PLEASE JUST CALM DOWN?
CRAP...!! WHY'S THIS GOTTA BE SO FREAKING EMBARRASSING ......!!?
BAM
UGH!
BLUSH

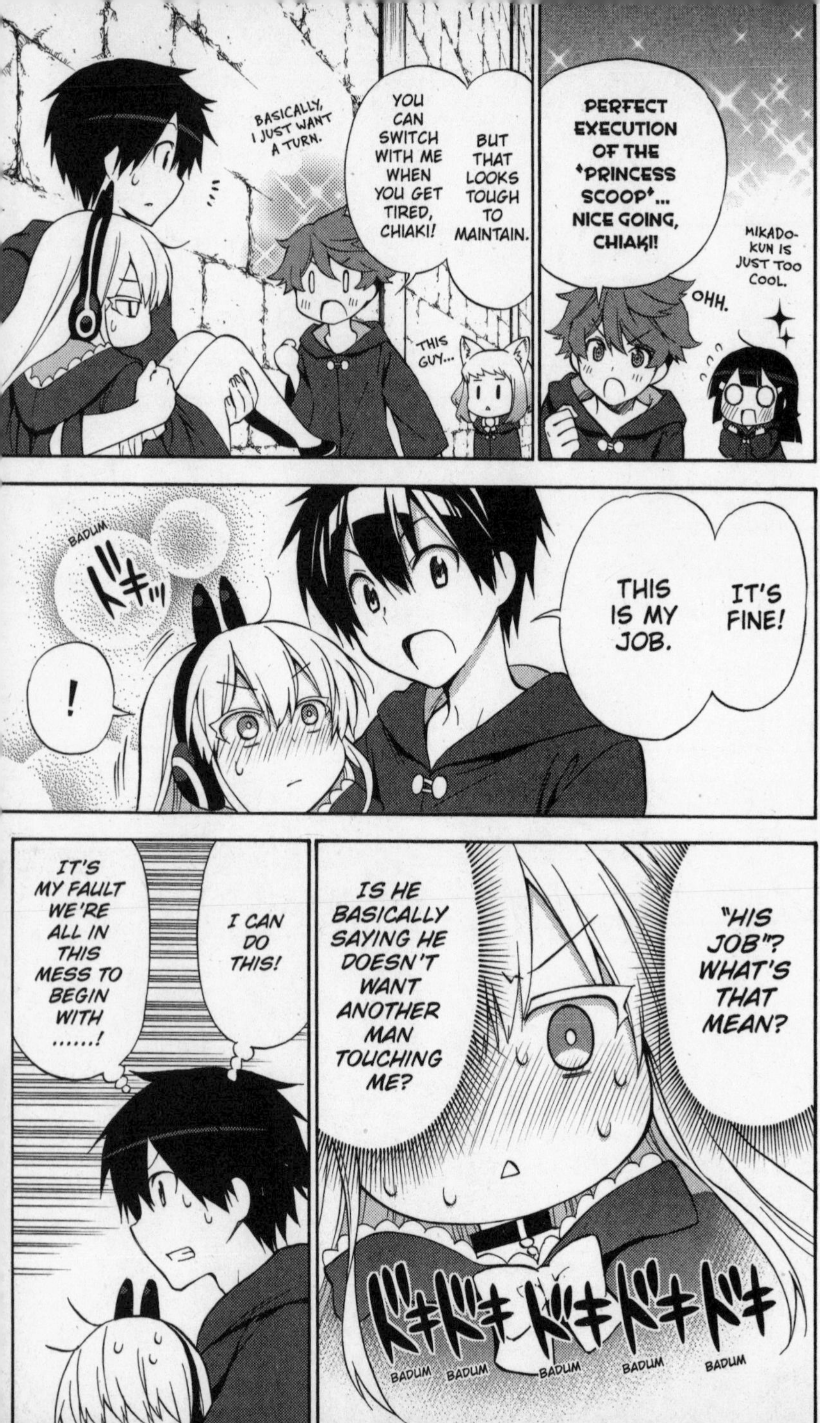
MIKADO-KUN IS JUST TOO COOL.
OHH.
PERFECT EXECUTION OF THE "PRINCESS SCOOP"... NICE GOING, CHIAKI!
THIS GUY...
BUT THAT LOOKS TOUGH TO MAINTAIN.
YOU CAN SWITCH WITH ME WHEN YOU GET TIRED, CHIAKI!
BASICALLY, I JUST WANT A TURN.
IT'S FINE!
THIS IS MY JOB.
BADUM
ドキッ
!
"HIS JOB"? WHAT'S THAT MEAN?
IS HE BASICALLY SAYING HE DOESN'T WANT ANOTHER MAN TOUCHING ME?
ドキドキドキドキドキ
BADUM BADUM BADUM BADUM BADUM
I CAN DO THIS!
IT'S MY FAULT WE'RE ALL IN THIS MESS TO BEGIN WITH ......!

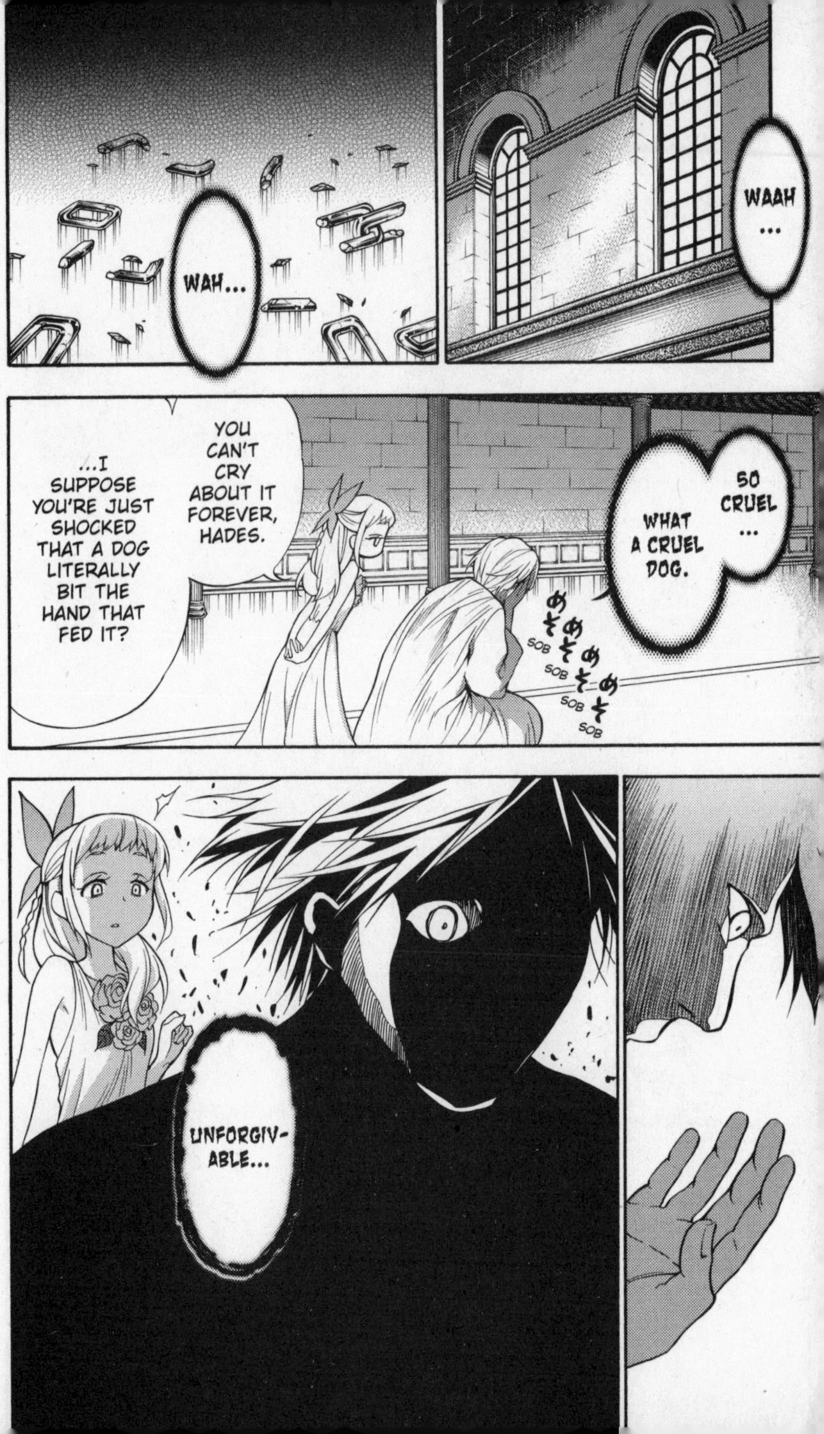
WAAH ...
WAH...
SO CRUEL ...
WHAT A CRUEL DOG.
めそめそめそめそ
SOB SOB SOB SOB
YOU CAN'T CRY ABOUT IT FOREVER, HADES.
...I SUPPOSE YOU'RE JUST SHOCKED THAT A DOG LITERALLY BIT THE HAND THAT FED IT?
UNFORGIV-ABLE...

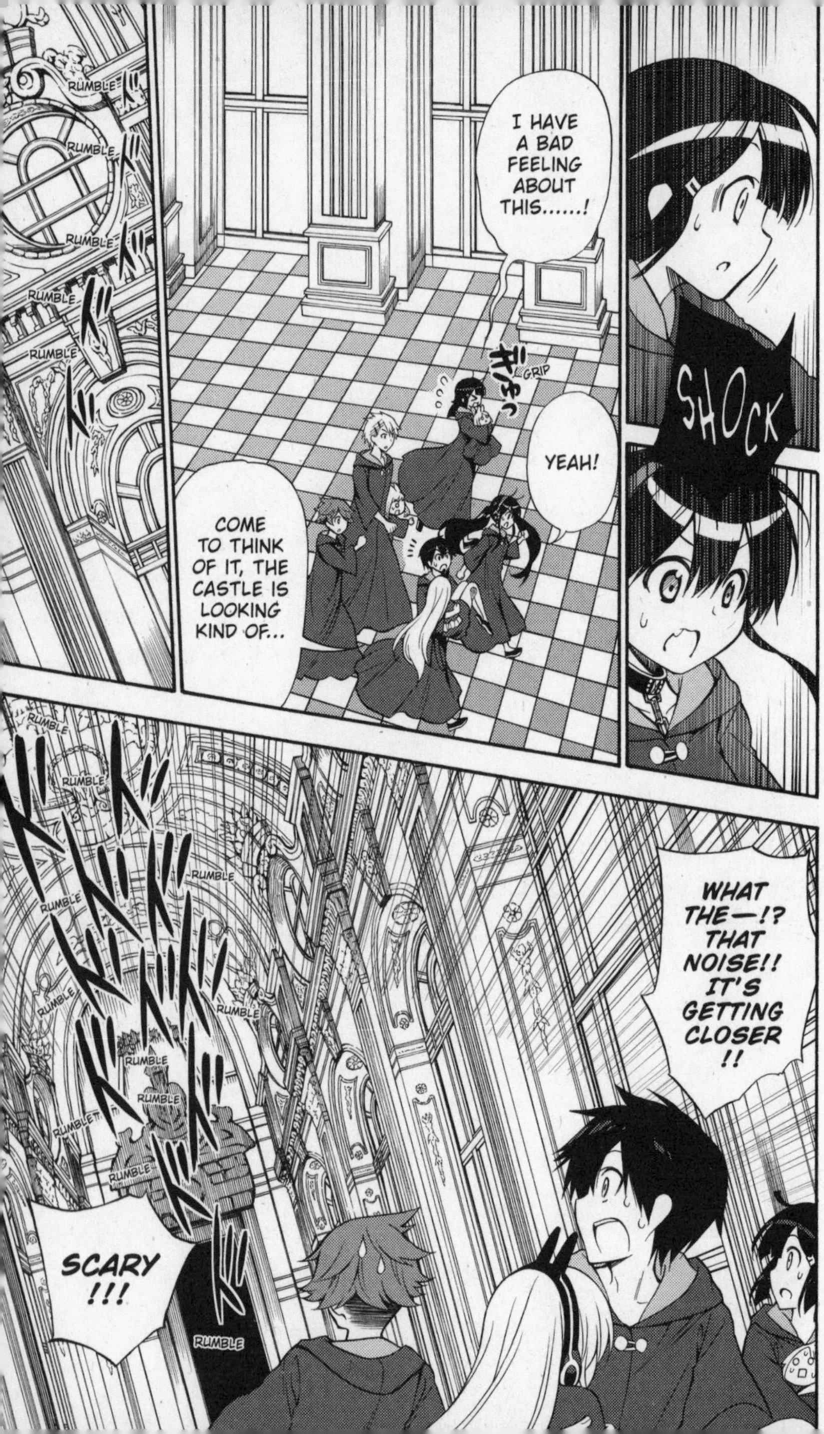

SHOCK
I HAVE A BAD FEELING ABOUT THIS......!
GRIP
YEAH!
COME TO THINK OF IT, THE CASTLE IS LOOKING KIND OF...
RUMBLE
RUMBLE
RUMBLE
RUMBLE
RUMBLE
WHAT THE—!? THAT NOISE!! IT'S GETTING CLOSER!!
RUMBLE
RUMBLE
RUMBLE
RUMBLE
RUMBLE
RUMBLE
RUMBLE
RUMBLE
RUMBLE
RUMBLE
SCARY!!!
RUMBLE

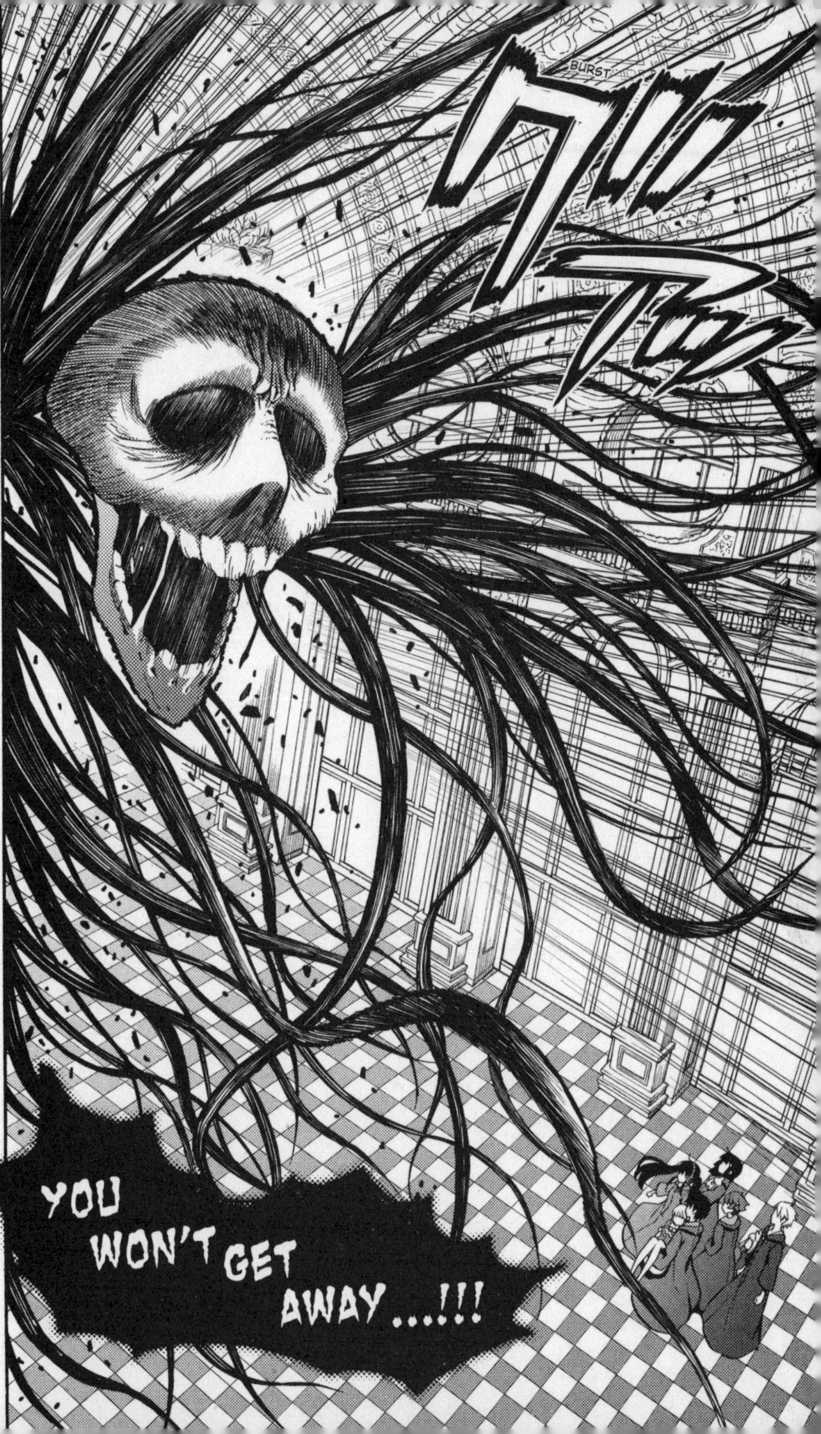
BURST
YOU WON'T GET AWAY...!!!

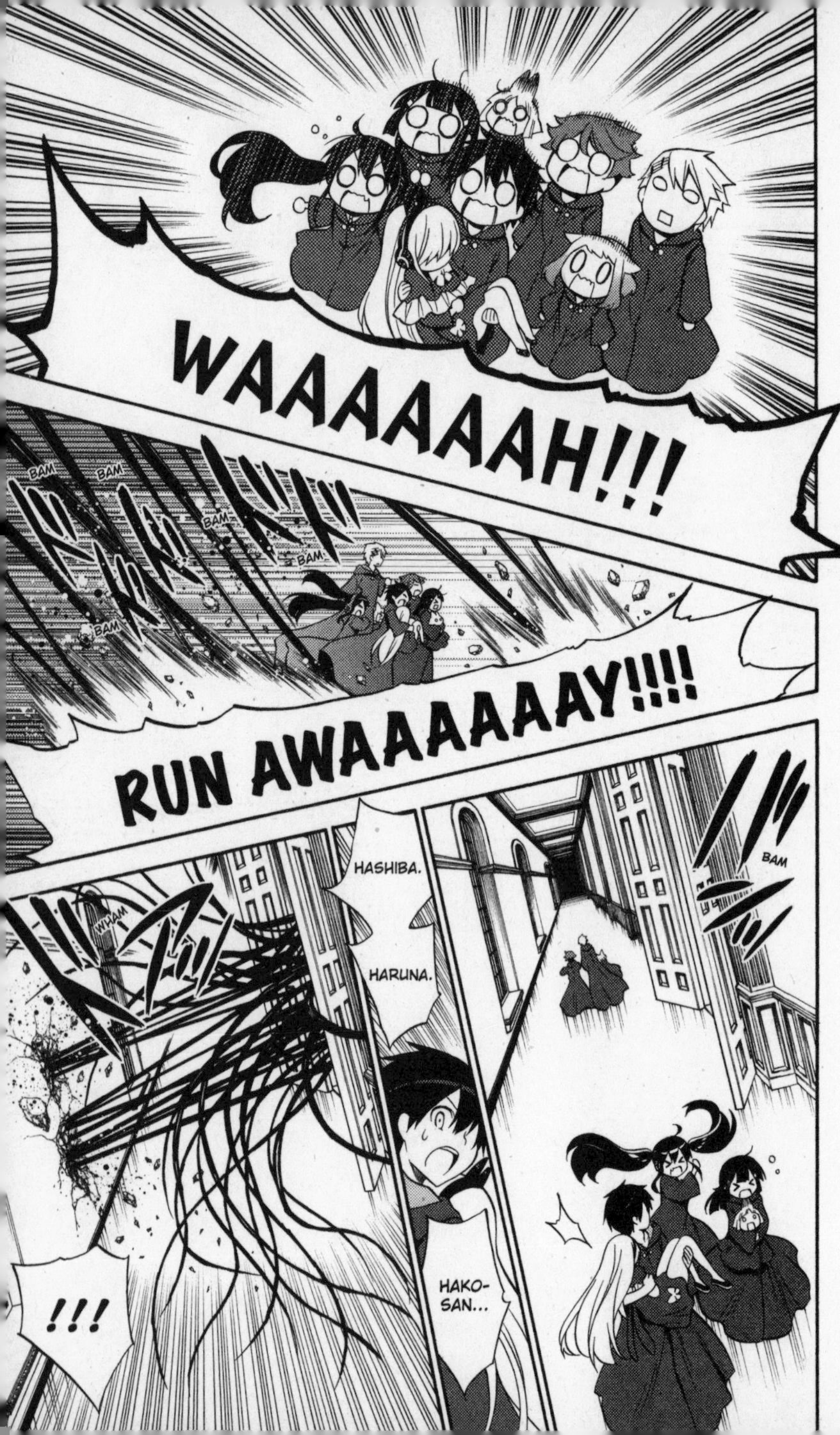
WAAAAAAAH!!!
RUN AWAAAAAAAY!!!!
BAM
BAM
BAM
BAM
BAM
BAM
HASHIBA.
HARUNA.
HAKO-SAN...
WHAM
!!!

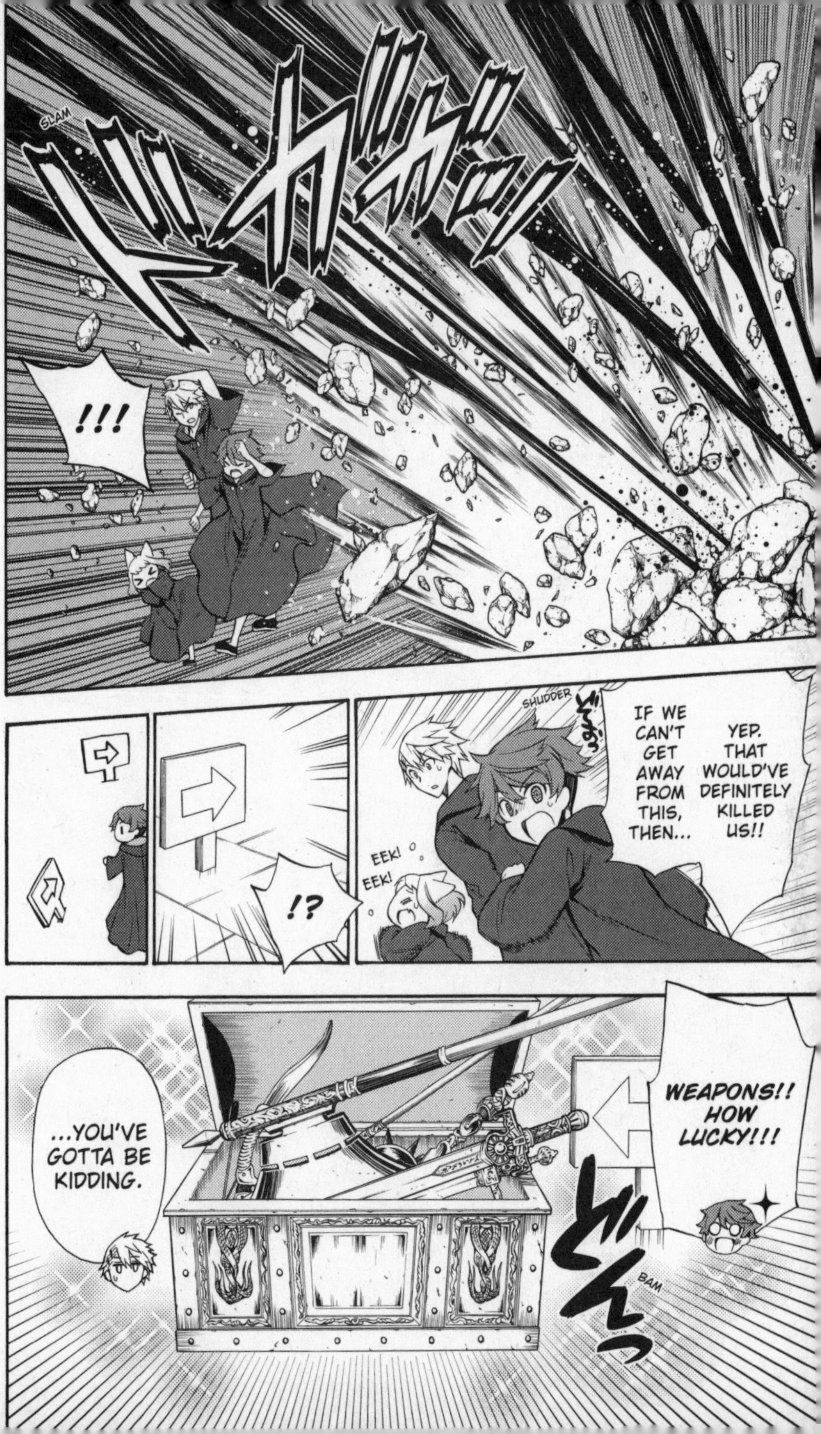
SLAM
!!!
SHUDDER
IF WE CAN'T GET AWAY FROM THIS, THEN...
YEP. THAT WOULD'VE DEFINITELY KILLED US!!
EEK!
EEK!
!?
WEAPONS!! HOW LUCKY!!!
BAM
...YOU'VE GOTTA BE KIDDING.

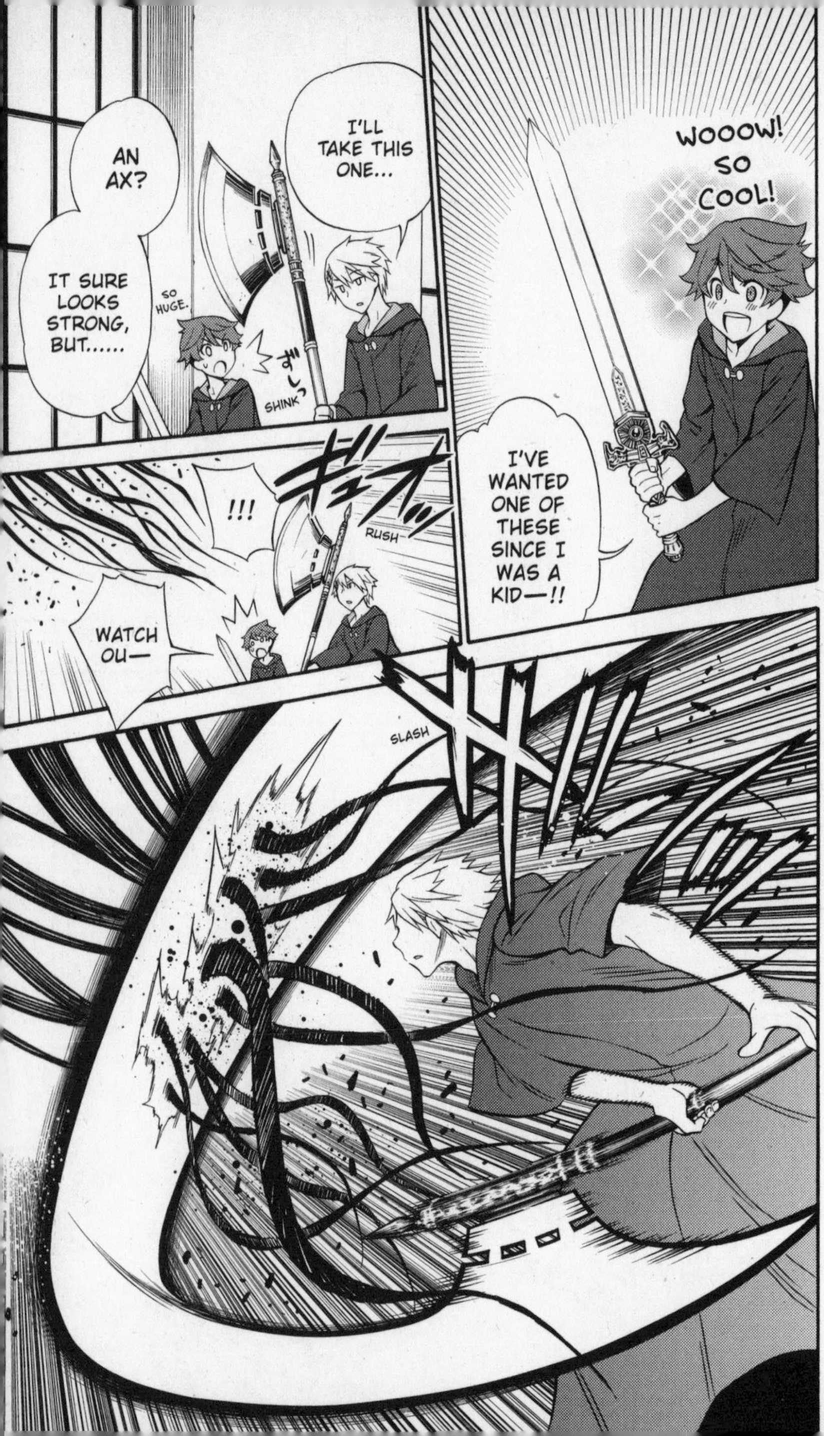
WOOOW! SO COOL!
I'VE WANTED ONE OF THESE SINCE I WAS A KID—!!
I'LL TAKE THIS ONE...
AN AX?
IT SURE LOOKS STRONG, BUT......
SO HUGE.
ずしっ
SHINK
!!!
RUSH
WATCH OU—
SLASH

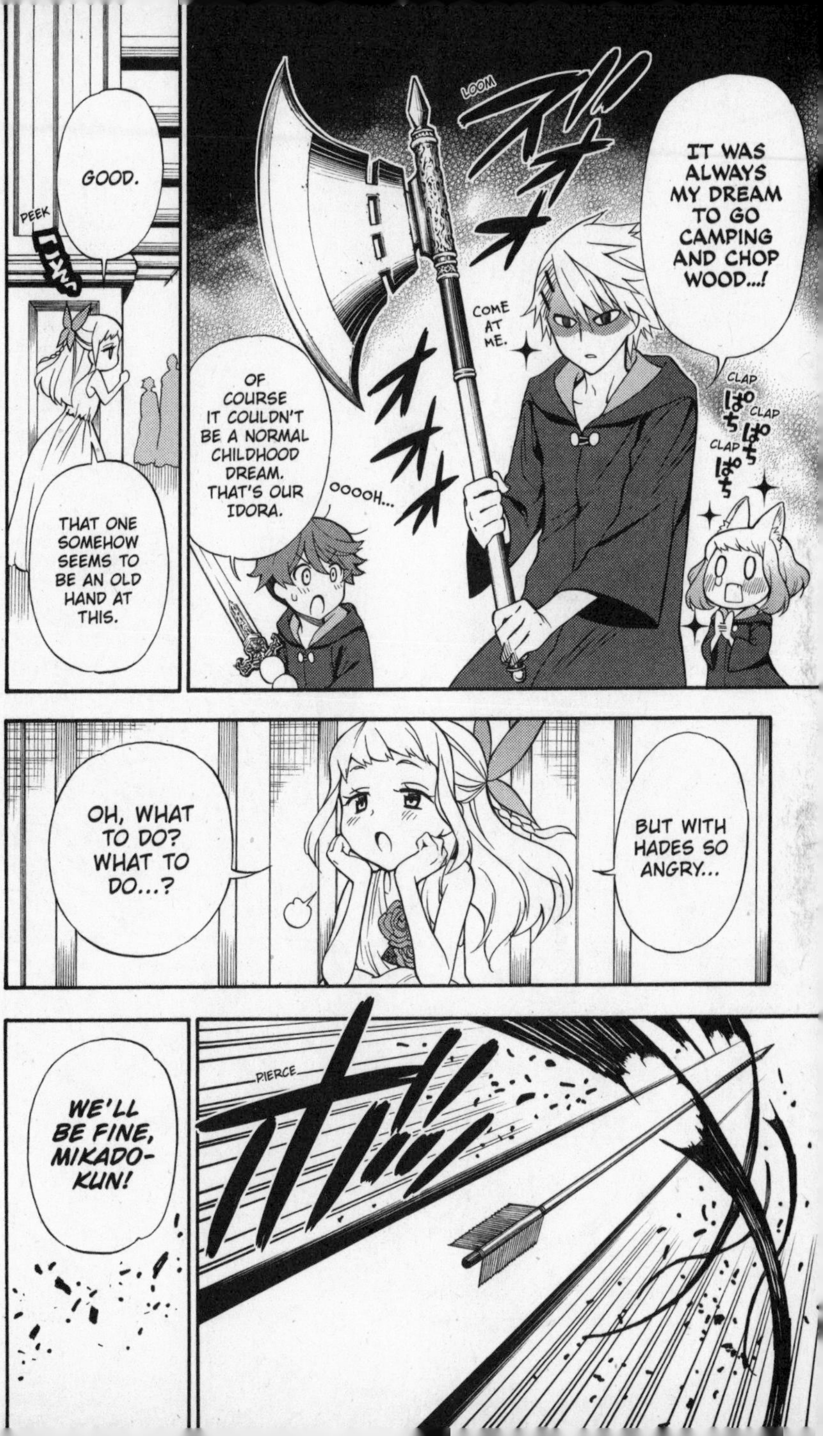
LOOM
IT WAS ALWAYS MY DREAM TO GO CAMPING AND CHOP WOOD...!
COME AT ME.
CLAP
CLAP
CLAP
OF COURSE IT COULDN'T BE A NORMAL CHILDHOOD DREAM. THAT'S OUR IDORA.
OOOOH...
GOOD.
PEEK
THAT ONE SOMEHOW SEEMS TO BE AN OLD HAND AT THIS.
BUT WITH HADES SO ANGRY...
OH, WHAT TO DO? WHAT TO DO...?
PIERCE
WE'LL BE FINE, MIKADO-KUN!

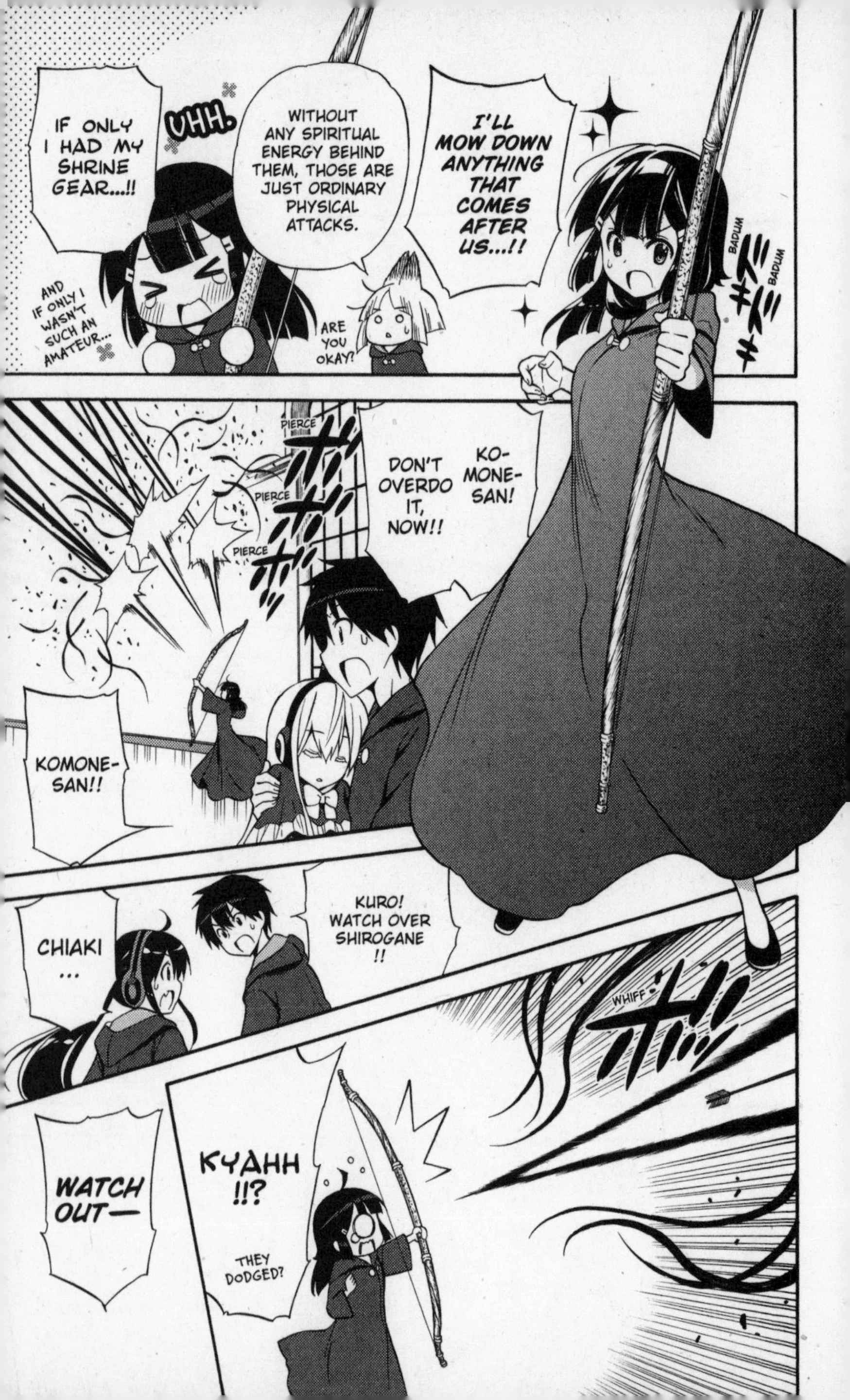
I'LL MOW DOWN ANYTHING THAT COMES AFTER US...!!
BADUM
BADUM
WITHOUT ANY SPIRITUAL ENERGY BEHIND THEM, THOSE ARE JUST ORDINARY PHYSICAL ATTACKS.
UHH.
IF ONLY I HAD MY SHRINE GEAR...!!
AND IF ONLY I WASN'T SUCH AN AMATEUR...
ARE YOU OKAY?
KO-MONE-SAN!
DON'T OVERDO IT, NOW!!
PIERCE
PIERCE
PIERCE
KOMONE-SAN!!
KURO! WATCH OVER SHIROGANE!!
CHIAKI...
WHIFF
KYAHH!!?
THEY DODGED?
WATCH OUT—

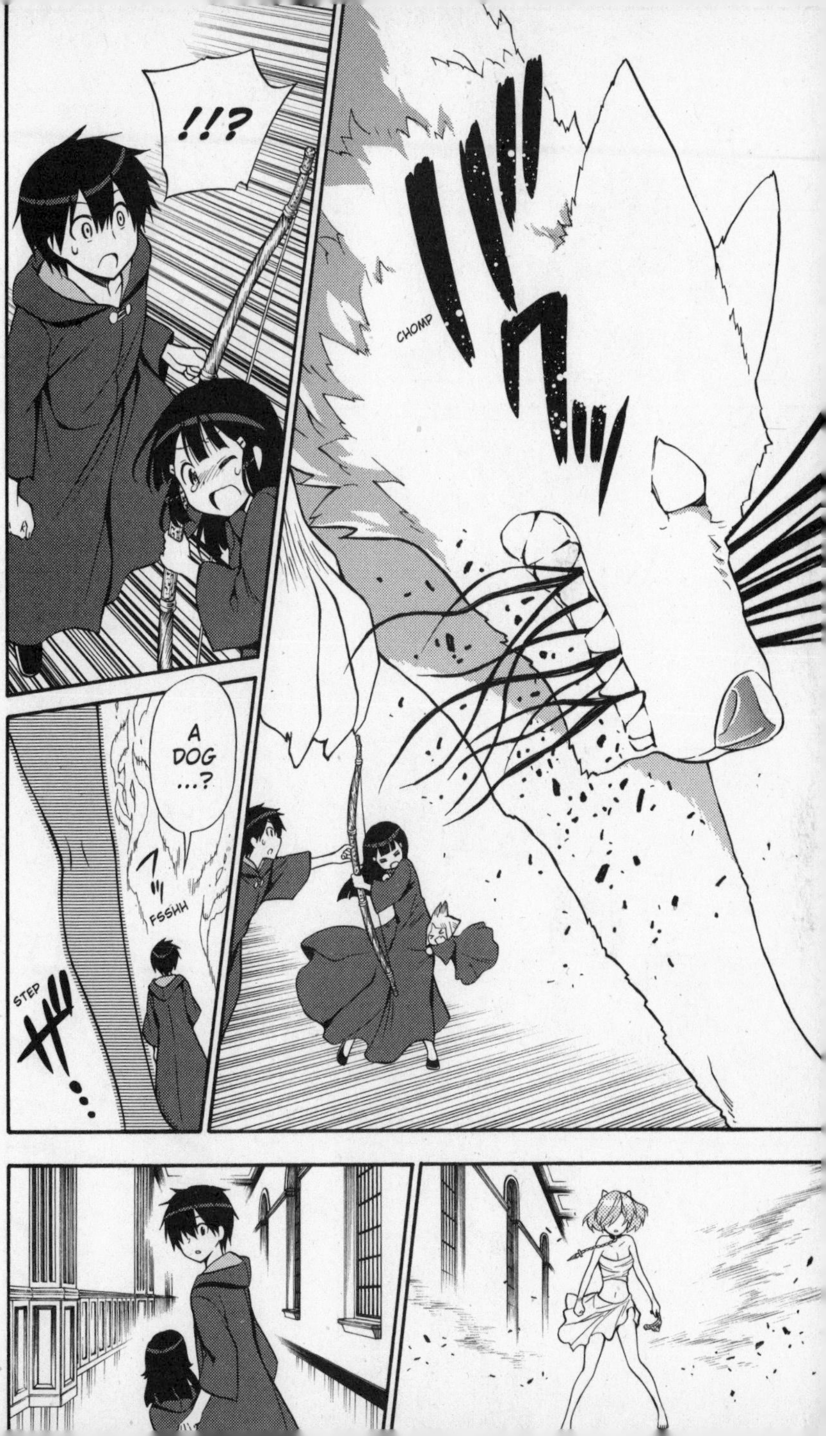
CHOMP
!!?
A DOG ...?
FSSHH
STEP
...

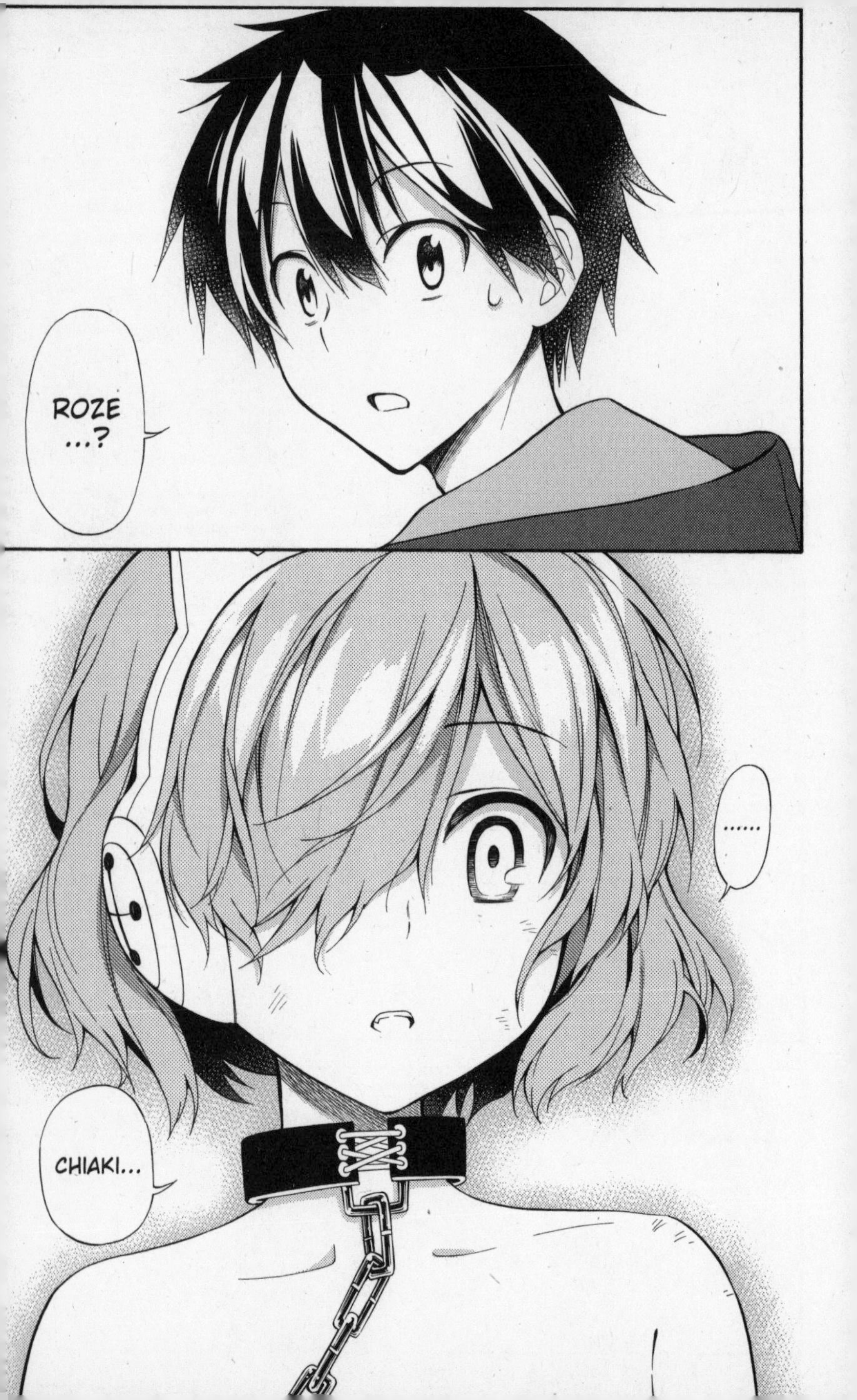
ROZE ...?
......
CHIAKI...

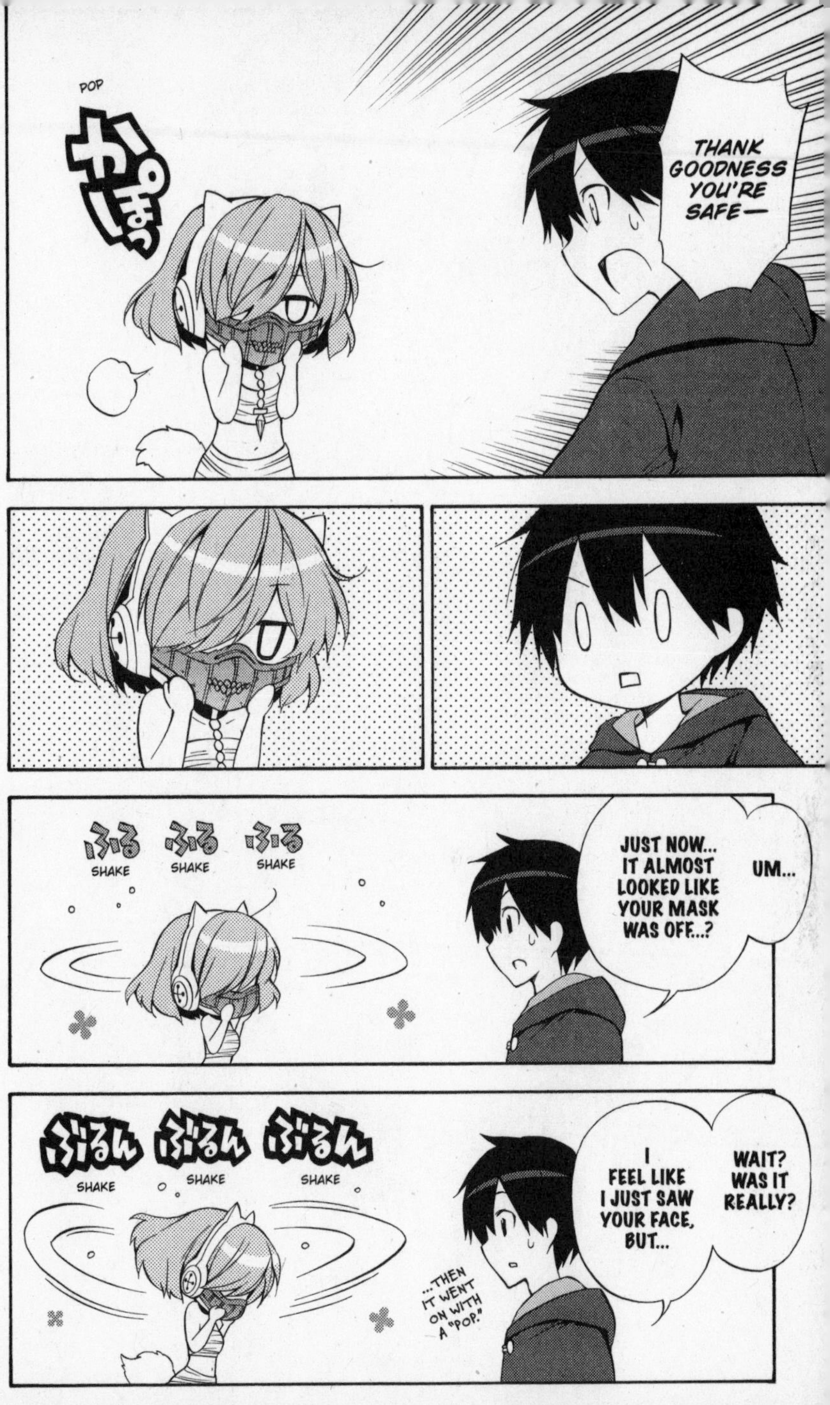
THANK GOODNESS YOU'RE SAFE—
かぽっ
POP
UM...
JUST NOW... IT ALMOST LOOKED LIKE YOUR MASK WAS OFF...?
ふる ふる ふる
SHAKE SHAKE SHAKE
WAIT? WAS IT REALLY?
I FEEL LIKE I JUST SAW YOUR FACE, BUT...
...THEN IT WENT ON WITH A "POP."
ぶるん ぶるん ぶるん
SHAKE SHAKE SHAKE

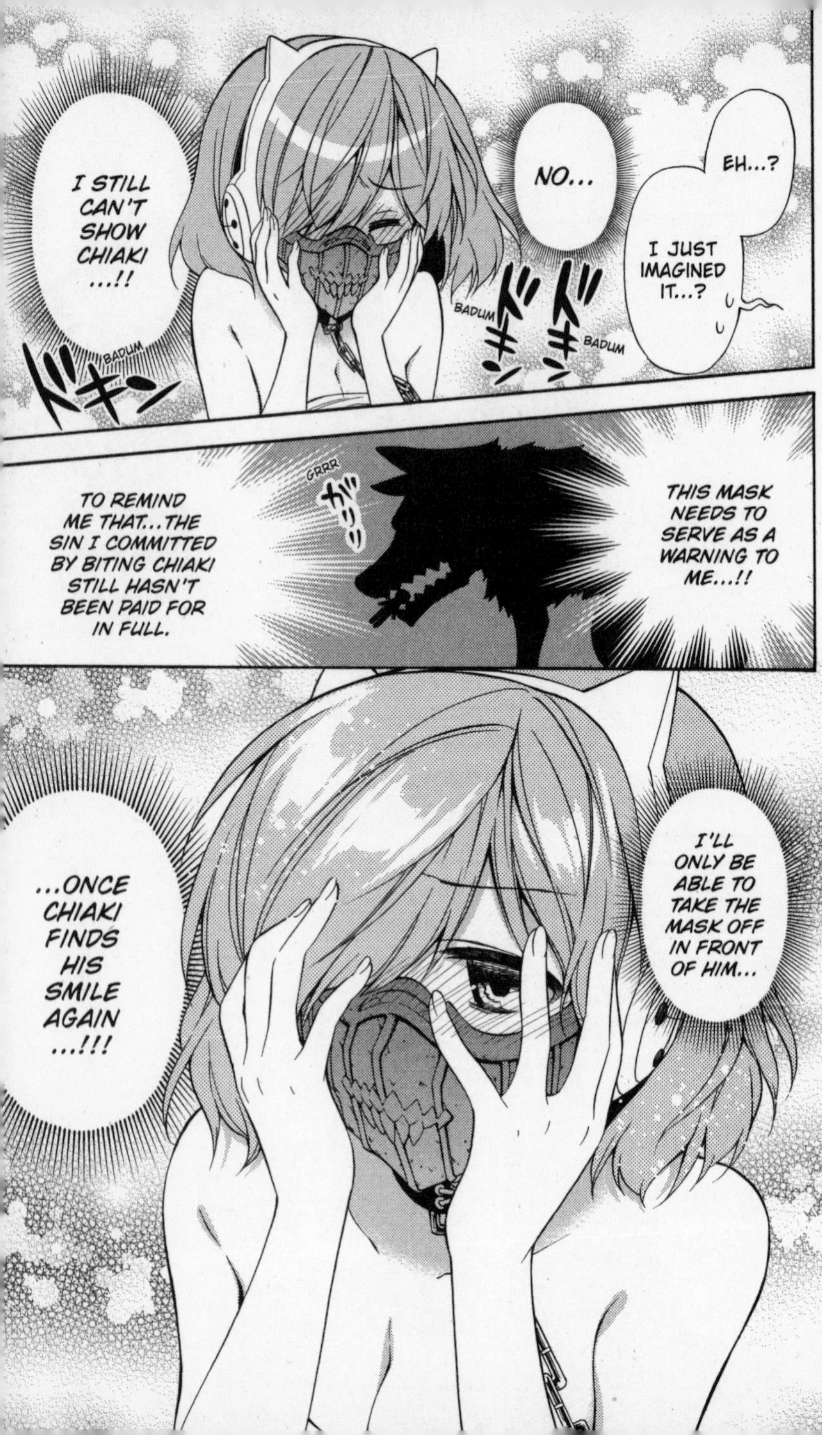
EH...? I JUST IMAGINED IT...?
BADUM
BADUM
NO...
BADUM
I STILL CAN'T SHOW CHIAKI ...!!
THIS MASK NEEDS TO SERVE AS A WARNING TO ME...!!
GRRR
TO REMIND ME THAT...THE SIN I COMMITTED BY BITING CHIAKI STILL HASN'T BEEN PAID FOR IN FULL.
I'LL ONLY BE ABLE TO TAKE THE MASK OFF IN FRONT OF HIM...
...ONCE CHIAKI FINDS HIS SMILE AGAIN ...!!!

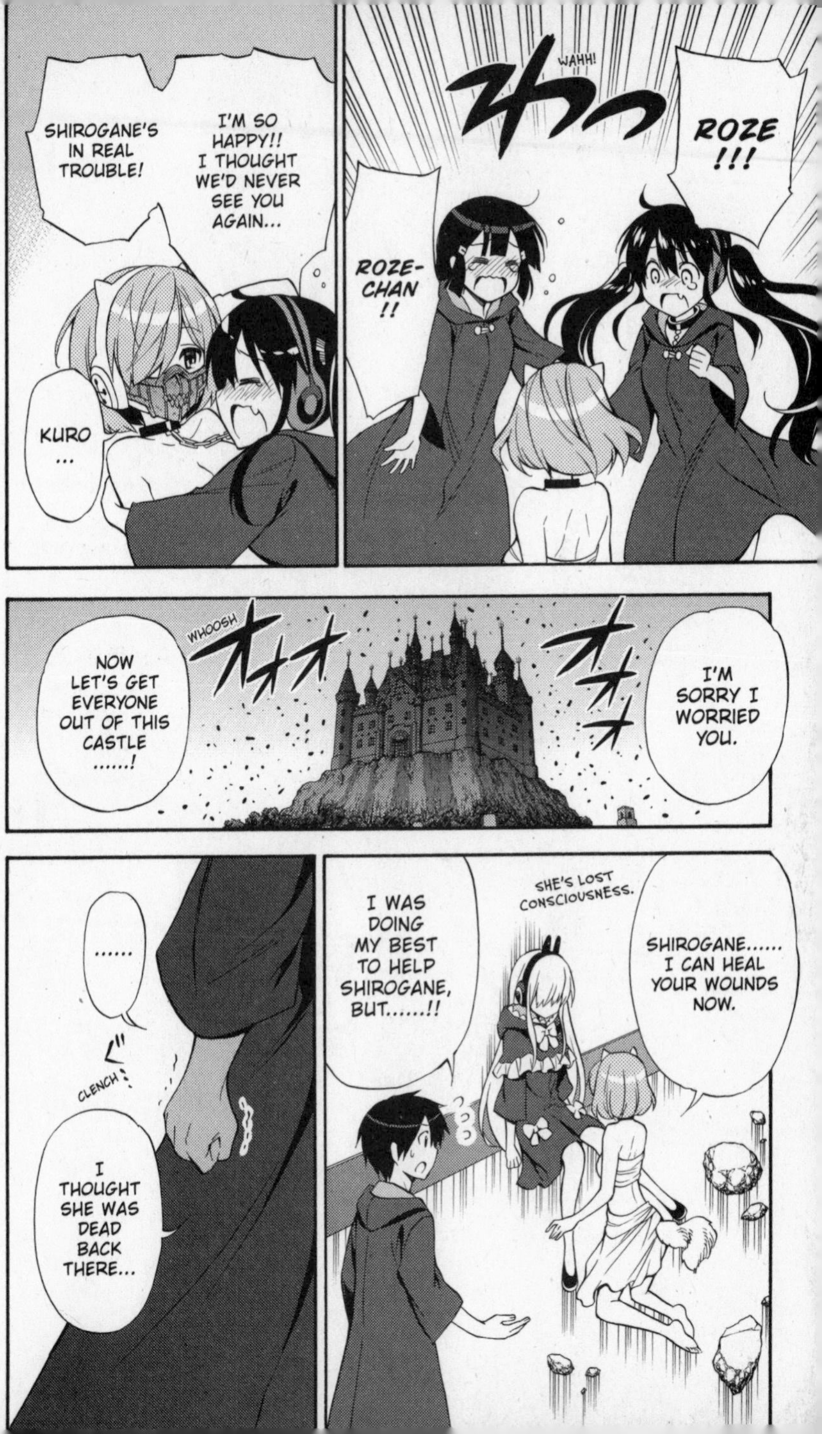
WAHH!
ROZE !!!
ROZE-CHAN !!
I'M SO HAPPY!! I THOUGHT WE'D NEVER SEE YOU AGAIN...
SHIROGANE'S IN REAL TROUBLE!
KURO ...
I'M SORRY I WORRIED YOU.
WHOOSH
NOW LET'S GET EVERYONE OUT OF THIS CASTLE ......!
SHIROGANE...... I CAN HEAL YOUR WOUNDS NOW.
SHE'S LOST CONSCIOUSNESS.
I WAS DOING MY BEST TO HELP SHIROGANE, BUT......!!
......
CLENCH
I THOUGHT SHE WAS DEAD BACK THERE...

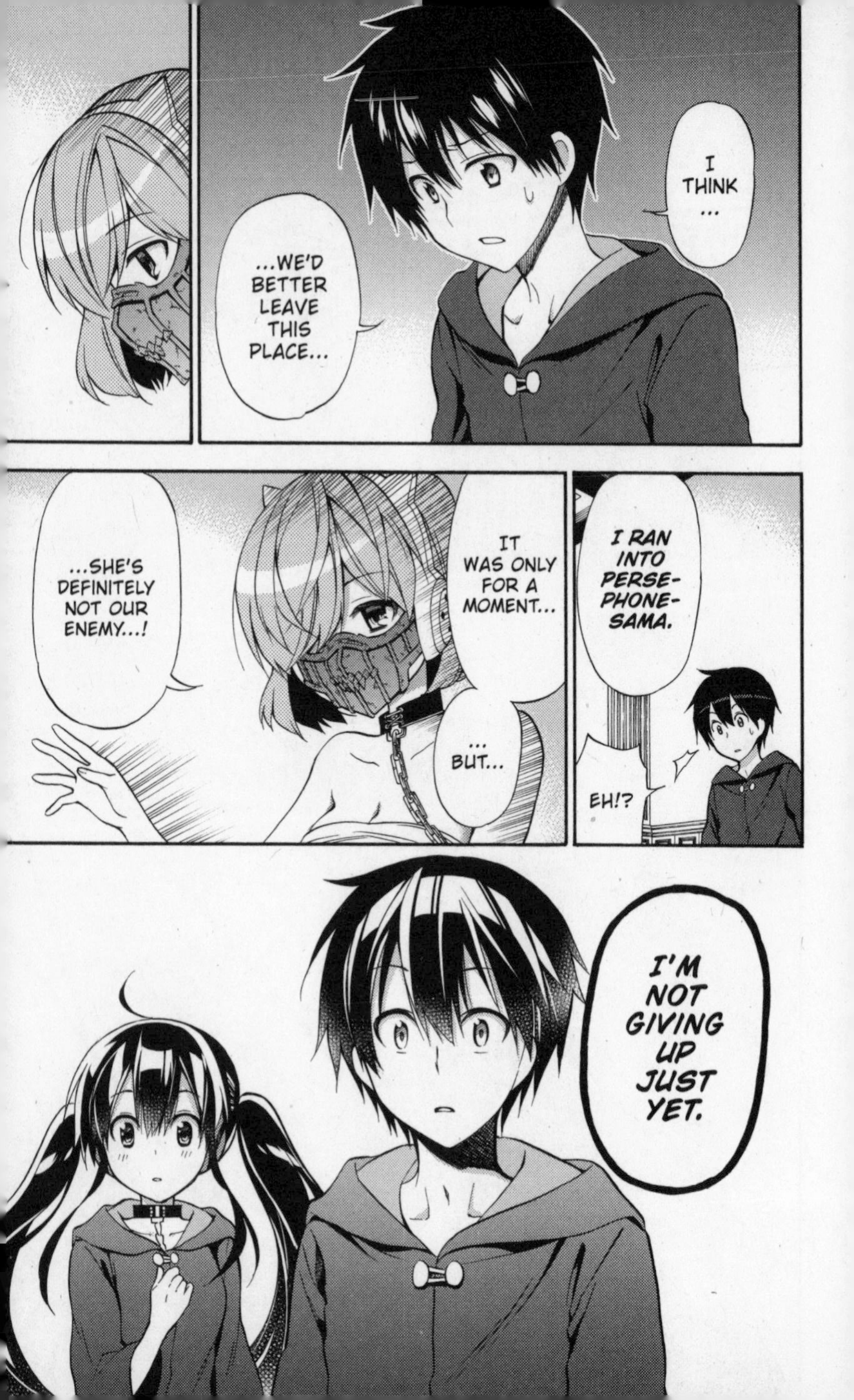
I THINK...
...WE'D BETTER LEAVE THIS PLACE...
I RAN INTO PERSE-PHONE-SAMA.
EH!?
IT WAS ONLY FOR A MOMENT...
...BUT...
...SHE'S DEFINITELY NOT OUR ENEMY...!
I'M NOT GIVING UP JUST YET.

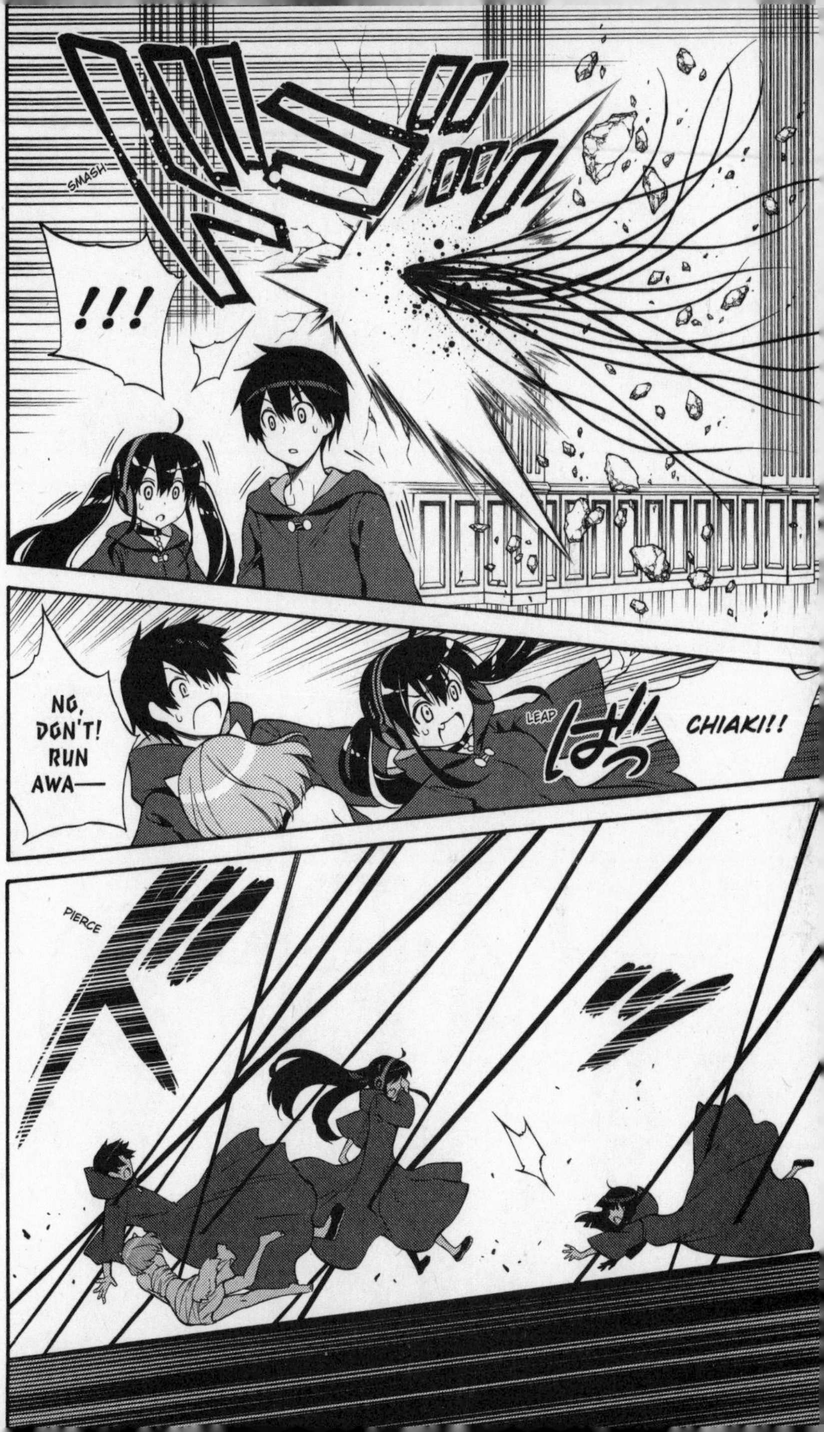
SMASH
!!!
CHIAKI!!
LEAP
NO, DON'T! RUN AWA—
PIERCE

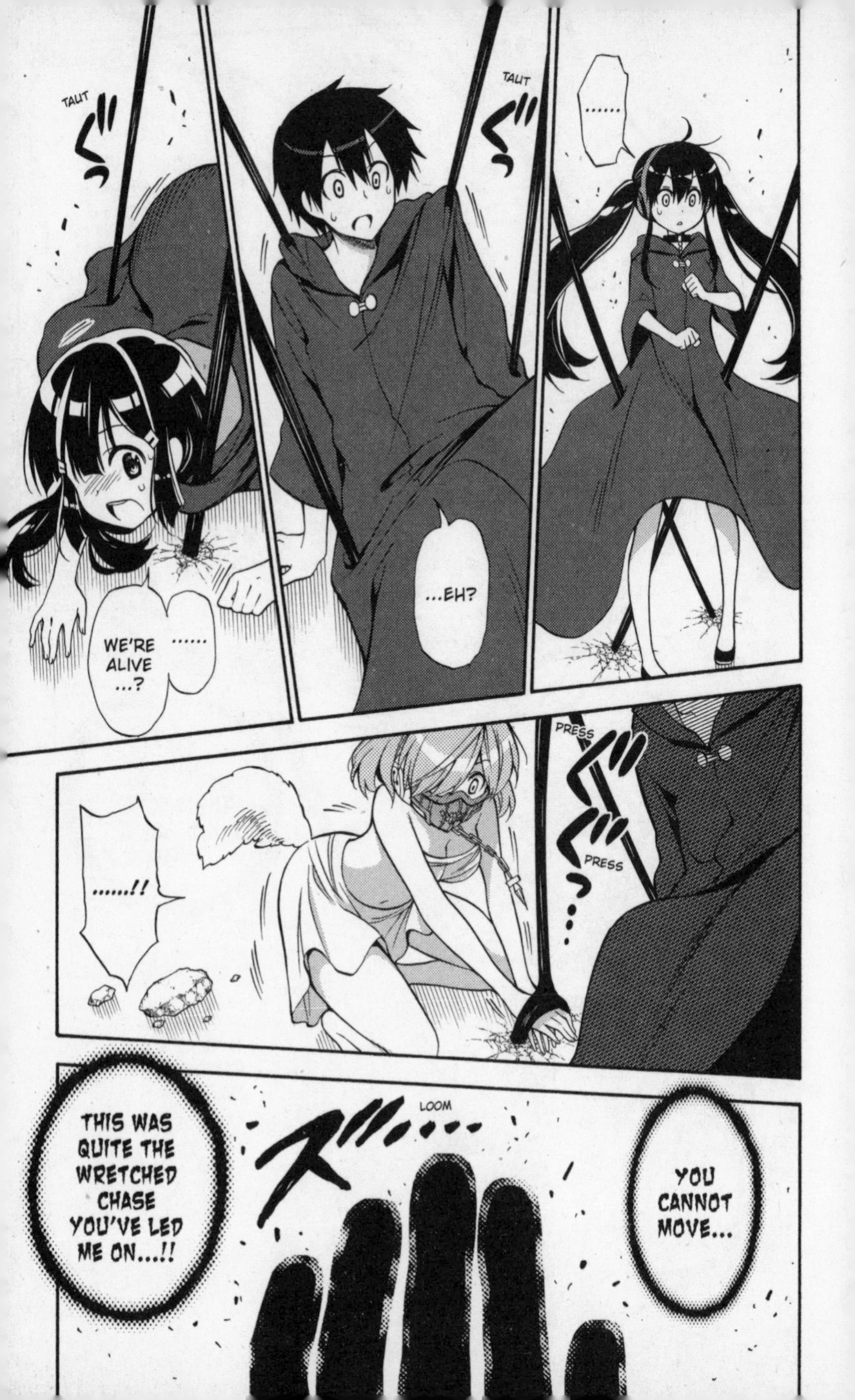
......
TAUT
...EH?
TAUT
......
WE'RE ALIVE ...?
PRESS
PRESS
......!!
YOU CANNOT MOVE...
LOOM
THIS WAS QUITE THE WRETCHED CHASE YOU'VE LED ME ON...!!

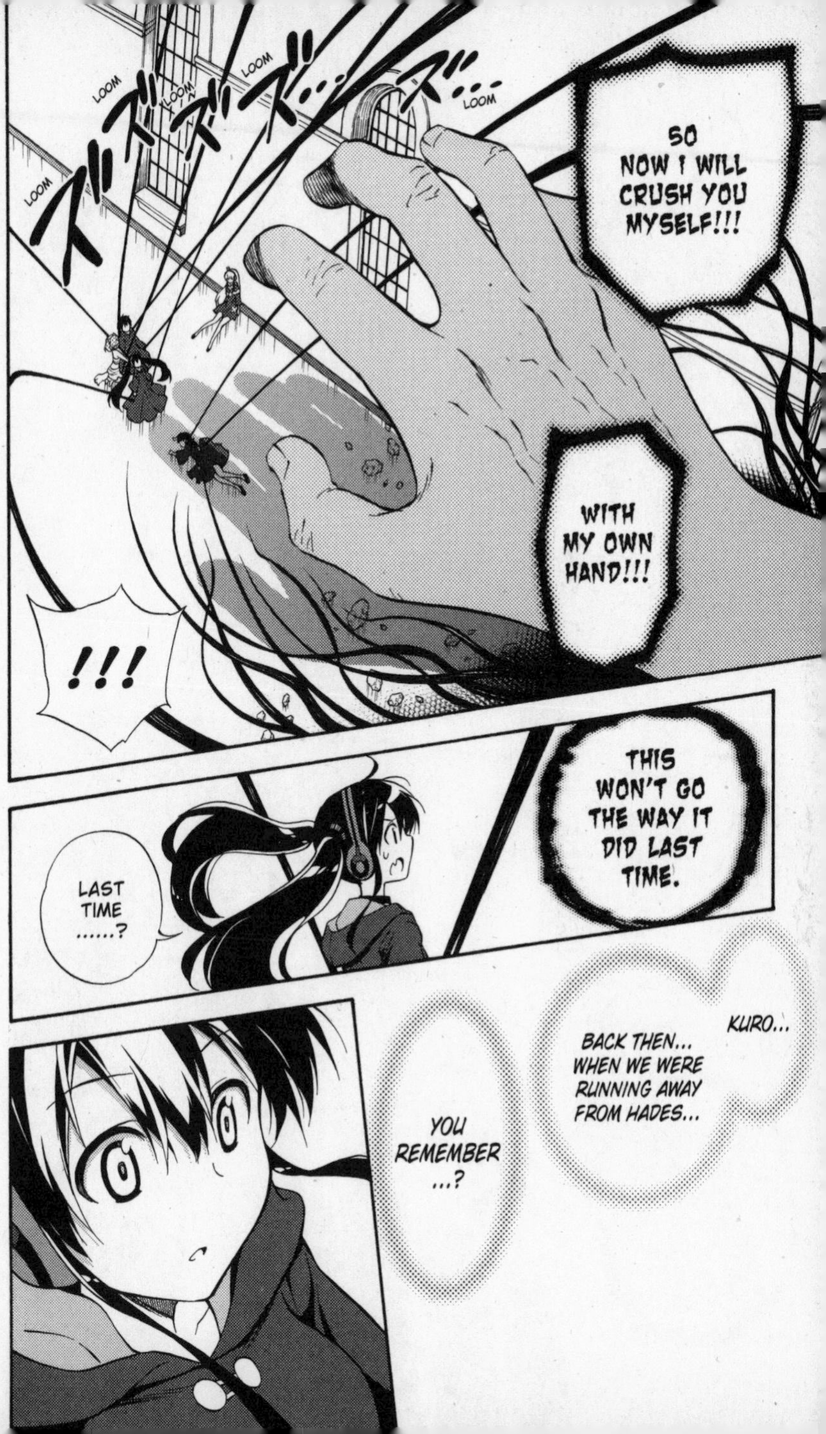
LOOM
LOOM
LOOM
LOOM
LOOM
SO NOW I WILL CRUSH YOU MYSELF!!!
WITH MY OWN HAND!!!
!!!
THIS WON'T GO THE WAY IT DID LAST TIME.
LAST TIME ......?
KURO...
BACK THEN... WHEN WE WERE RUNNING AWAY FROM HADES...
YOU REMEMBER ...?

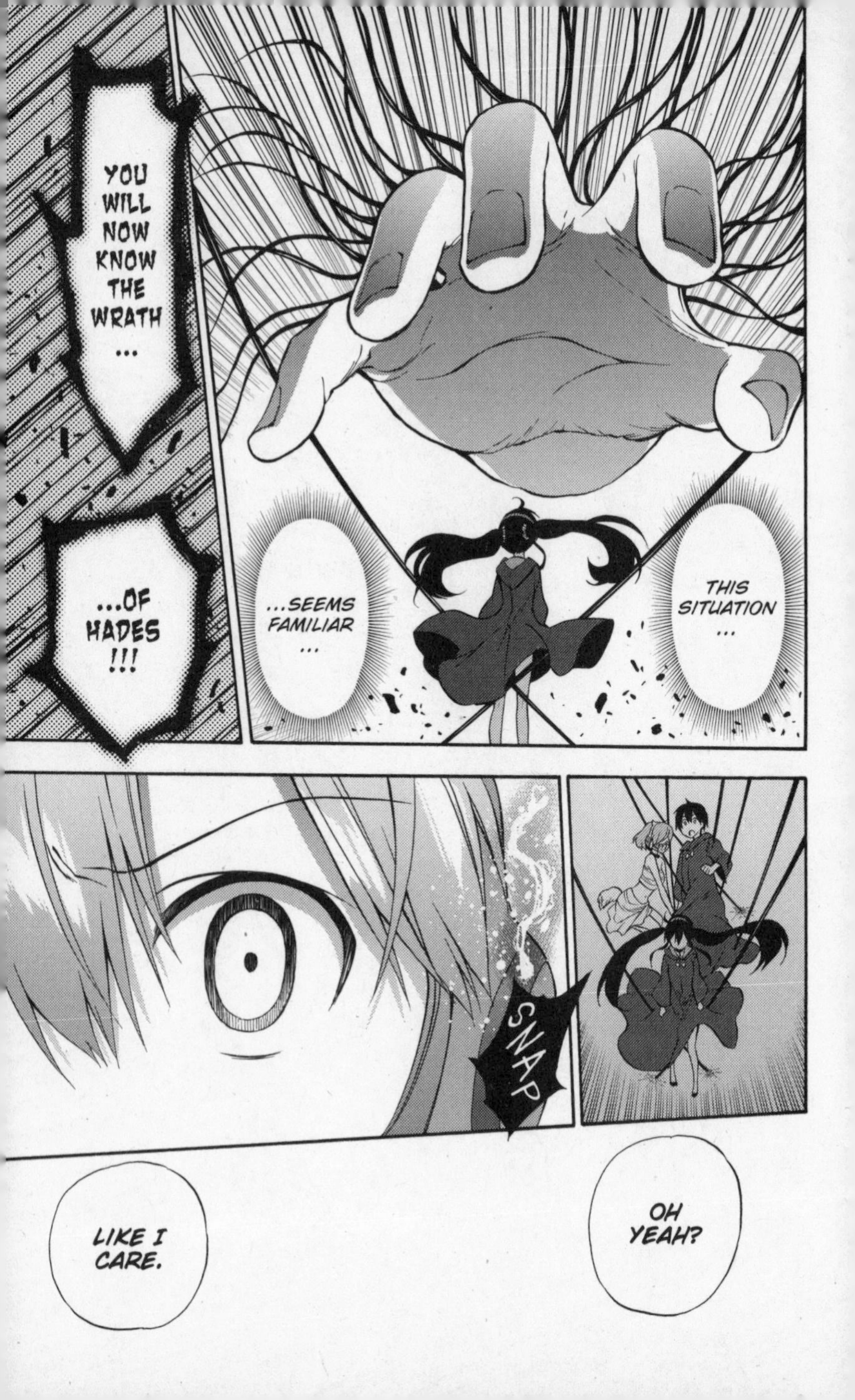
THIS SITUATION ...
...SEEMS FAMILIAR ...
YOU WILL NOW KNOW THE WRATH ...
...OF HADES !!!
SNAP
OH YEAH?
LIKE I CARE.

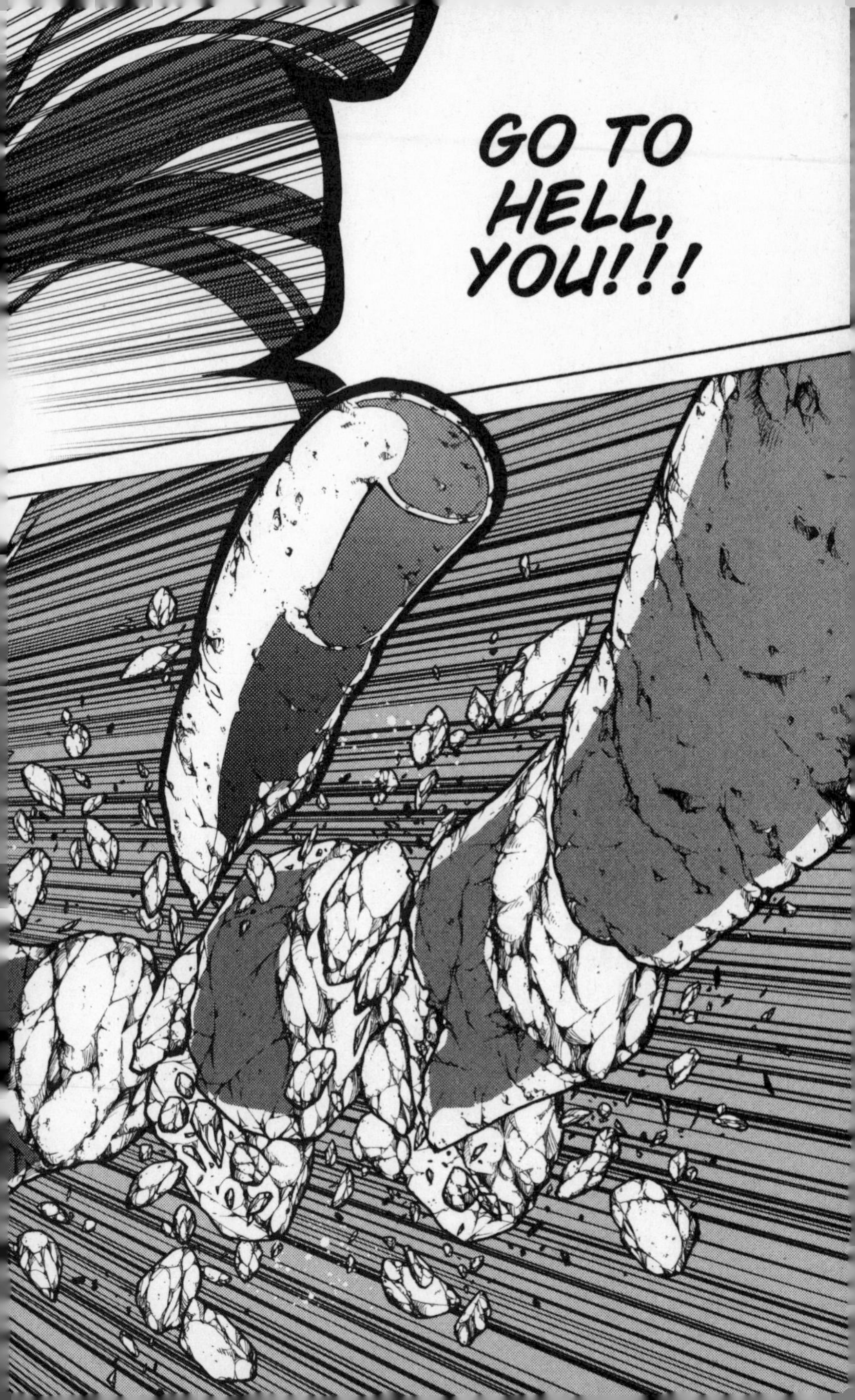
GO TO HELL, YOU!!!

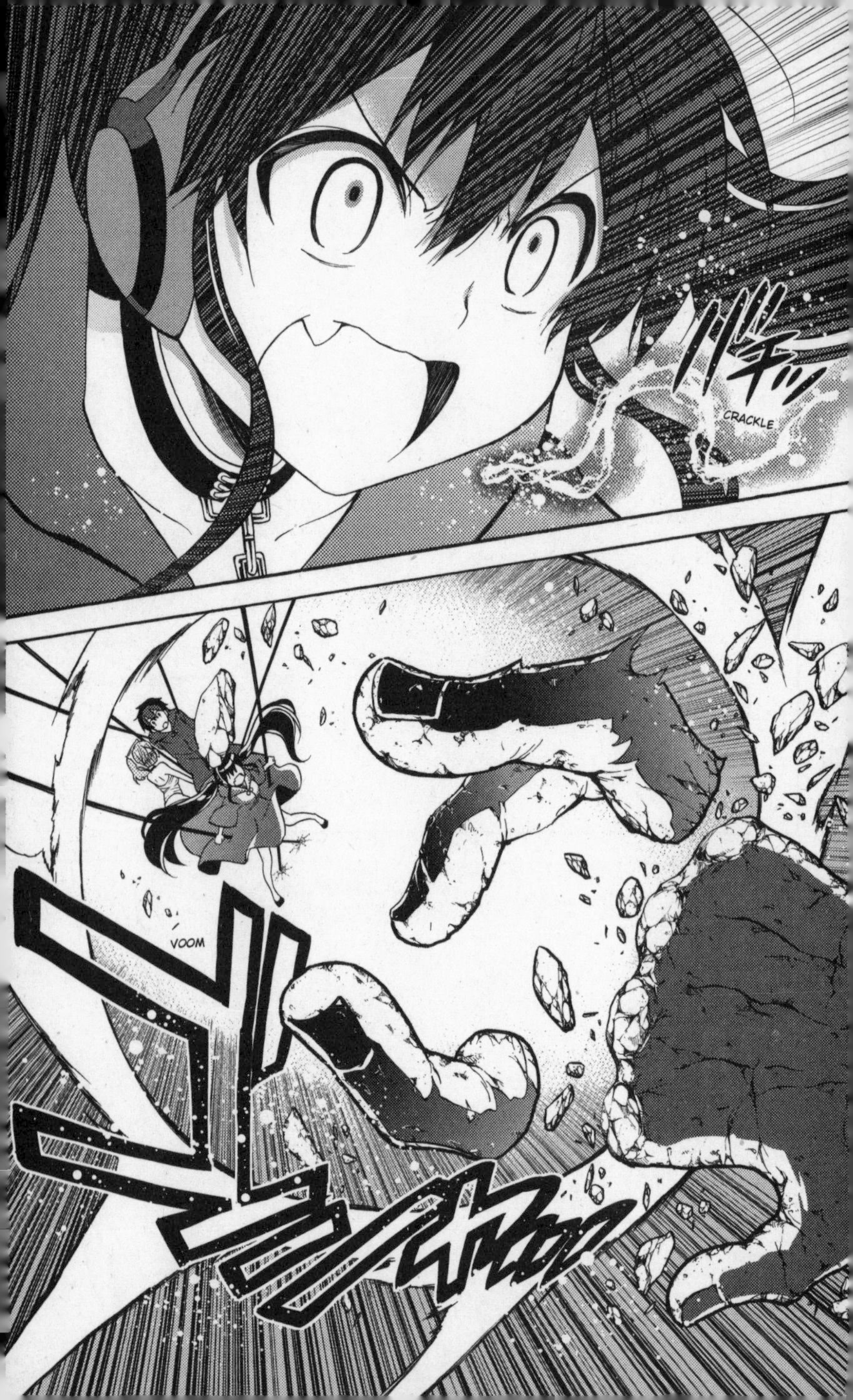
CRACKLE
VOOM

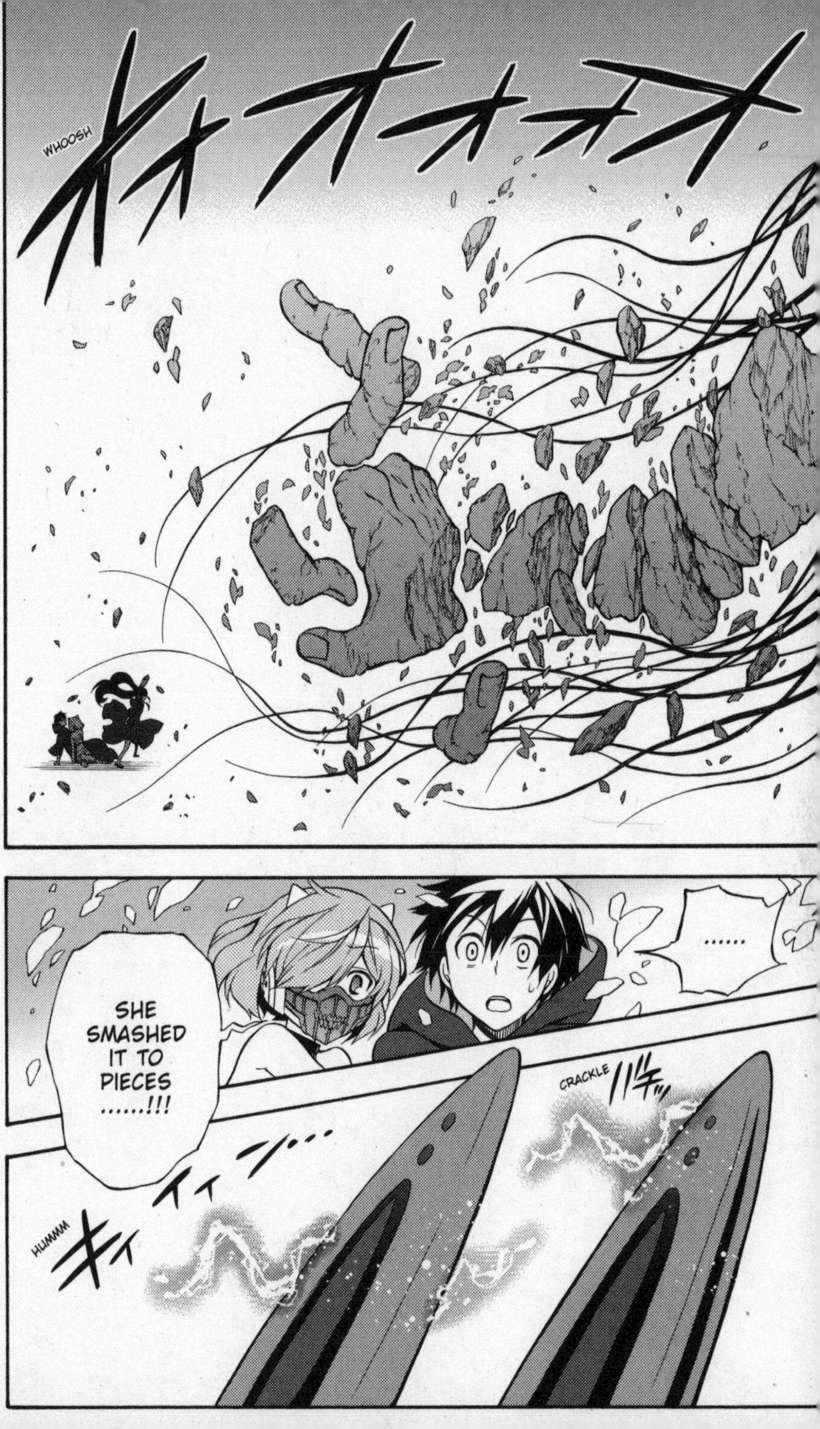

WHOOSH
......
SHE SMASHED IT TO PIECES ......!!!
CRACKLE
HUMMM

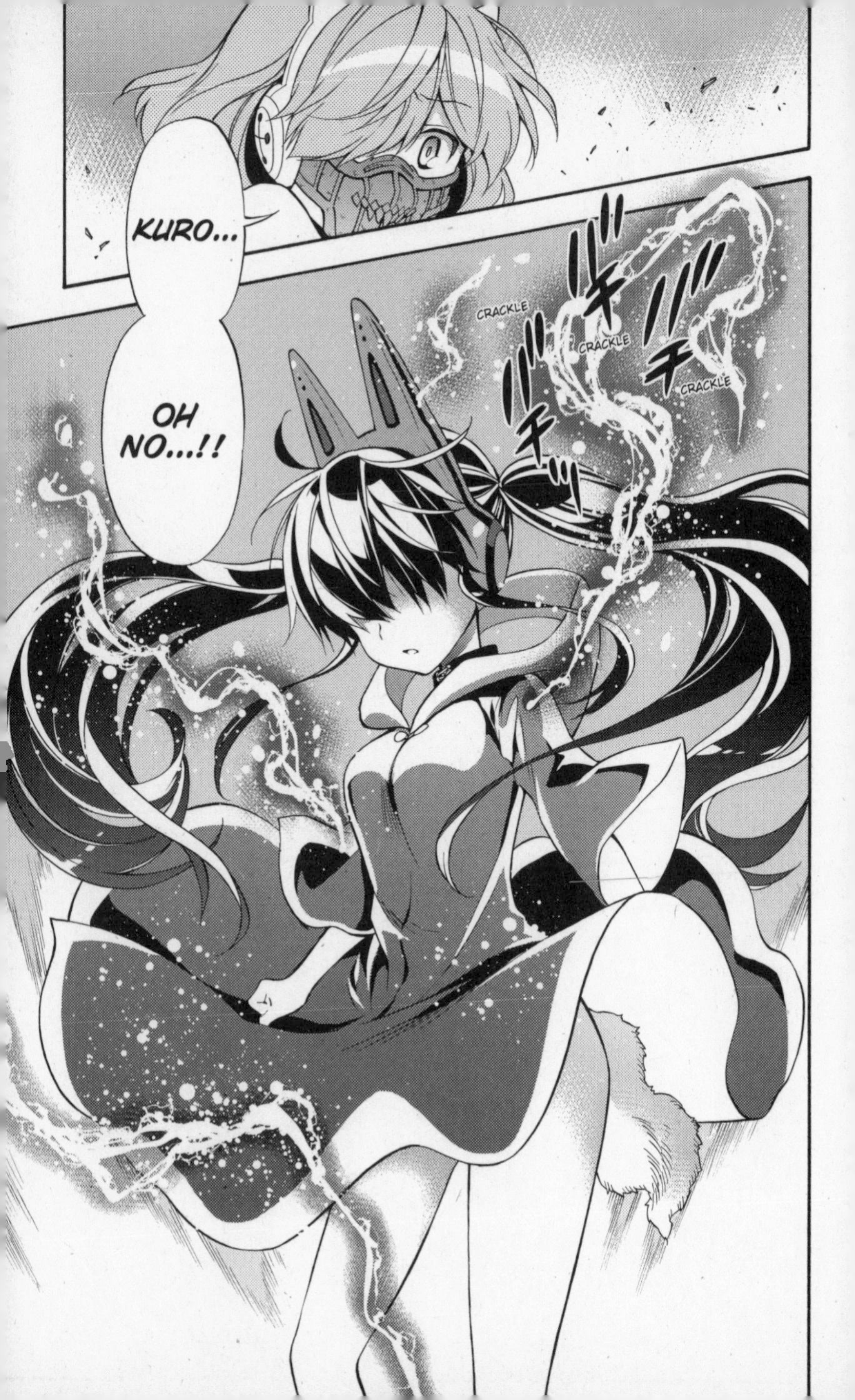
KURO...
OH NO...!!
CRACKLE
CRACKLE
CRACKLE

TODAY'S CERBERUS 🐾

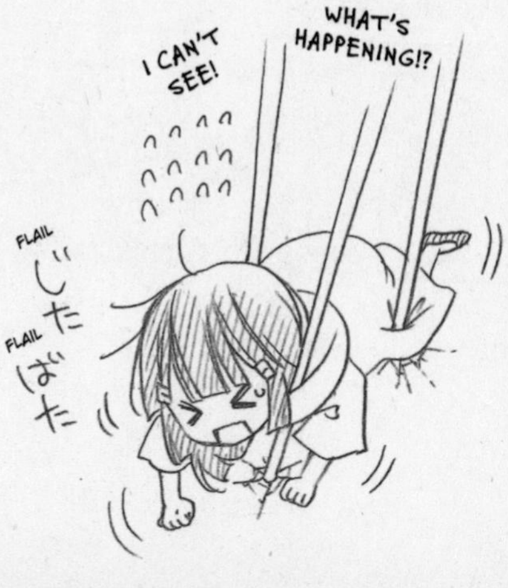
WHAT'S HAPPENING!?
I CAN'T SEE!
FLAIL
じた
FLAIL
ばた

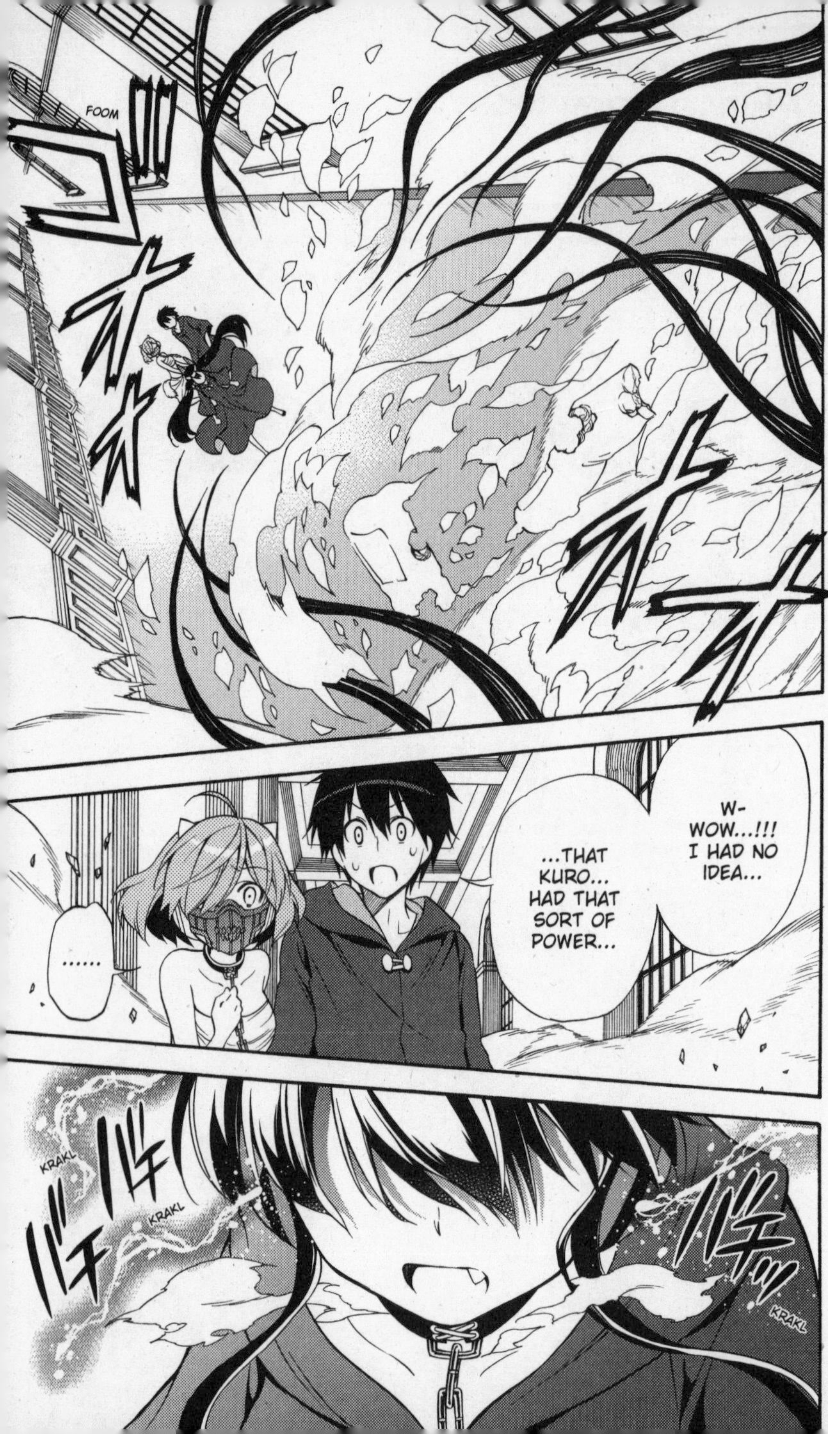
FOOM
W-
WOW...!!!
I HAD NO
IDEA...
...THAT
KURO...
HAD THAT
SORT OF
POWER...
......
KRAKL
KRAKL
KRAKL

CHAPTER 36: A MIRACLE THAT NIGHT

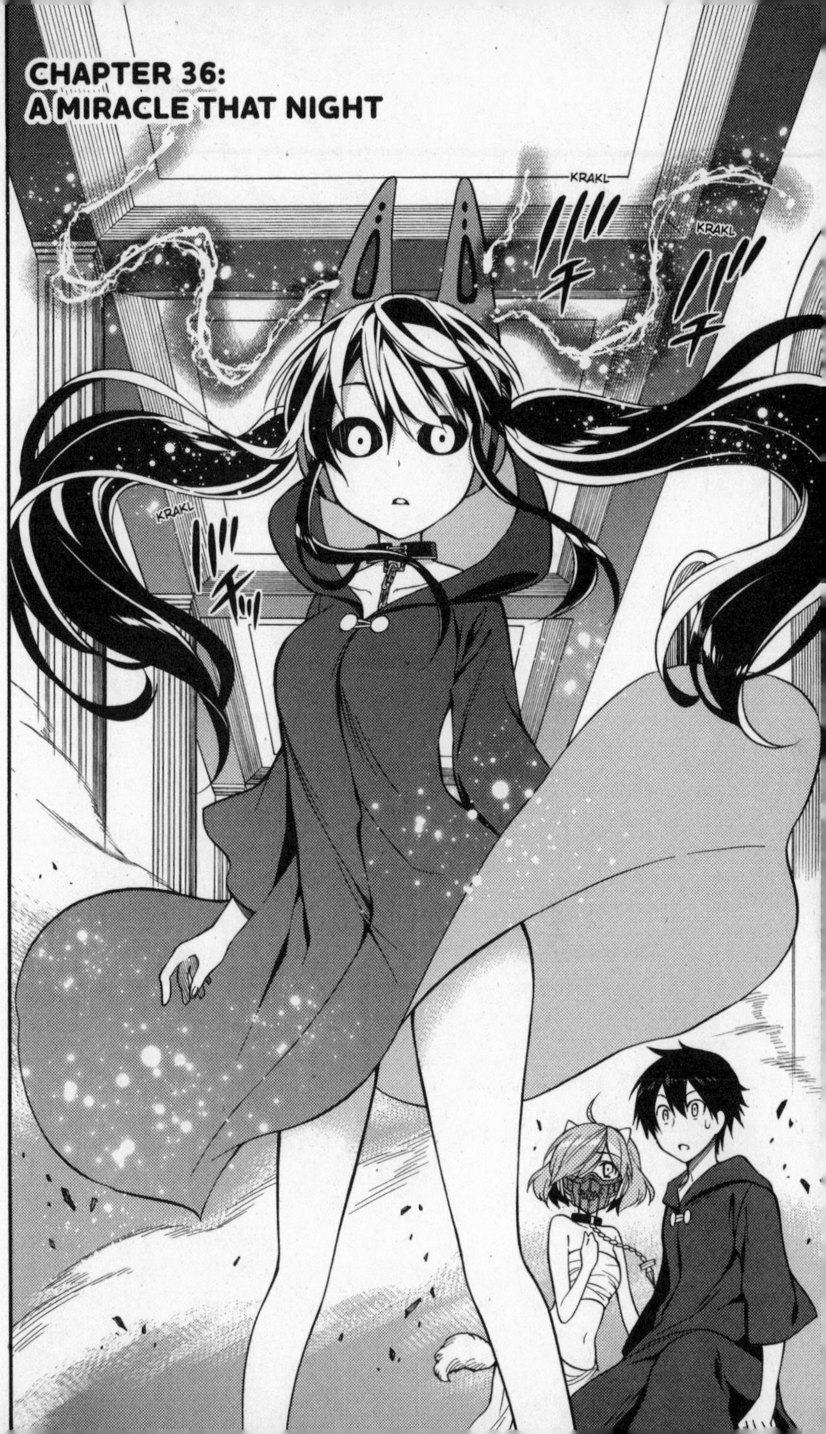
KRAKL
KRAKL
KRAKL

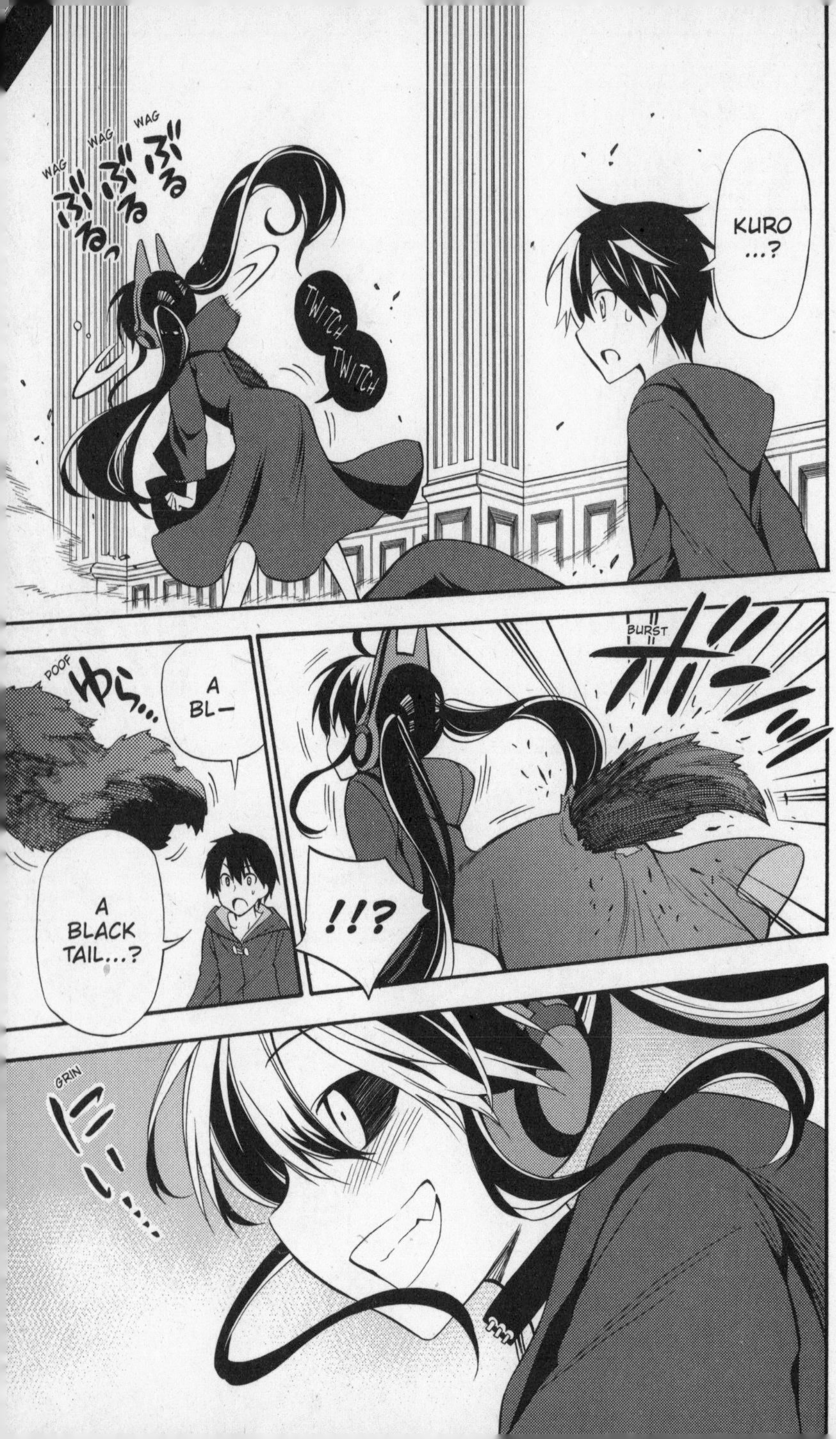
KURO ...?
TWITCH TWITCH
WAG WAG WAG
ぶるぶるぶるっ
BURST
!!?
POOF
ゆら…
A BL—
A BLACK TAIL...?
GRIN
にぃぃ…

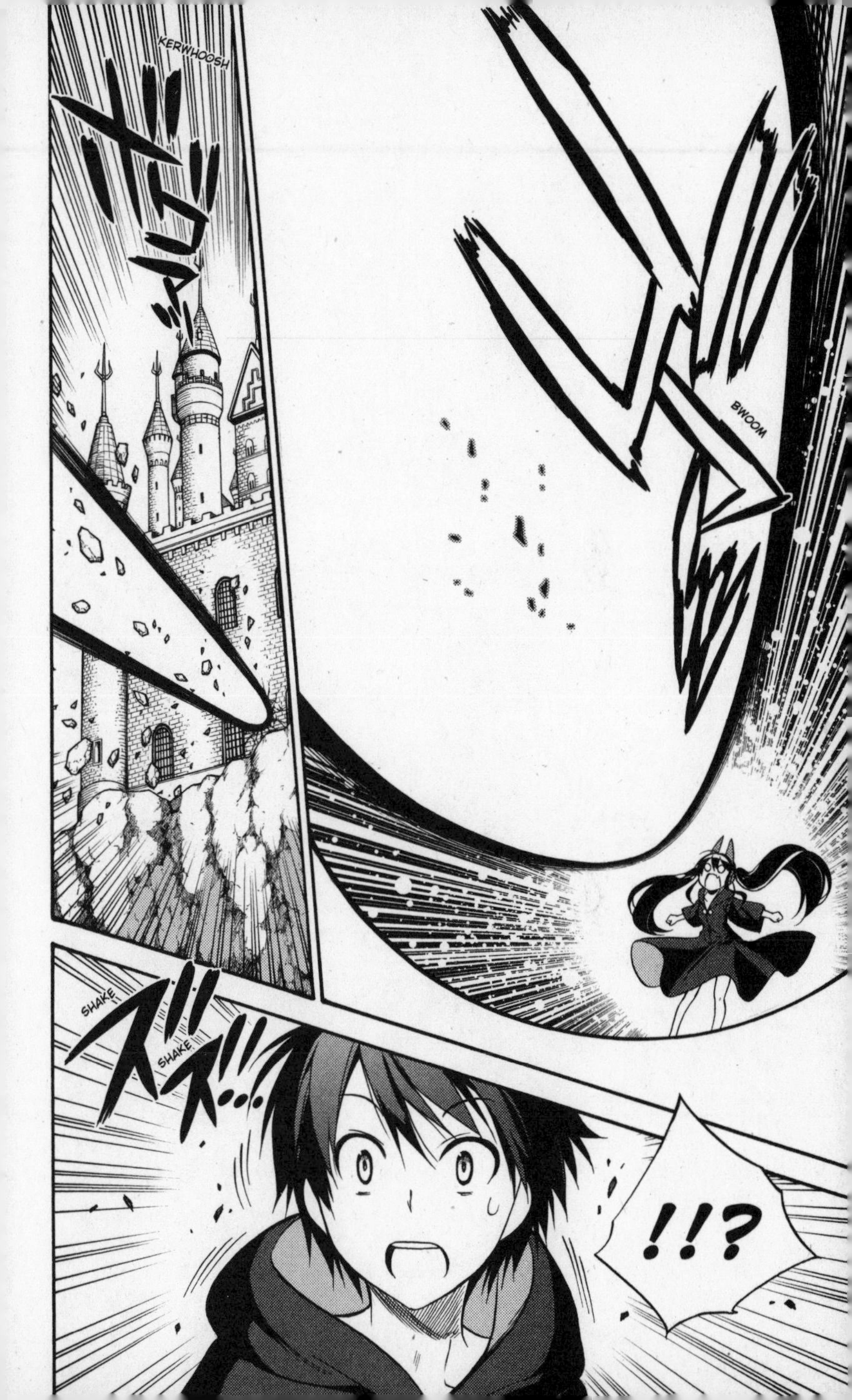
BWOOM
KERWHOOSH
SHAKE
SHAKE
!!?

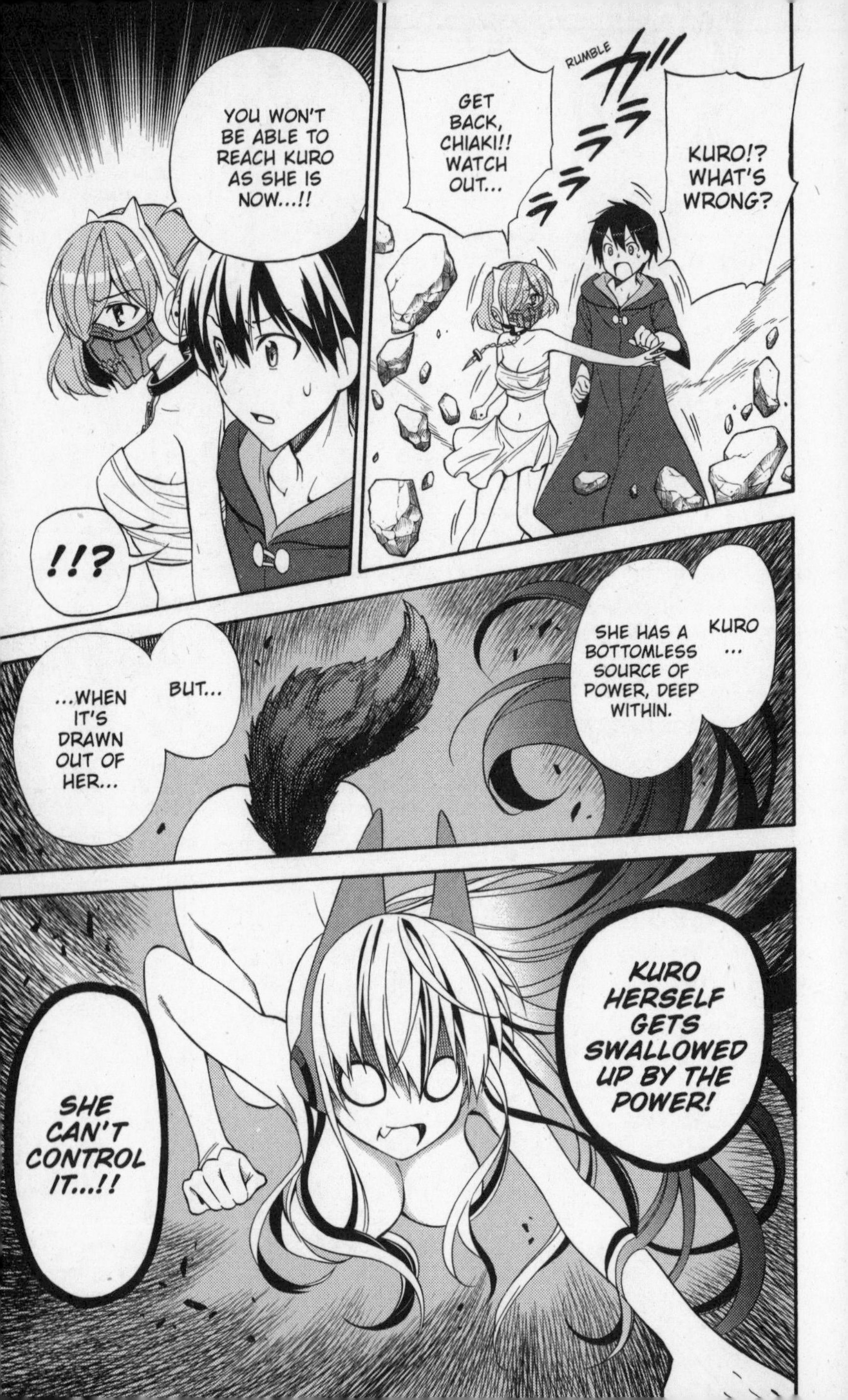
KURO!? WHAT'S WRONG?
RUMBLE
GET BACK, CHIAKI!! WATCH OUT...
YOU WON'T BE ABLE TO REACH KURO AS SHE IS NOW...!!
!!?
KURO...
SHE HAS A BOTTOMLESS SOURCE OF POWER, DEEP WITHIN.
BUT...
...WHEN IT'S DRAWN OUT OF HER...
KURO HERSELF GETS SWALLOWED UP BY THE POWER!
SHE CAN'T CONTROL IT...!!

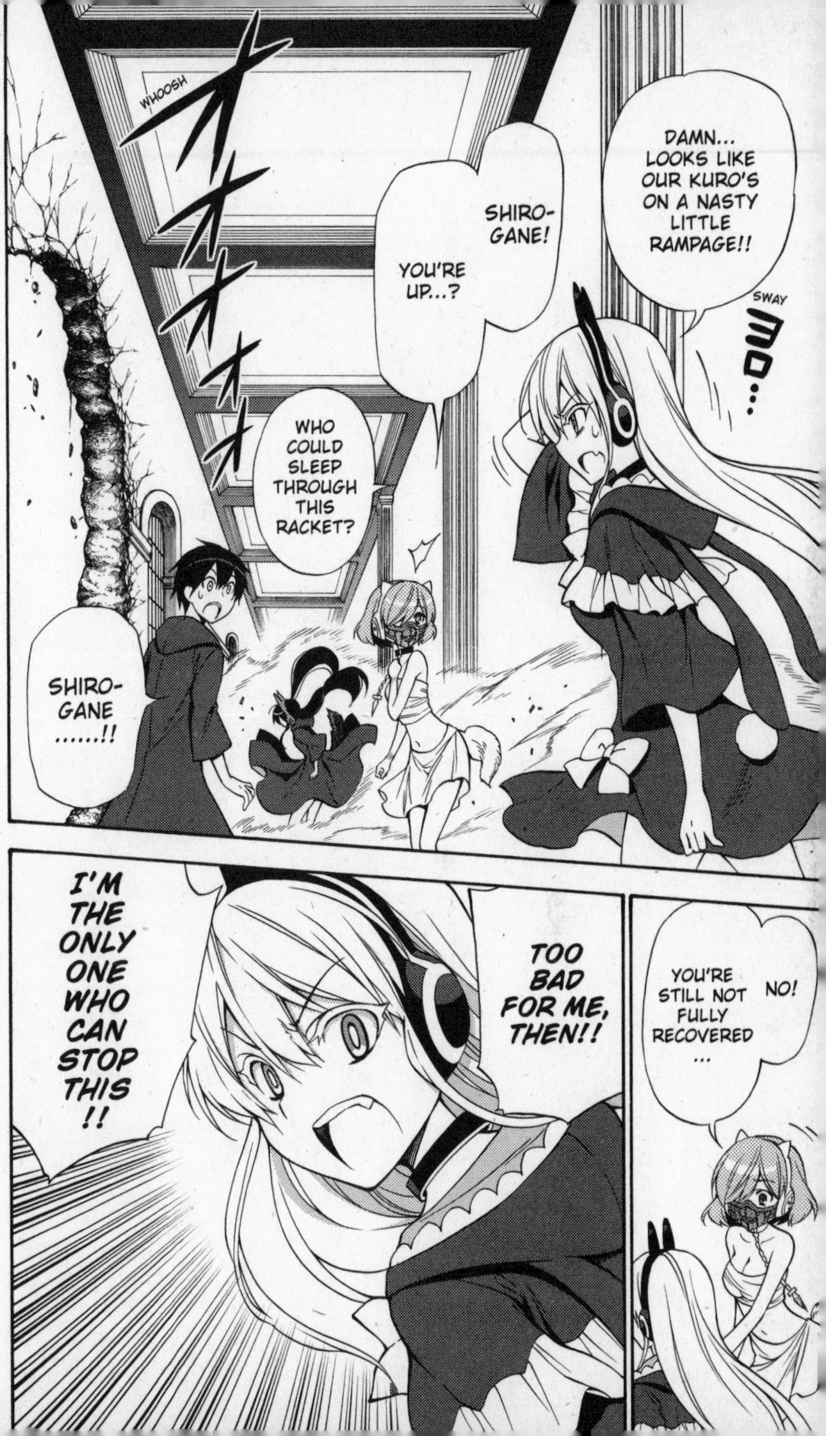
DAMN... LOOKS LIKE OUR KURO'S ON A NASTY LITTLE RAMPAGE!!
SWAY
SHIRO-GANE! YOU'RE UP...?
WHO COULD SLEEP THROUGH THIS RACKET?
WHOOSH
SHIRO-GANE ......!!
NO! YOU'RE STILL NOT FULLY RECOVERED ...
TOO BAD FOR ME, THEN!!
I'M THE ONLY ONE WHO CAN STOP THIS!!

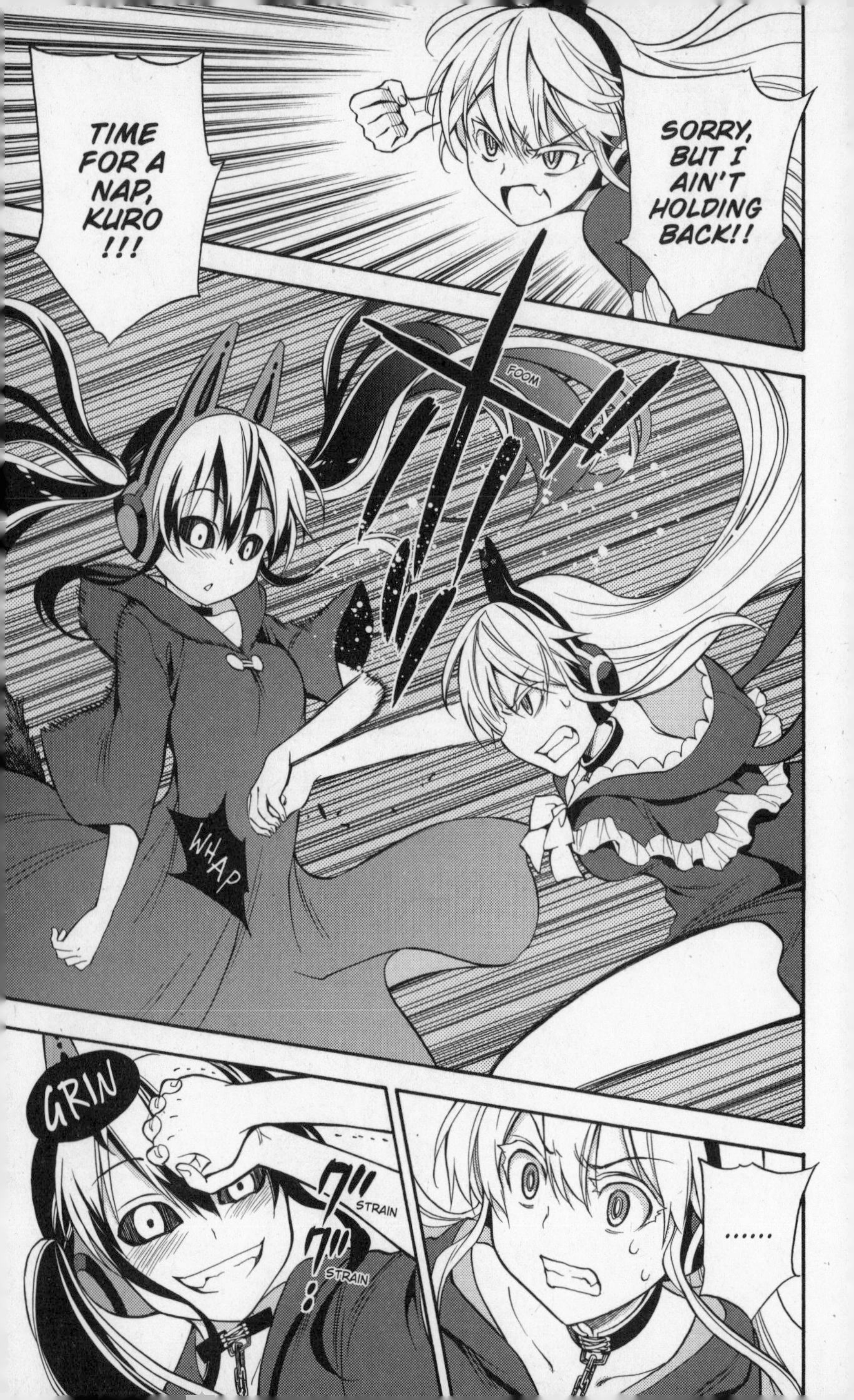
SORRY, BUT I AIN'T HOLDING BACK!!
TIME FOR A NAP, KURO!!!
FOOM
WHAP
......
GRIN
STRAIN
STRAIN

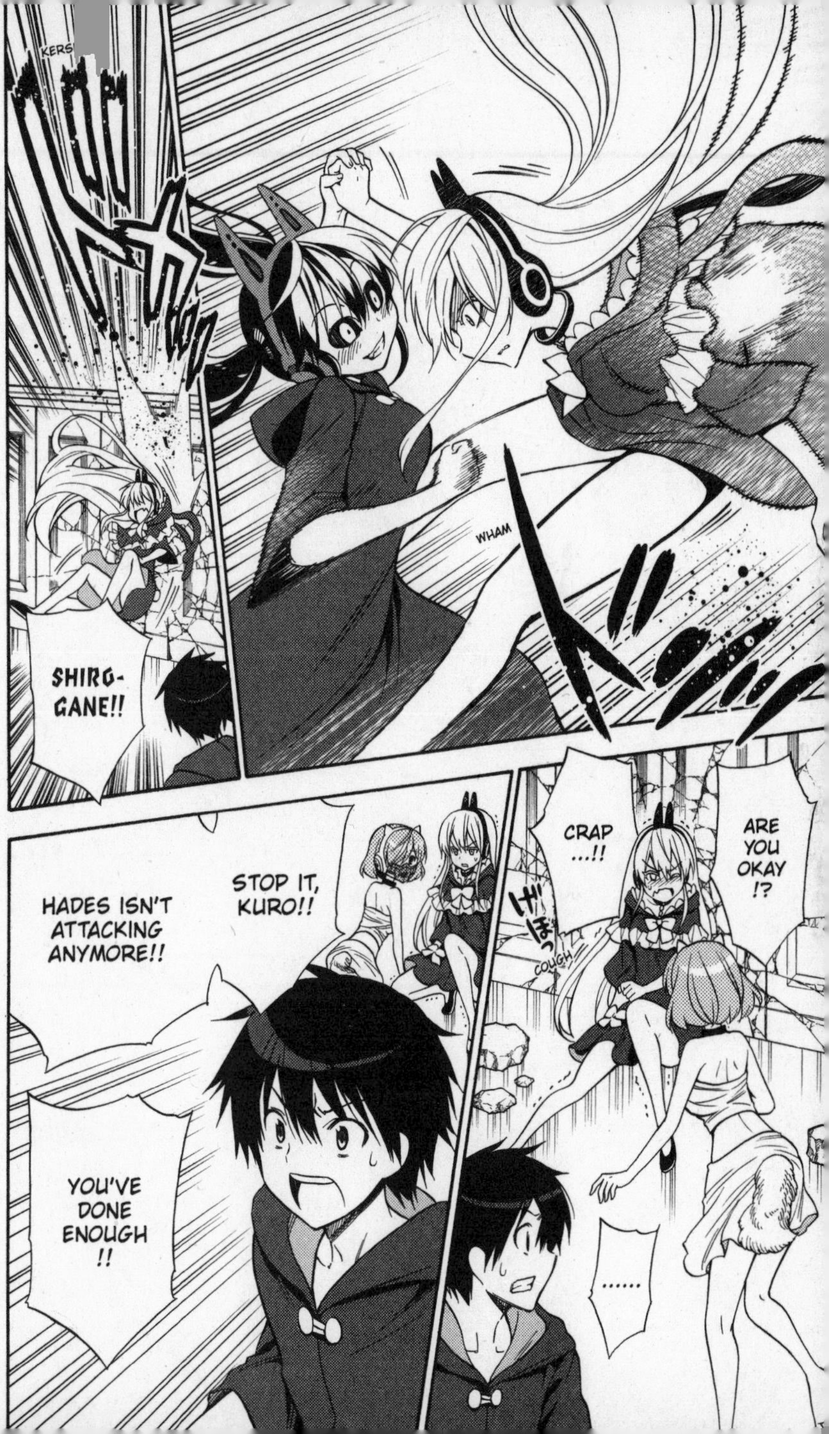
WHAM
KERS
SHIRO-GANE!!
ARE YOU OKAY!?
CRAP ...!!
げほっ
COUGH
......
STOP IT, KURO!!
HADES ISN'T ATTACKING ANYMORE!!
YOU'VE DONE ENOUGH!!

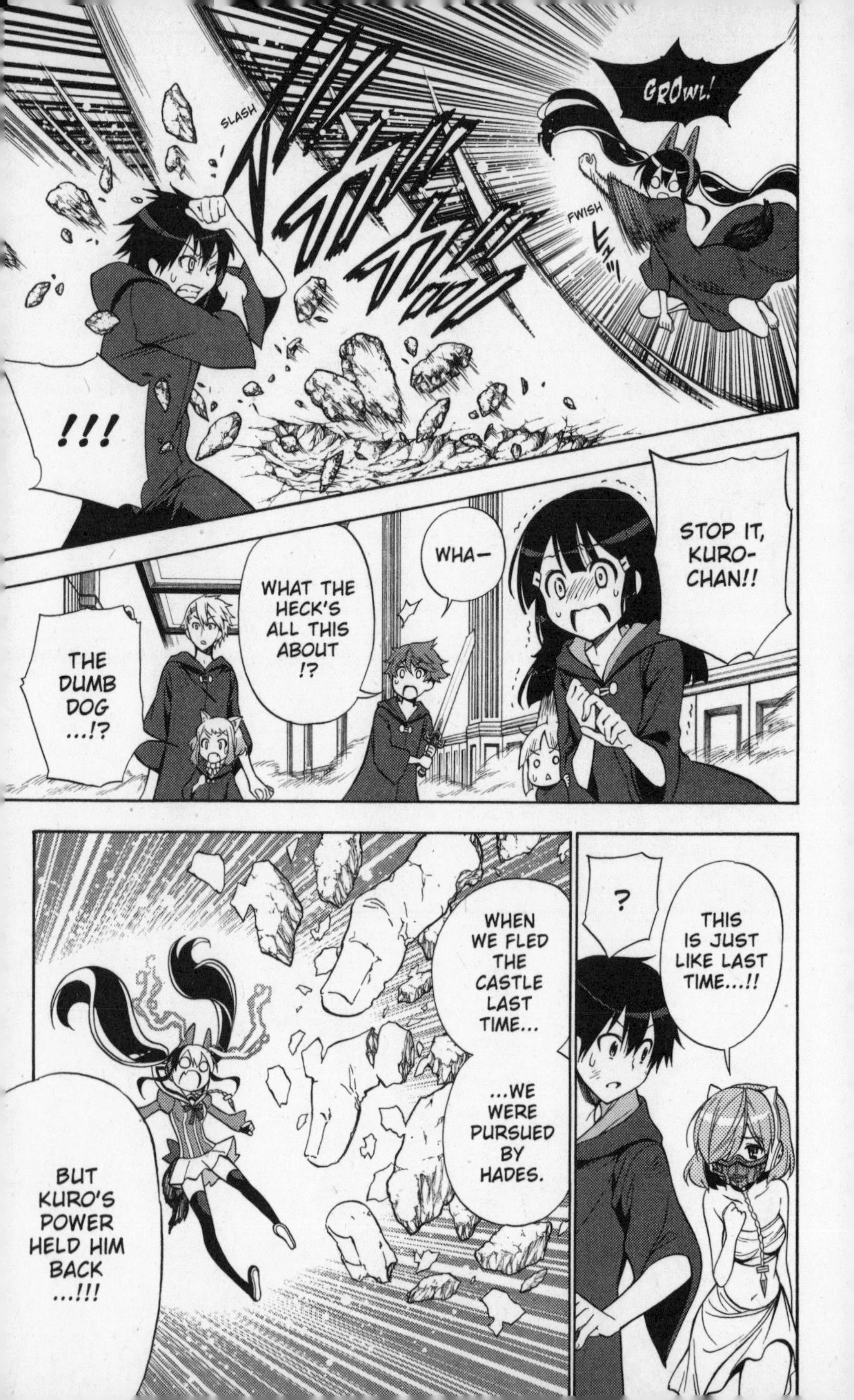
GROWL!
FWISH
SLASH
!!!
STOP IT, KURO-CHAN!!
WHA—
WHAT THE HECK'S ALL THIS ABOUT !?
THE DUMB DOG ...!?
THIS IS JUST LIKE LAST TIME...!!
?
WHEN WE FLED THE CASTLE LAST TIME...
...WE WERE PURSUED BY HADES.
BUT KURO'S POWER HELD HIM BACK ...!!!

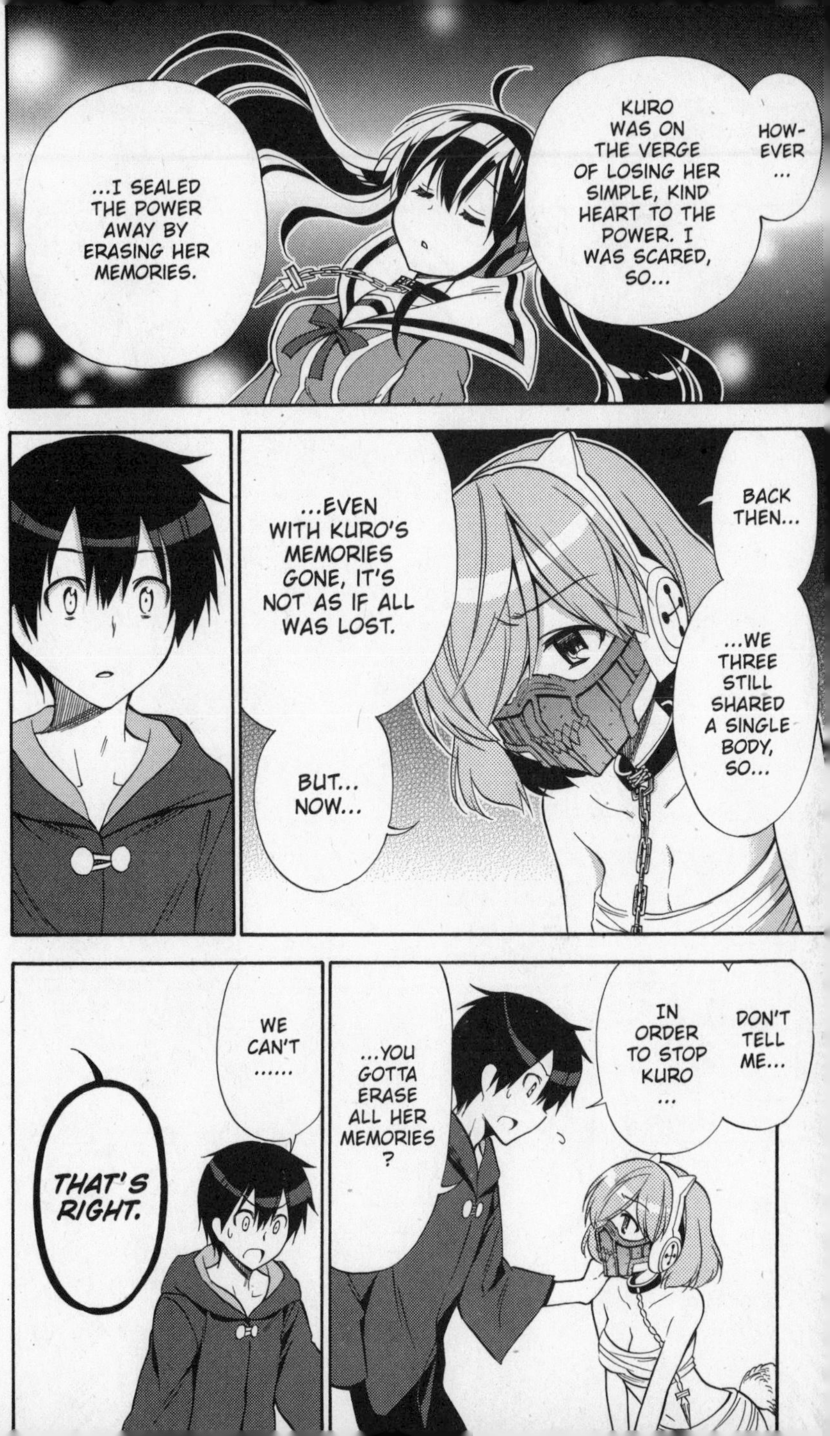
HOW-EVER ...
KURO WAS ON THE VERGE OF LOSING HER SIMPLE, KIND HEART TO THE POWER. I WAS SCARED, SO...
...I SEALED THE POWER AWAY BY ERASING HER MEMORIES.
BACK THEN...
...WE THREE STILL SHARED A SINGLE BODY, SO...
...EVEN WITH KURO'S MEMORIES GONE, IT'S NOT AS IF ALL WAS LOST.
BUT... NOW...
DON'T TELL ME...
IN ORDER TO STOP KURO ...
...YOU GOTTA ERASE ALL HER MEMORIES ?
WE CAN'T ......
THAT'S RIGHT.

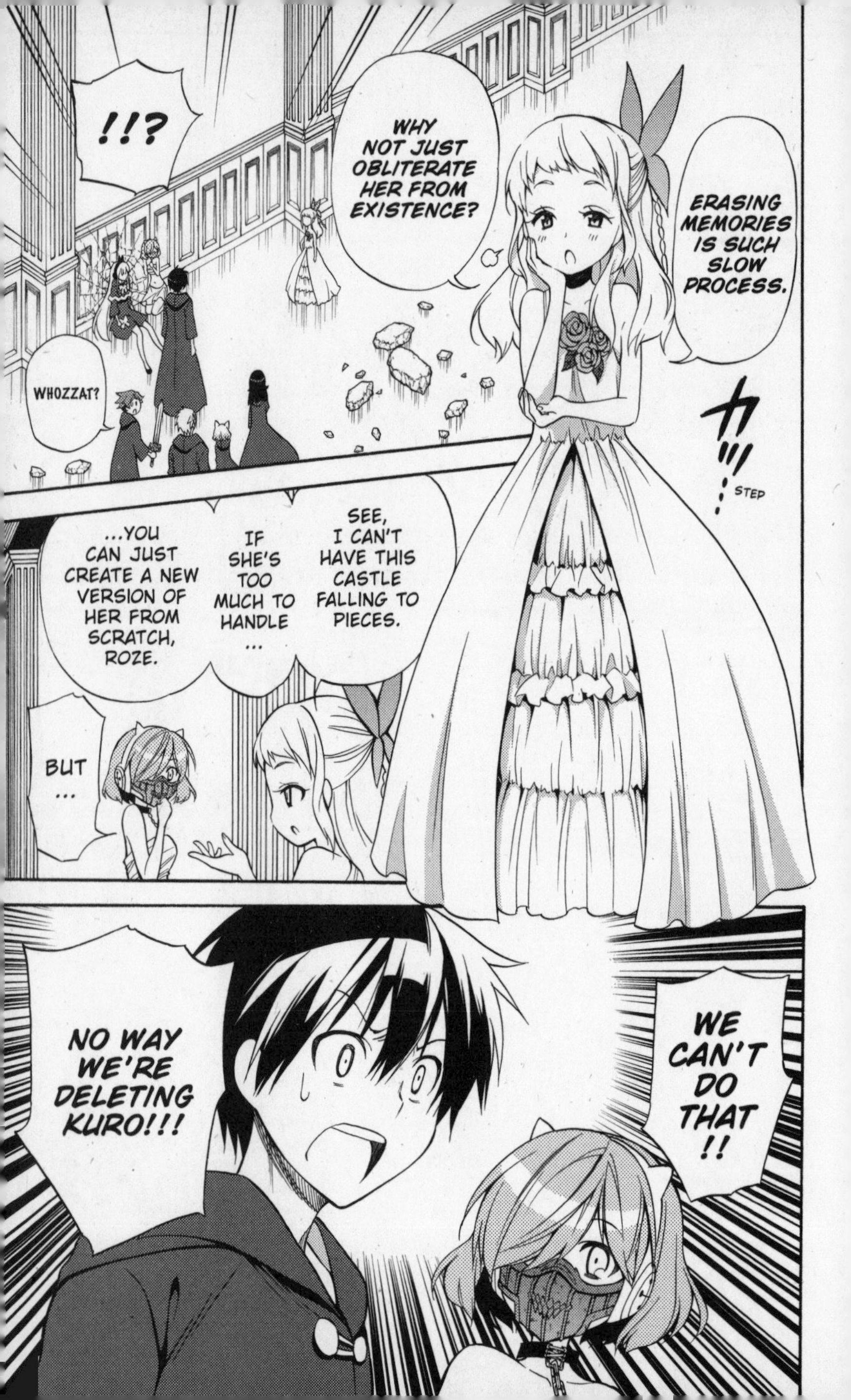
ERASING MEMORIES IS SUCH SLOW PROCESS.
WHY NOT JUST OBLITERATE HER FROM EXISTENCE?
!!?
WHOZZAT?
STEP
SEE, I CAN'T HAVE THIS CASTLE FALLING TO PIECES.
IF SHE'S TOO MUCH TO HANDLE ...
...YOU CAN JUST CREATE A NEW VERSION OF HER FROM SCRATCH, ROZE.
BUT ...
WE CAN'T DO THAT!!
NO WAY WE'RE DELETING KURO!!!

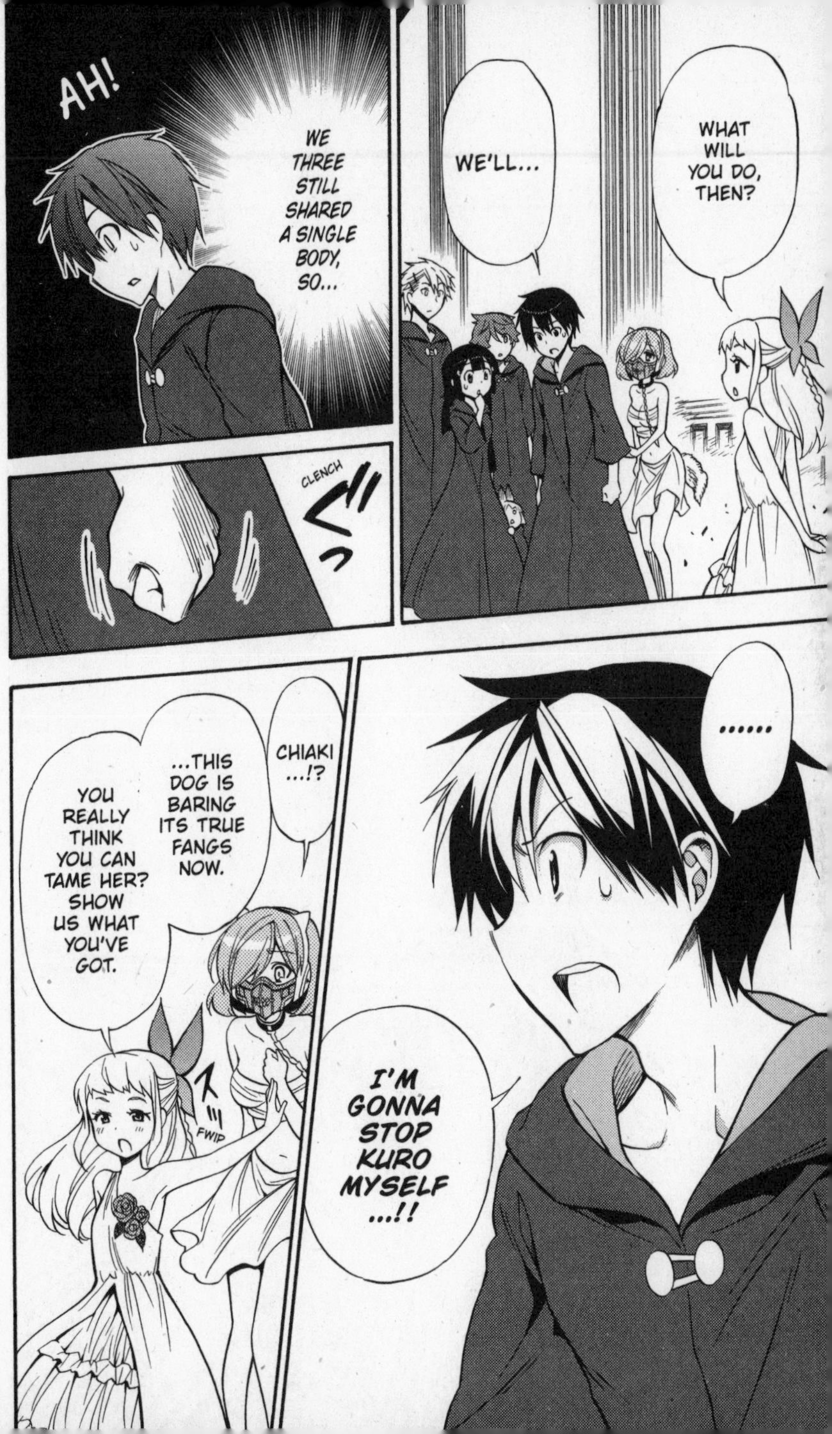
WHAT WILL YOU DO, THEN?
WE'LL...
AH!
WE THREE STILL SHARED A SINGLE BODY, SO...
CLENCH
......
I'M GONNA STOP KURO MYSELF ...!!
CHIAKI ...!?
...THIS DOG IS BARING ITS TRUE FANGS NOW.
YOU REALLY THINK YOU CAN TAME HER? SHOW US WHAT YOU'VE GOT.
FWIP

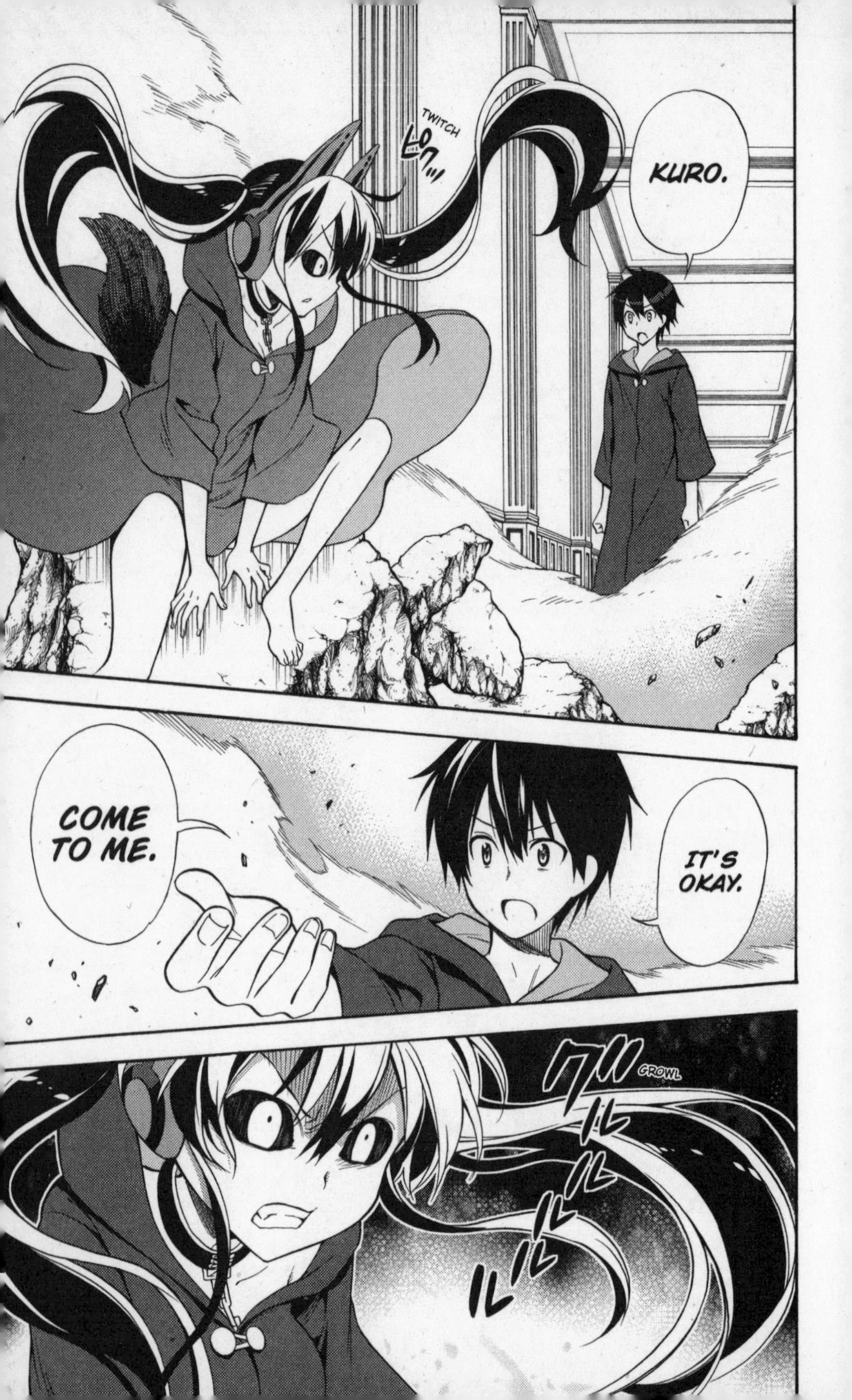
KURO.
TWITCH
IT'S OKAY.
COME TO ME.
GROWL

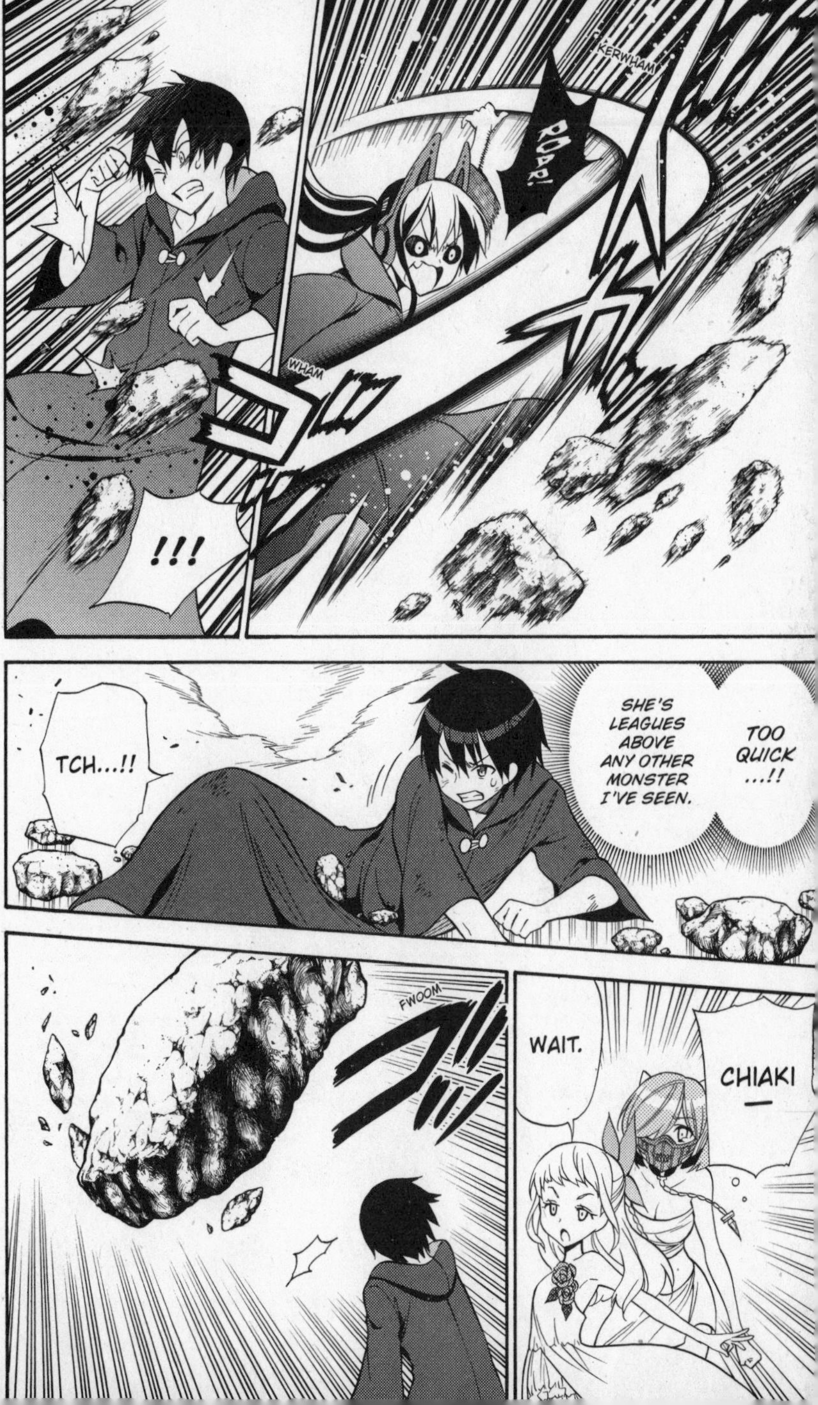
KERWHAM
ROAR!
WHAM
!!!
TOO QUICK ...!!
SHE'S LEAGUES ABOVE ANY OTHER MONSTER I'VE SEEN.
TCH...!!
CHIAKI —
WAIT.
FWOOM

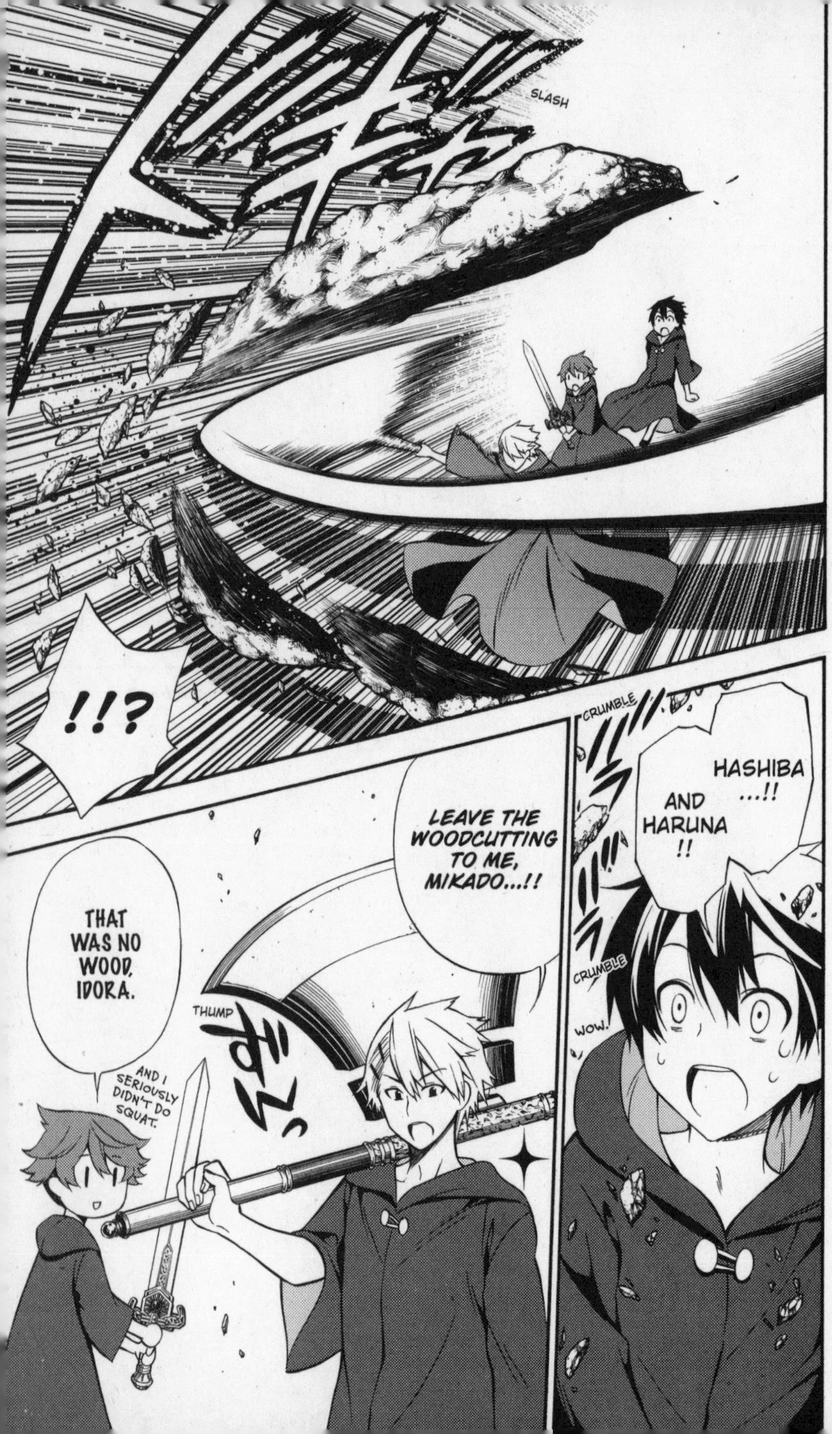
SLASH
!!?
CRUMBLE
HASHIBA ...!!
AND HARUNA !!
CRUMBLE
WOW.
LEAVE THE WOODCUTTING TO ME, MIKADO...!!
THUMP
THAT WAS NO WOOD, IDORA.
AND I SERIOUSLY DIDN'T DO SQUAT.

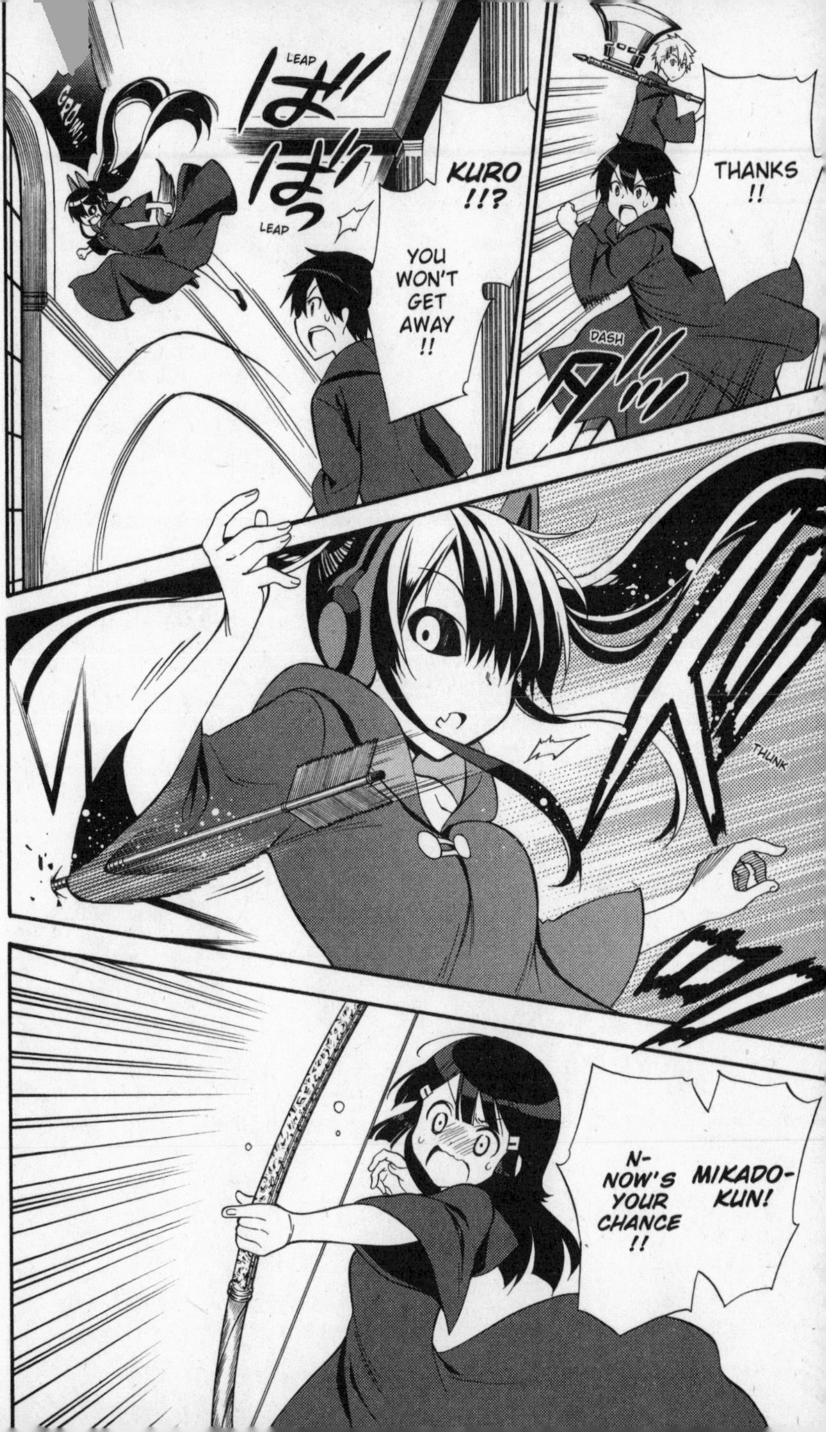
THANKS !!
DASH
ダッ
KURO !!?
YOU WON'T GET AWAY !!
LEAP
ばっ
ばっ
LEAP
GROWL!
THUNK
MIKADO-KUN!
N-NOW'S YOUR CHANCE !!

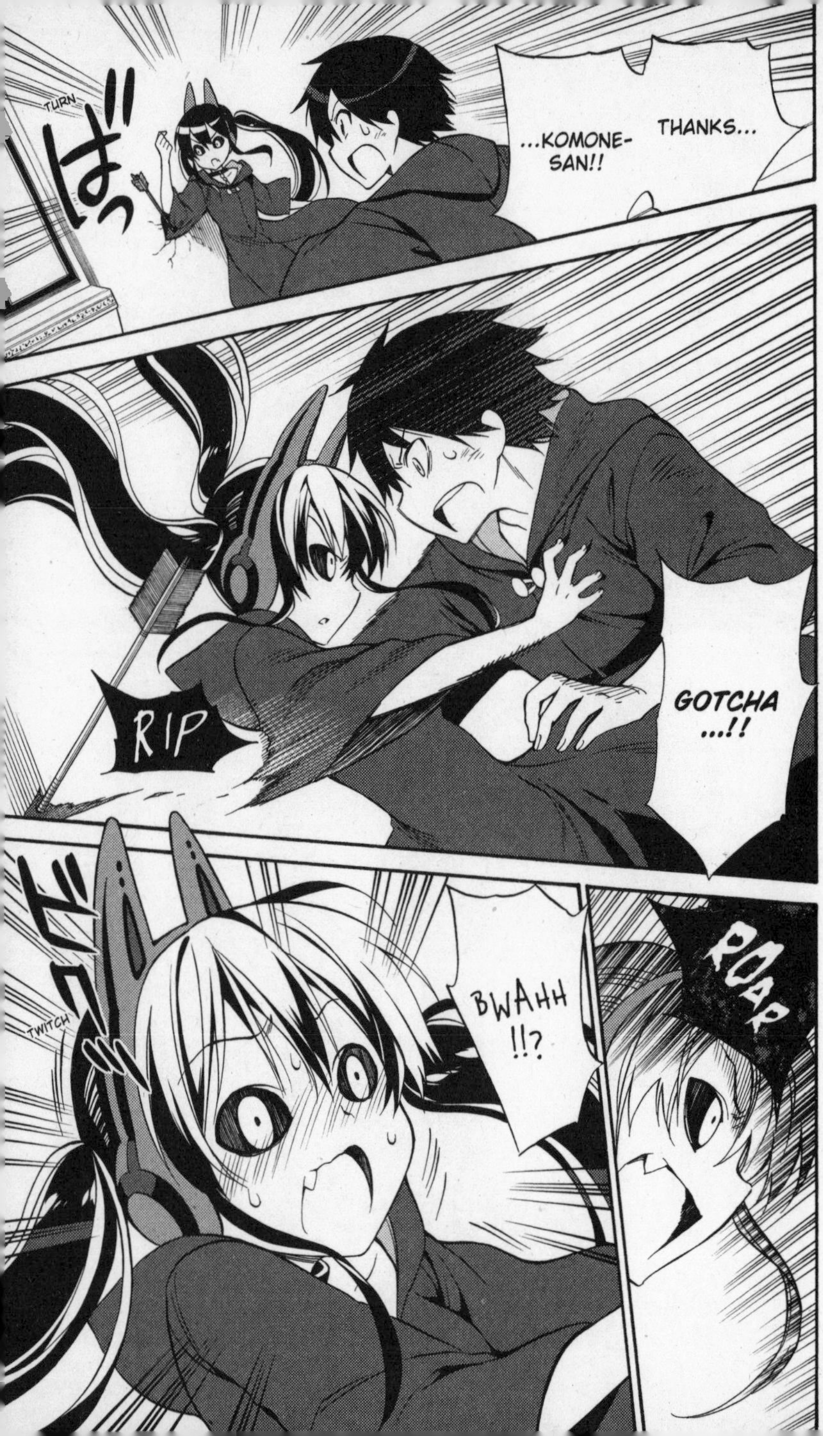
THANKS...
...KOMONE-SAN!!
TURN
ばっ
GOTCHA...!!
RIP
ROAR
BWAHH!!?
TWITCH

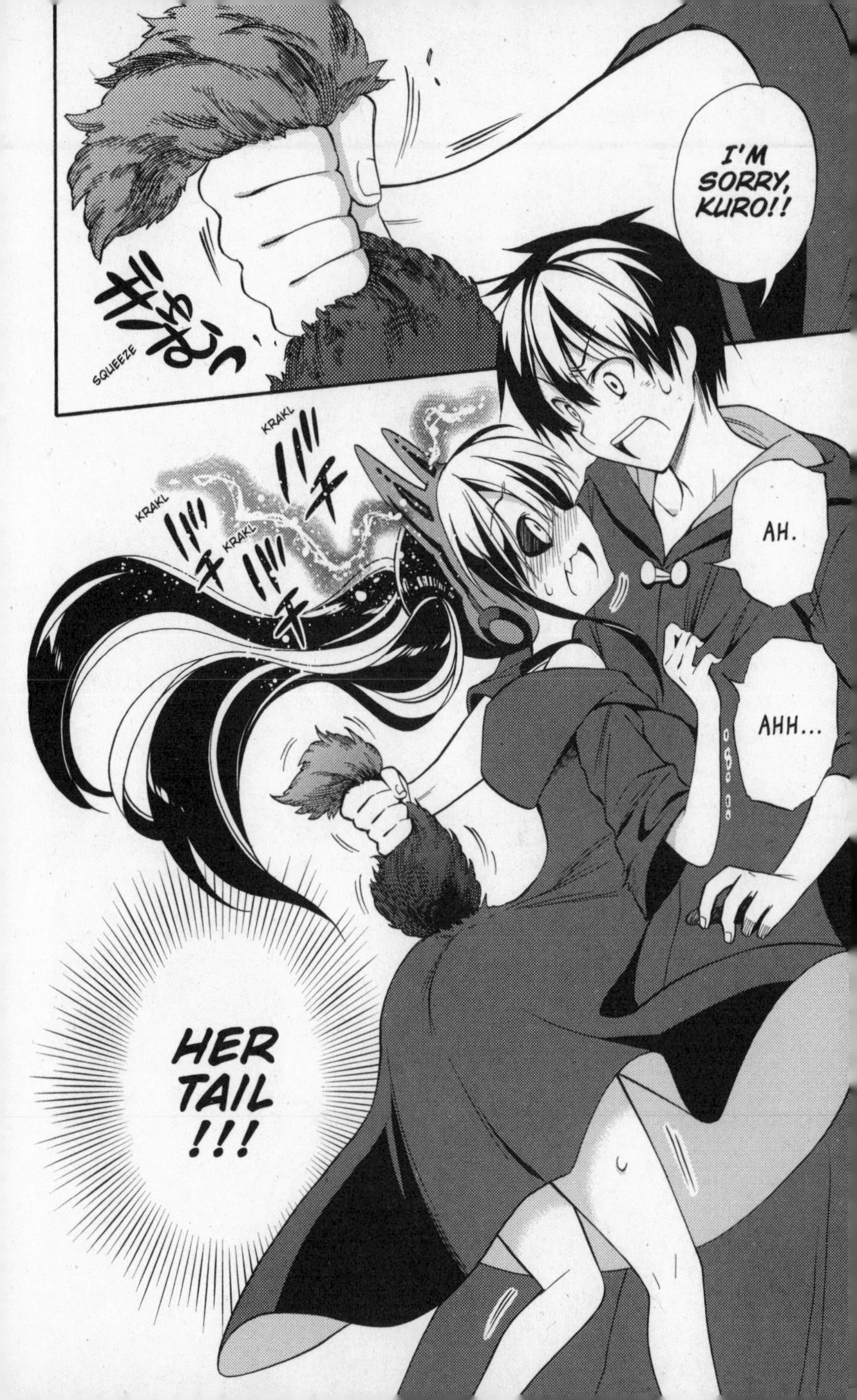
I'M SORRY, KURO!!
SQUEEZE
AH.
AHH...
KRAKL
KRAKL
KRAKL
HER TAIL!!!

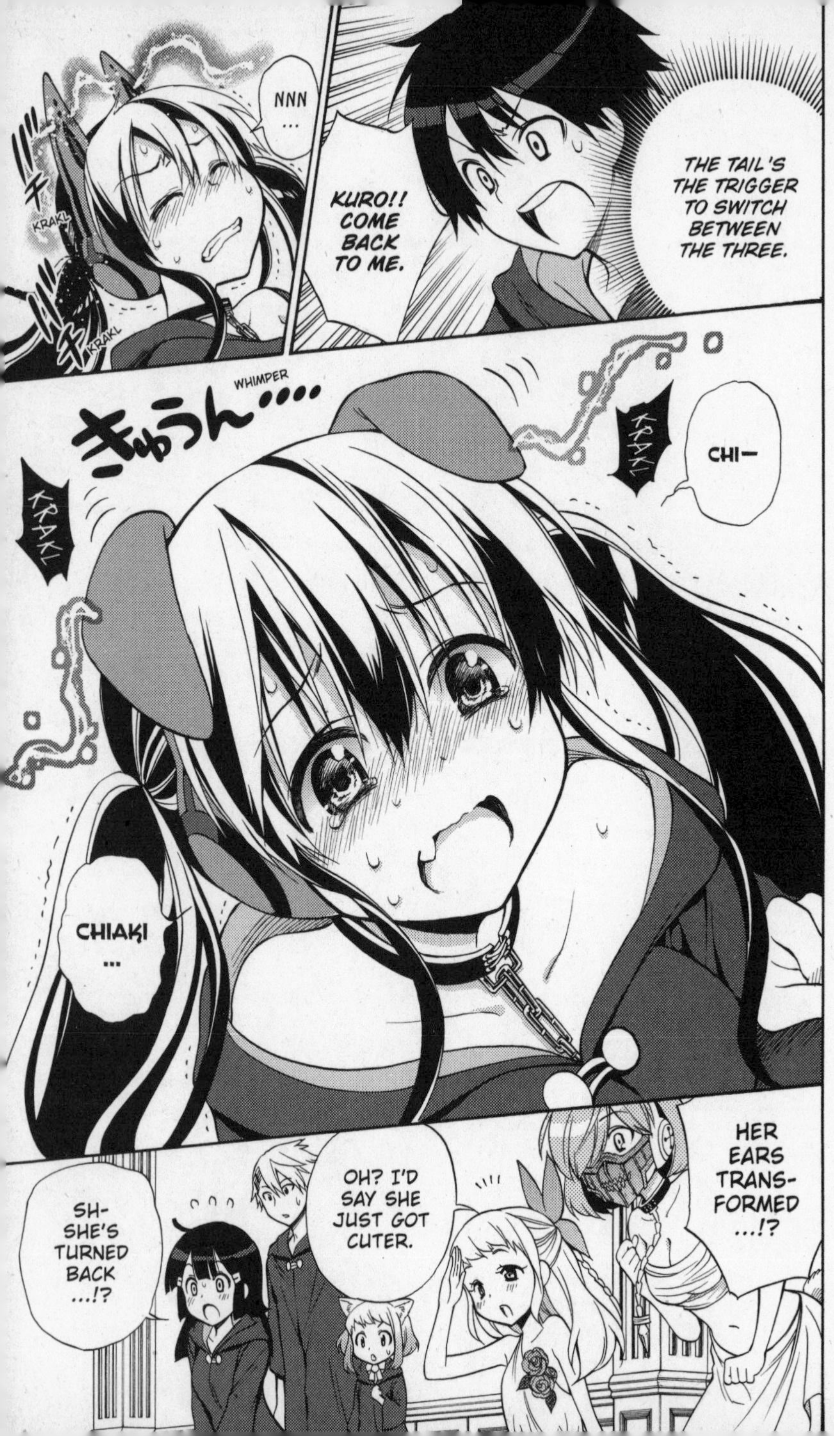
THE TAIL'S THE TRIGGER TO SWITCH BETWEEN THE THREE.
KURO!! COME BACK TO ME.
NNN ...
KRAKL
KRAKL
CHI—
KRAKL
WHIMPER
きゅうん・・・・
KRAKL
CHIAKI ...
HER EARS TRANS-FORMED ...!?
OH? I'D SAY SHE JUST GOT CUTER.
SH-SHE'S TURNED BACK ...!?

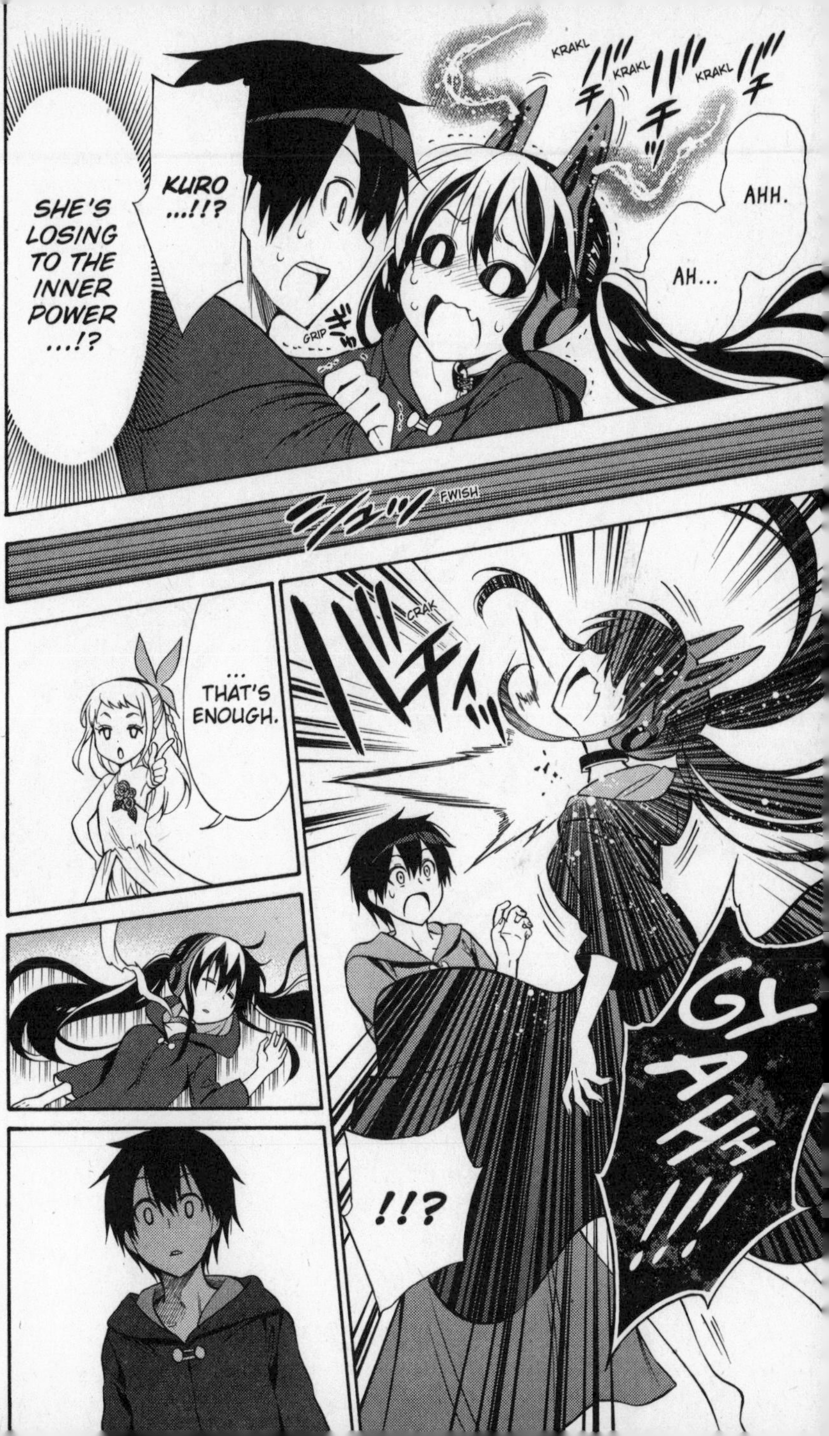
KRAKL
KRAKL
KRAKL
AHH.
AH...
GRIP
KURO ...!!?
SHE'S LOSING TO THE INNER POWER ...!?
FWISH
CRAK
GYAHH!!!
!!?
... THAT'S ENOUGH.

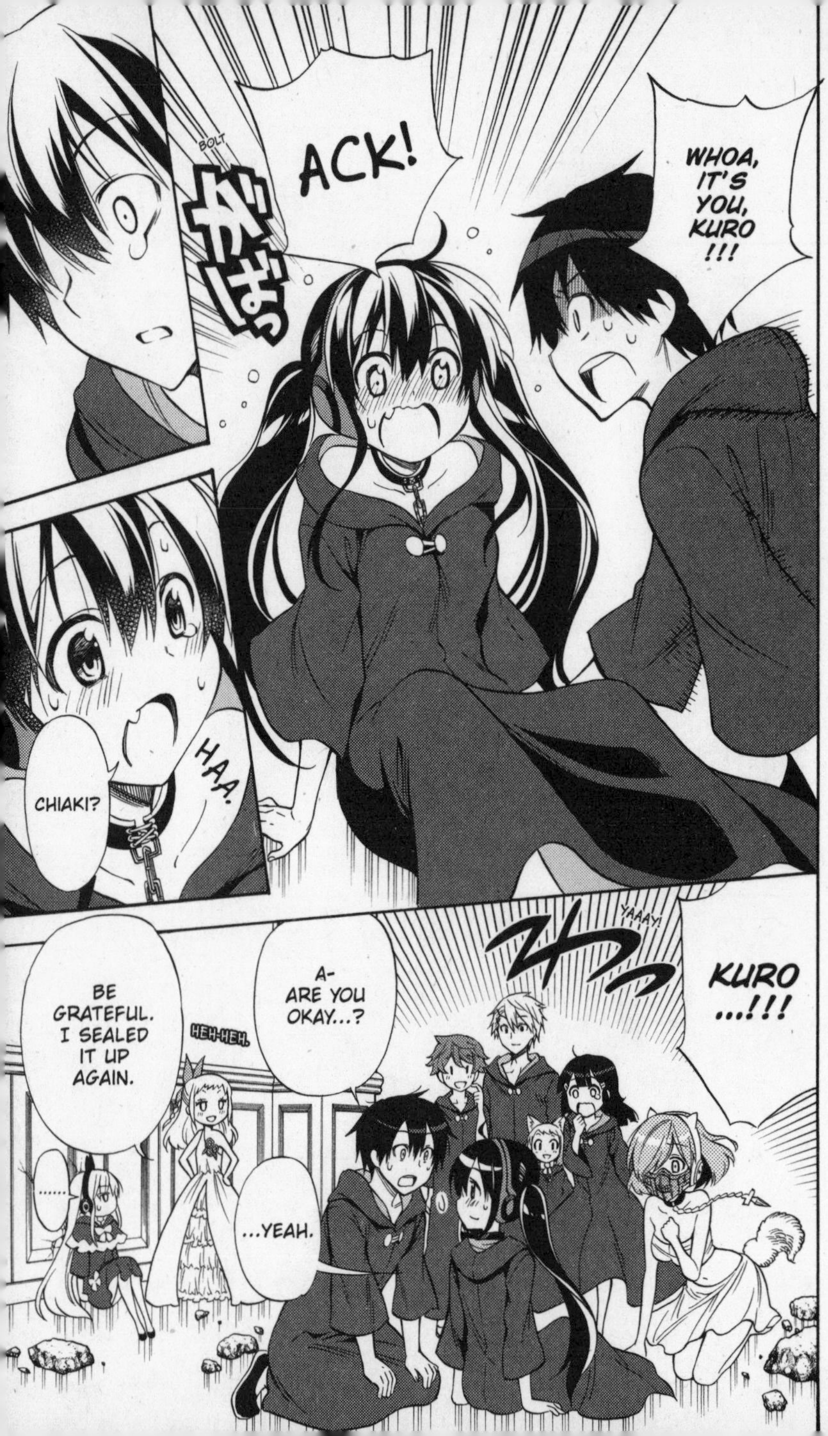
WHOA, IT'S YOU, KURO !!!
ACK!
BOLT
かぽっ
HAA.
CHIAKI?
KURO ...!!!
YAAAY!
A- ARE YOU OKAY...?
BE GRATEFUL. I SEALED IT UP AGAIN.
HEH-HEH.
...YEAH.
......

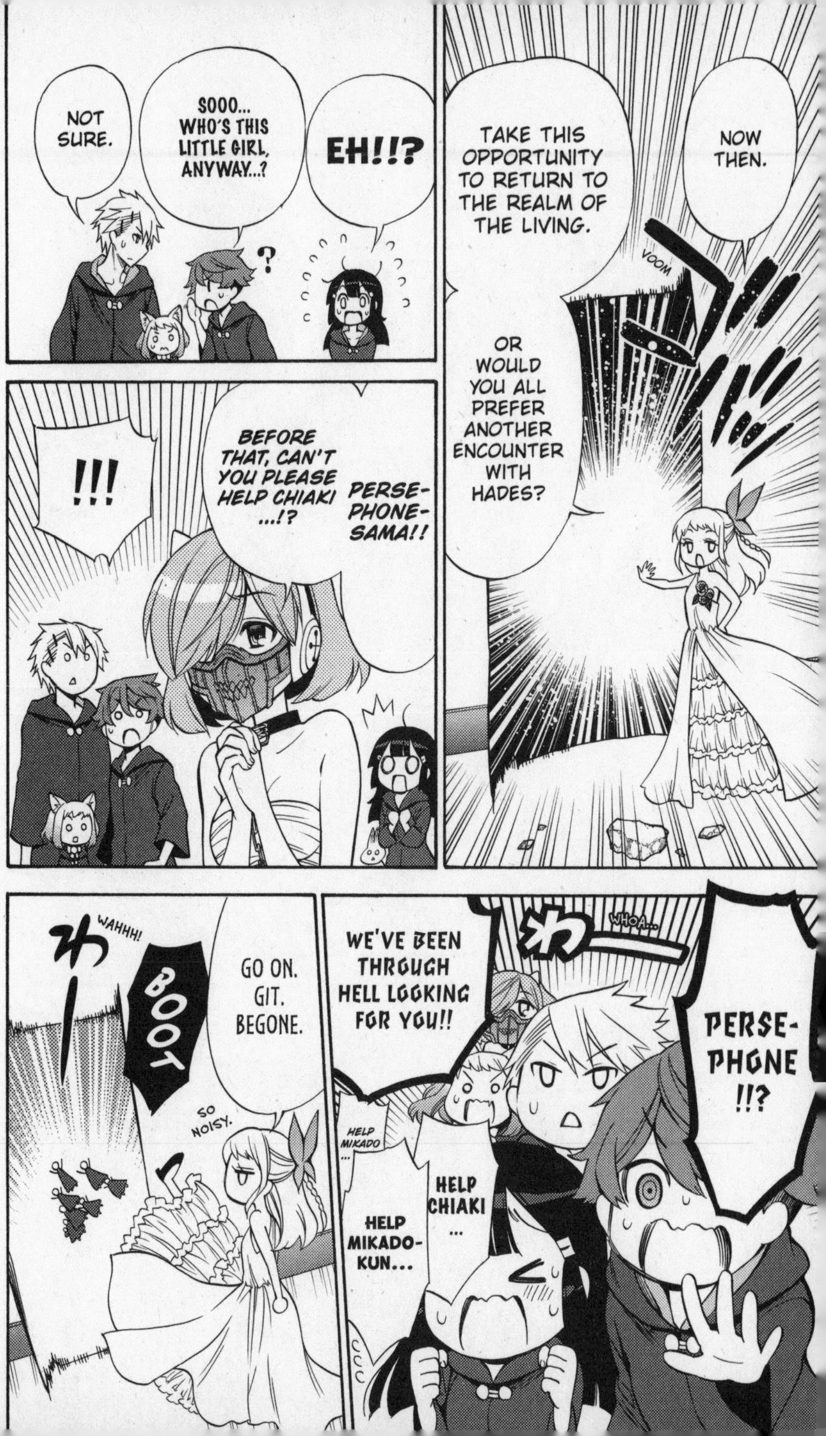
NOW THEN.
TAKE THIS OPPORTUNITY TO RETURN TO THE REALM OF THE LIVING.
VOOM
OR WOULD YOU ALL PREFER ANOTHER ENCOUNTER WITH HADES?
EH!!?
SOOO... WHO'S THIS LITTLE GIRL, ANYWAY...?
NOT SURE.
PERSE-PHONE-SAMA!!
BEFORE THAT, CAN'T YOU PLEASE HELP CHIAKI ...!?
!!!
PERSE-PHONE !!?
わー
WHOA...
WE'VE BEEN THROUGH HELL LOOKING FOR YOU!!
HELP CHIAKI ...
HELP MIKADO ...
HELP MIKADO-KUN...
GO ON. GIT. BEGONE.
SO NOISY.
BOOT
わー
WAHHH!

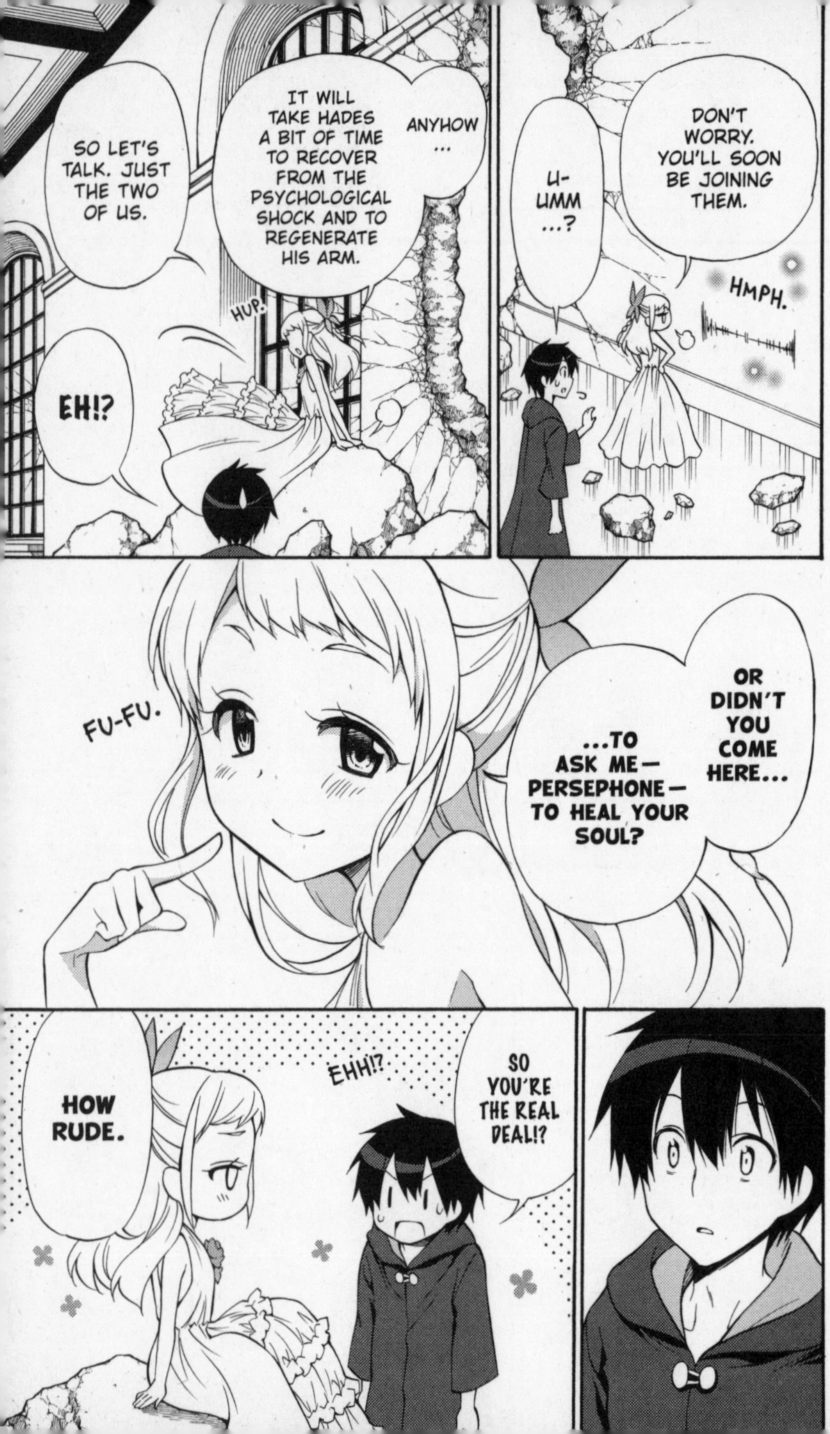
DON'T WORRY. YOU'LL SOON BE JOINING THEM.
U-UMM...?
HMPH.
ANYHOW...
IT WILL TAKE HADES A BIT OF TIME TO RECOVER FROM THE PSYCHOLOGICAL SHOCK AND TO REGENERATE HIS ARM.
SO LET'S TALK. JUST THE TWO OF US.
HUP.
EH!?
OR DIDN'T YOU COME HERE...
...TO ASK ME—PERSEPHONE—TO HEAL YOUR SOUL?
FU-FU.
SO YOU'RE THE REAL DEAL!?
EHH!?
HOW RUDE.

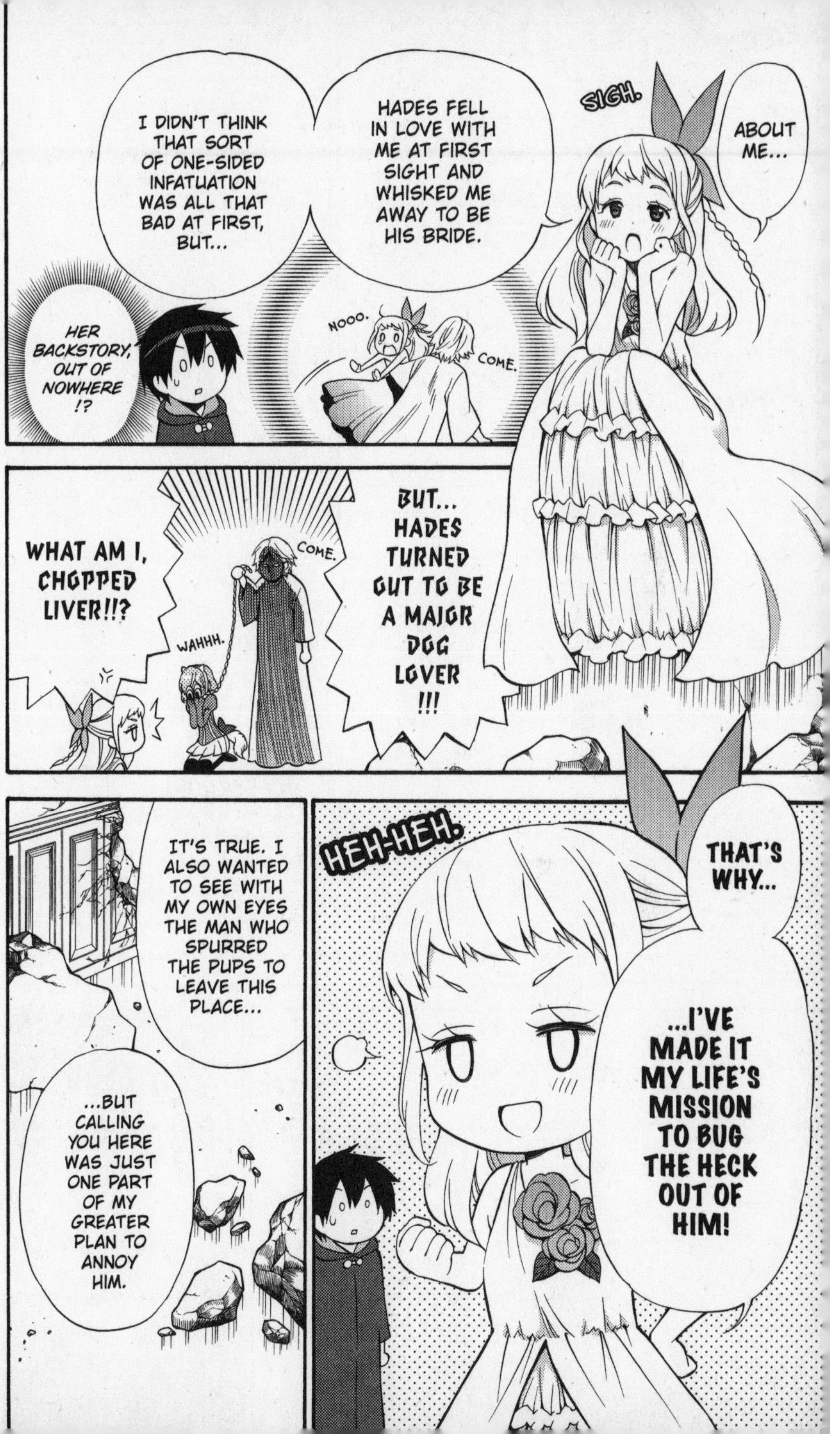
SIGH.
ABOUT ME...
HADES FELL IN LOVE WITH ME AT FIRST SIGHT AND WHISKED ME AWAY TO BE HIS BRIDE.
I DIDN'T THINK THAT SORT OF ONE-SIDED INFATUATION WAS ALL THAT BAD AT FIRST, BUT...
NOOO.
COME.
HER BACKSTORY, OUT OF NOWHERE!?
BUT... HADES TURNED OUT TO BE A MAJOR DOG LOVER!!!
COME.
WAHHH.
WHAT AM I, CHOPPED LIVER!!?
HEH-HEH.
THAT'S WHY...
...I'VE MADE IT MY LIFE'S MISSION TO BUG THE HECK OUT OF HIM!
IT'S TRUE. I ALSO WANTED TO SEE WITH MY OWN EYES THE MAN WHO SPURRED THE PUPS TO LEAVE THIS PLACE...
...BUT CALLING YOU HERE WAS JUST ONE PART OF MY GREATER PLAN TO ANNOY HIM.

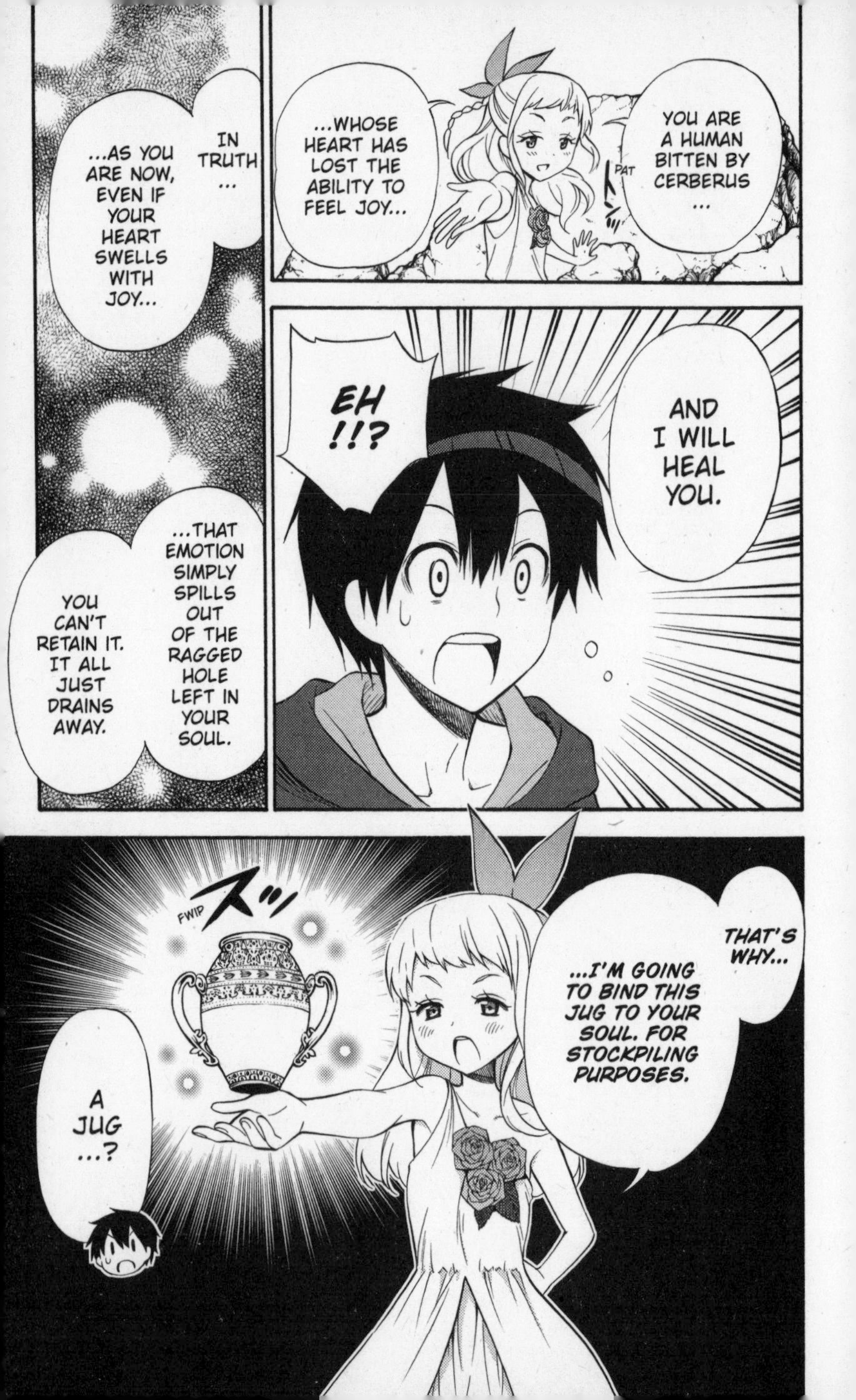
YOU ARE A HUMAN BITTEN BY CERBERUS ...
PAT
...WHOSE HEART HAS LOST THE ABILITY TO FEEL JOY...
AND I WILL HEAL YOU.
EH !!?
IN TRUTH ...
...AS YOU ARE NOW, EVEN IF YOUR HEART SWELLS WITH JOY...
...THAT EMOTION SIMPLY SPILLS OUT OF THE RAGGED HOLE LEFT IN YOUR SOUL.
YOU CAN'T RETAIN IT. IT ALL JUST DRAINS AWAY.
THAT'S WHY...
...I'M GOING TO BIND THIS JUG TO YOUR SOUL. FOR STOCKPILING PURPOSES.
FWIP
A JUG ...?

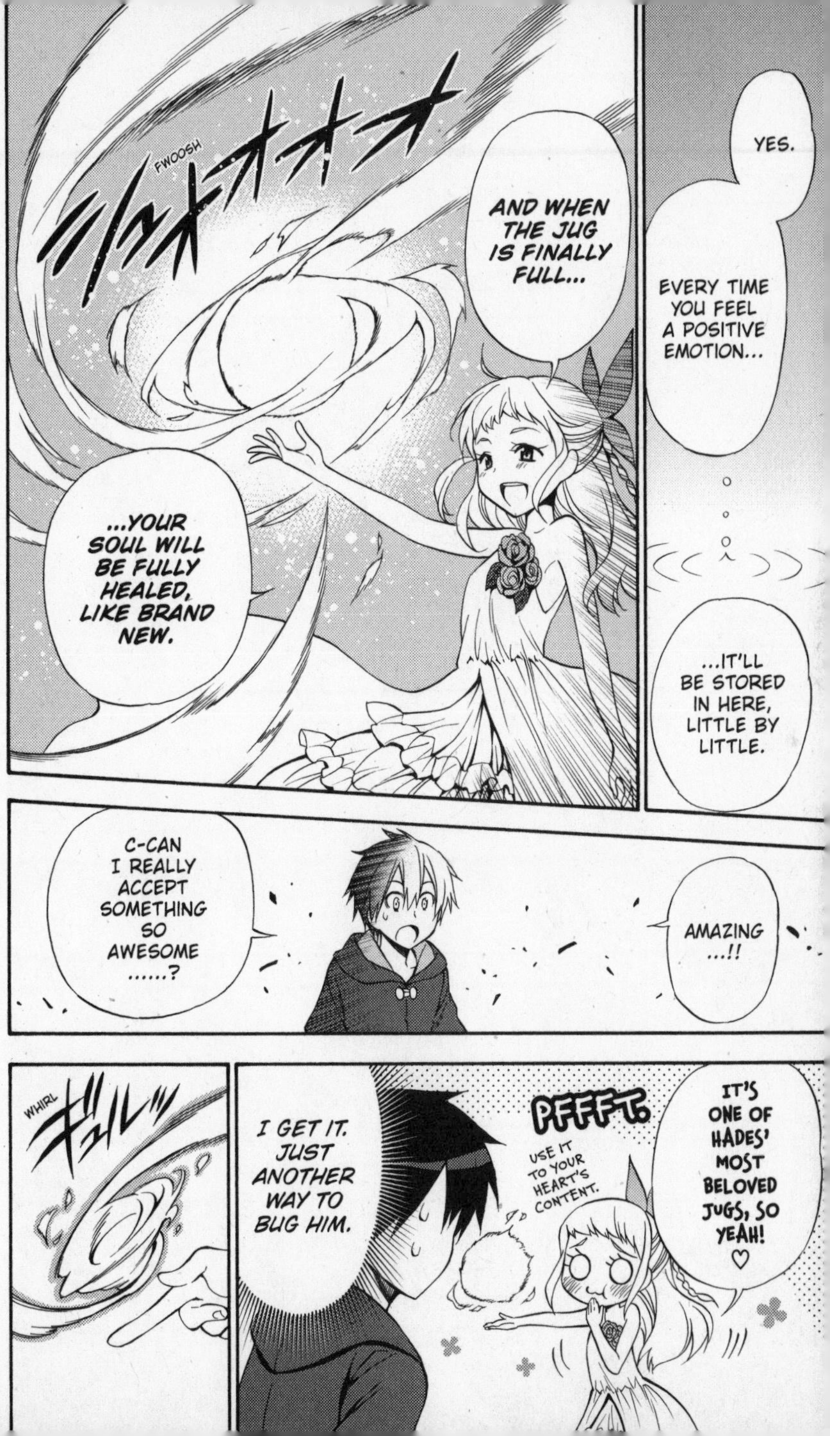
YES.
EVERY TIME YOU FEEL A POSITIVE EMOTION...
...IT'LL BE STORED IN HERE, LITTLE BY LITTLE.
FWOOSH
AND WHEN THE JUG IS FINALLY FULL...
...YOUR SOUL WILL BE FULLY HEALED, LIKE BRAND NEW.
AMAZING ...!!
C-CAN I REALLY ACCEPT SOMETHING SO AWESOME ......?
IT'S ONE OF HADES' MOST BELOVED JUGS, SO YEAH! ♡
PFFFT.
USE IT TO YOUR HEART'S CONTENT.
I GET IT. JUST ANOTHER WAY TO BUG HIM.
WHIRL

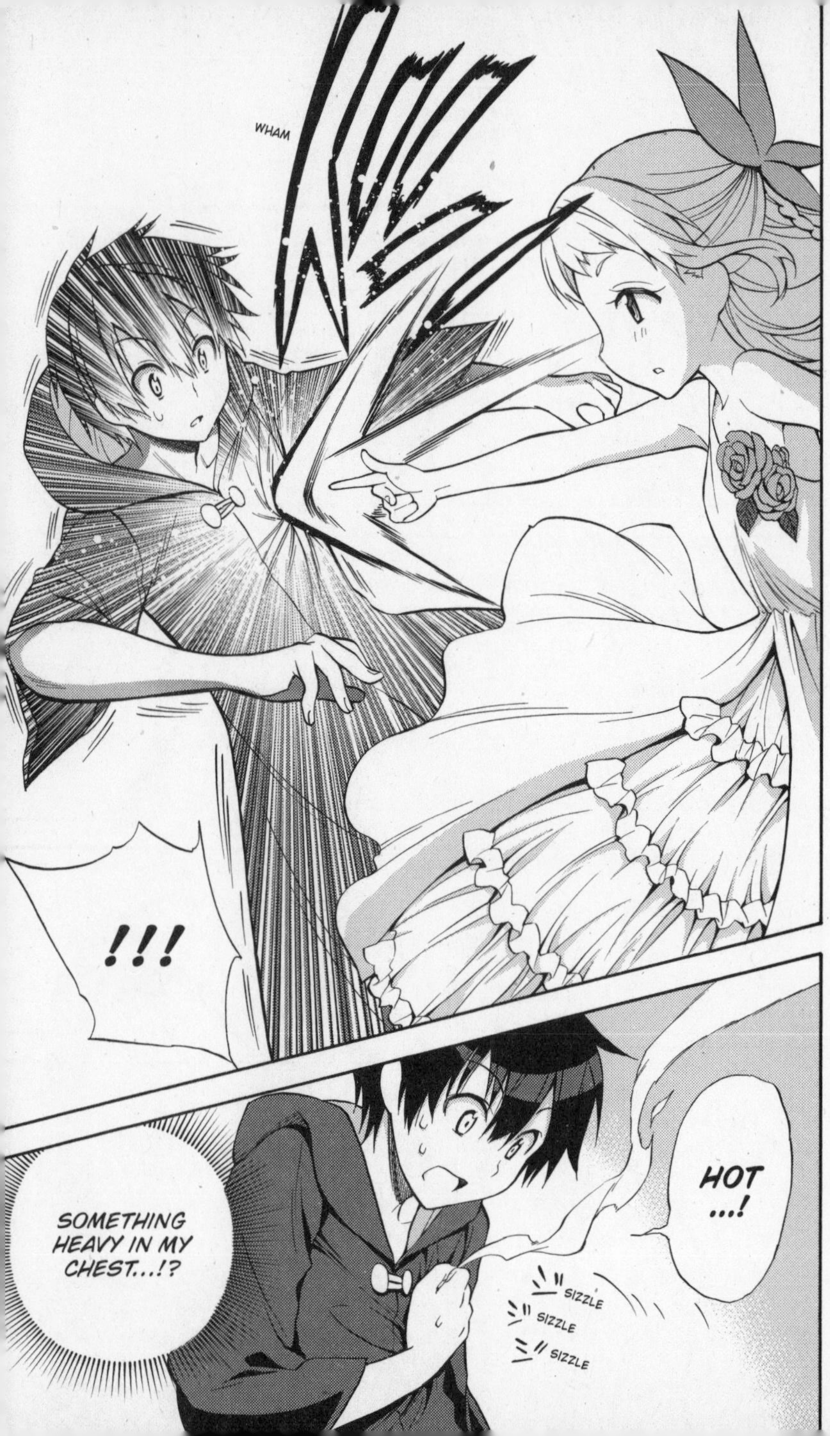
WHAM
!!!
HOT ...!
SOMETHING HEAVY IN MY CHEST...!?
SIZZLE
SIZZLE
SIZZLE

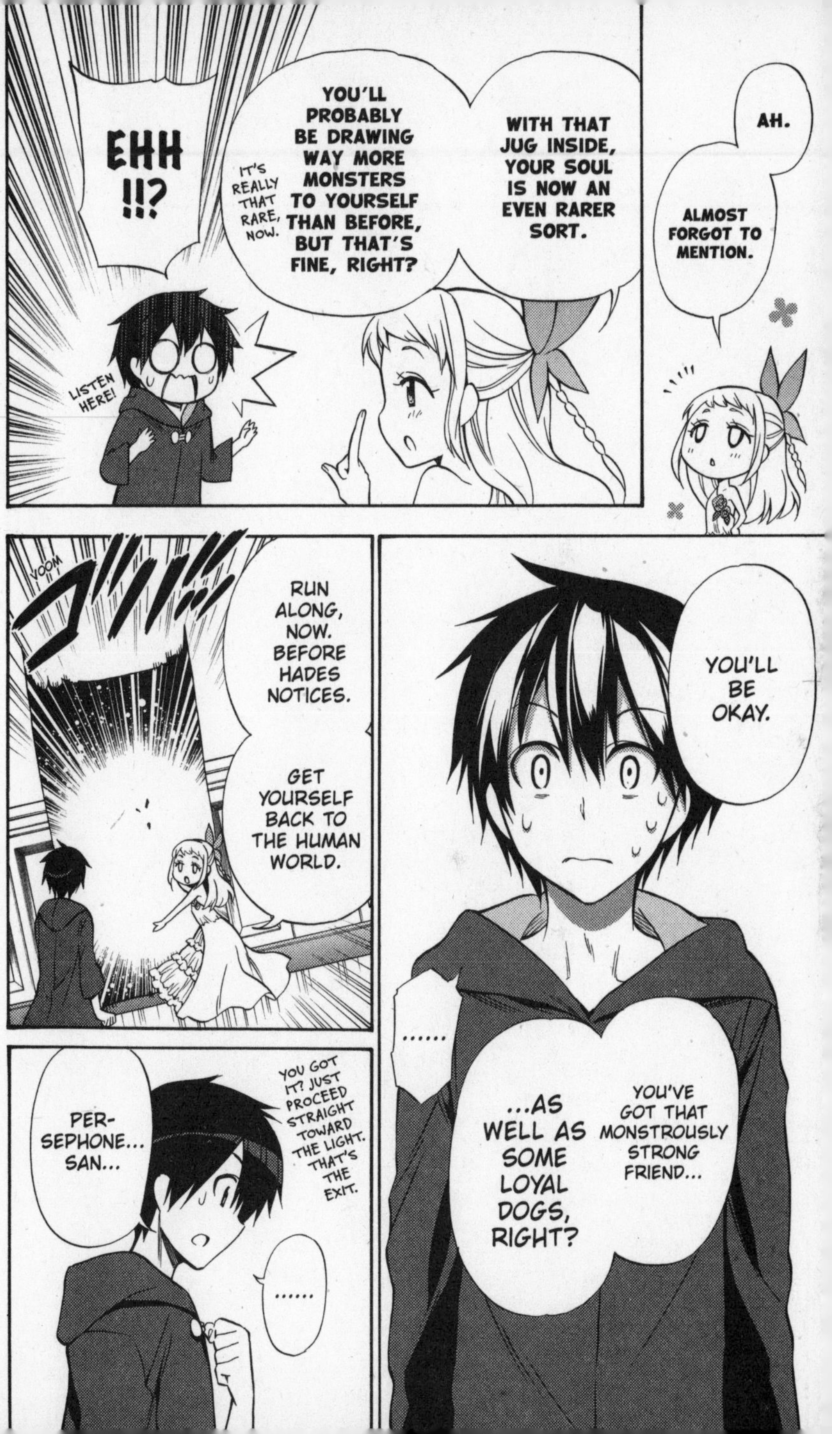
AH.
ALMOST FORGOT TO MENTION.
WITH THAT JUG INSIDE, YOUR SOUL IS NOW AN EVEN RARER SORT.
YOU'LL PROBABLY BE DRAWING WAY MORE MONSTERS TO YOURSELF THAN BEFORE, BUT THAT'S FINE, RIGHT?
IT'S REALLY THAT RARE, NOW.
EHH !!?
LISTEN HERE!
YOU'LL BE OKAY.
......
YOU'VE GOT THAT MONSTROUSLY STRONG FRIEND...
...AS WELL AS SOME LOYAL DOGS, RIGHT?
VOOM
RUN ALONG, NOW. BEFORE HADES NOTICES.
GET YOURSELF BACK TO THE HUMAN WORLD.
YOU GOT IT? JUST PROCEED STRAIGHT TOWARD THE LIGHT. THAT'S THE EXIT.
PER-SEPHONE... SAN...
......

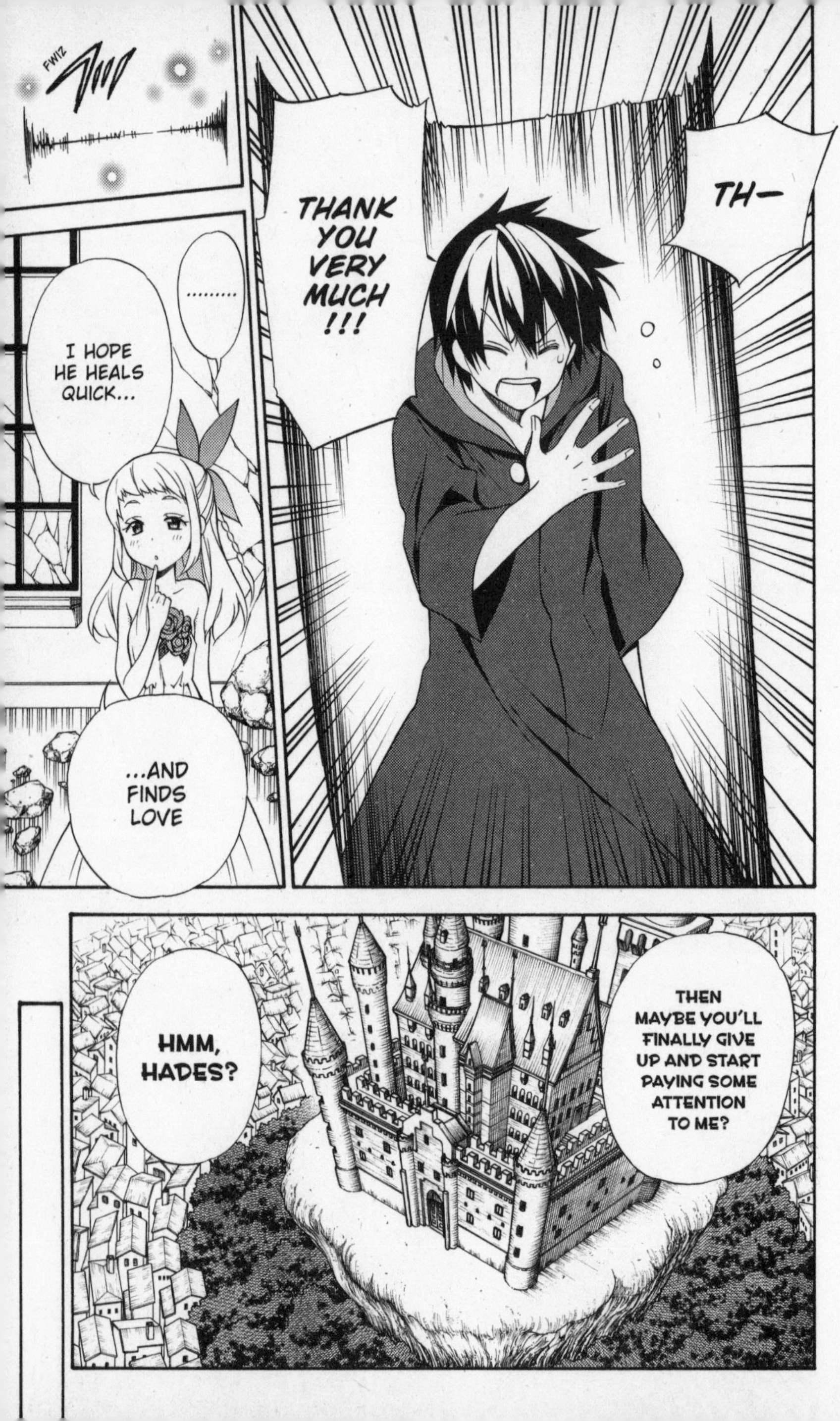
TH—
THANK YOU VERY MUCH!!!
FWIZ
....
I HOPE HE HEALS QUICK...
...AND FINDS LOVE
THEN MAYBE YOU'LL FINALLY GIVE UP AND START PAYING SOME ATTENTION TO ME?
HMM, HADES?

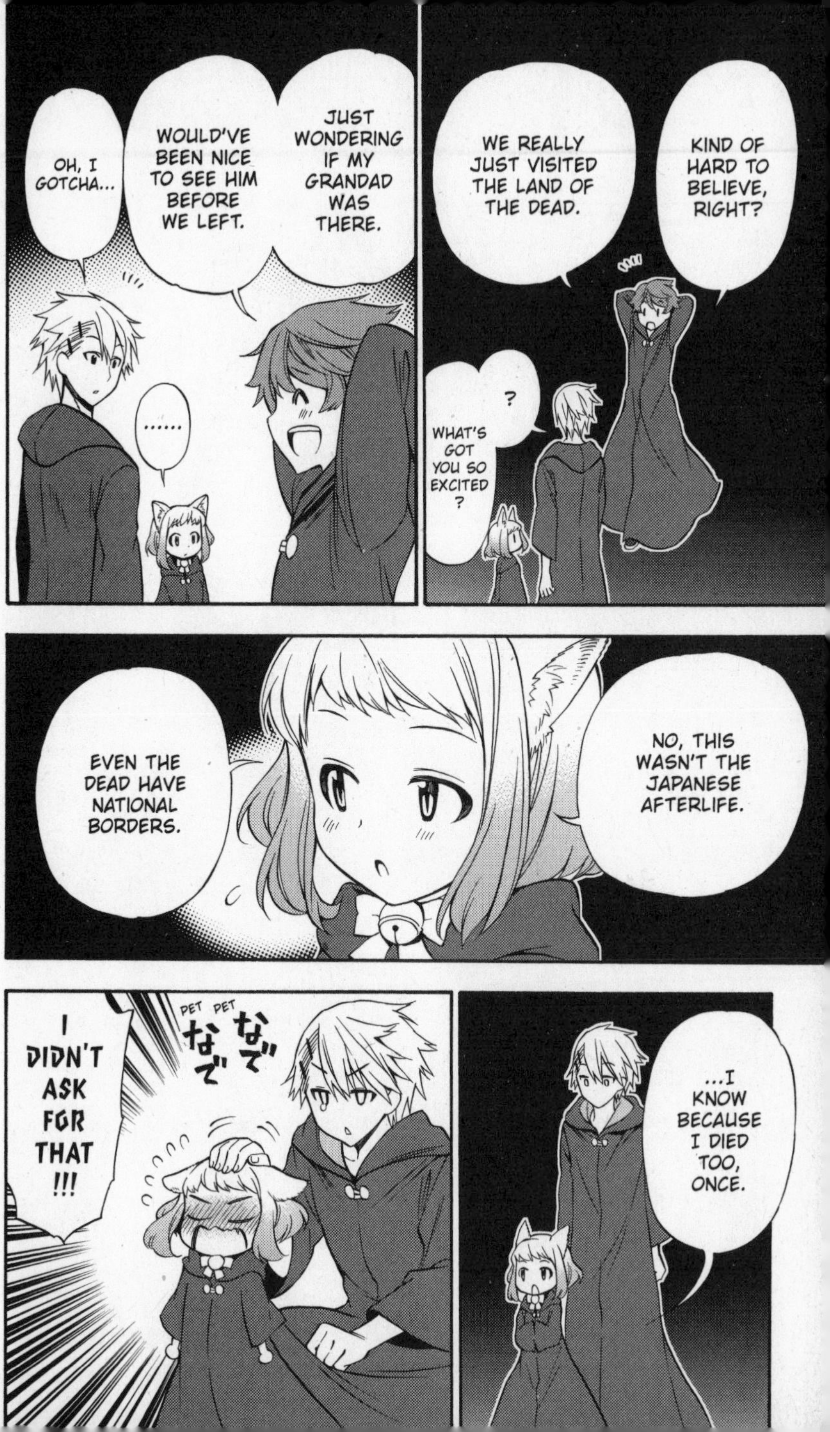
KIND OF HARD TO BELIEVE, RIGHT?
WE REALLY JUST VISITED THE LAND OF THE DEAD.
?
WHAT'S GOT YOU SO EXCITED?
JUST WONDERING IF MY GRANDAD WAS THERE.
WOULD'VE BEEN NICE TO SEE HIM BEFORE WE LEFT.
OH, I GOTCHA...
......
NO, THIS WASN'T THE JAPANESE AFTERLIFE.
EVEN THE DEAD HAVE NATIONAL BORDERS.
...I KNOW BECAUSE I DIED TOO, ONCE.
なでなで
PET PET
I DIDN'T ASK FOR THAT!!!

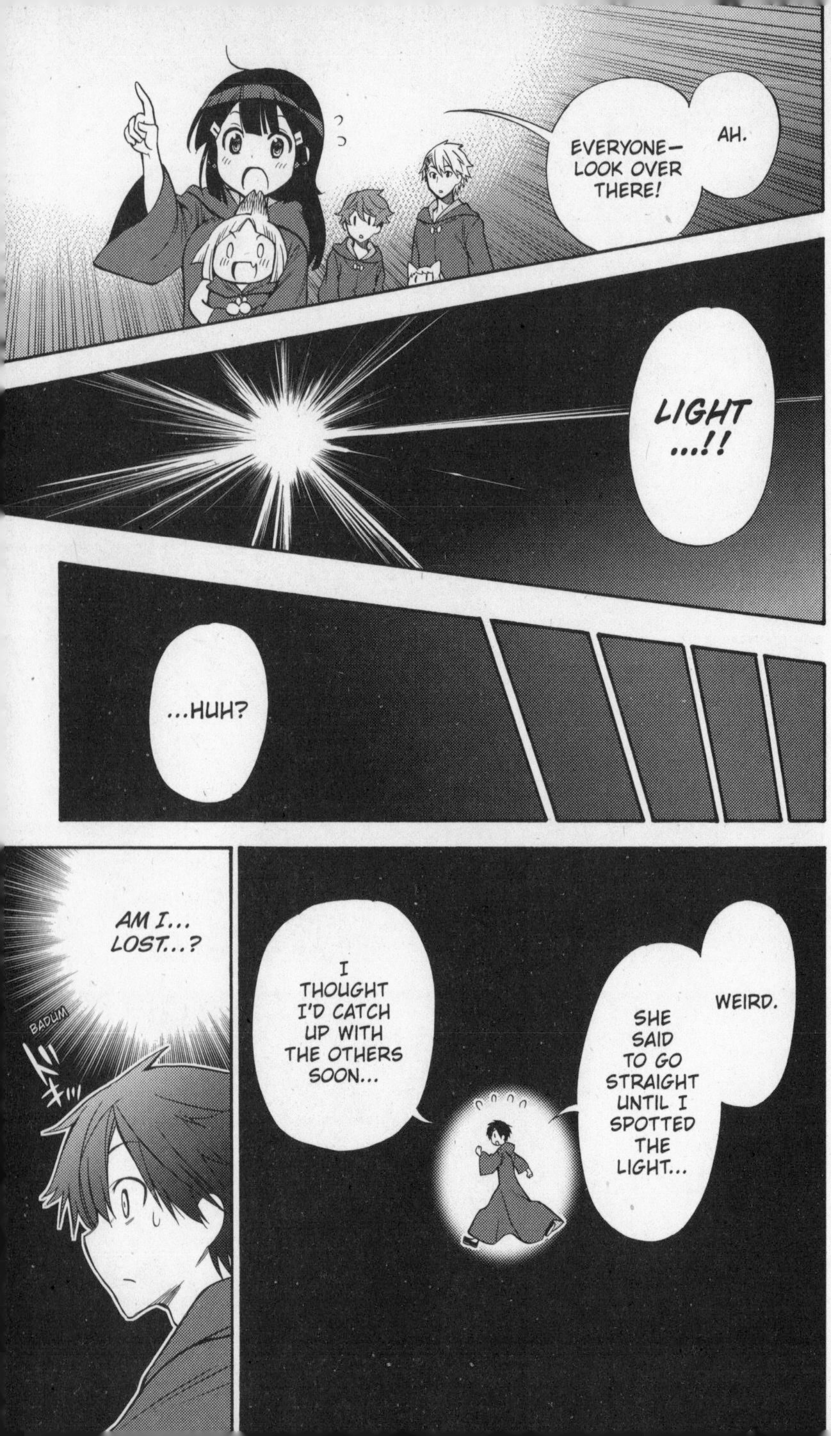
AH.
EVERYONE—LOOK OVER THERE!
LIGHT ...!!
...HUH?
WEIRD.
SHE SAID TO GO STRAIGHT UNTIL I SPOTTED THE LIGHT...
I THOUGHT I'D CATCH UP WITH THE OTHERS SOON...
AM I... LOST...?
BADUM

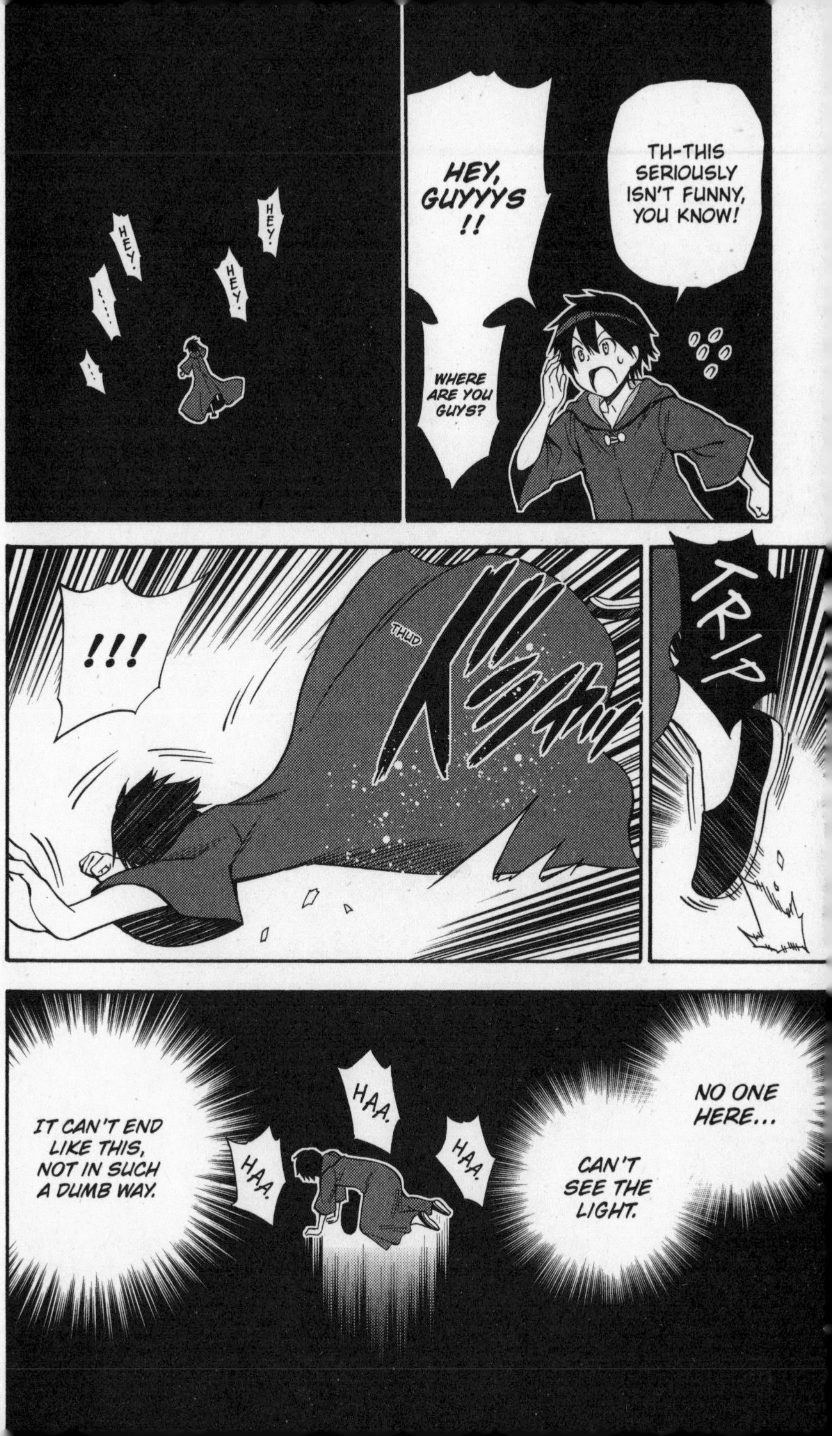
TH-THIS SERIOUSLY ISN'T FUNNY, YOU KNOW!
HEY, GUYYYS!!
WHERE ARE YOU GUYS?
HEY!
HEY.
HEY.
TRIP
THUD
!!!
NO ONE HERE...
CAN'T SEE THE LIGHT.
HAA.
HAA.
HAA.
IT CAN'T END LIKE THIS, NOT IN SUCH A DUMB WAY.

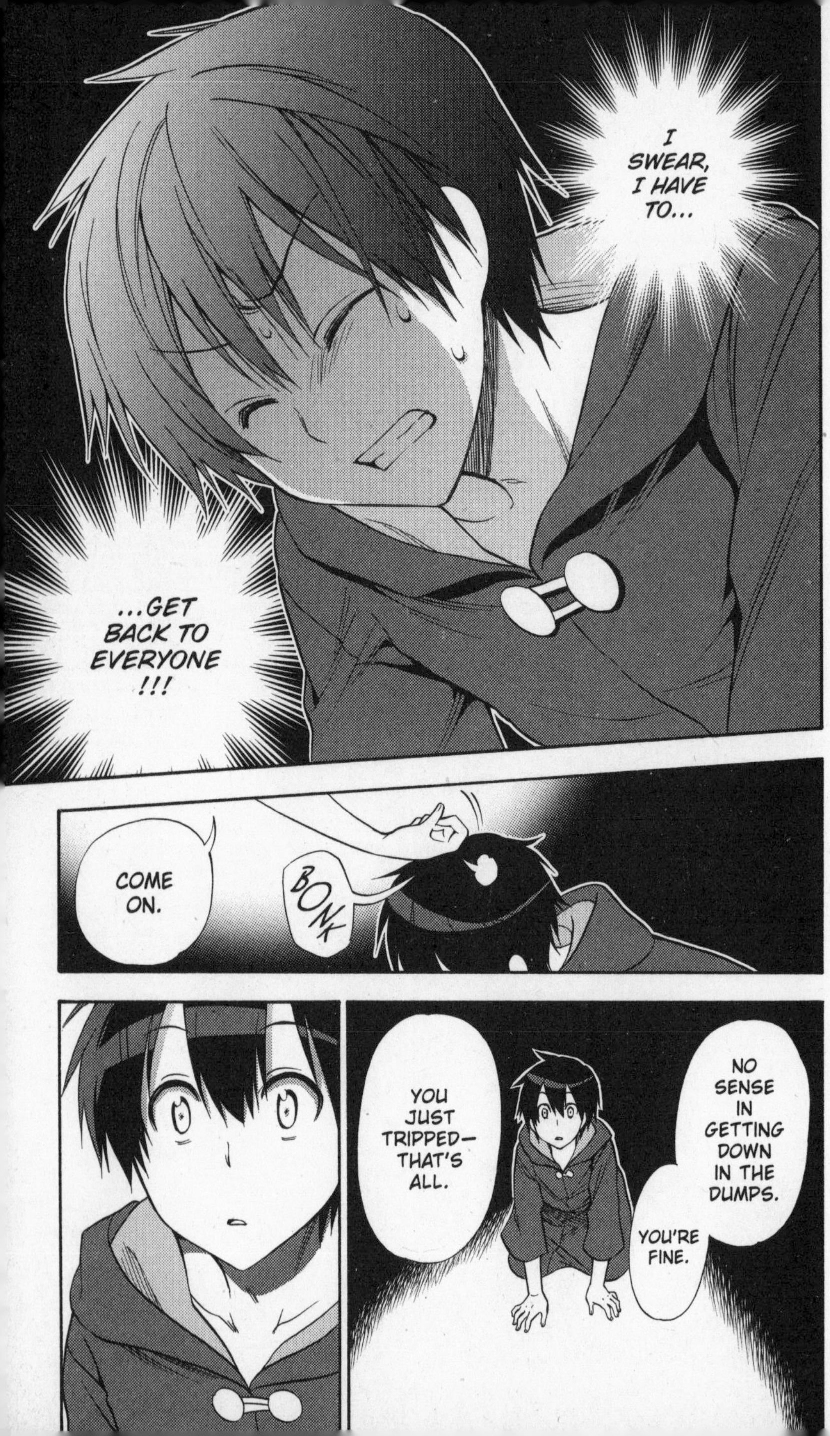
I SWEAR, I HAVE TO...
...GET BACK TO EVERYONE!!!
BONK
COME ON.
NO SENSE IN GETTING DOWN IN THE DUMPS.
YOU'RE FINE.
YOU JUST TRIPPED—THAT'S ALL.

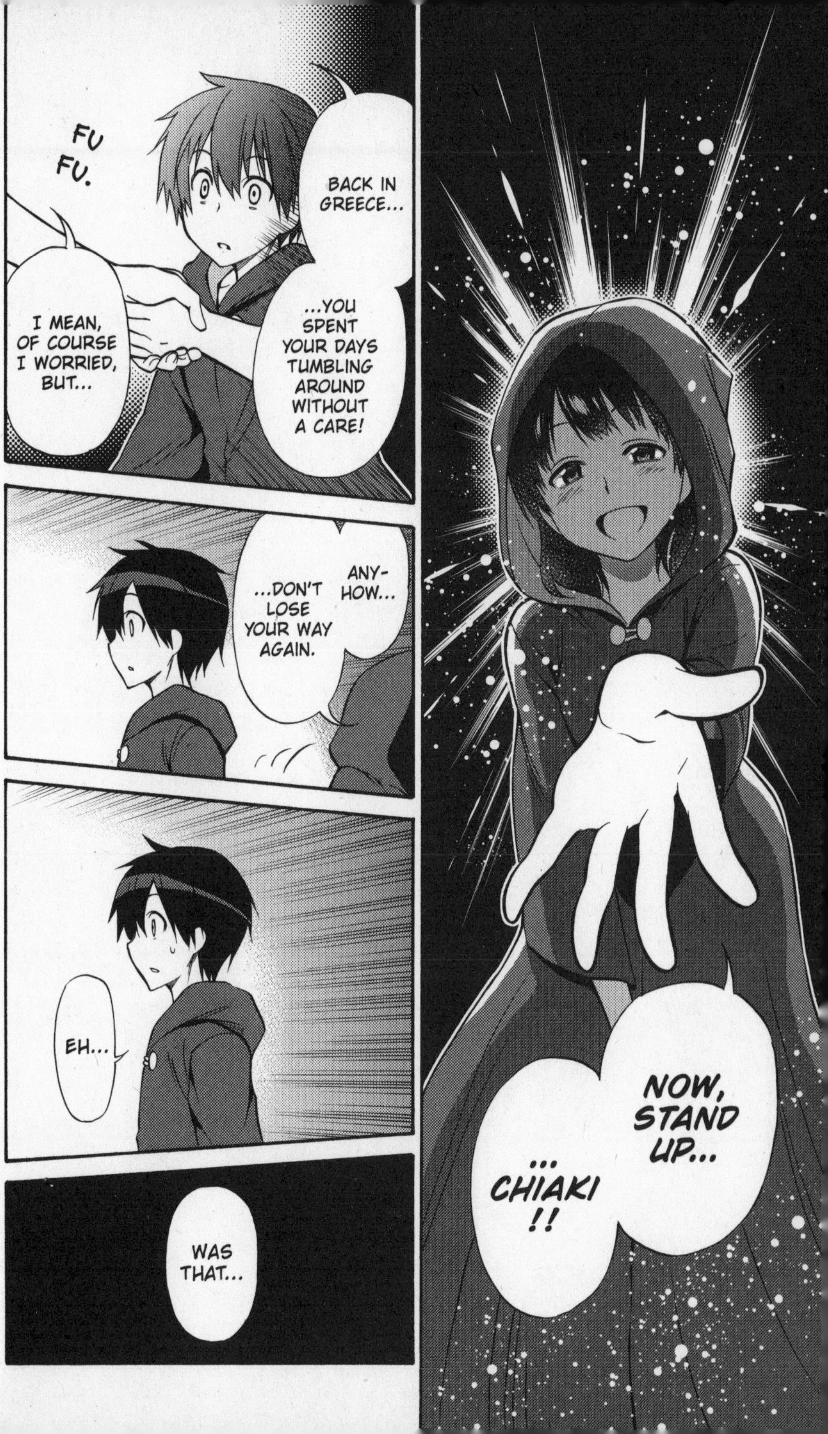
NOW, STAND UP... ...CHIAKI!!
BACK IN GREECE...
...YOU SPENT YOUR DAYS TUMBLING AROUND WITHOUT A CARE!
FU FU.
I MEAN, OF COURSE I WORRIED, BUT...
ANY-HOW...
...DON'T LOSE YOUR WAY AGAIN.
EH...
WAS THAT...

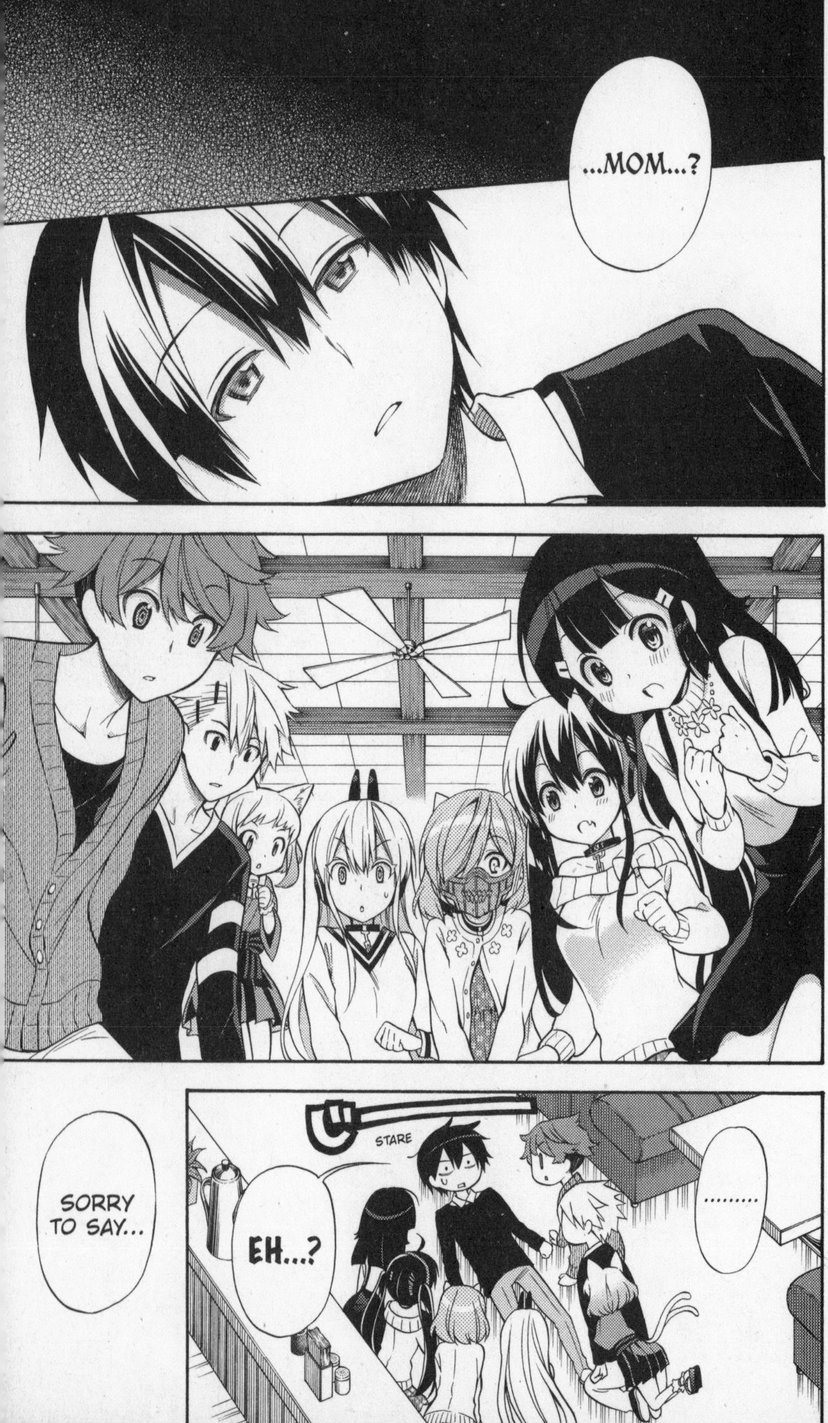
...MOM...?
....
STARE
EH...?
SORRY TO SAY...

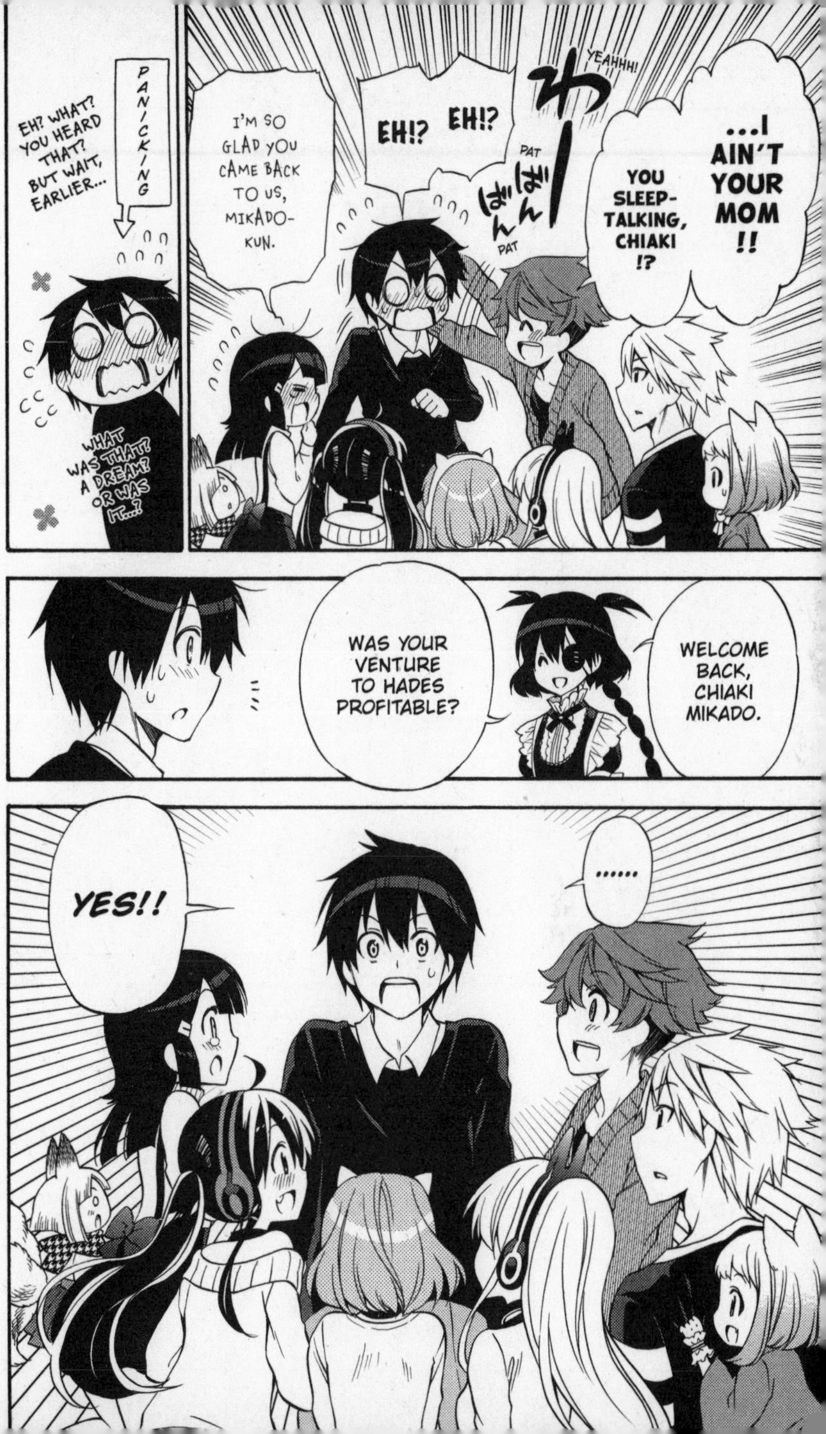
...I AIN'T YOUR MOM!!
YEAHHH!
わー
YOU SLEEP-TALKING, CHIAKI!?
PAT ばん ばん PAT
EH!? EH!?
I'M SO GLAD YOU CAME BACK TO US, MIKADO-KUN.
PANICKING
EH? WHAT? YOU HEARD THAT? BUT WAIT, EARLIER...
WHAT WAS THAT? A DREAM? OR WAS IT...?
WELCOME BACK, CHIAKI MIKADO.
WAS YOUR VENTURE TO HADES PROFITABLE?
......
YES!!

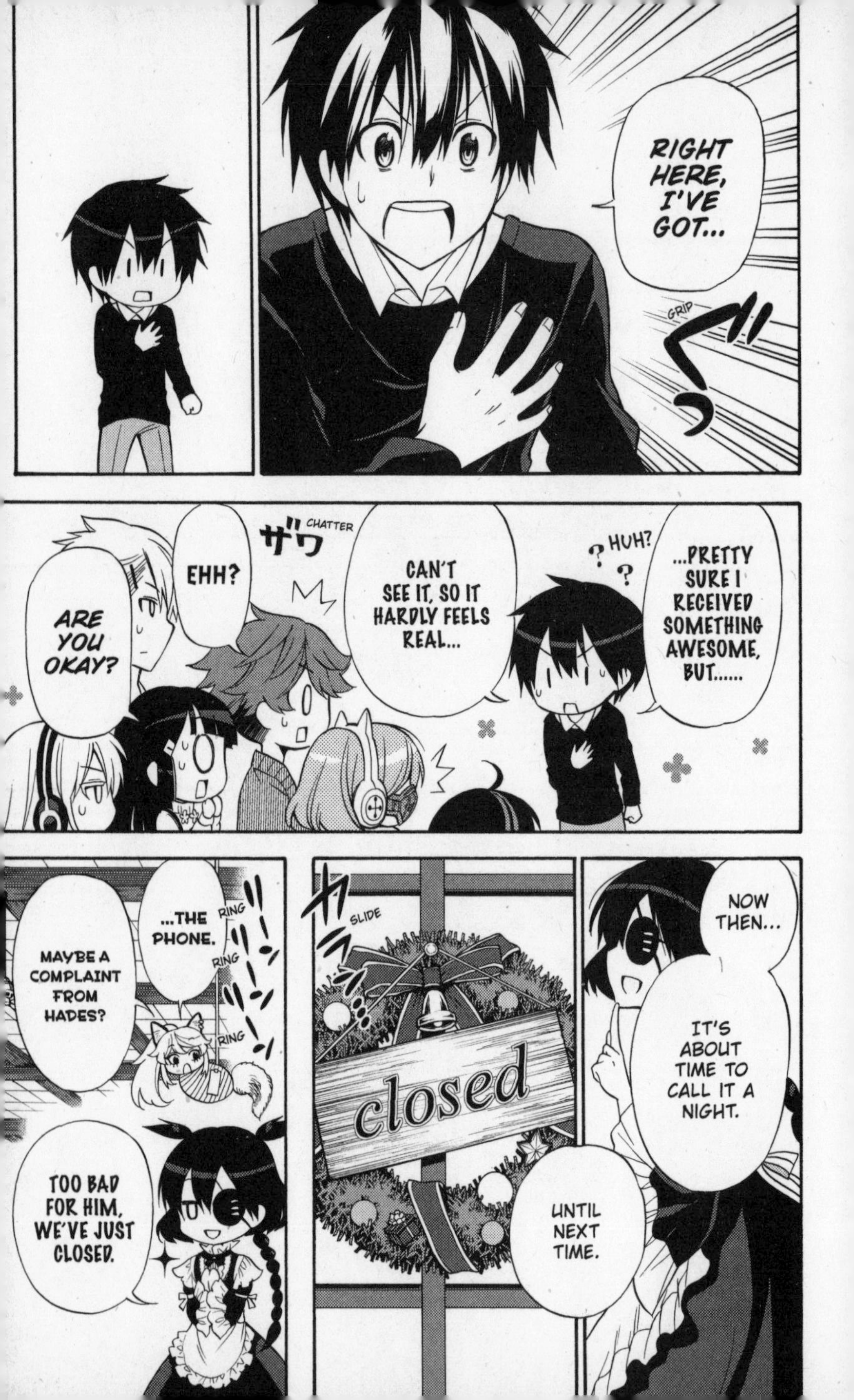
RIGHT HERE, I'VE GOT...
GRIP
...PRETTY SURE I RECEIVED SOMETHING AWESOME, BUT......
HUH?
CAN'T SEE IT, SO IT HARDLY FEELS REAL...
CHATTER
EHH?
ARE YOU OKAY?
NOW THEN...
IT'S ABOUT TIME TO CALL IT A NIGHT.
UNTIL NEXT TIME.
SLIDE
closed
...THE PHONE.
RING
RING
RING
MAYBE A COMPLAINT FROM HADES?
TOO BAD FOR HIM, WE'VE JUST CLOSED.

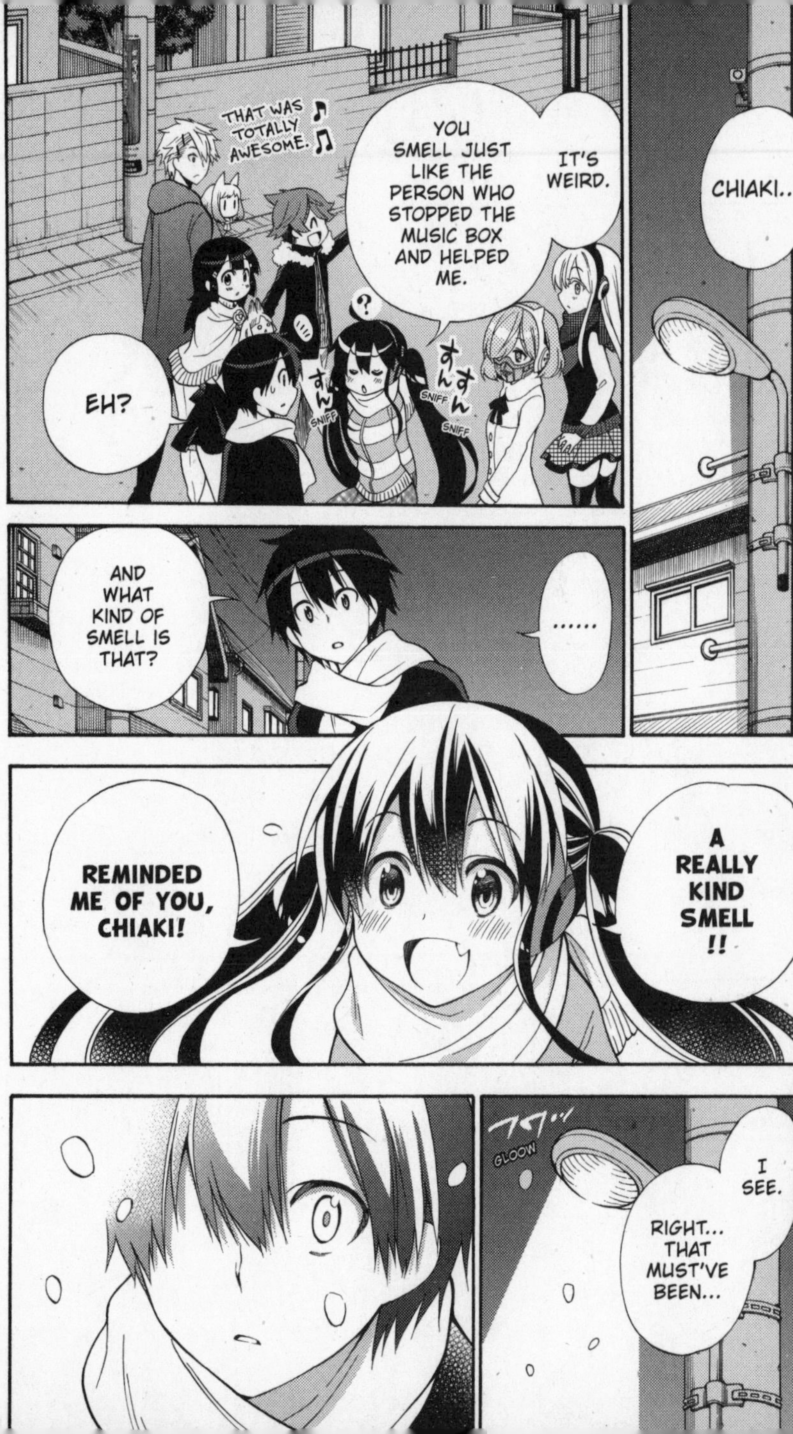
CHIAKI...
IT'S WEIRD.
YOU SMELL JUST LIKE THE PERSON WHO STOPPED THE MUSIC BOX AND HELPED ME.
THAT WAS TOTALLY AWESOME. ♪ ♫
すんすん SNIFF SNIFF
すん SNIFF
?
EH?
......
AND WHAT KIND OF SMELL IS THAT?
A REALLY KIND SMELL !!
REMINDED ME OF YOU, CHIAKI!
フワッ GLOOW
I SEE.
RIGHT... THAT MUST'VE BEEN...

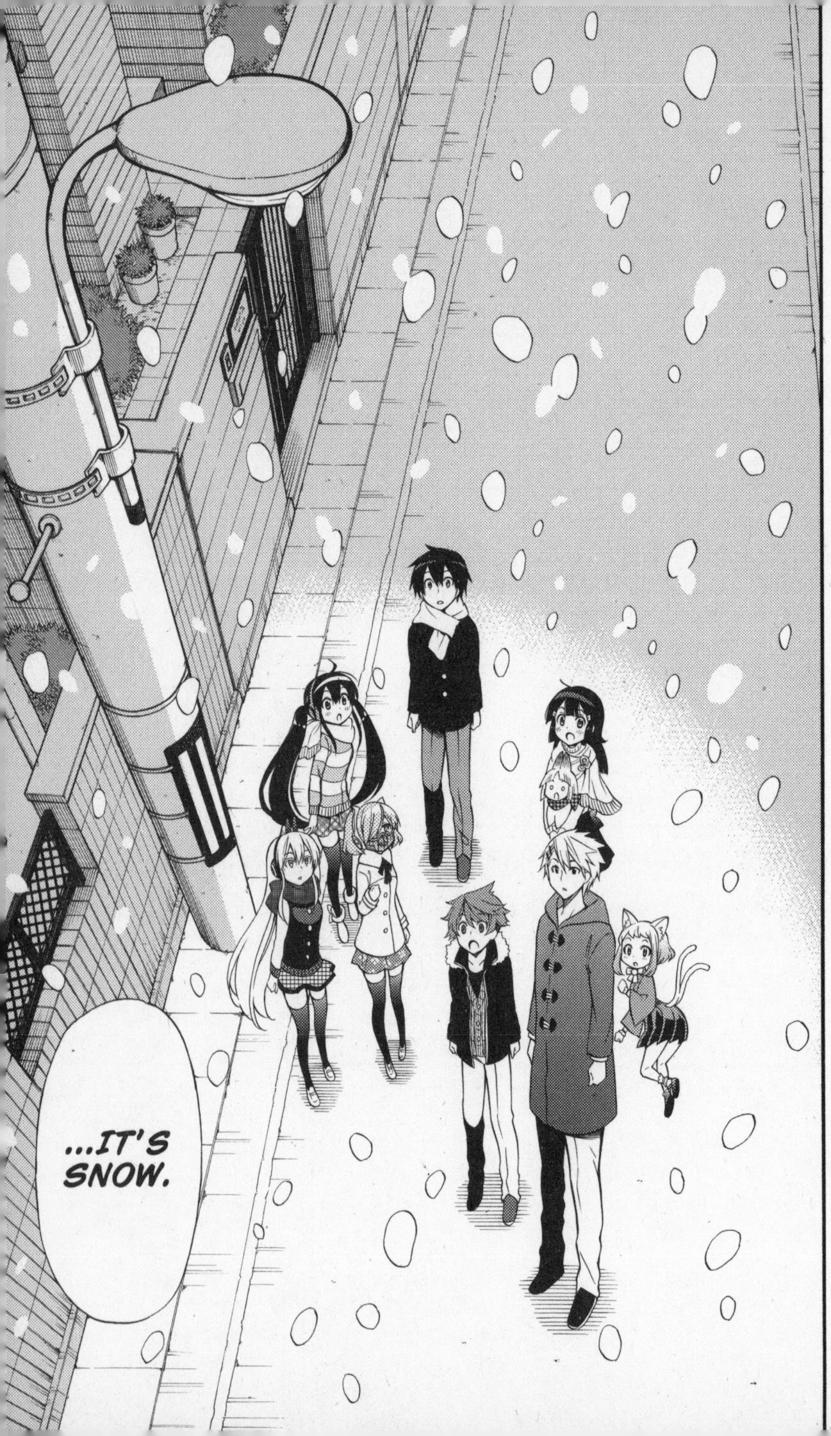
...IT'S SNOW.

OHHH.

SO PRETTY...

WOW, AMAZING!!

WE'RE GONNA HAVE A WHITE CHRISTMAS!

IT'S THE REMAINS OF THE DEAD.

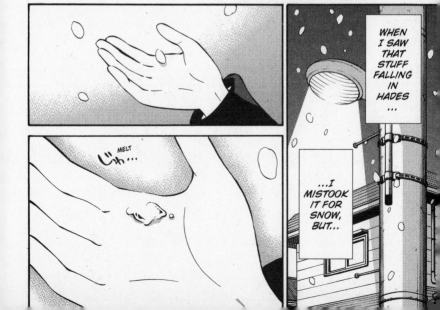

MELT
じゅ...

WHEN I SAW THAT STUFF FALLING IN HADES...

...I MISTOOK IT FOR SNOW, BUT...

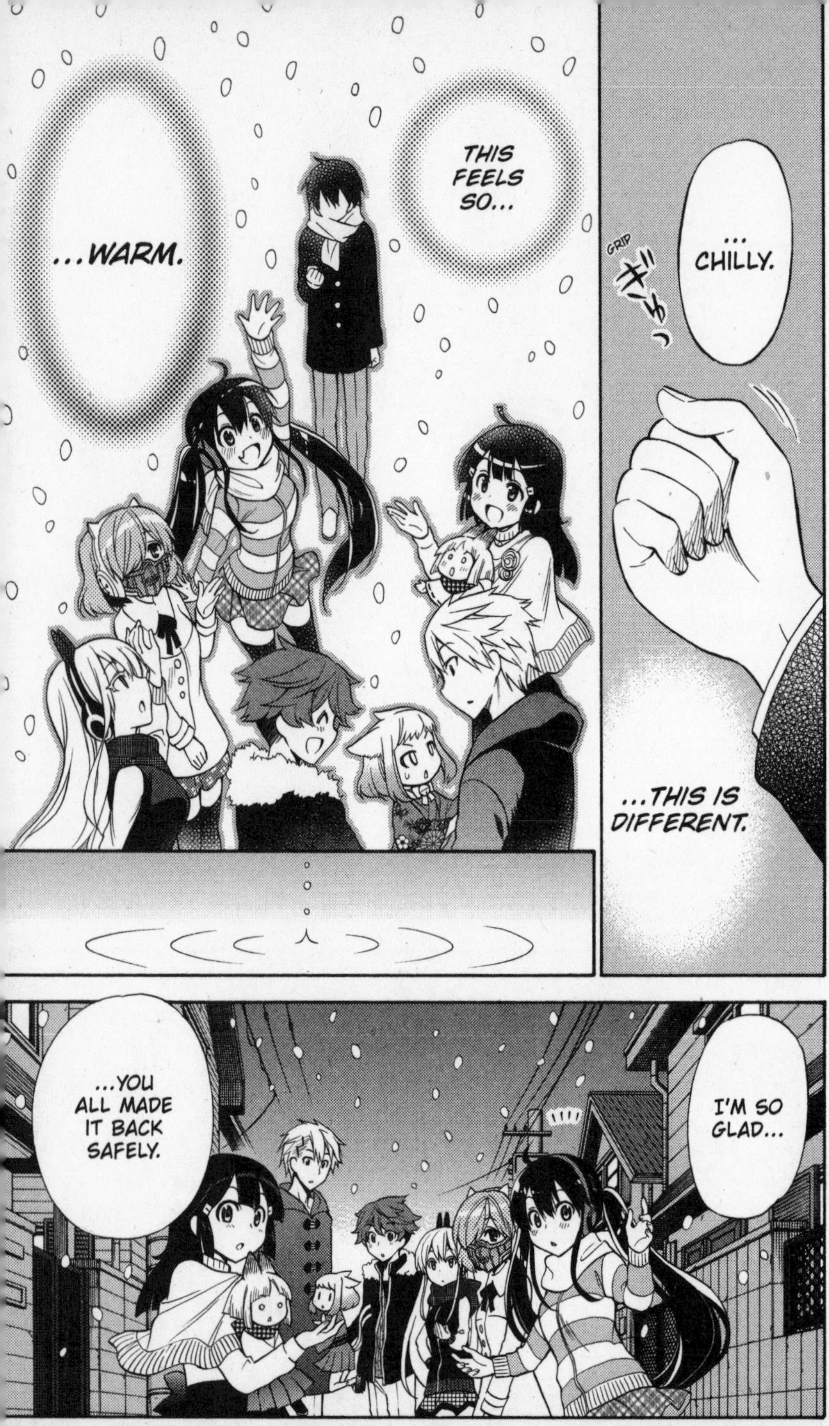
... CHILLY.
GRIP
ギュッ
...THIS IS DIFFERENT.
THIS FEELS SO...
...WARM.
I'M SO GLAD...
...YOU ALL MADE IT BACK SAFELY.

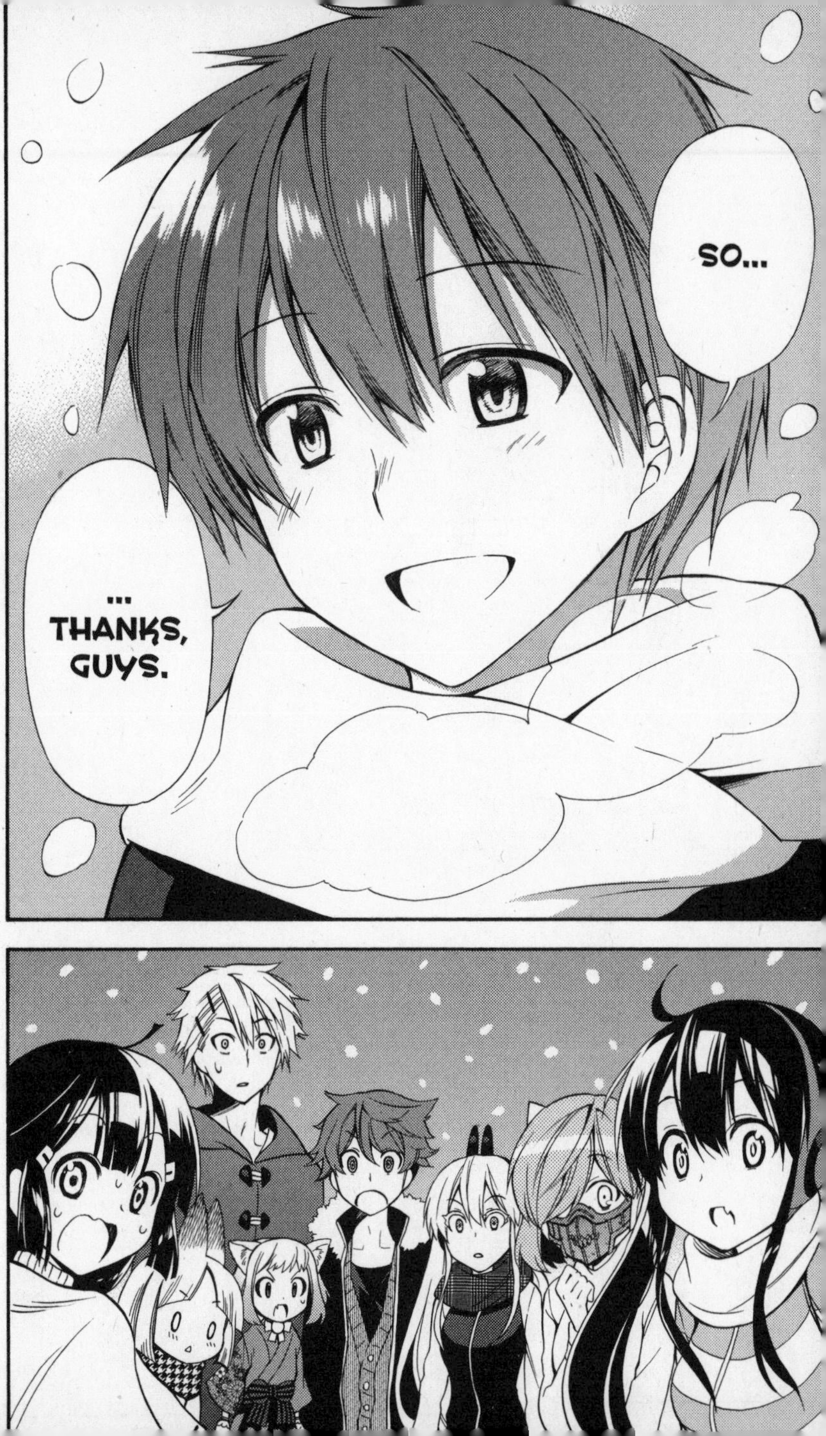
SO...
... THANKS, GUYS.

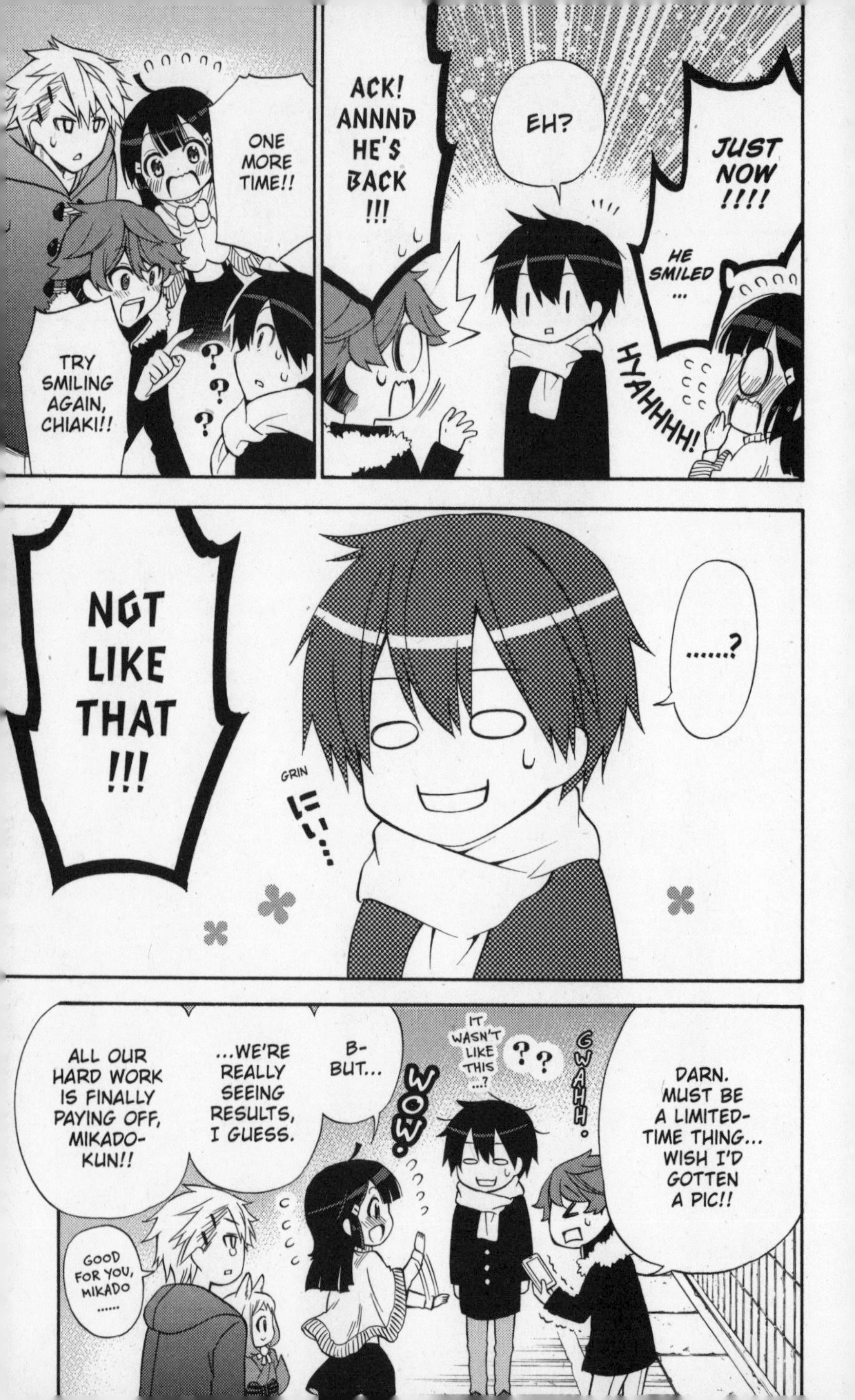
JUST NOW!!!!
EH?
ACK! ANNND HE'S BACK!!!
HE SMILED...
HYAHHHH!
ONE MORE TIME!!
TRY SMILING AGAIN, CHIAKI!!
......?
GRIN
にぃ…
NOT LIKE THAT!!!
DARN. MUST BE A LIMITED-TIME THING... WISH I'D GOTTEN A PIC!!
GWAHH.
IT WASN'T LIKE THIS ...?
WOW!
B-BUT...
...WE'RE REALLY SEEING RESULTS, I GUESS.
ALL OUR HARD WORK IS FINALLY PAYING OFF, MIKADO-KUN!!
GOOD FOR YOU, MIKADO ......

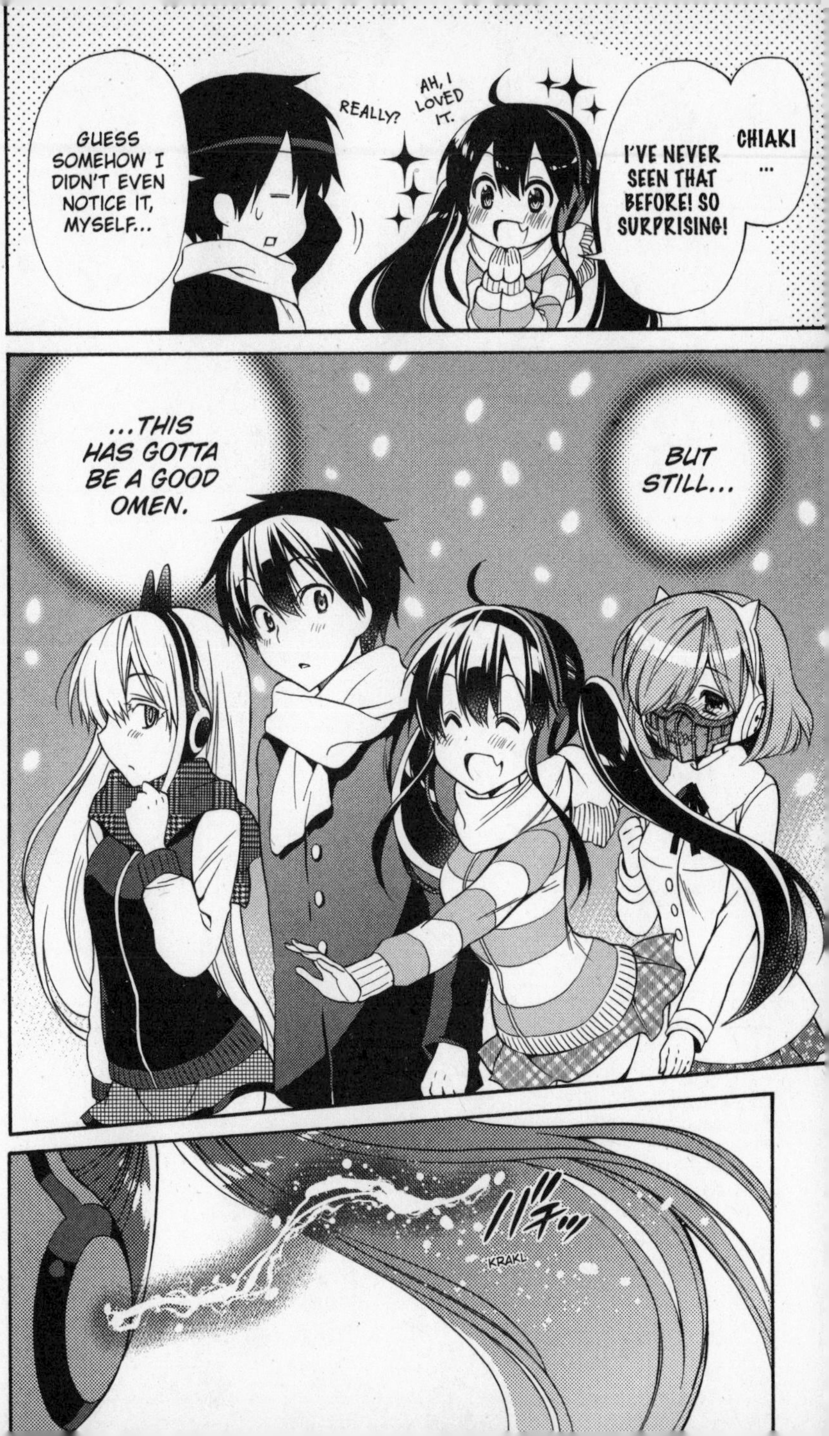
CHIAKI ...
I'VE NEVER SEEN THAT BEFORE! SO SURPRISING!
AH, I LOVED IT.
REALLY?
GUESS SOMEHOW I DIDN'T EVEN NOTICE IT, MYSELF...
BUT STILL...
...THIS HAS GOTTA BE A GOOD OMEN.
バチッ
KRAKL

TODAY'S CERBERUS

HEY. WE NEED TO TALK.
I SWEAR I DON'T KNOW ANYTHING ABOUT A BUNNY COSTUME.
...RIGHT. THOUGHT SO. WE'RE GONNA SETTLE THIS, YOU AND ME.

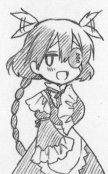

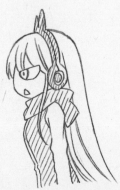

TODAY'S CERBERUS

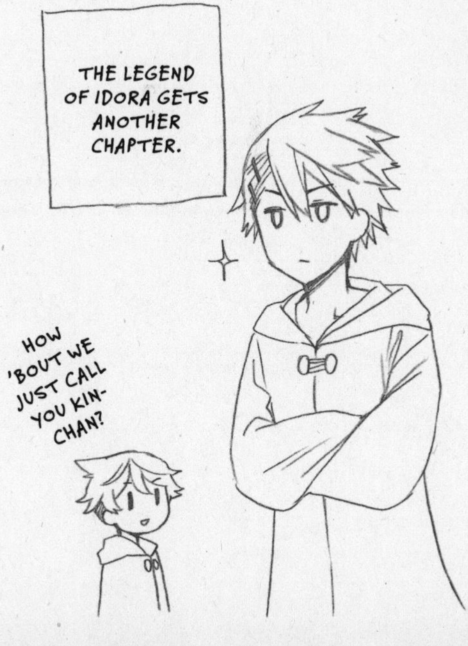
THE LEGEND OF IDORA GETS ANOTHER CHAPTER.
HOW 'BOUT WE JUST CALL YOU KIN-CHAN?

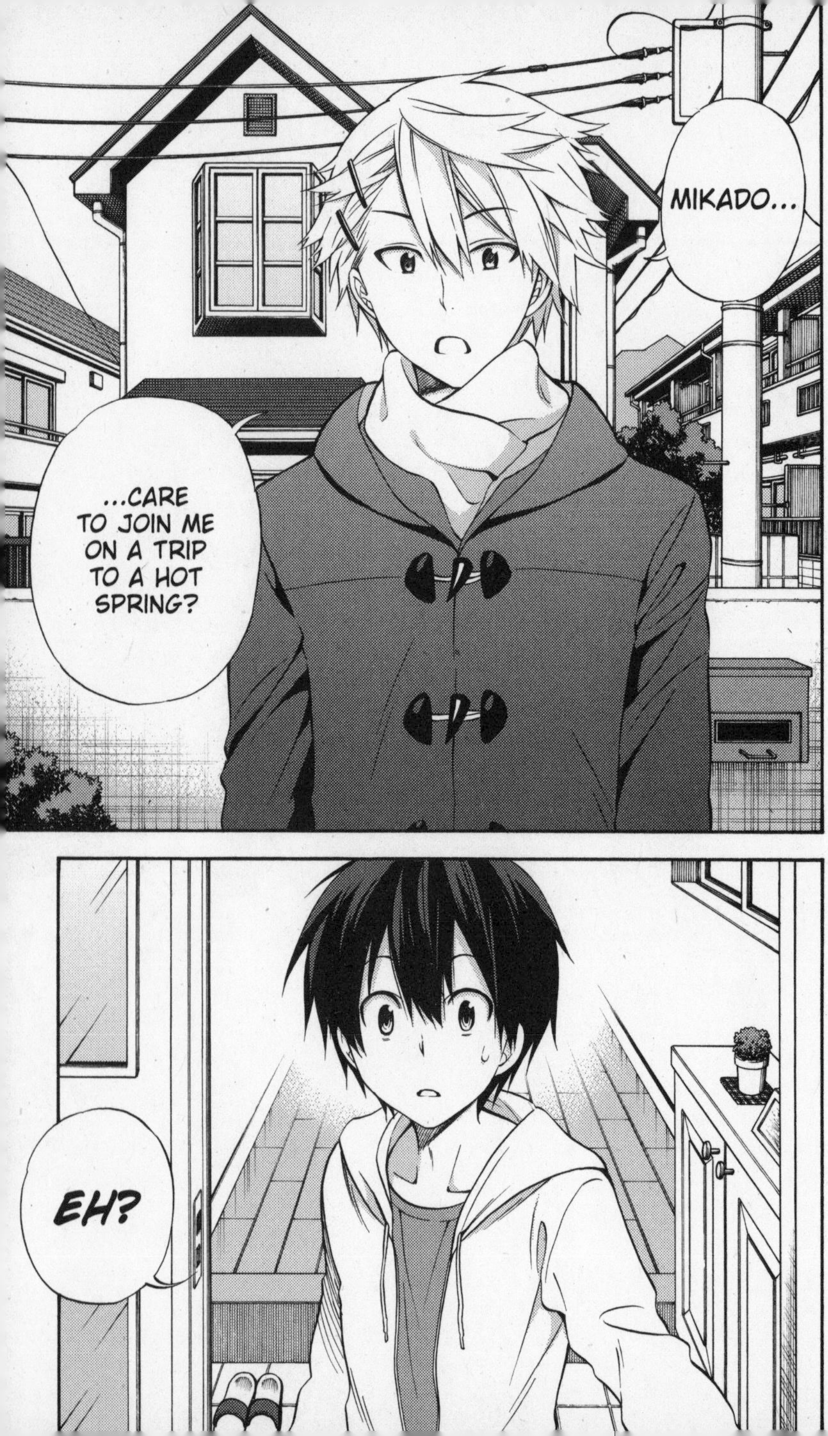
MIKADO...
...CARE TO JOIN ME ON A TRIP TO A HOT SPRING?
EH?

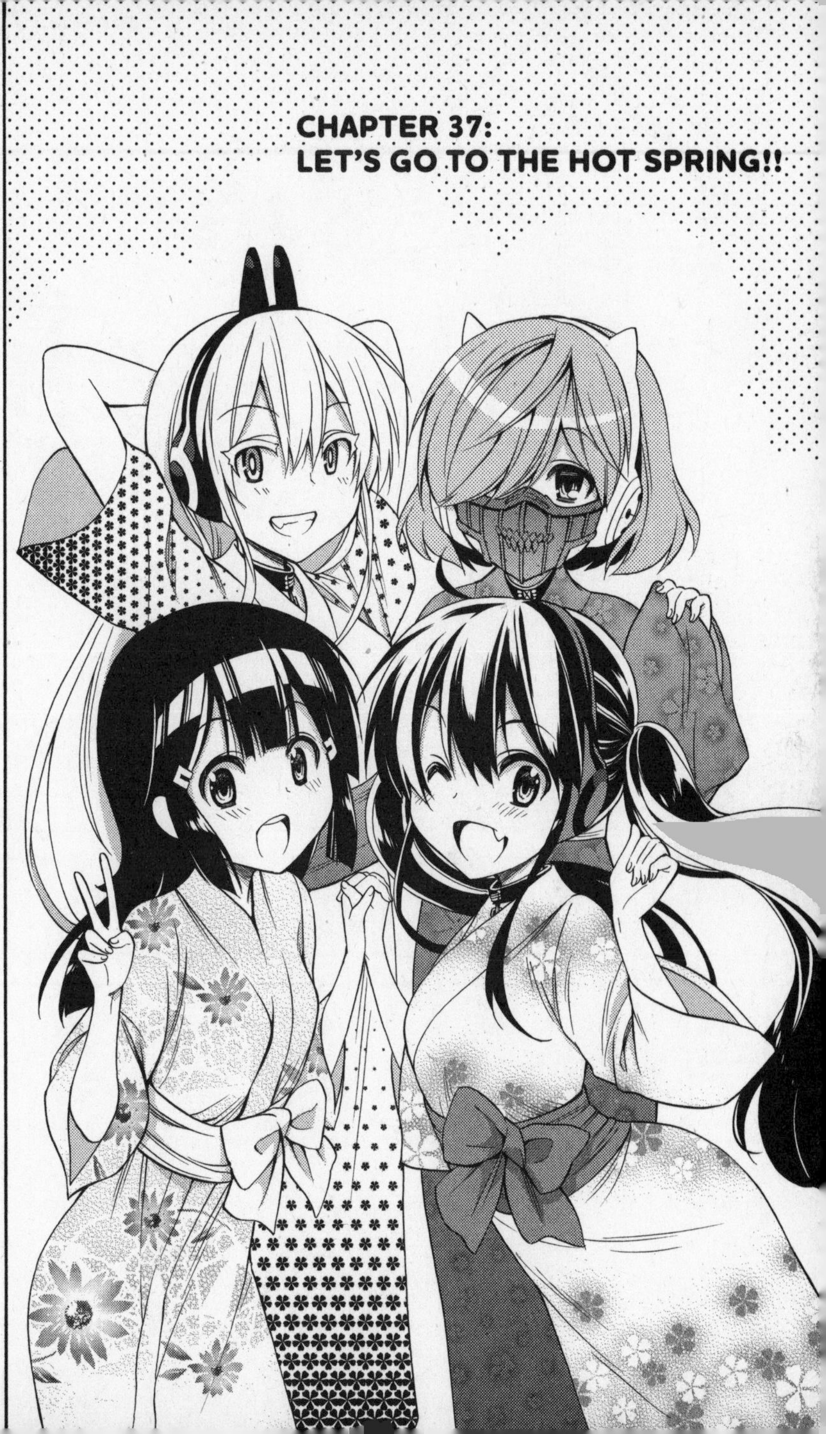
CHAPTER 37:
LET'S GO TO THE HOT SPRING!!

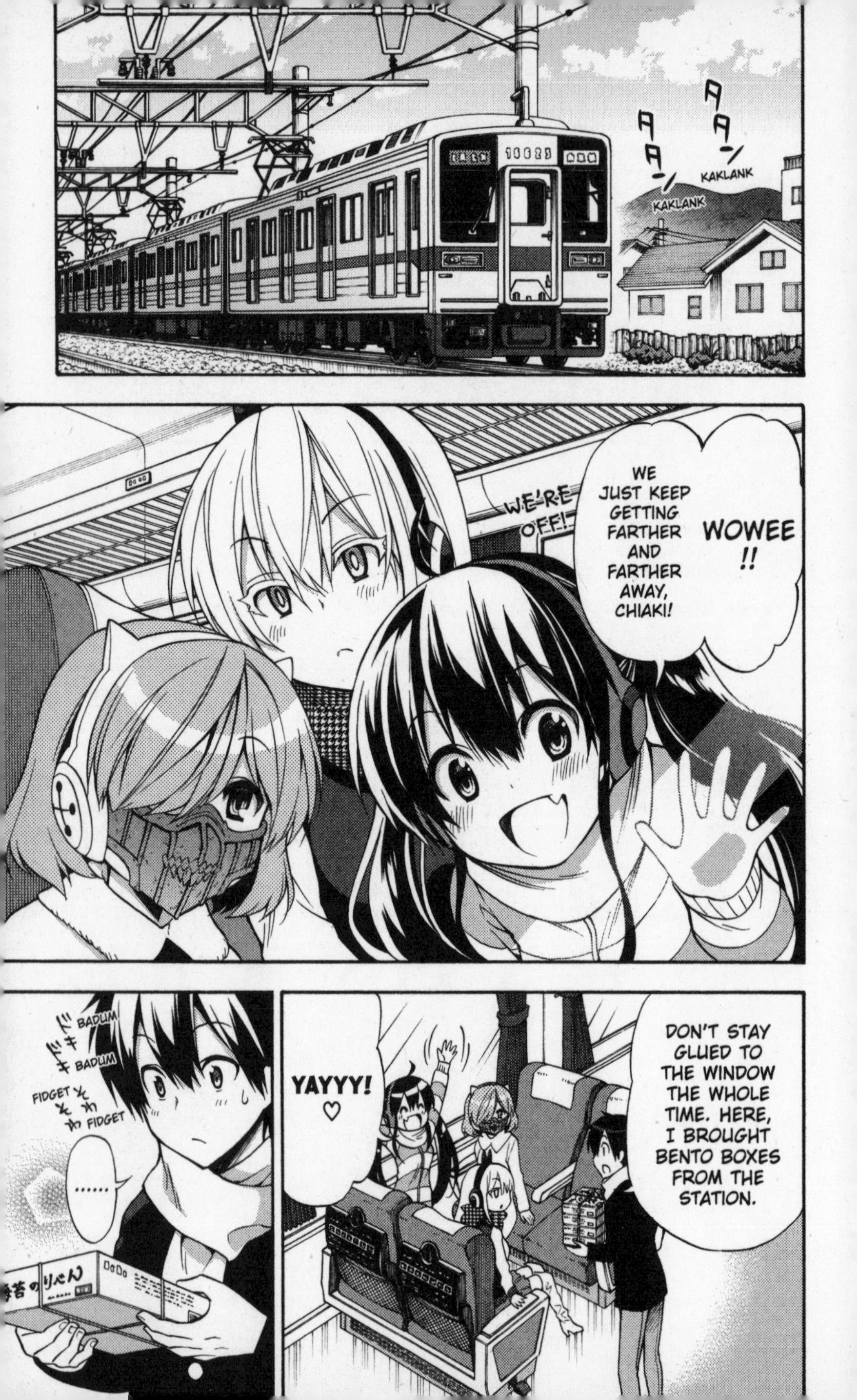
KAKLANK
KAKLANK
WOWEE !!
WE JUST KEEP GETTING FARTHER AND FARTHER AWAY, CHIAKI!
WE'RE OFF!
DON'T STAY GLUED TO THE WINDOW THE WHOLE TIME. HERE, I BROUGHT BENTO BOXES FROM THE STATION.
YAYYY! ♡
BADUM
BADUM
FIDGET
FIDGET
......

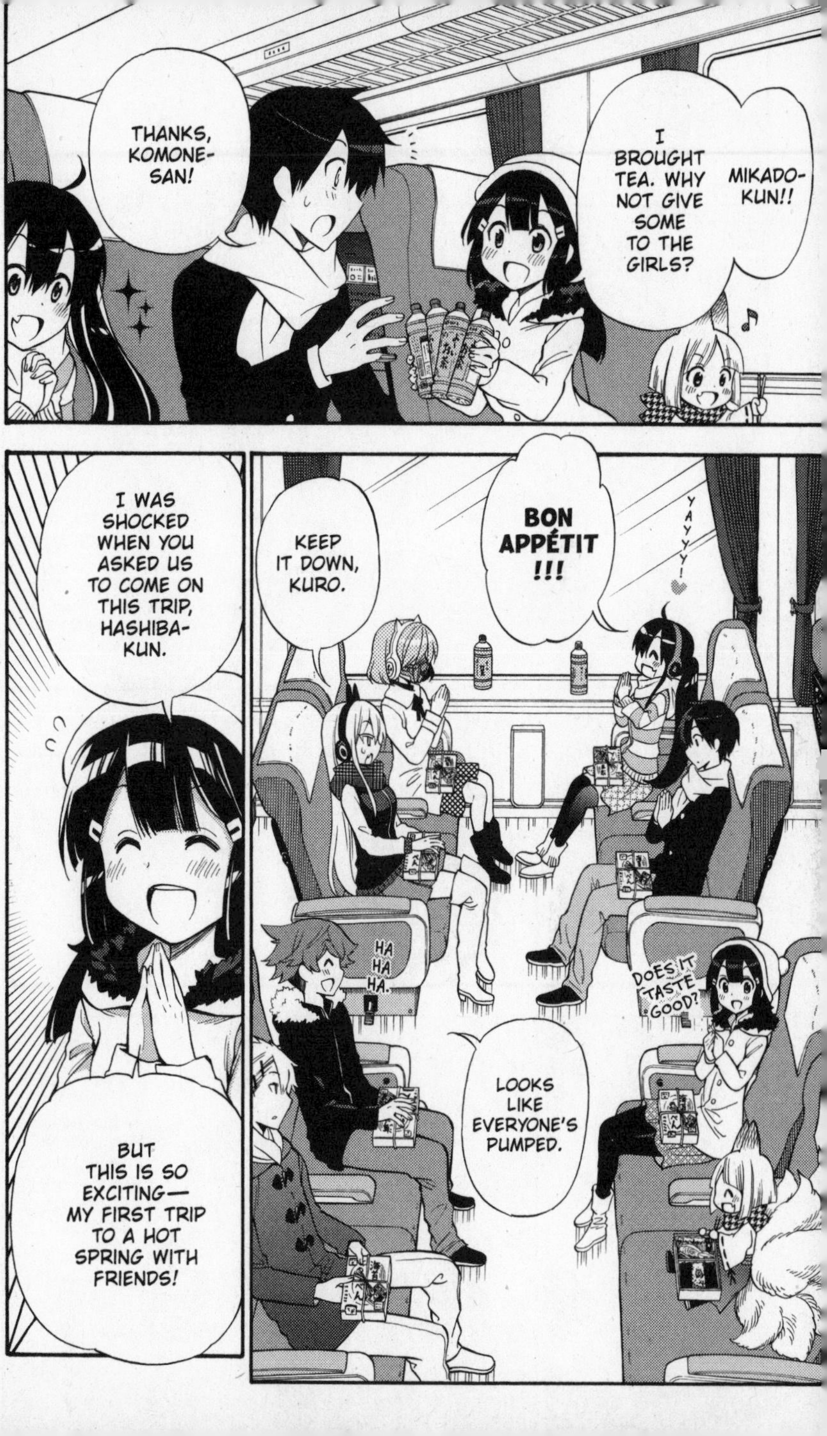
MIKADO-KUN!!
I BROUGHT TEA. WHY NOT GIVE SOME TO THE GIRLS?
THANKS, KOMONE-SAN!
YAYYY!
BON APPÉTIT!!!
KEEP IT DOWN, KURO.
DOES IT TASTE GOOD?
HA HA HA.
LOOKS LIKE EVERYONE'S PUMPED.
I WAS SHOCKED WHEN YOU ASKED US TO COME ON THIS TRIP, HASHIBA-KUN.
BUT THIS IS SO EXCITING—MY FIRST TRIP TO A HOT SPRING WITH FRIENDS!

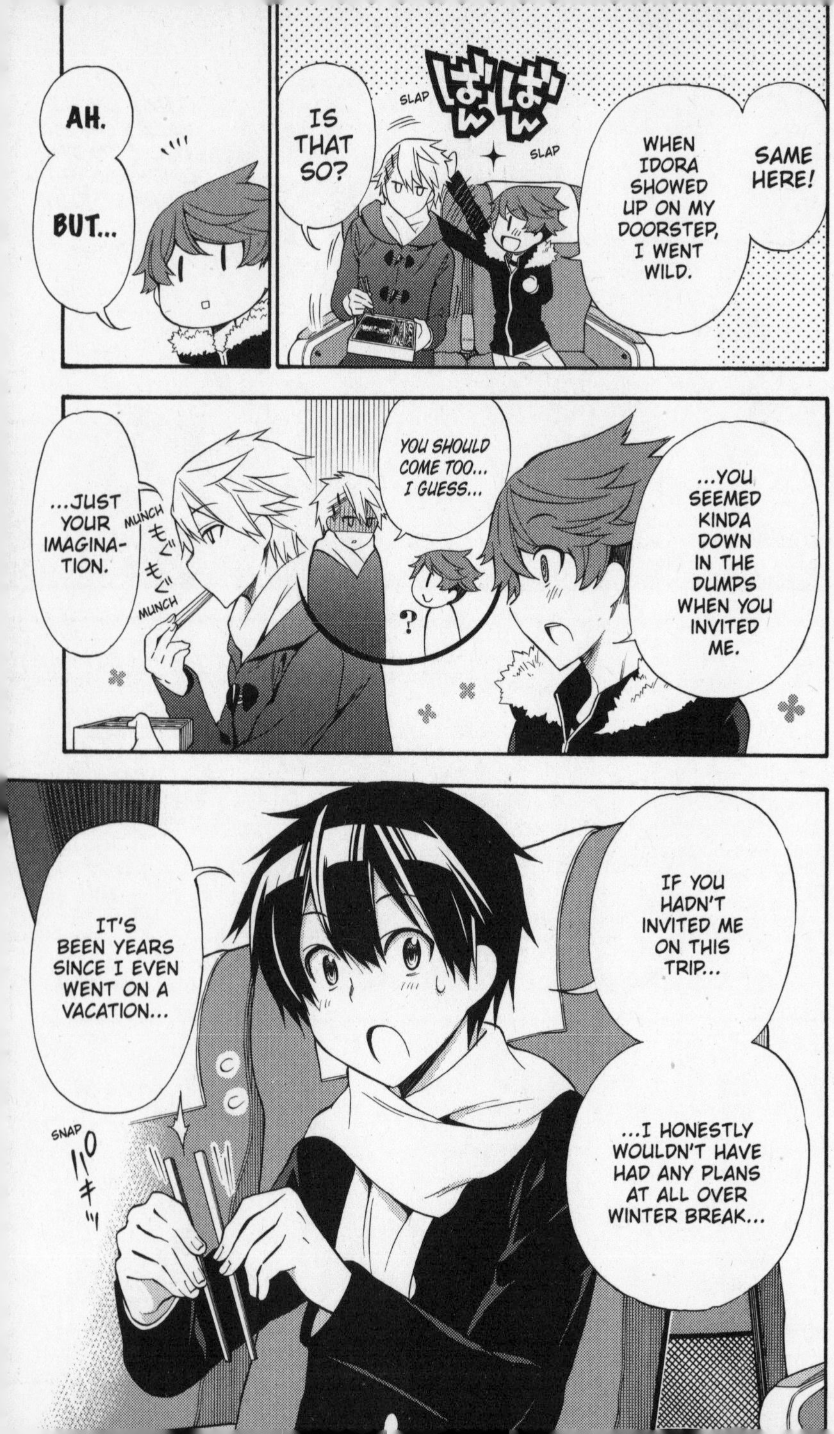
SAME HERE!
WHEN IDORA SHOWED UP ON MY DOORSTEP, I WENT WILD.
ばんばん
SLAP
SLAP
IS THAT SO?
AH.
BUT...
...YOU SEEMED KINDA DOWN IN THE DUMPS WHEN YOU INVITED ME.
YOU SHOULD COME TOO... I GUESS...
?
MUNCH もぐもぐ MUNCH
...JUST YOUR IMAGINATION.
IF YOU HADN'T INVITED ME ON THIS TRIP...
...I HONESTLY WOULDN'T HAVE HAD ANY PLANS AT ALL OVER WINTER BREAK...
IT'S BEEN YEARS SINCE I EVEN WENT ON A VACATION...
SNAP パキッ

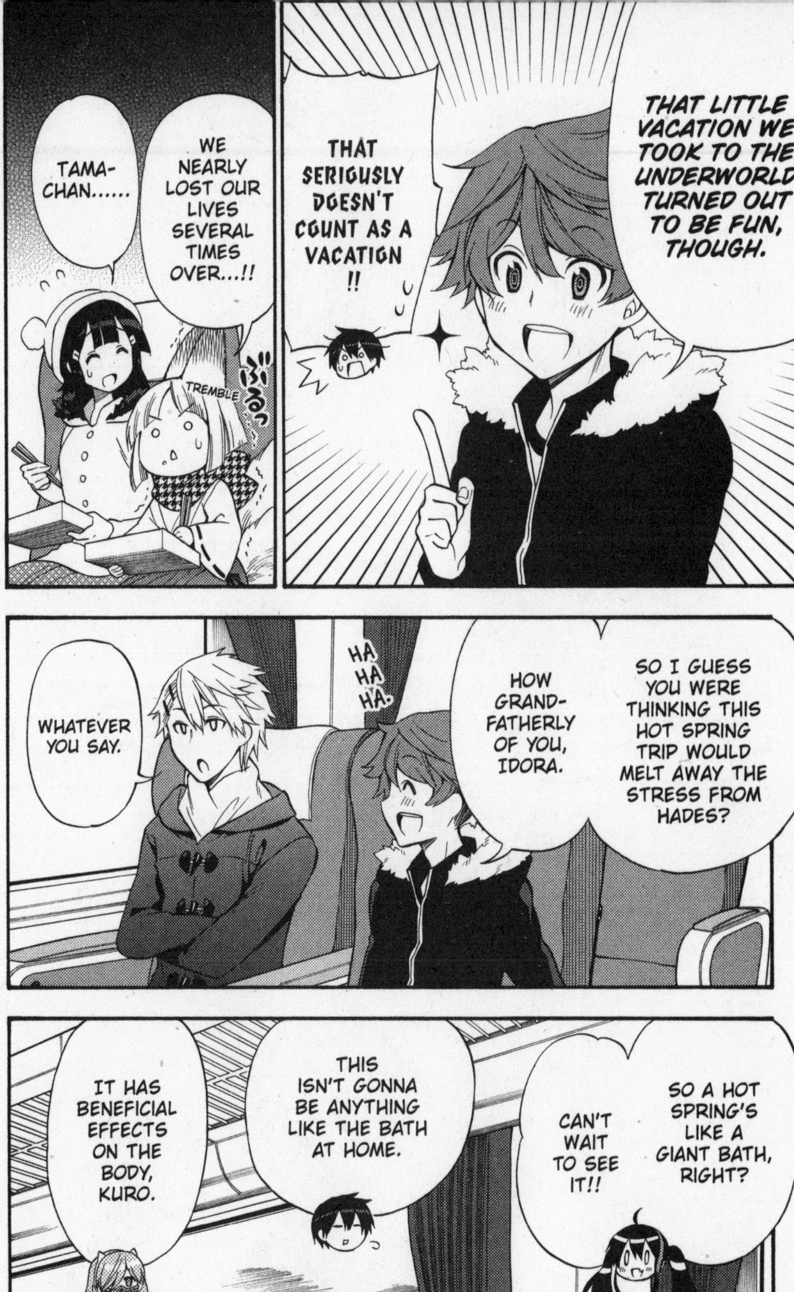
THAT LITTLE VACATION WE TOOK TO THE UNDERWORLD TURNED OUT TO BE FUN, THOUGH.
THAT SERIOUSLY DOESN'T COUNT AS A VACATION !!
WE NEARLY LOST OUR LIVES SEVERAL TIMES OVER...!!
TAMA-CHAN......
TREMBLE
ぶるっ
SO I GUESS YOU WERE THINKING THIS HOT SPRING TRIP WOULD MELT AWAY THE STRESS FROM HADES?
HOW GRAND-FATHERLY OF YOU, IDORA.
HA HA HA.
WHATEVER YOU SAY.
SO A HOT SPRING'S LIKE A GIANT BATH, RIGHT?
CAN'T WAIT TO SEE IT!!
THIS ISN'T GONNA BE ANYTHING LIKE THE BATH AT HOME.
IT HAS BENEFICIAL EFFECTS ON THE BODY, KURO.

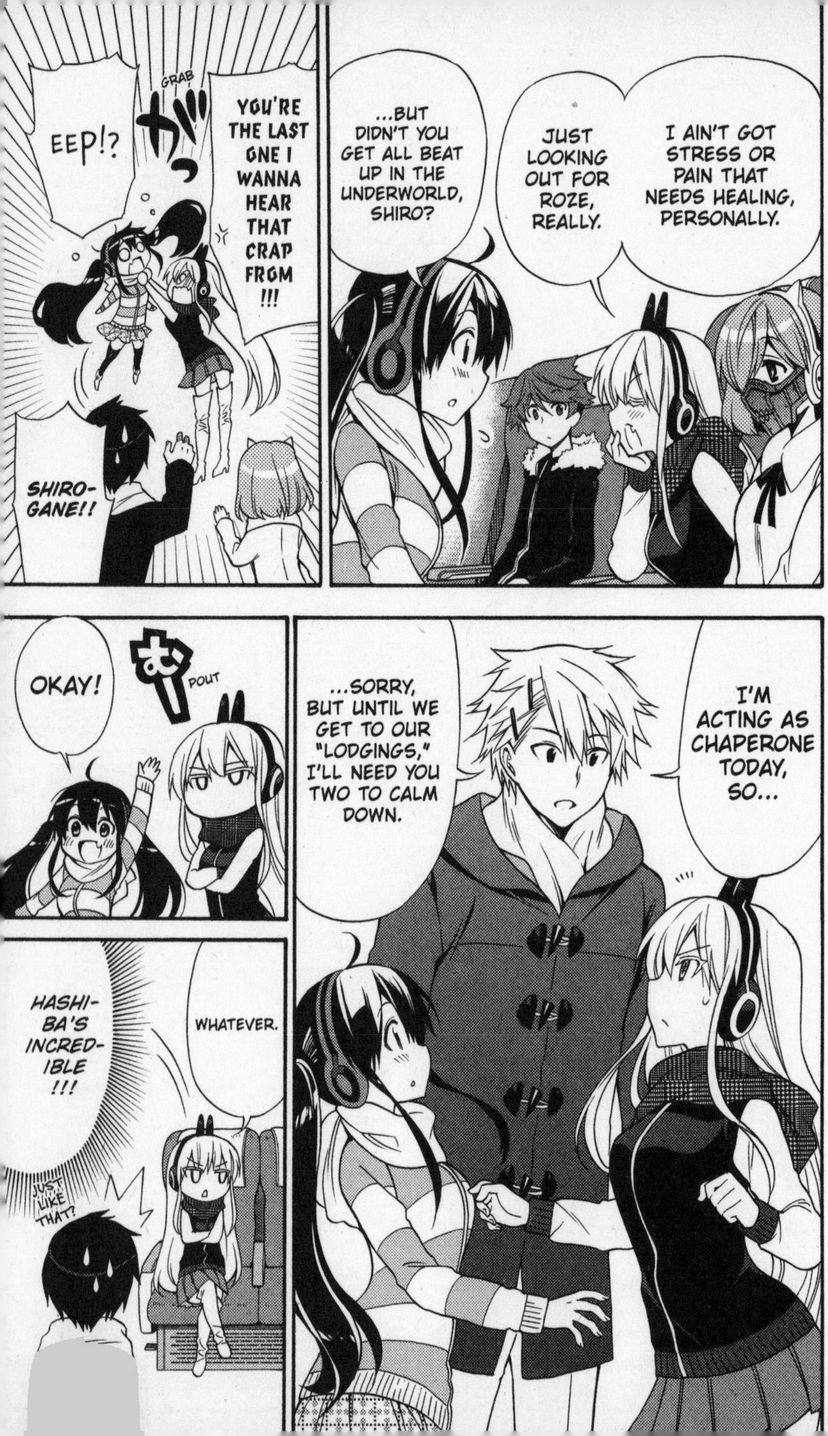
I AIN'T GOT STRESS OR PAIN THAT NEEDS HEALING, PERSONALLY.
JUST LOOKING OUT FOR ROZE, REALLY.
...BUT DIDN'T YOU GET ALL BEAT UP IN THE UNDERWORLD, SHIRO?
YOU'RE THE LAST ONE I WANNA HEAR THAT CRAP FROM!!!
GRAB
EEP!?
SHIRO-GANE!!
I'M ACTING AS CHAPERONE TODAY, SO...
...SORRY, BUT UNTIL WE GET TO OUR "LODGINGS," I'LL NEED YOU TWO TO CALM DOWN.
POUT
OKAY!
WHATEVER.
HASHIBA'S INCREDIBLE!!!
JUST LIKE THAT?

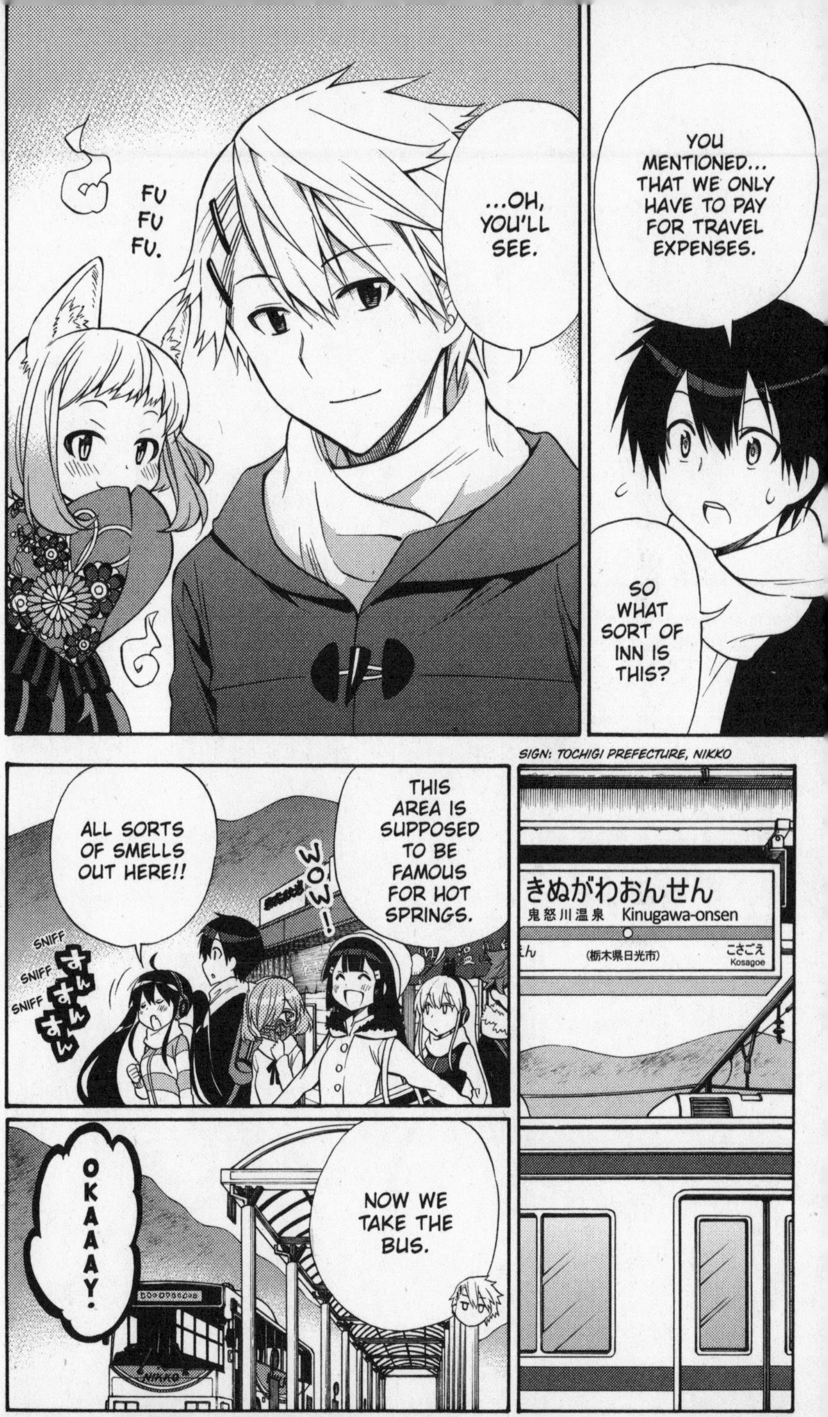
YOU MENTIONED... THAT WE ONLY HAVE TO PAY FOR TRAVEL EXPENSES.
SO WHAT SORT OF INN IS THIS?
...OH, YOU'LL SEE.
FU FU FU.
SIGN: TOCHIGI PREFECTURE, NIKKO
きぬがわおんせん
鬼怒川温泉 Kinugawa-onsen
(栃木県日光市)
こさごえ Kosagoe
THIS AREA IS SUPPOSED TO BE FAMOUS FOR HOT SPRINGS.
WOW!
ALL SORTS OF SMELLS OUT HERE!!
すんすんすん
SNIFF SNIFF SNIFF
NOW WE TAKE THE BUS.
OKAAAY.

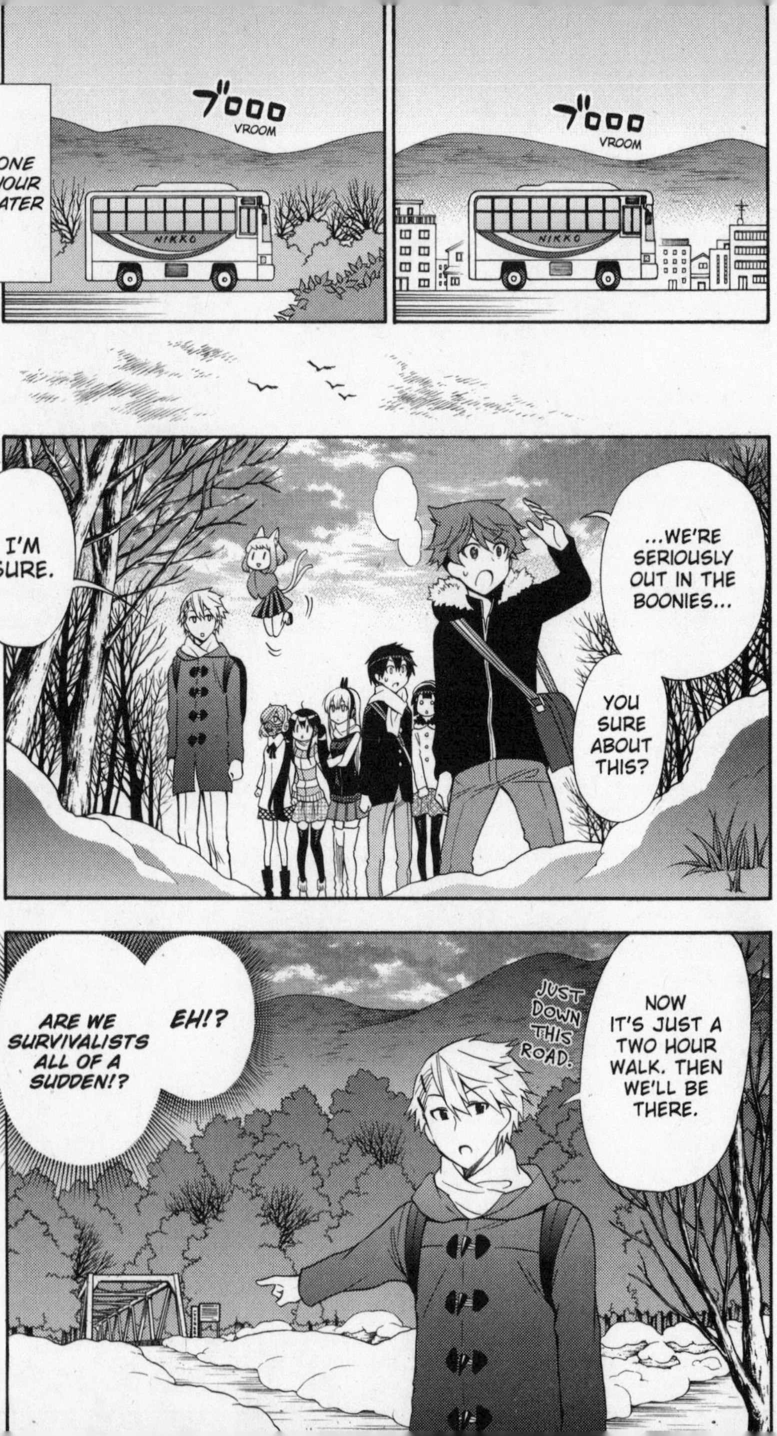
VROOM
ONE HOUR LATER
VROOM
...WE'RE SERIOUSLY OUT IN THE BOONIES...
YOU SURE ABOUT THIS?
I'M SURE.
NOW IT'S JUST A TWO HOUR WALK. THEN WE'LL BE THERE.
JUST DOWN THIS ROAD.
EH!?
ARE WE SURVIVALISTS ALL OF A SUDDEN!?

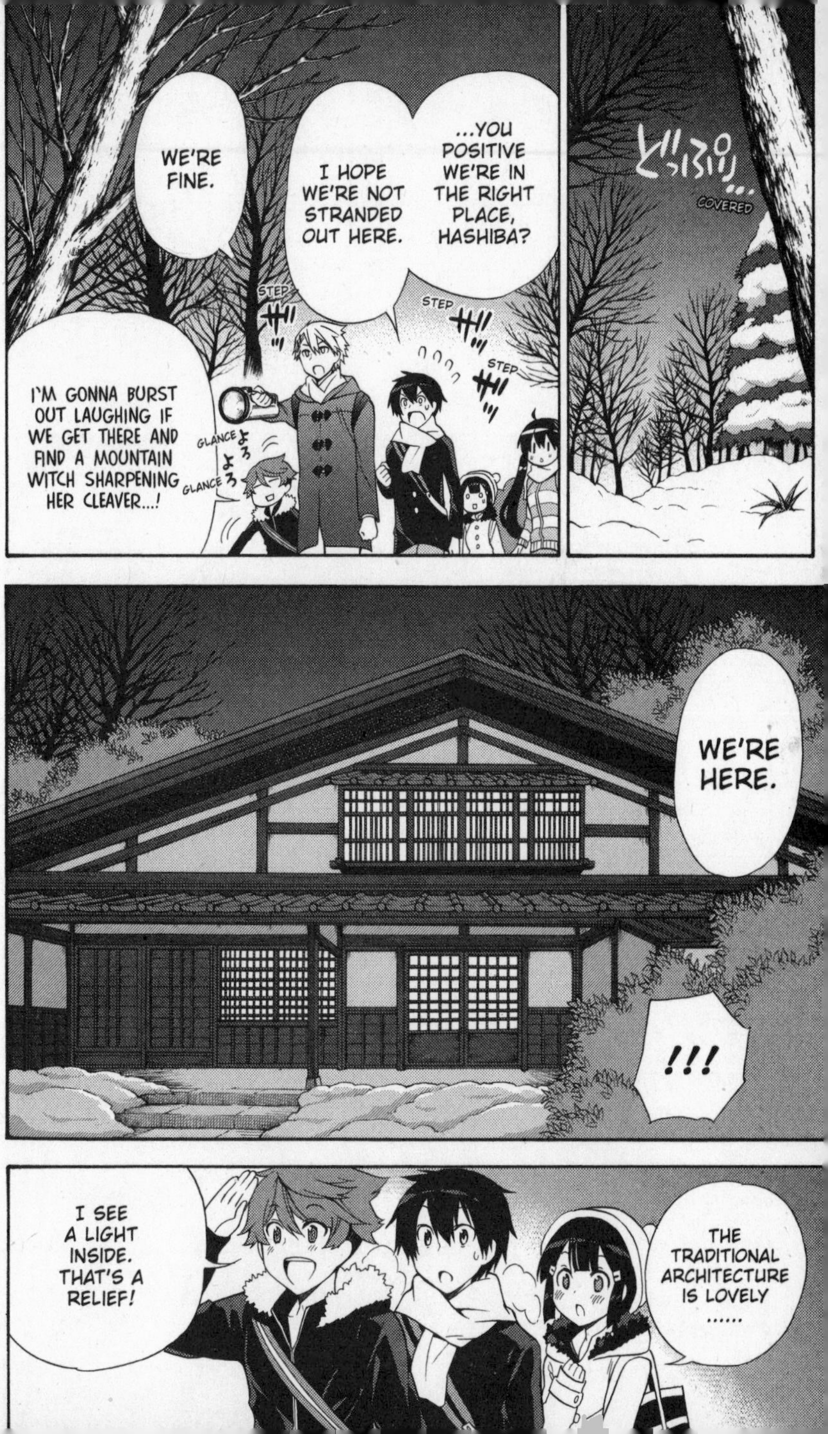

どっぷり…
COVERED
...YOU POSITIVE WE'RE IN THE RIGHT PLACE, HASHIBA?
I HOPE WE'RE NOT STRANDED OUT HERE.
WE'RE FINE.
STEP
STEP
STEP
I'M GONNA BURST OUT LAUGHING IF WE GET THERE AND FIND A MOUNTAIN WITCH SHARPENING HER CLEAVER...!
GLANCE よろ
GLANCE よろ
WE'RE HERE.
!!!
THE TRADITIONAL ARCHITECTURE IS LOVELY ......
I SEE A LIGHT INSIDE. THAT'S A RELIEF!

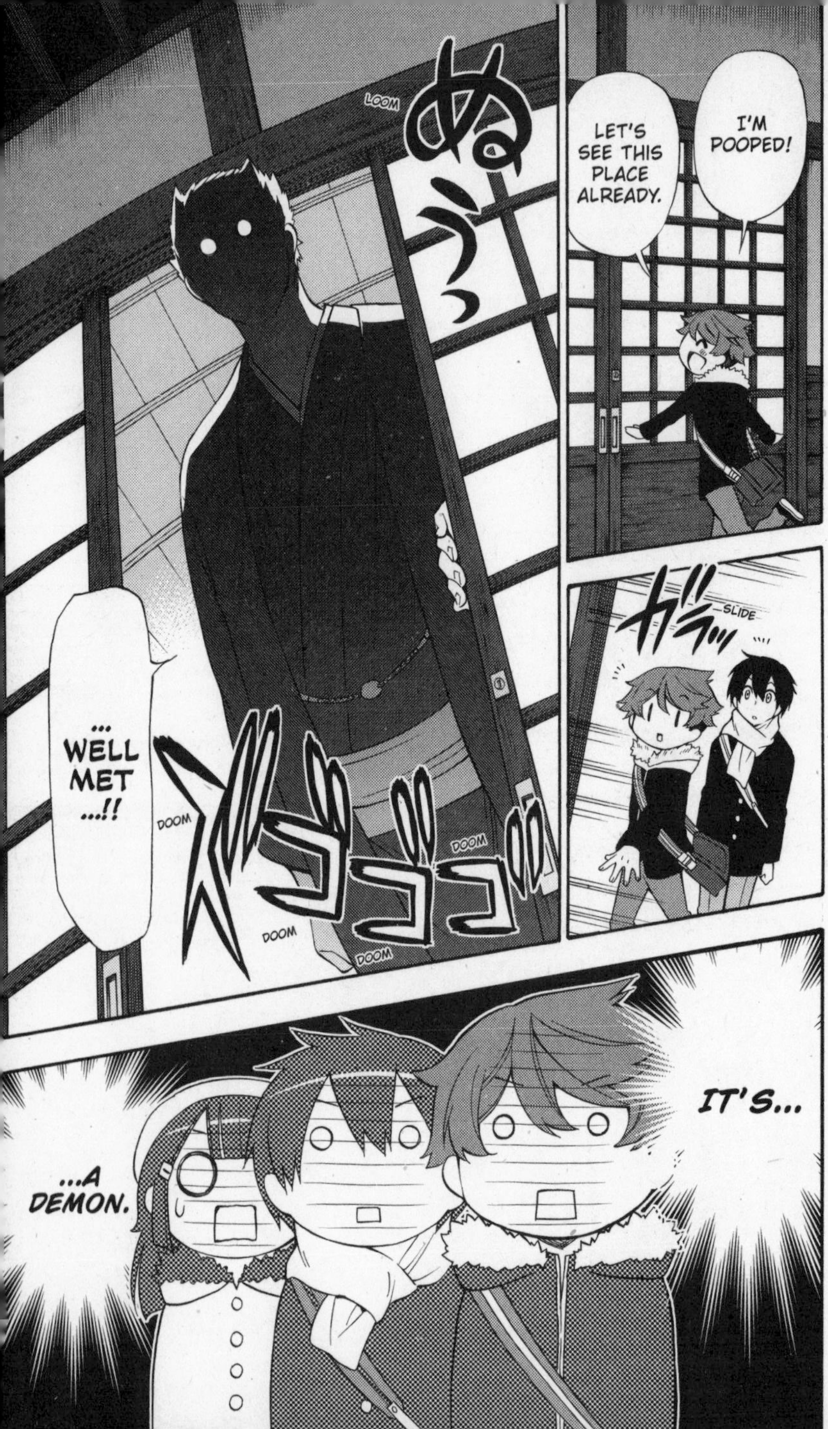
I'M POOPED!
LET'S SEE THIS PLACE ALREADY.
SLIDE
LOOM
DOOM
DOOM
DOOM
DOOM
...WELL MET ...!!
IT'S...
...A DEMON.

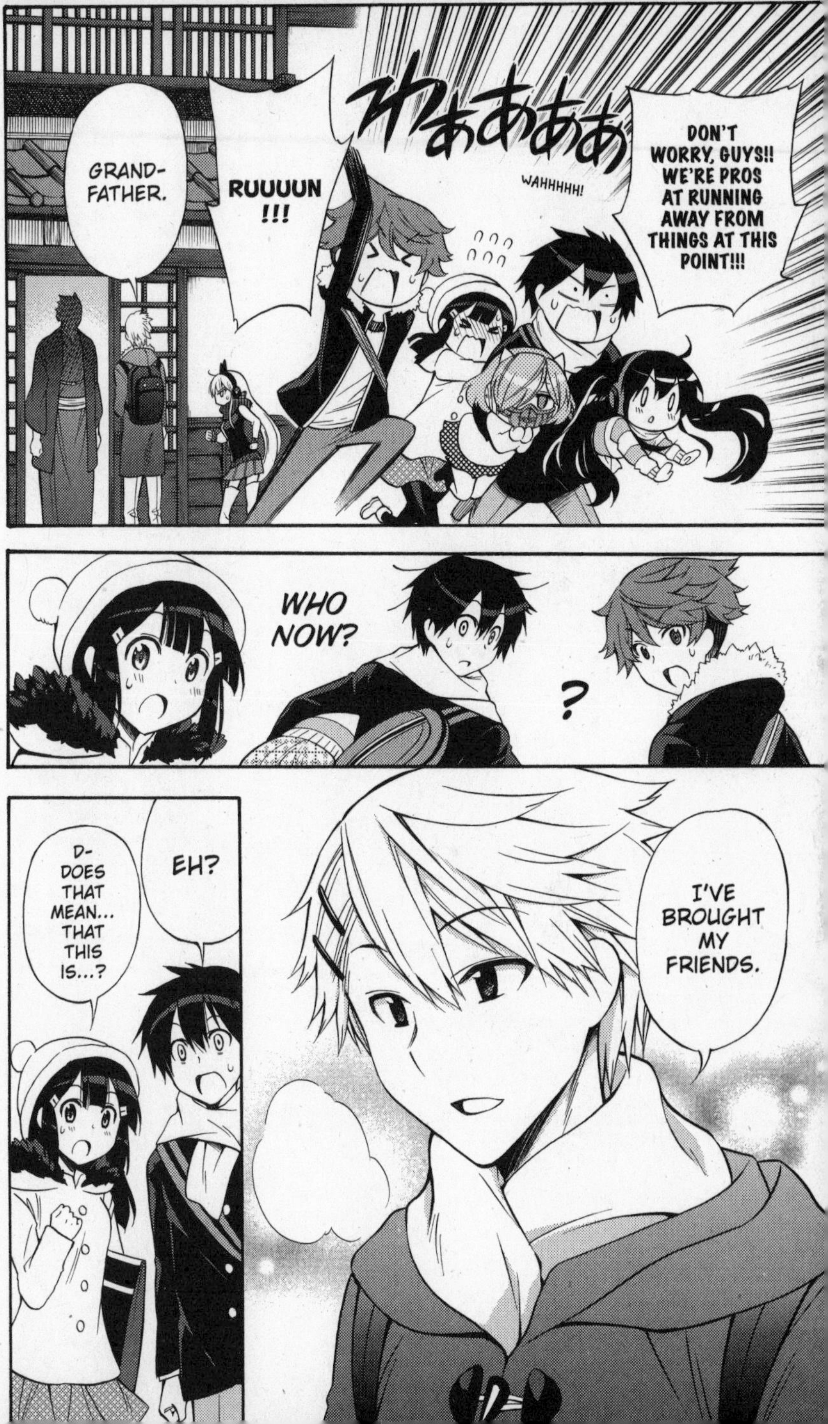
DON'T WORRY, GUYS!! WE'RE PROS AT RUNNING AWAY FROM THINGS AT THIS POINT!!!
WAHHHHH!
RUUUUN !!!
GRAND-FATHER.
?
WHO NOW?
I'VE BROUGHT MY FRIENDS.
EH?
D-DOES THAT MEAN... THAT THIS IS...?

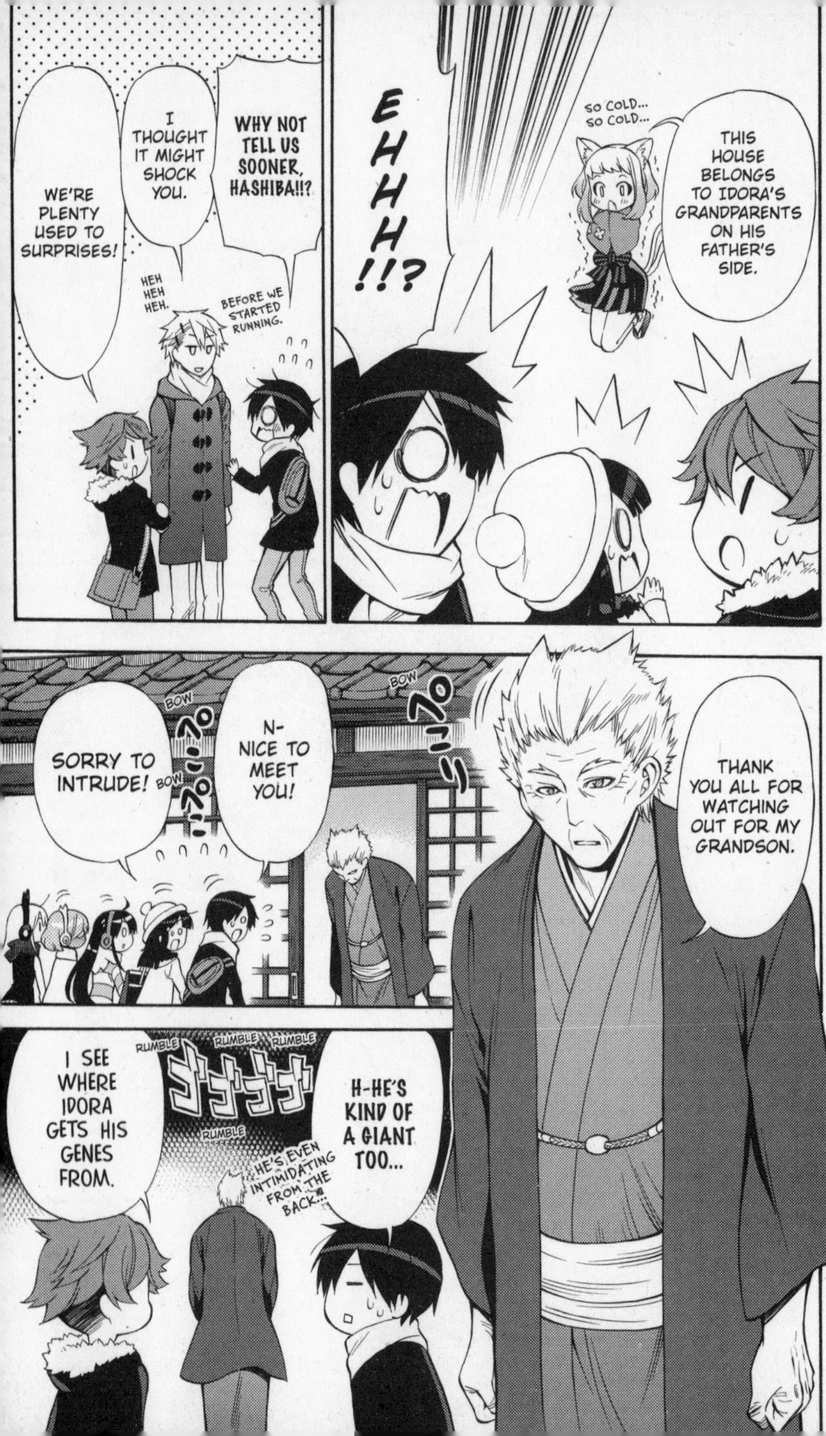
SO COLD... SO COLD...
THIS HOUSE BELONGS TO IDORA'S GRANDPARENTS ON HIS FATHER'S SIDE.
EHHHH!!?
WHY NOT TELL US SOONER, HASHIBA!!?
BEFORE WE STARTED RUNNING.
I THOUGHT IT MIGHT SHOCK YOU.
HEH HEH HEH.
WE'RE PLENTY USED TO SURPRISES!
THANK YOU ALL FOR WATCHING OUT FOR MY GRANDSON.
BOW
N-NICE TO MEET YOU!
BOW
BOW
SORRY TO INTRUDE!
RUMBLE RUMBLE RUMBLE
RUMBLE
H-HE'S KIND OF A GIANT TOO...
HE'S EVEN INTIMIDATING FROM THE BACK...
I SEE WHERE IDORA GETS HIS GENES FROM.

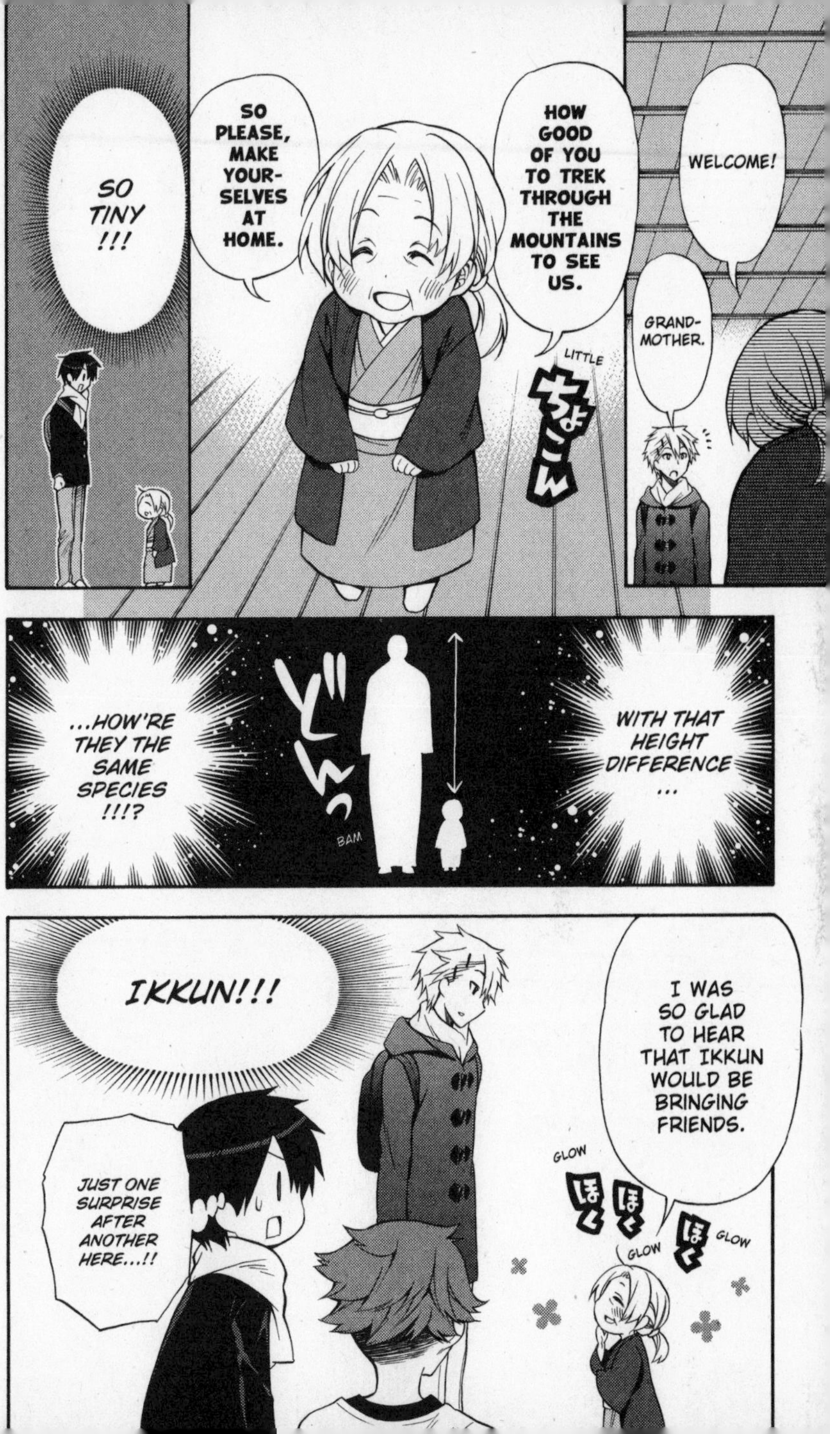
WELCOME!
GRAND-MOTHER.
HOW GOOD OF YOU TO TREK THROUGH THE MOUNTAINS TO SEE US.
SO PLEASE, MAKE YOUR-SELVES AT HOME.
ちょこん
LITTLE
SO TINY!!!
WITH THAT HEIGHT DIFFERENCE...
どんっ
BAM
...HOW'RE THEY THE SAME SPECIES!!!?
I WAS SO GLAD TO HEAR THAT IKKUN WOULD BE BRINGING FRIENDS.
ほくほくほく
GLOW GLOW GLOW
IKKUN!!!
JUST ONE SURPRISE AFTER ANOTHER HERE...!!

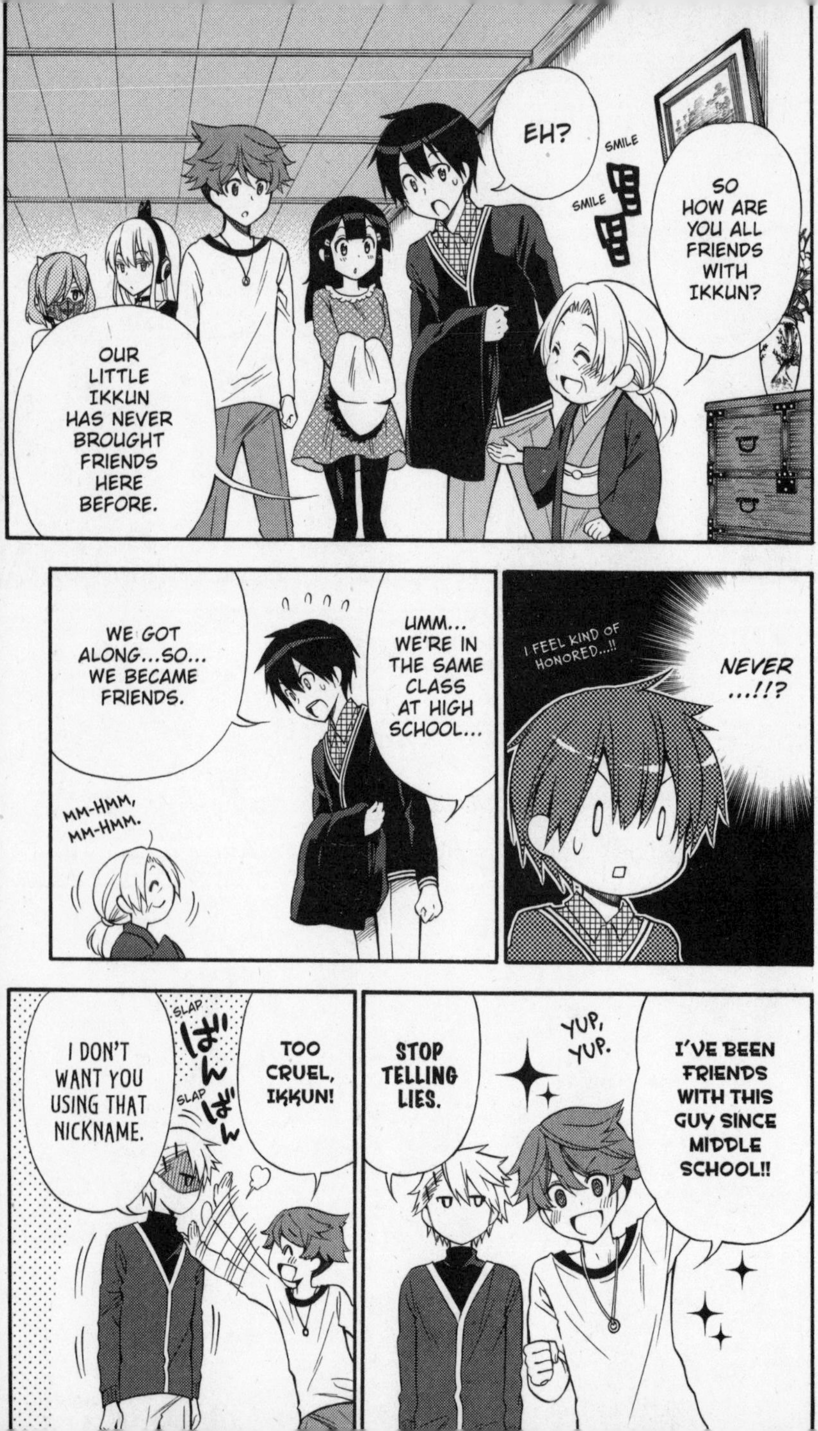
SO HOW ARE YOU ALL FRIENDS WITH IKKUN?
SMILE
SMILE
EH?
OUR LITTLE IKKUN HAS NEVER BROUGHT FRIENDS HERE BEFORE.
NEVER...!!?
I FEEL KIND OF HONORED...!!
UMM... WE'RE IN THE SAME CLASS AT HIGH SCHOOL...
WE GOT ALONG...SO... WE BECAME FRIENDS.
MM-HMM, MM-HMM.
I'VE BEEN FRIENDS WITH THIS GUY SINCE MIDDLE SCHOOL!!
YUP, YUP.
STOP TELLING LIES.
TOO CRUEL, IKKUN!
SLAP
ばん
SLAP
ばん
I DON'T WANT YOU USING THAT NICKNAME.

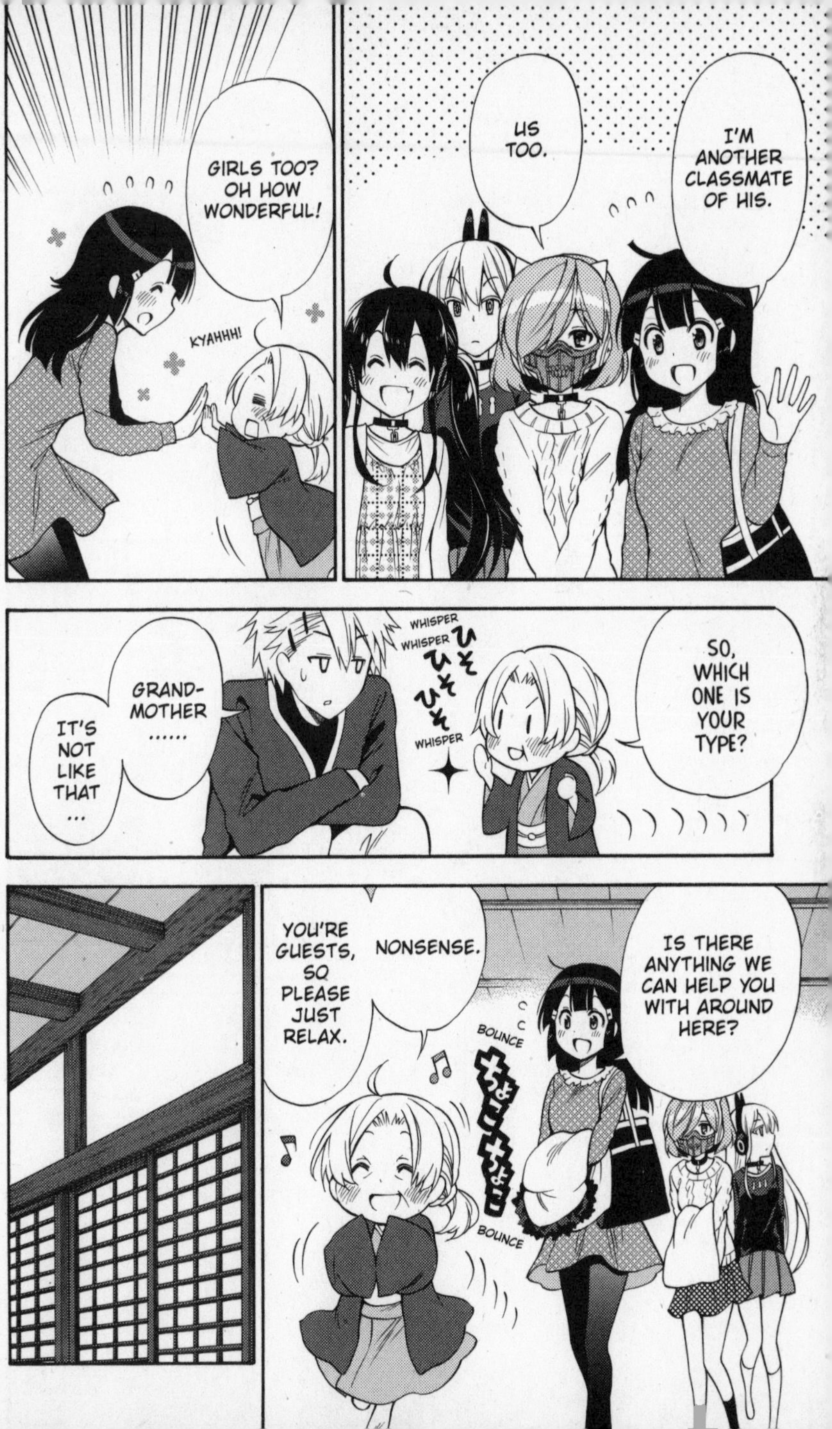
I'M ANOTHER CLASSMATE OF HIS.
US TOO.
GIRLS TOO? OH HOW WONDERFUL!
KYAHHH!
SO, WHICH ONE IS YOUR TYPE?
WHISPER WHISPER ひそひそ WHISPER
ひそ
GRAND-MOTHER ......
IT'S NOT LIKE THAT ...
IS THERE ANYTHING WE CAN HELP YOU WITH AROUND HERE?
NONSENSE.
YOU'RE GUESTS, SO PLEASE JUST RELAX.
BOUNCE ちょこちょこ BOUNCE

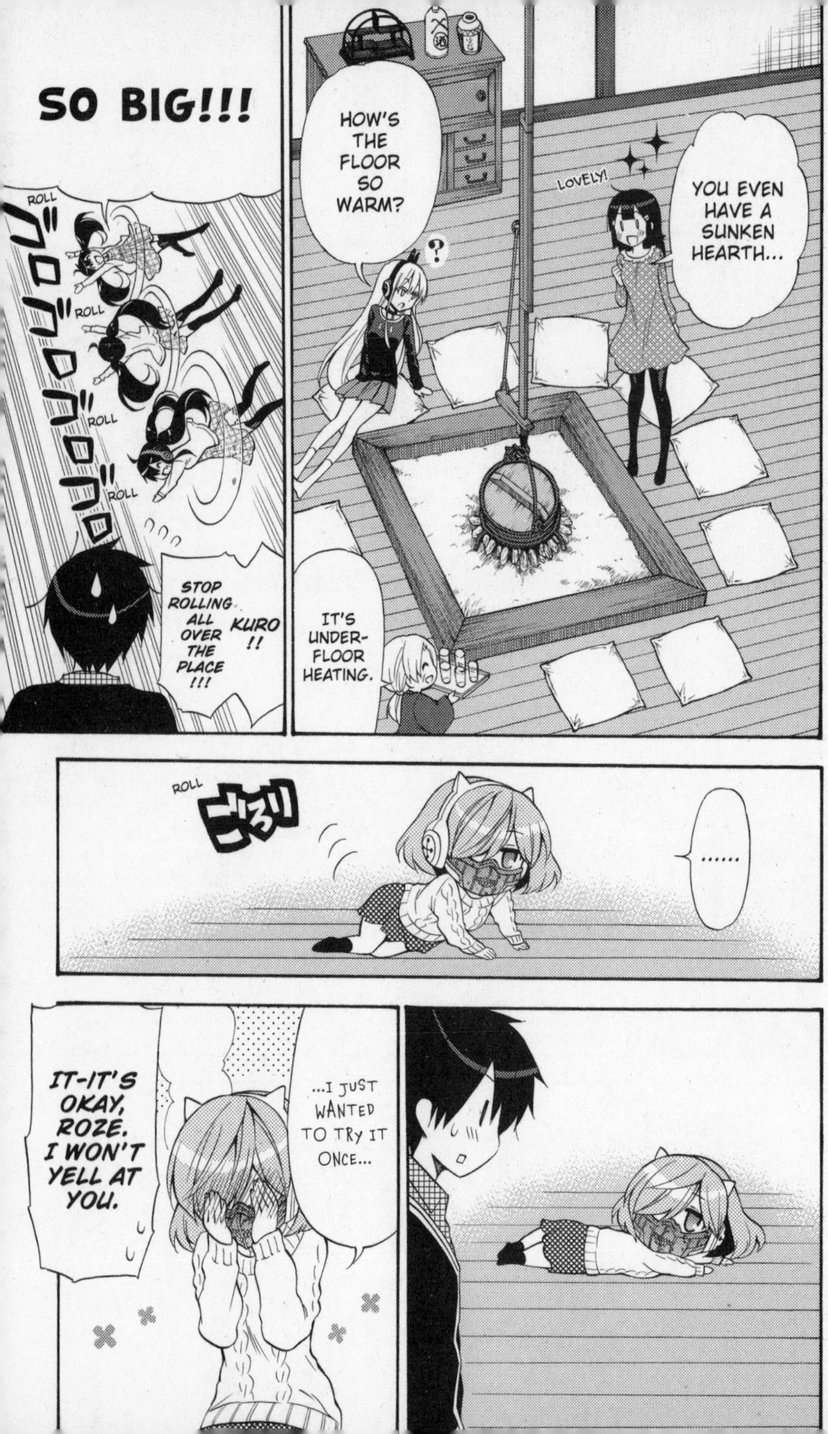

YOU EVEN HAVE A SUNKEN HEARTH...
LOVELY!
HOW'S THE FLOOR SO WARM?
IT'S UNDER-FLOOR HEATING.
SO BIG!!!
ROLL
ROLL
ROLL
ROLL
KURO!! STOP ROLLING ALL OVER THE PLACE!!!
......
ROLL
ごろり
...I JUST WANTED TO TRY IT ONCE...
IT-IT'S OKAY, ROZE. I WON'T YELL AT YOU.

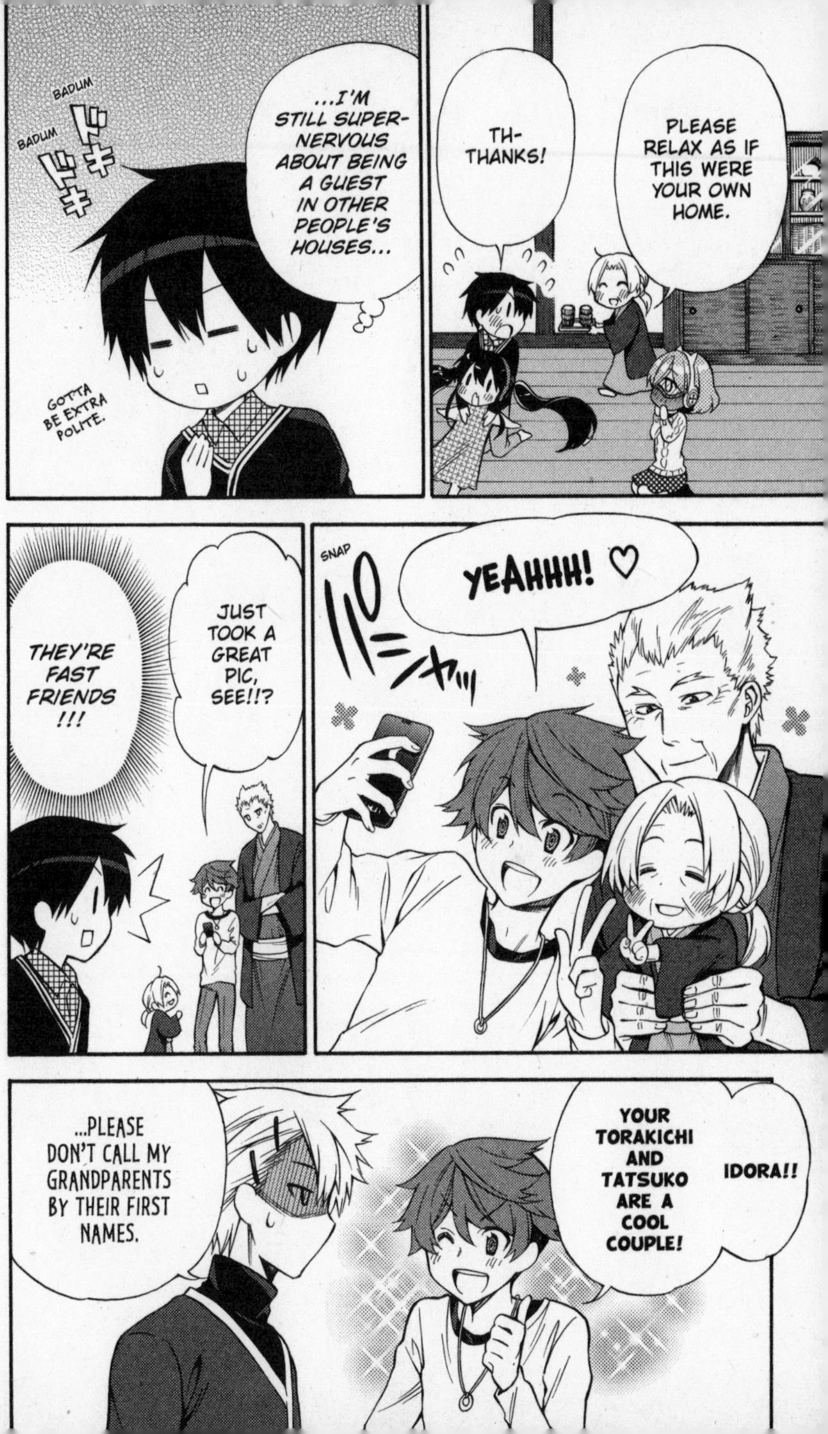
PLEASE RELAX AS IF THIS WERE YOUR OWN HOME.
TH- THANKS!
...I'M STILL SUPER-NERVOUS ABOUT BEING A GUEST IN OTHER PEOPLE'S HOUSES...
BADUM
BADUM
GOTTA BE EXTRA POLITE.
SNAP
YEAHHH! ♡
JUST TOOK A GREAT PIC, SEE!!?
THEY'RE FAST FRIENDS!!!
YOUR TORAKICHI AND TATSUKO ARE A COOL COUPLE!
IDORA!!
...PLEASE DON'T CALL MY GRANDPARENTS BY THEIR FIRST NAMES.

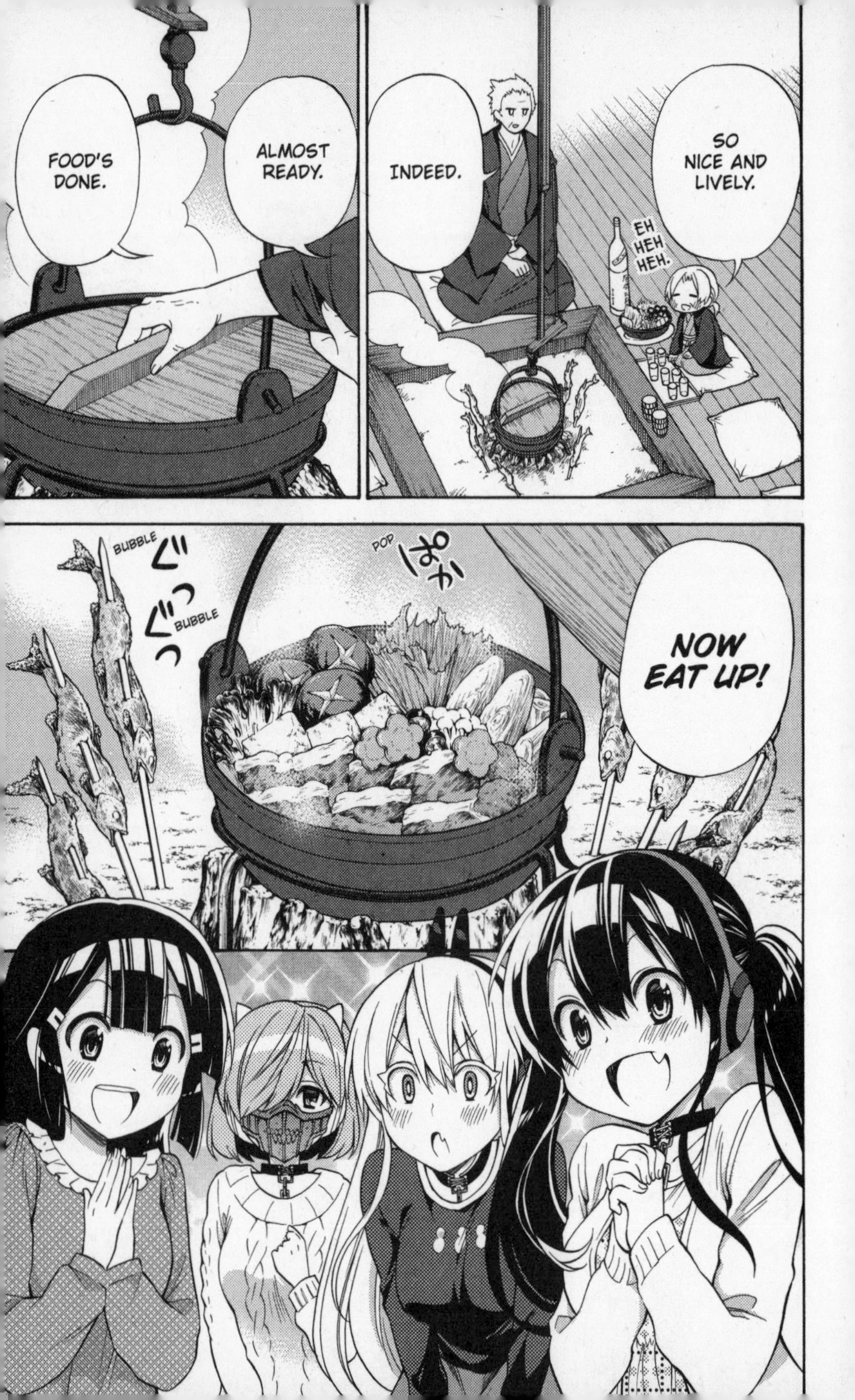
SO NICE AND LIVELY.
EH HEH HEH.
INDEED.
ALMOST READY.
FOOD'S DONE.
NOW EAT UP!
POP ぱか
BUBBLE ぐつ
BUBBLE ぐつ

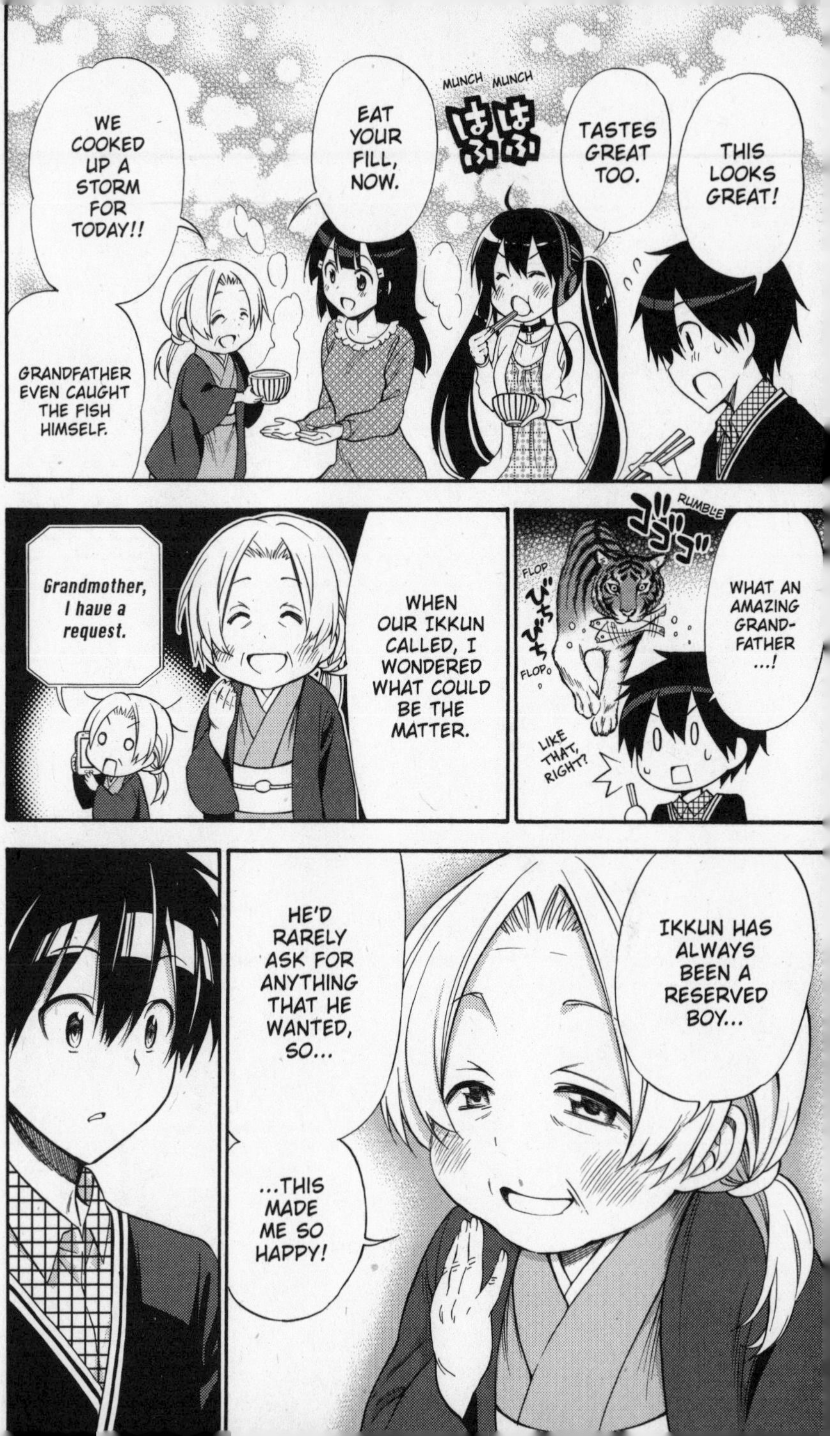
THIS LOOKS GREAT!
TASTES GREAT TOO.
MUNCH MUNCH
はふはふ
EAT YOUR FILL, NOW.
WE COOKED UP A STORM FOR TODAY!!
GRANDFATHER EVEN CAUGHT THE FISH HIMSELF.
WHAT AN AMAZING GRAND-FATHER ...!
RUMBLE
ゴゴゴ
FLOP
びちびち
FLOP
LIKE THAT, RIGHT?
WHEN OUR IKKUN CALLED, I WONDERED WHAT COULD BE THE MATTER.
Grandmother, I have a request.
IKKUN HAS ALWAYS BEEN A RESERVED BOY...
HE'D RARELY ASK FOR ANYTHING THAT HE WANTED, SO...
...THIS MADE ME SO HAPPY!

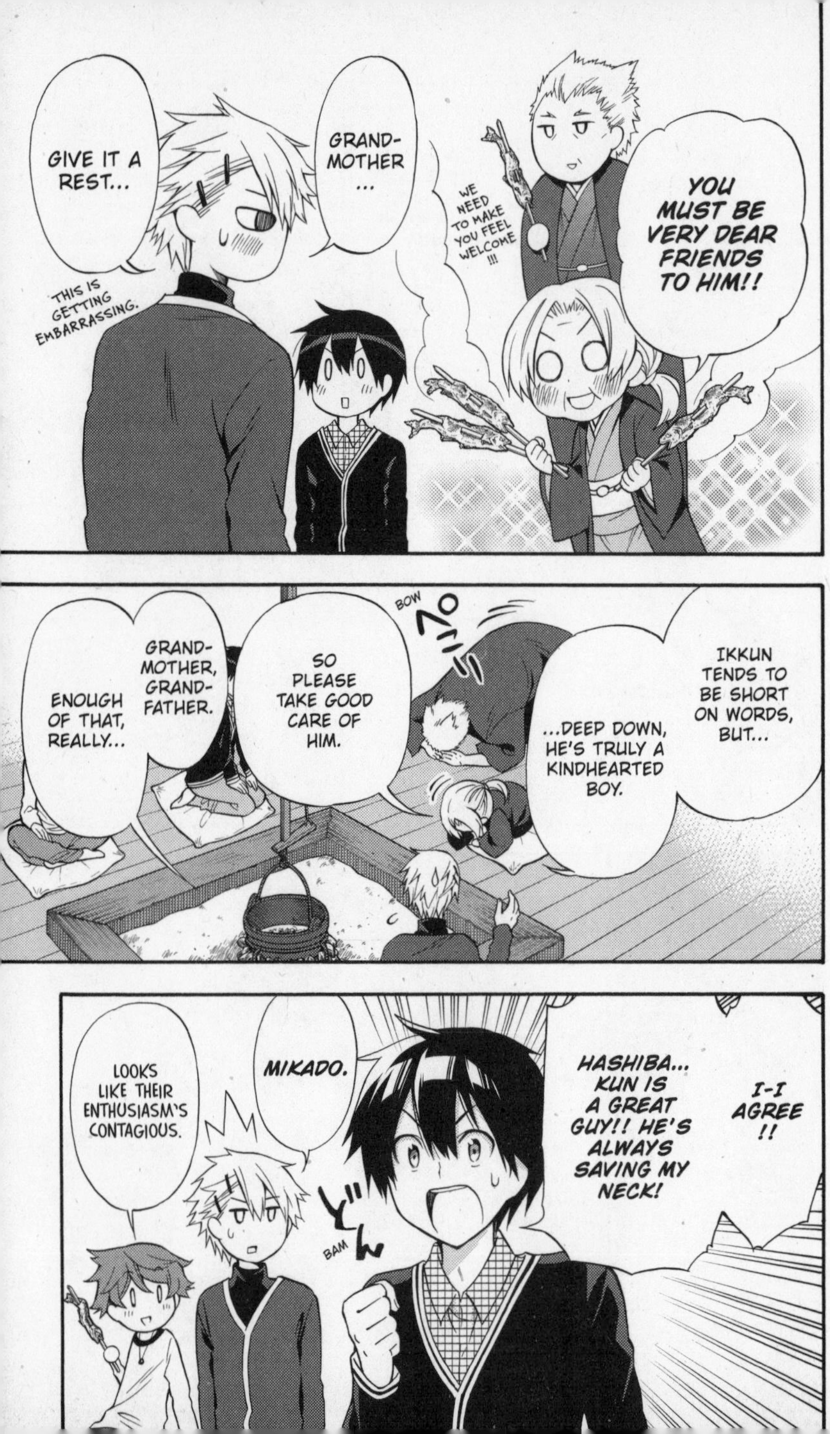
YOU MUST BE VERY DEAR FRIENDS TO HIM!!
WE NEED TO MAKE YOU FEEL WELCOME!!!
GRAND-MOTHER...
GIVE IT A REST...
THIS IS GETTING EMBARRASSING.
IKKUN TENDS TO BE SHORT ON WORDS, BUT...
...DEEP DOWN, HE'S TRULY A KINDHEARTED BOY.
BOW
SO PLEASE TAKE GOOD CARE OF HIM.
GRAND-MOTHER, GRAND-FATHER.
ENOUGH OF THAT, REALLY...
I-I AGREE!!
HASHIBA... KUN IS A GREAT GUY!! HE'S ALWAYS SAVING MY NECK!
BAM
MIKADO.
LOOKS LIKE THEIR ENTHUSIASM'S CONTAGIOUS.

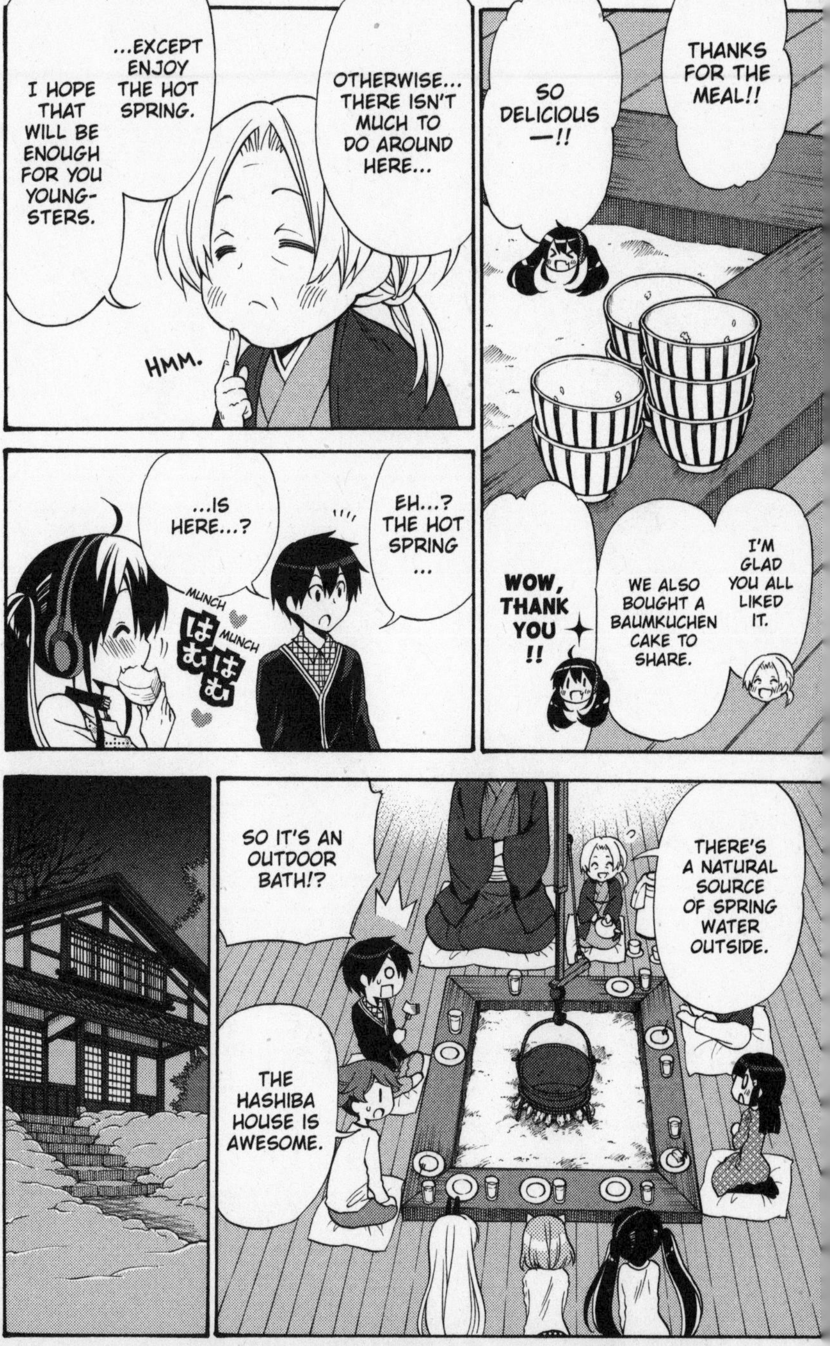
THANKS FOR THE MEAL!!
SO DELICIOUS—!!
I'M GLAD YOU ALL LIKED IT.
WE ALSO BOUGHT A BAUMKUCHEN CAKE TO SHARE.
WOW, THANK YOU!!
OTHERWISE... THERE ISN'T MUCH TO DO AROUND HERE...
...EXCEPT ENJOY THE HOT SPRING.
I HOPE THAT WILL BE ENOUGH FOR YOU YOUNG-STERS.
HMM.
EH...? THE HOT SPRING...
...IS HERE...?
MUNCH
MUNCH
はむはむ
THERE'S A NATURAL SOURCE OF SPRING WATER OUTSIDE.
SO IT'S AN OUTDOOR BATH!?
THE HASHIBA HOUSE IS AWESOME.

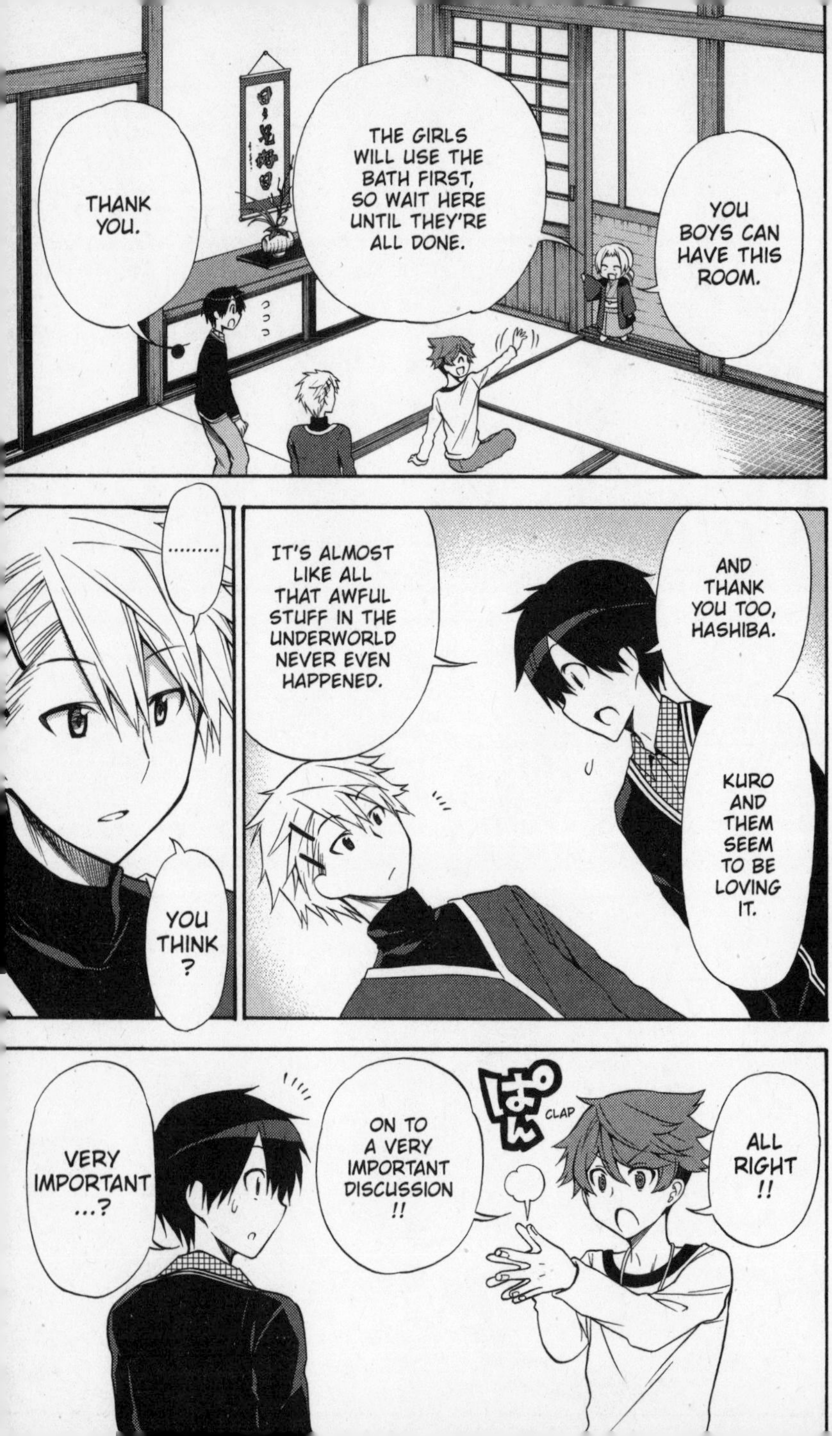
YOU BOYS CAN HAVE THIS ROOM.
THE GIRLS WILL USE THE BATH FIRST, SO WAIT HERE UNTIL THEY'RE ALL DONE.
THANK YOU.
AND THANK YOU TOO, HASHIBA.
KURO AND THEM SEEM TO BE LOVING IT.
IT'S ALMOST LIKE ALL THAT AWFUL STUFF IN THE UNDERWORLD NEVER EVEN HAPPENED.
....
YOU THINK?
ALL RIGHT!!
ぱん
CLAP
ON TO A VERY IMPORTANT DISCUSSION!!
VERY IMPORTANT...?

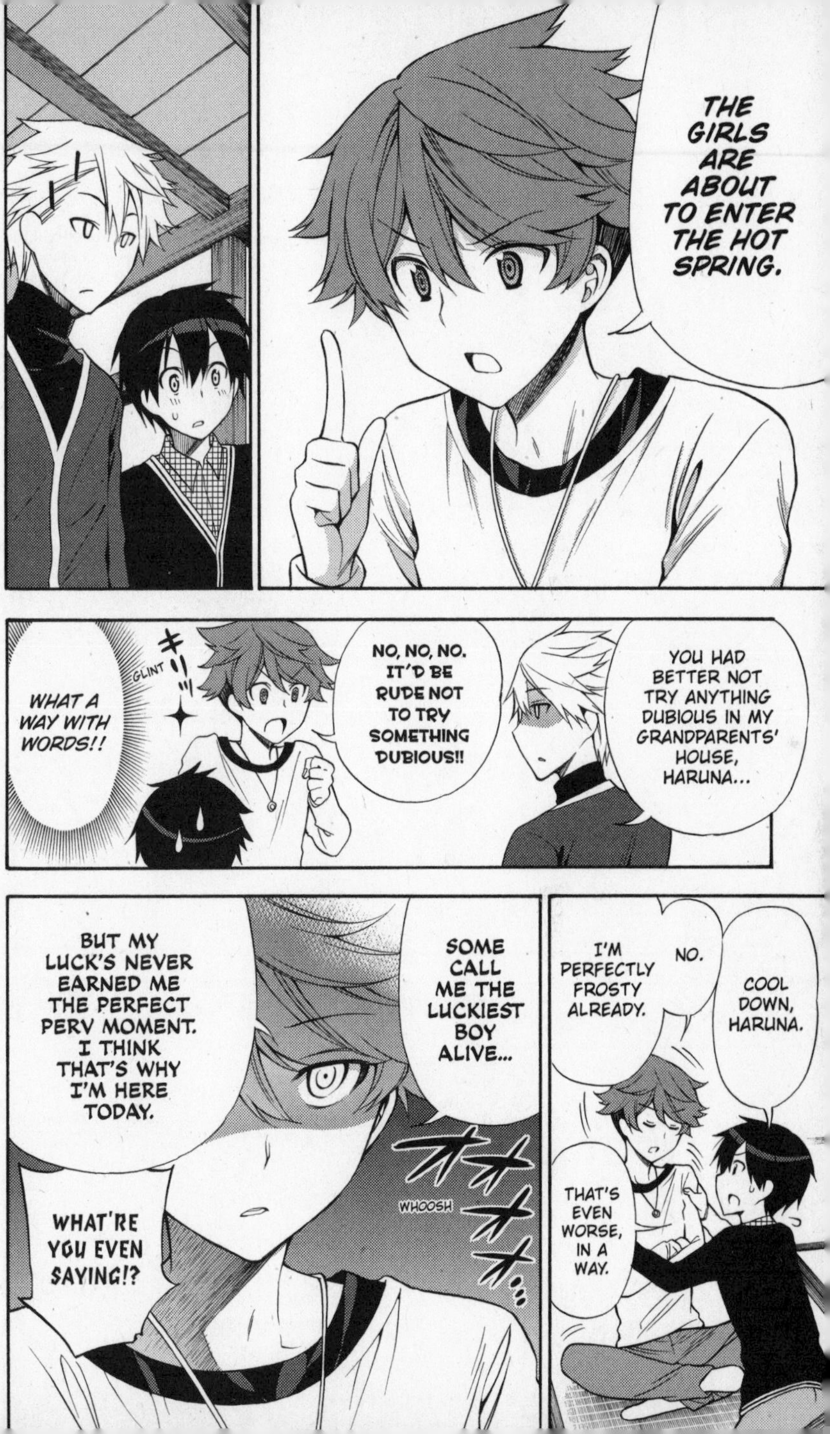
THE GIRLS ARE ABOUT TO ENTER THE HOT SPRING.
YOU HAD BETTER NOT TRY ANYTHING DUBIOUS IN MY GRANDPARENTS' HOUSE, HARUNA...
NO, NO, NO. IT'D BE RUDE NOT TO TRY SOMETHING DUBIOUS!!
GLINT
WHAT A WAY WITH WORDS!!
COOL DOWN, HARUNA.
NO.
I'M PERFECTLY FROSTY ALREADY.
THAT'S EVEN WORSE, IN A WAY.
SOME CALL ME THE LUCKIEST BOY ALIVE...
BUT MY LUCK'S NEVER EARNED ME THE PERFECT PERV MOMENT. I THINK THAT'S WHY I'M HERE TODAY.
WHOOSH
WHAT'RE YOU EVEN SAYING!?

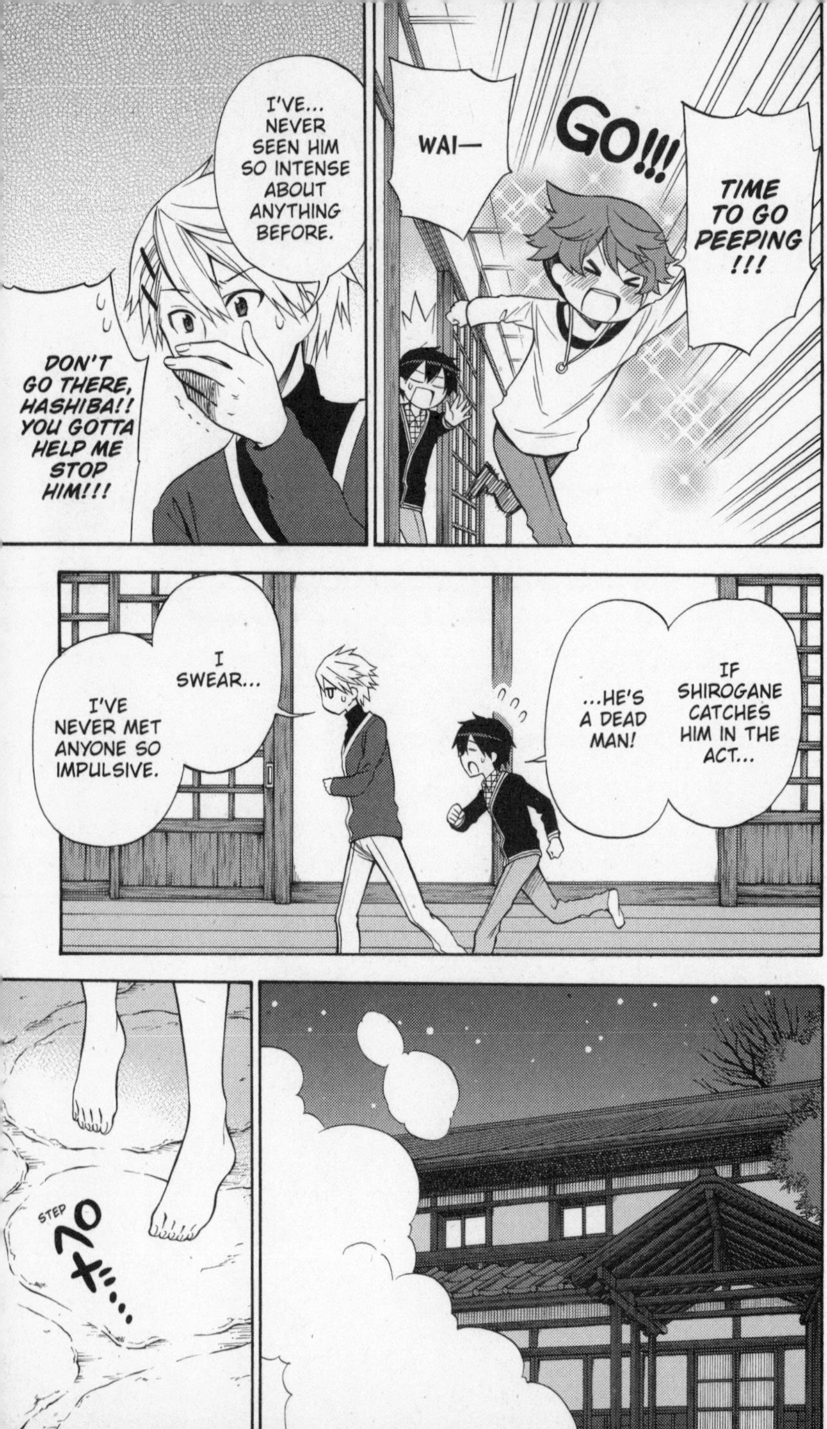
TIME TO GO PEEPING!!!
GO!!!
WAI—
I'VE... NEVER SEEN HIM SO INTENSE ABOUT ANYTHING BEFORE.
DON'T GO THERE, HASHIBA!! YOU GOTTA HELP ME STOP HIM!!!
IF SHIROGANE CATCHES HIM IN THE ACT...
...HE'S A DEAD MAN!
I SWEAR...
I'VE NEVER MET ANYONE SO IMPULSIVE.
STEP

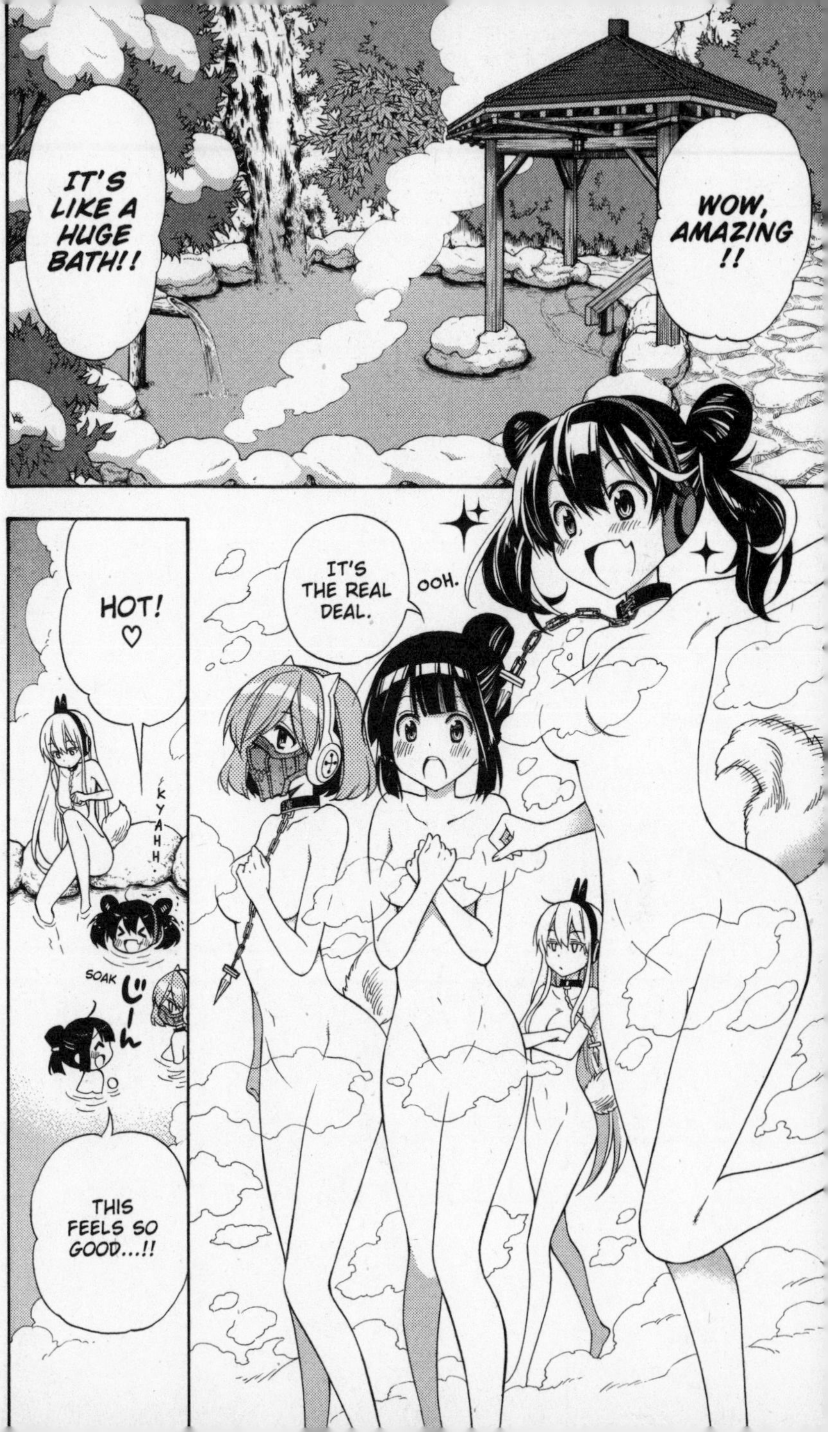
WOW, AMAZING!!
IT'S LIKE A HUGE BATH!!
OOH.
IT'S THE REAL DEAL.
HOT! ♡
KYAHH
SOAK
じーん
THIS FEELS SO GOOD...!!

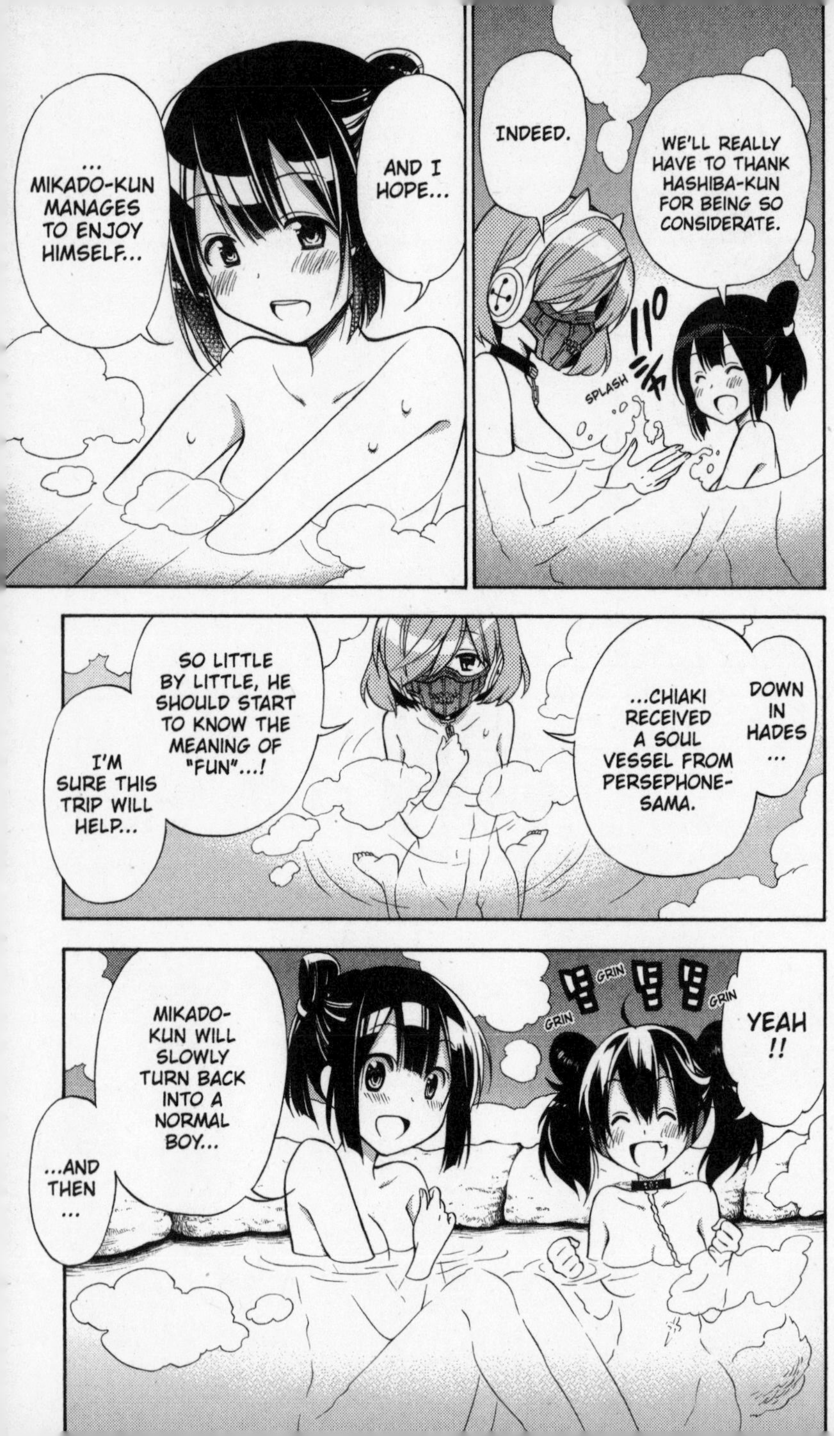
WE'LL REALLY HAVE TO THANK HASHIBA-KUN FOR BEING SO CONSIDERATE.
INDEED.
SPLASH
AND I HOPE...
...MIKADO-KUN MANAGES TO ENJOY HIMSELF...
DOWN IN HADES...
...CHIAKI RECEIVED A SOUL VESSEL FROM PERSEPHONE-SAMA.
SO LITTLE BY LITTLE, HE SHOULD START TO KNOW THE MEANING OF "FUN"...!
I'M SURE THIS TRIP WILL HELP...
...AND THEN...
MIKADO-KUN WILL SLOWLY TURN BACK INTO A NORMAL BOY...
GRIN
GRIN
GRIN
YEAH!!

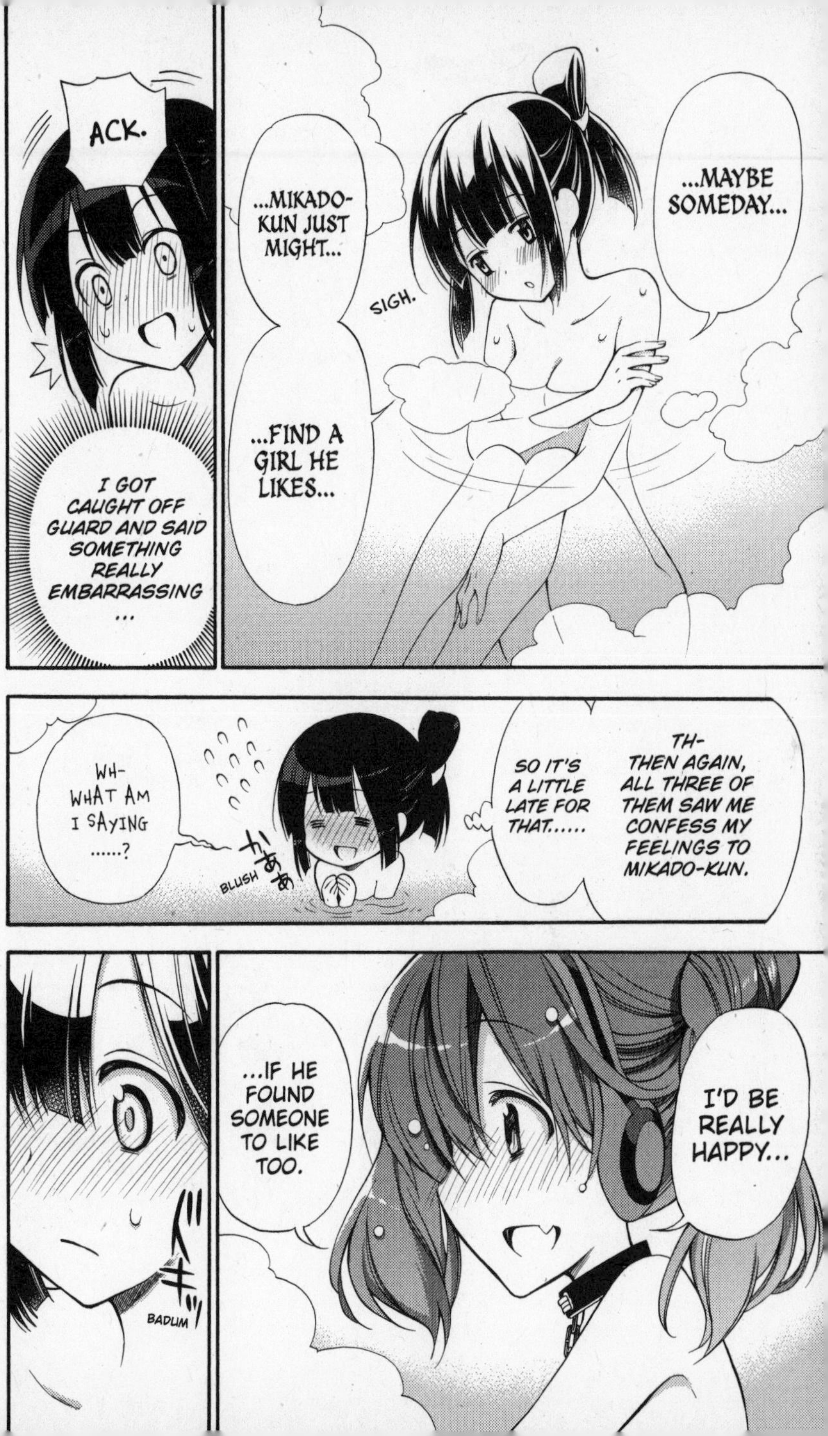
...MAYBE SOMEDAY...
SIGH.
...MIKADO-KUN JUST MIGHT...
...FIND A GIRL HE LIKES...
ACK.
I GOT CAUGHT OFF GUARD AND SAID SOMETHING REALLY EMBARRASSING ...
TH- THEN AGAIN, ALL THREE OF THEM SAW ME CONFESS MY FEELINGS TO MIKADO-KUN.
SO IT'S A LITTLE LATE FOR THAT......
かあぁ
BLUSH
WH- WHAT AM I SAYING ......?
I'D BE REALLY HAPPY...
...IF HE FOUND SOMEONE TO LIKE TOO.
BADUM

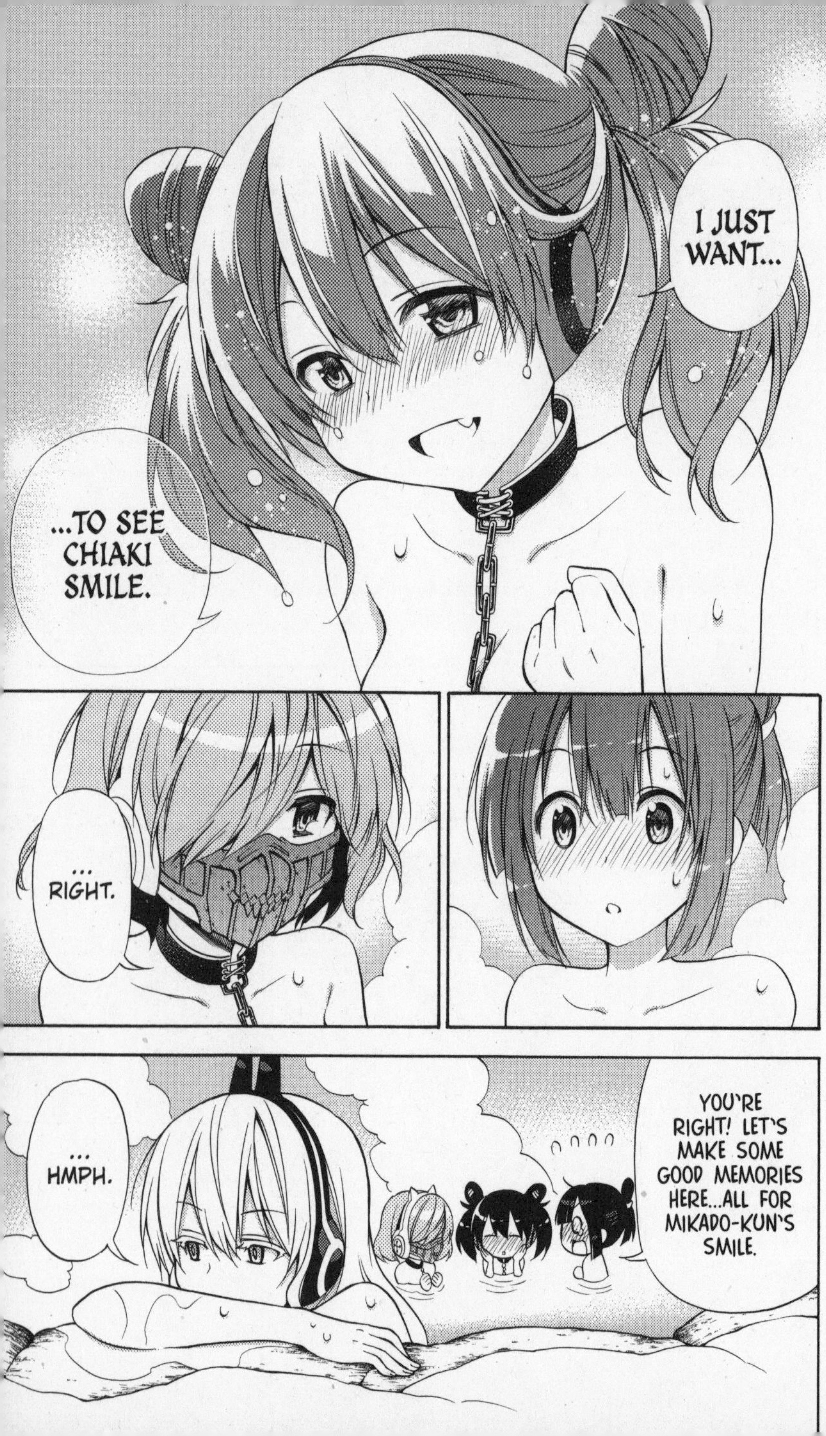
I JUST WANT...
...TO SEE CHIAKI SMILE.
... RIGHT.
YOU'RE RIGHT! LET'S MAKE SOME GOOD MEMORIES HERE...ALL FOR MIKADO-KUN'S SMILE.
... HMPH.

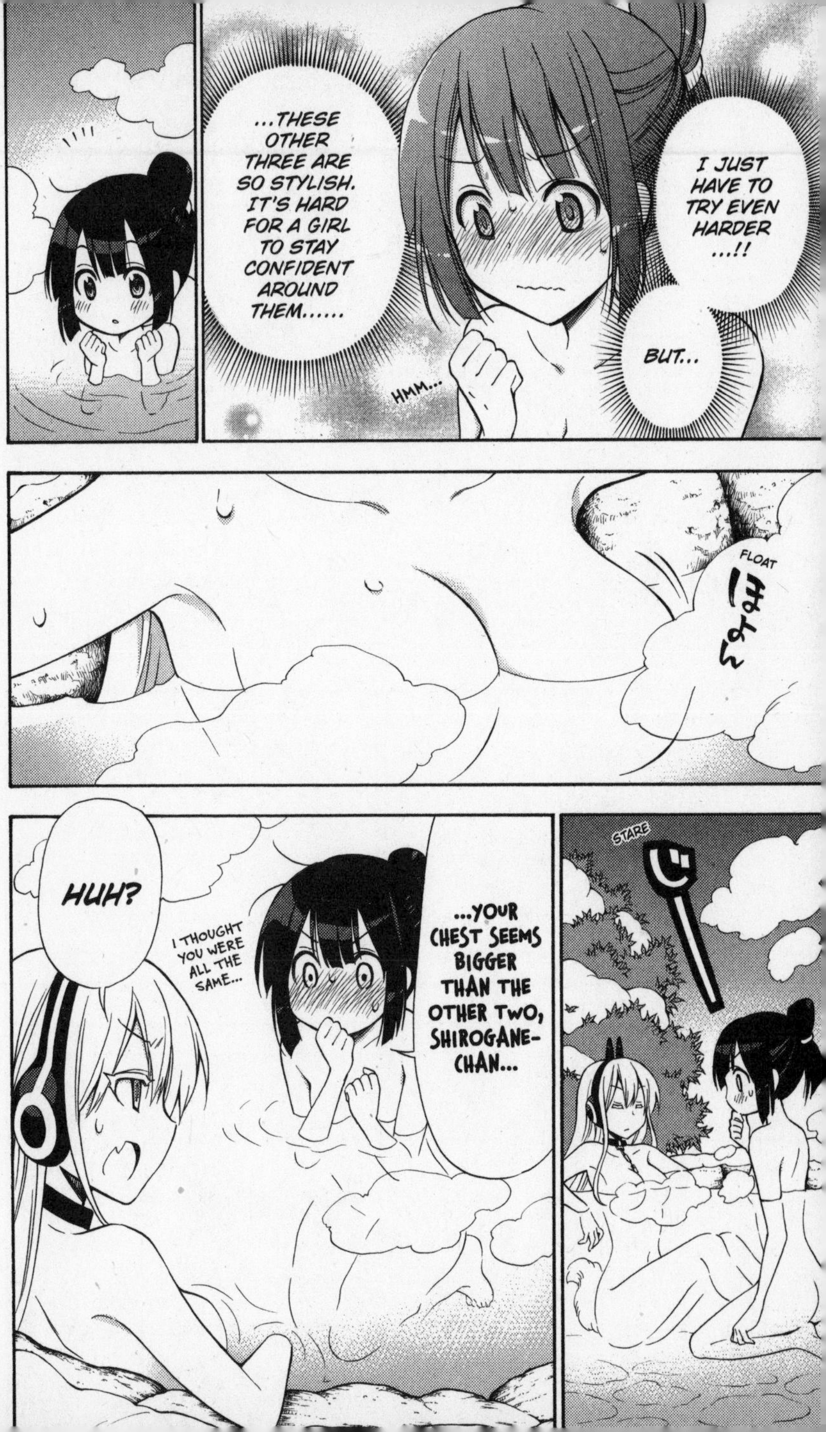
I JUST HAVE TO TRY EVEN HARDER ...!!
BUT...
...THESE OTHER THREE ARE SO STYLISH. IT'S HARD FOR A GIRL TO STAY CONFIDENT AROUND THEM......
HMM...
FLOAT
ほよん
STARE
...YOUR CHEST SEEMS BIGGER THAN THE OTHER TWO, SHIROGANE-CHAN...
HUH?
I THOUGHT YOU WERE ALL THE SAME...

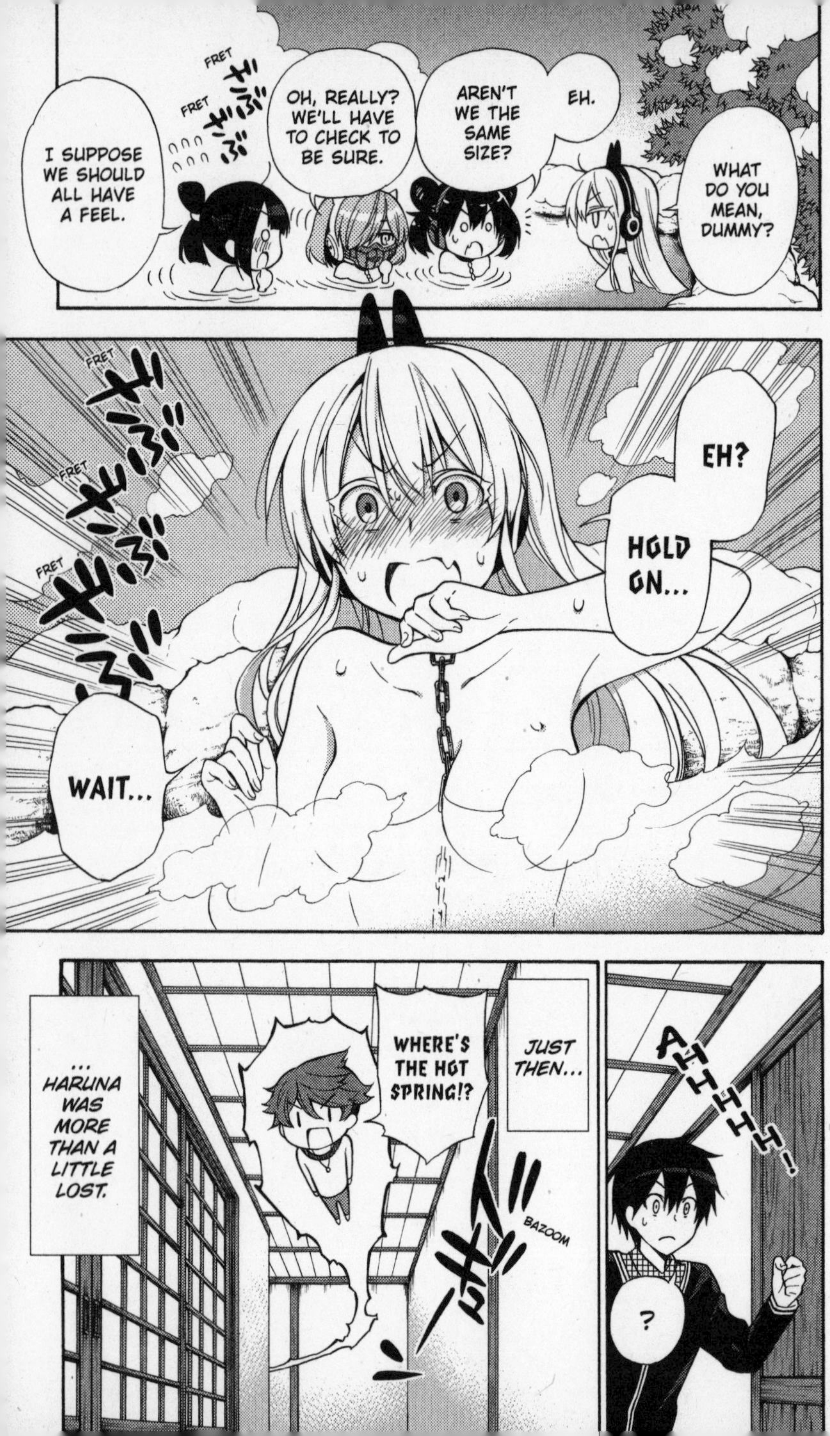
WHAT DO YOU MEAN, DUMMY?
EH.
AREN'T WE THE SAME SIZE?
OH, REALLY? WE'LL HAVE TO CHECK TO BE SURE.
FRET
FRET
I SUPPOSE WE SHOULD ALL HAVE A FEEL.
EH?
HOLD ON...
FRET
FRET
FRET
WAIT...
AHHHHHH!
?
BAZOOM
JUST THEN...
WHERE'S THE HOT SPRING!?
...HARUNA WAS MORE THAN A LITTLE LOST.

TODAY'S CERBERUS 🐾

HOW RELAXING...
THIS IS NICE...

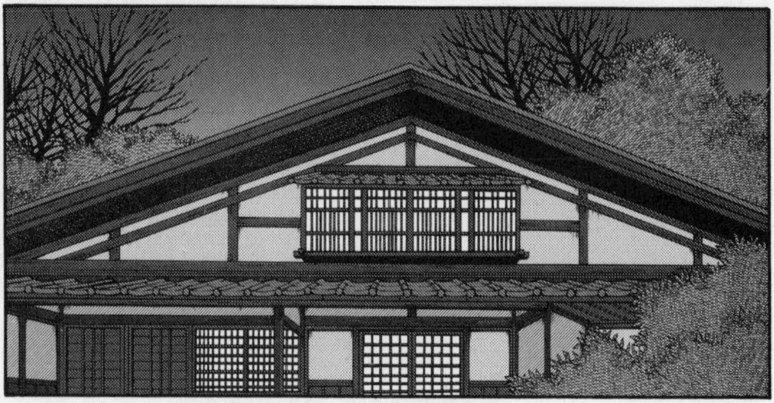

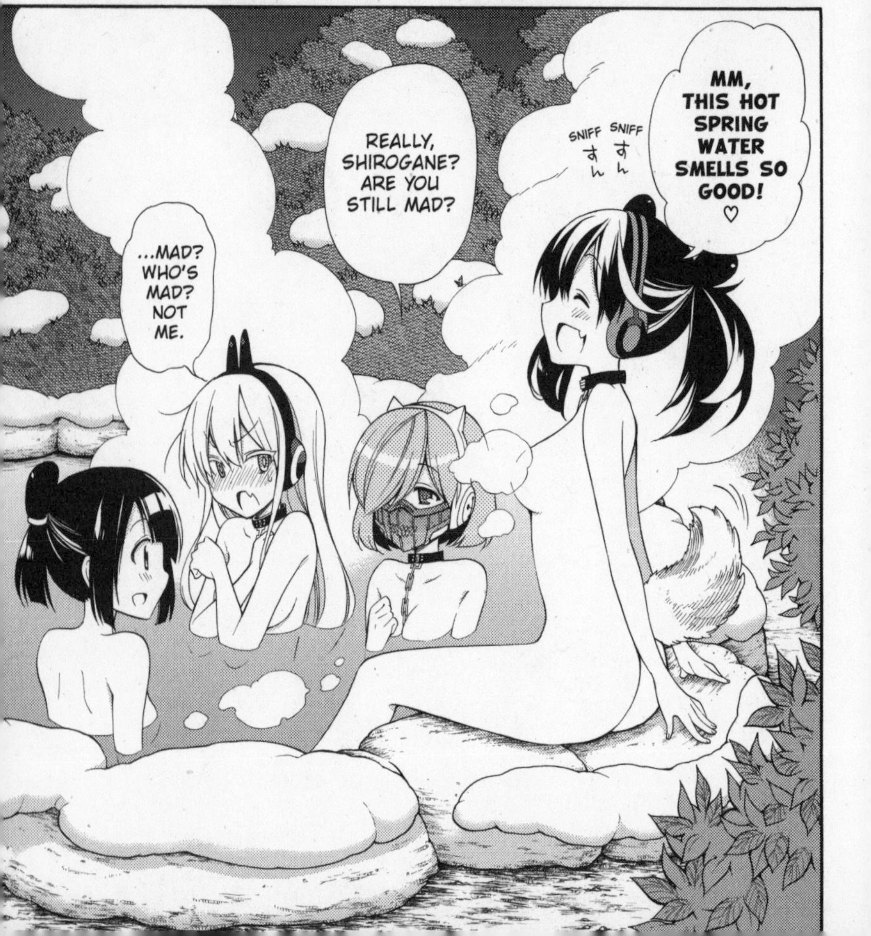
MM, THIS HOT SPRING WATER SMELLS SO GOOD! ♡
SNIFF SNIFF
すん すん
REALLY, SHIROGANE? ARE YOU STILL MAD?
...MAD? WHO'S MAD? NOT ME.

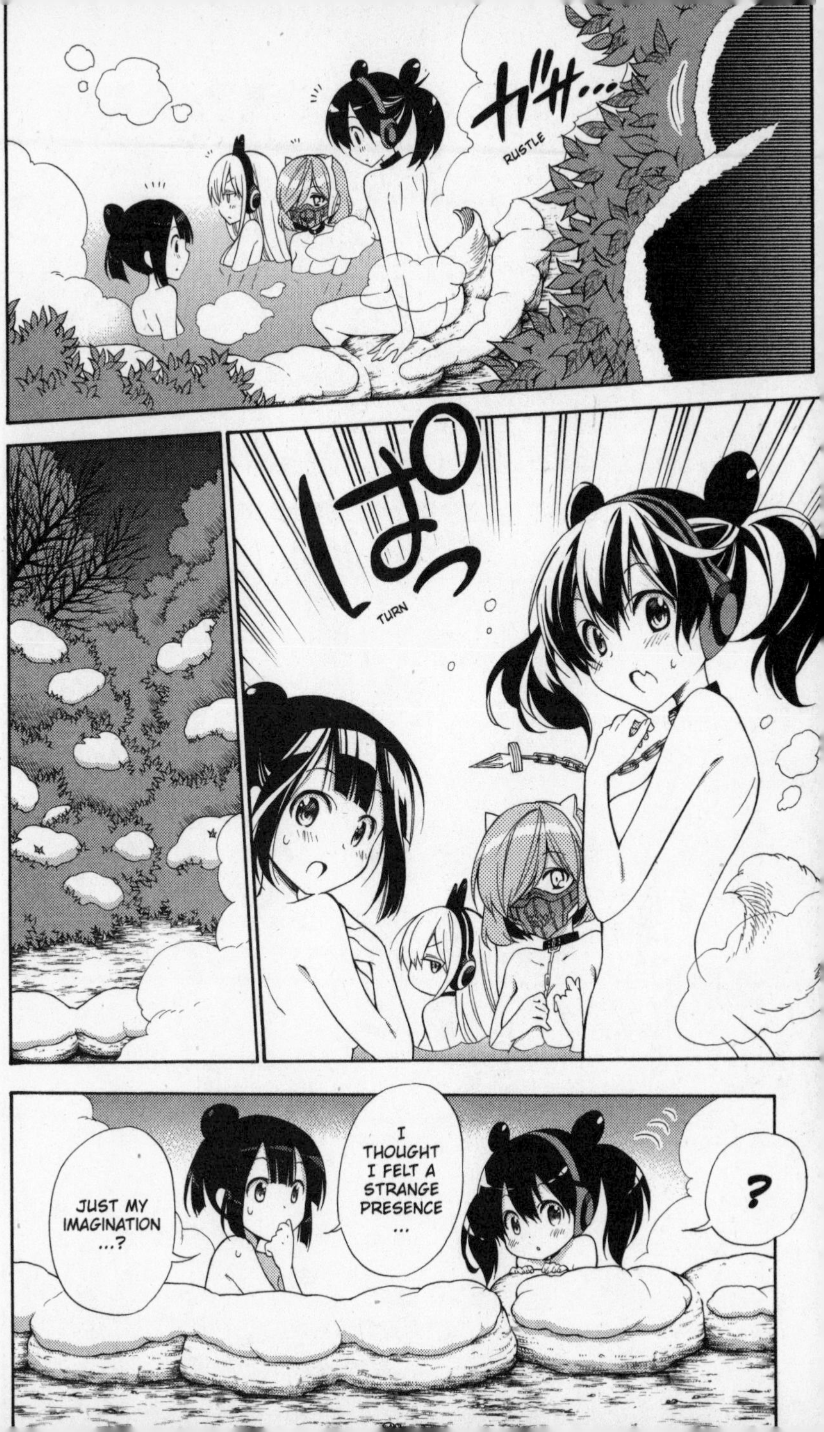
ガサ…
RUSTLE
ぱっ
TURN
?
I THOUGHT I FELT A STRANGE PRESENCE...
JUST MY IMAGINATION...?

CHAPTER 38: MEMORIES OF WINTER

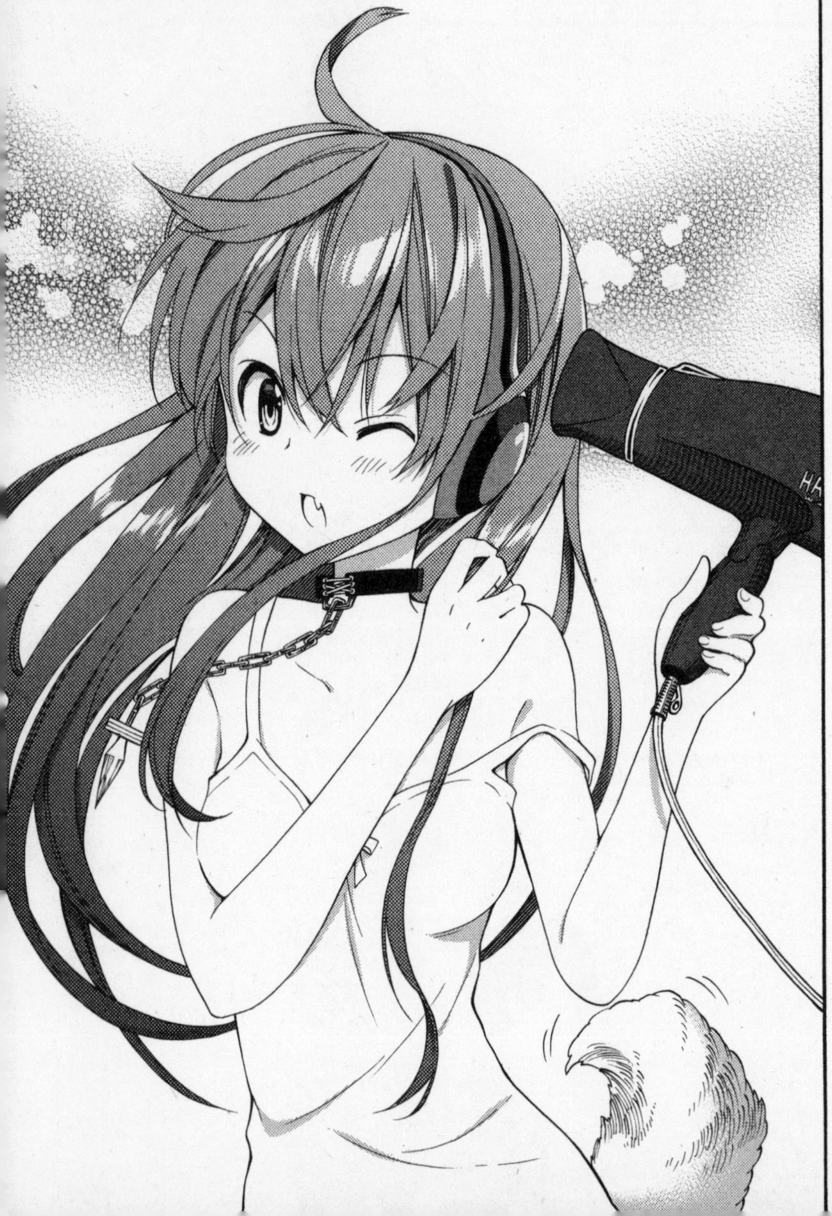

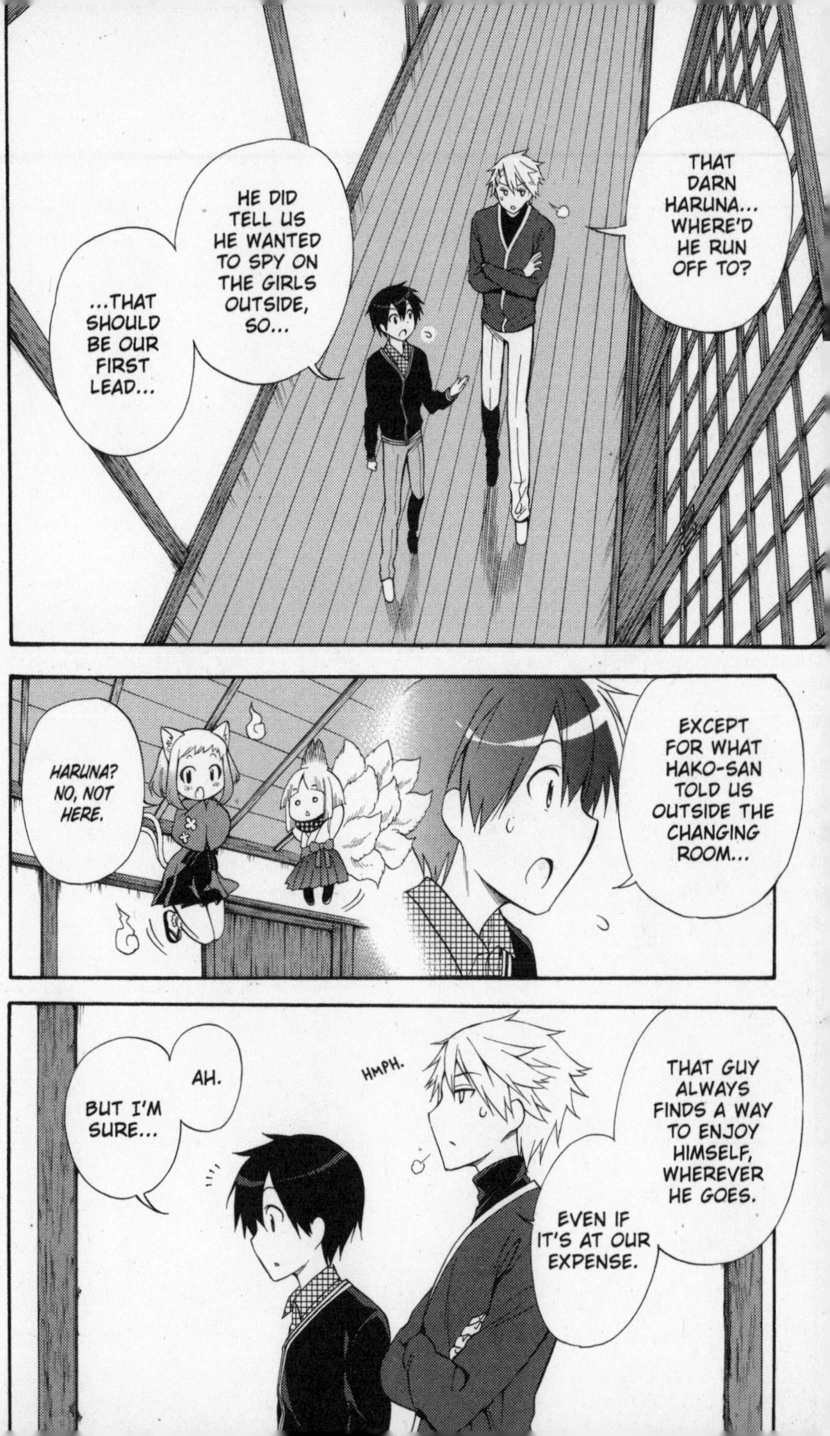
THAT DARN HARUNA... WHERE'D HE RUN OFF TO?
HE DID TELL US HE WANTED TO SPY ON THE GIRLS OUTSIDE, SO...
...THAT SHOULD BE OUR FIRST LEAD...
EXCEPT FOR WHAT HAKO-SAN TOLD US OUTSIDE THE CHANGING ROOM...
HARUNA? NO, NOT HERE.
THAT GUY ALWAYS FINDS A WAY TO ENJOY HIMSELF, WHEREVER HE GOES.
EVEN IF IT'S AT OUR EXPENSE.
HMPH.
AH.
BUT I'M SURE...

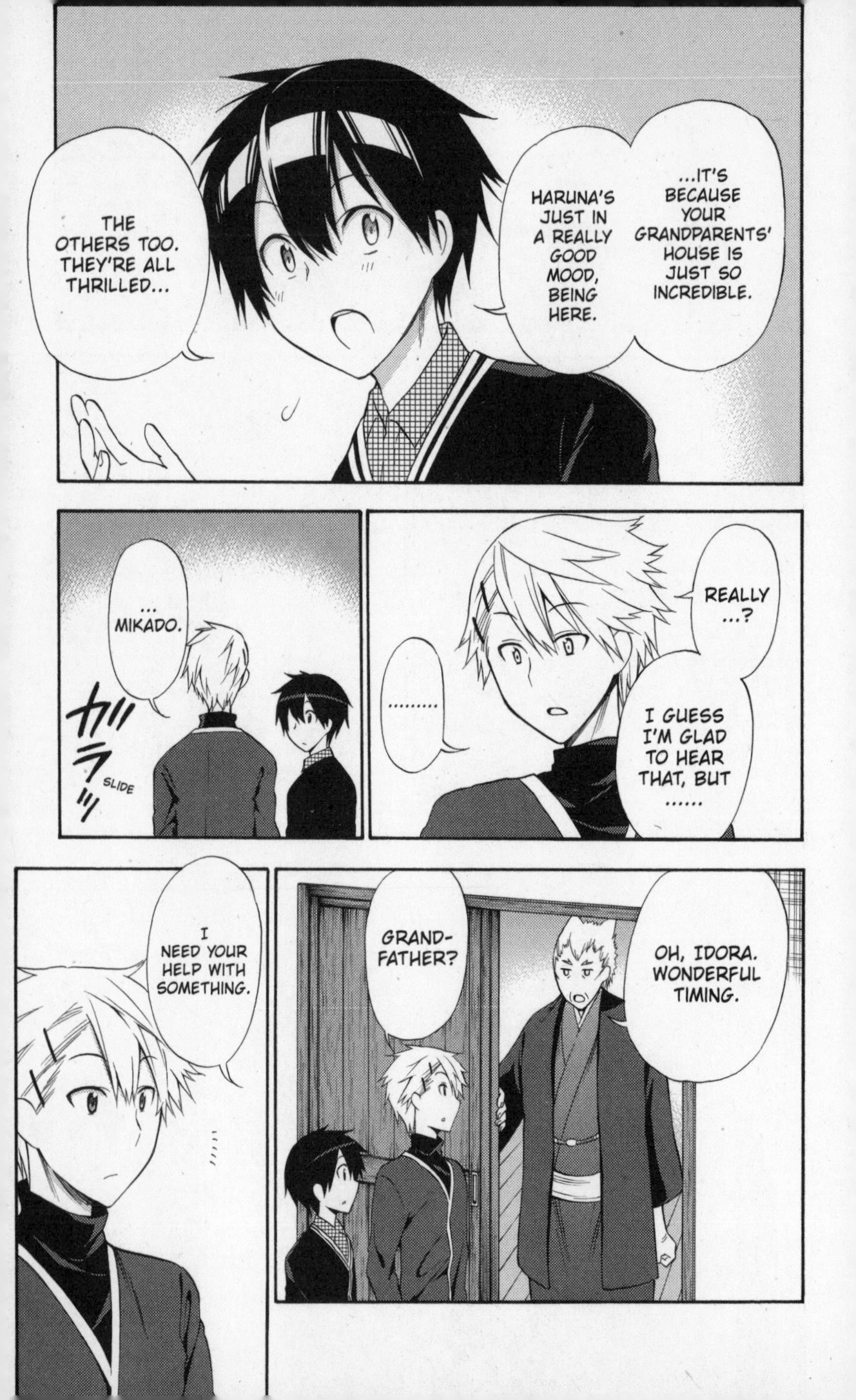
...IT'S BECAUSE YOUR GRANDPARENTS' HOUSE IS JUST SO INCREDIBLE.
HARUNA'S JUST IN A REALLY GOOD MOOD, BEING HERE.
THE OTHERS TOO. THEY'RE ALL THRILLED...
REALLY ...?
I GUESS I'M GLAD TO HEAR THAT, BUT ......
....
SLIDE
... MIKADO.
OH, IDORA. WONDERFUL TIMING.
GRAND-FATHER?
I NEED YOUR HELP WITH SOMETHING.

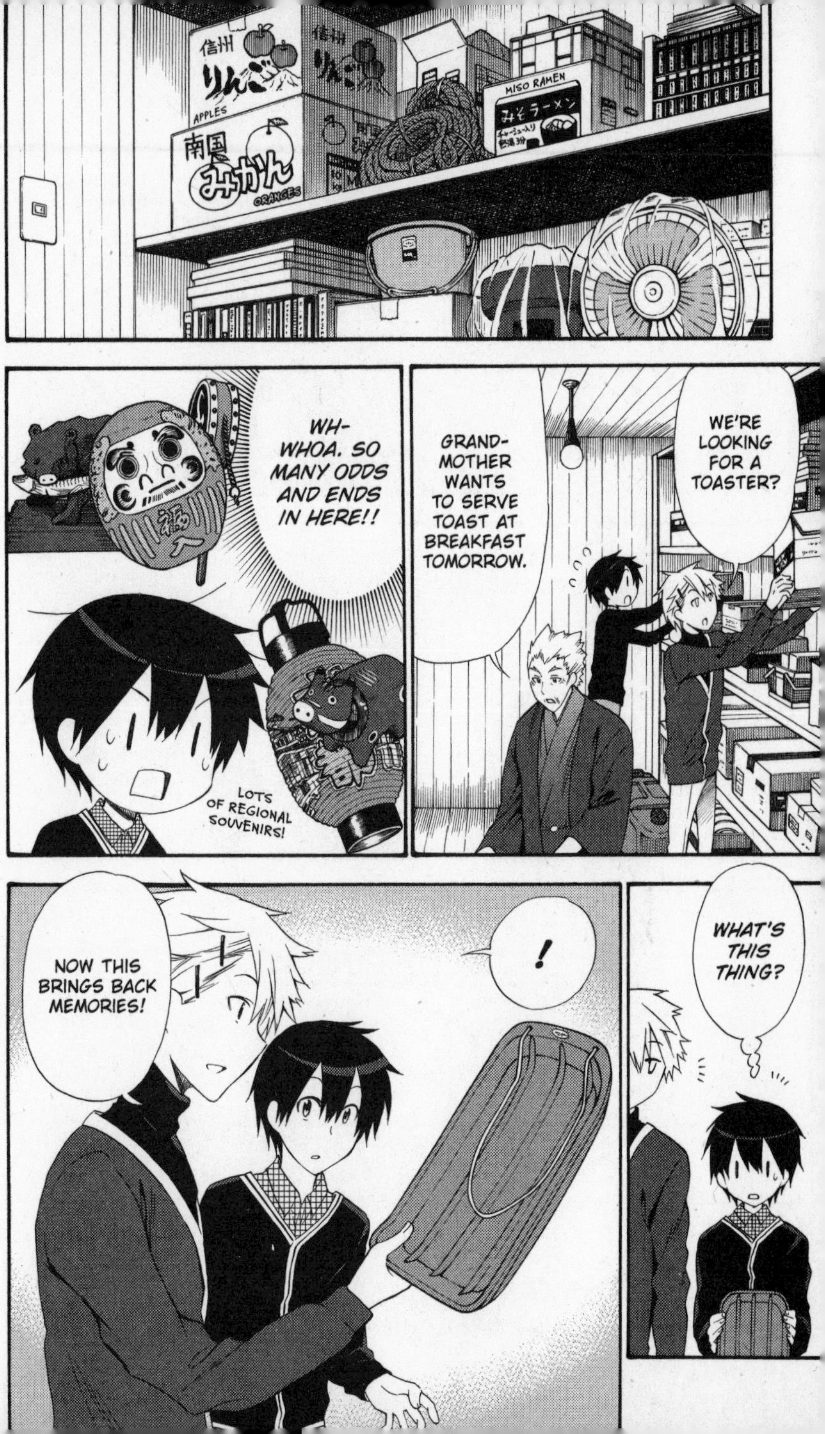
信州 りんご
APPLES
南国 みかん
ORANGES
MISO RAMEN
みそラーメン
WE'RE LOOKING FOR A TOASTER?
GRANDMOTHER WANTS TO SERVE TOAST AT BREAKFAST TOMORROW.
WH-WHOA. SO MANY ODDS AND ENDS IN HERE!!
LOTS OF REGIONAL SOUVENIRS!
WHAT'S THIS THING?
!
NOW THIS BRINGS BACK MEMORIES!

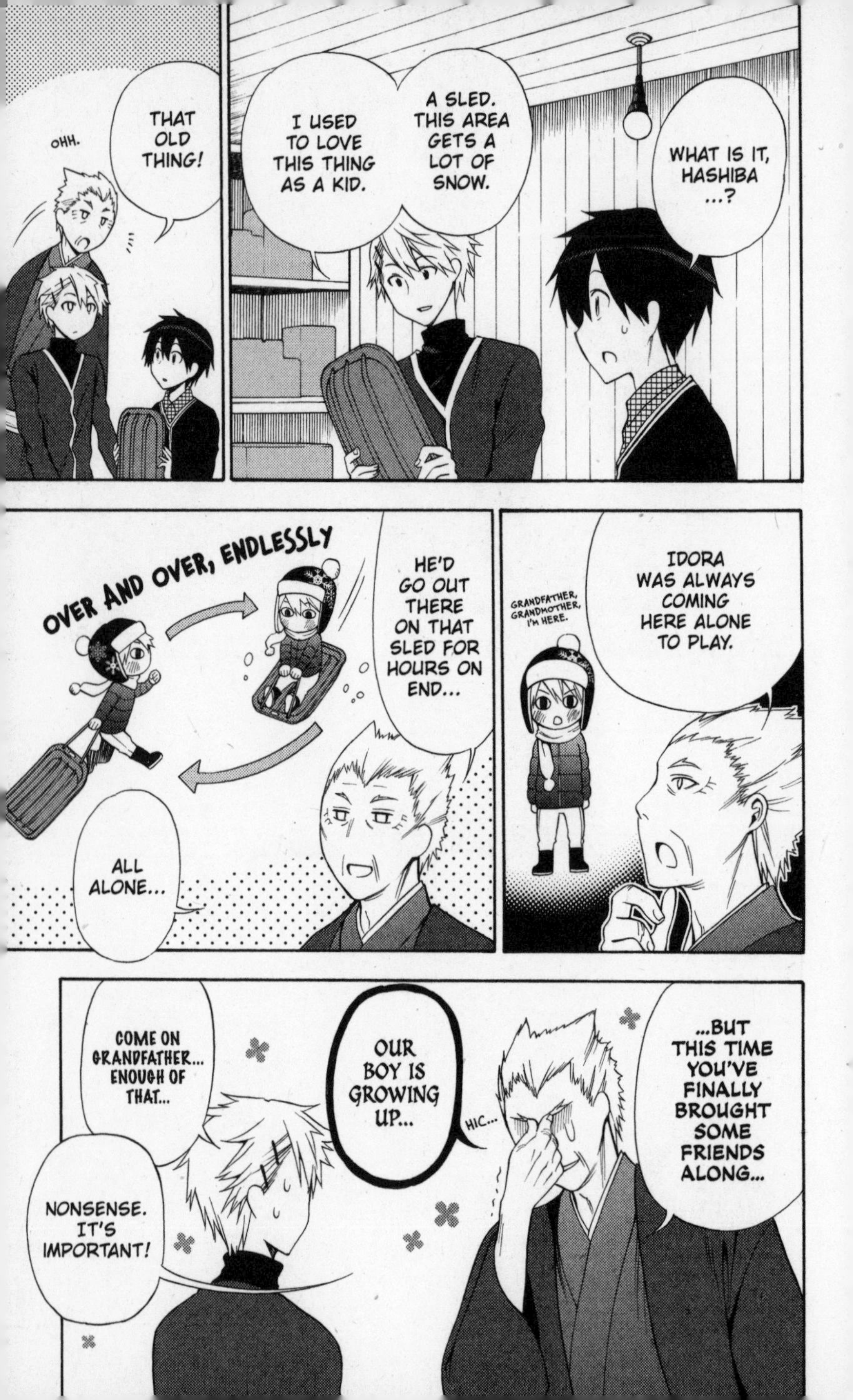
WHAT IS IT, HASHIBA ...?
A SLED. THIS AREA GETS A LOT OF SNOW.
I USED TO LOVE THIS THING AS A KID.
THAT OLD THING!
OHH.
IDORA WAS ALWAYS COMING HERE ALONE TO PLAY.
GRANDFATHER, GRANDMOTHER, I'M HERE.
HE'D GO OUT THERE ON THAT SLED FOR HOURS ON END...
OVER AND OVER, ENDLESSLY
ALL ALONE...
...BUT THIS TIME YOU'VE FINALLY BROUGHT SOME FRIENDS ALONG...
OUR BOY IS GROWING UP...
HIC...
COME ON GRANDFATHER... ENOUGH OF THAT...
NONSENSE. IT'S IMPORTANT!

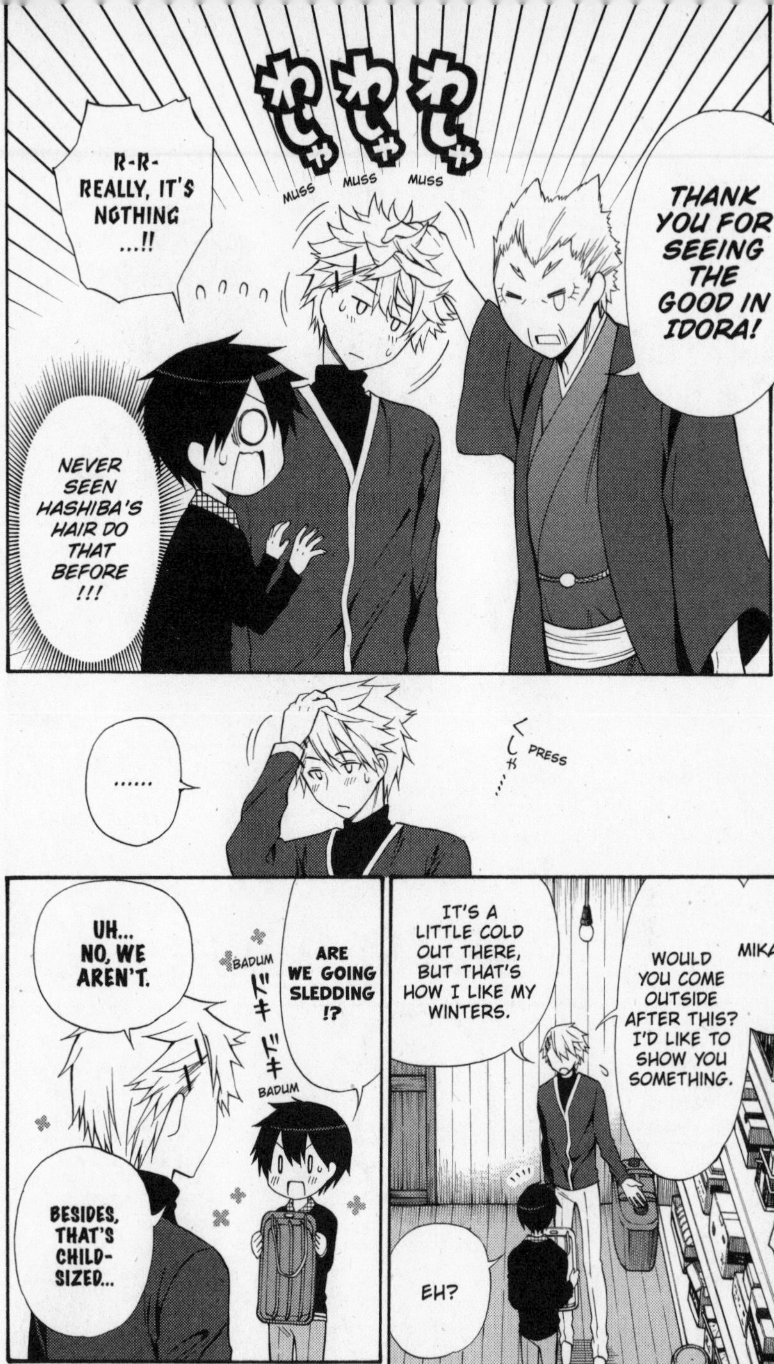
THANK YOU FOR SEEING THE GOOD IN IDORA!
わしゃわしゃわしゃ
MUSS MUSS MUSS
R-R-REALLY, IT'S NOTHING ...!!
NEVER SEEN HASHIBA'S HAIR DO THAT BEFORE !!!
くしゃ…
PRESS
......
MIKADO.
WOULD YOU COME OUTSIDE AFTER THIS? I'D LIKE TO SHOW YOU SOMETHING.
IT'S A LITTLE COLD OUT THERE, BUT THAT'S HOW I LIKE MY WINTERS.
EH?
ARE WE GOING SLEDDING !?
ドキドキ
BADUM BADUM
UH... NO, WE AREN'T.
BESIDES, THAT'S CHILD-SIZED...

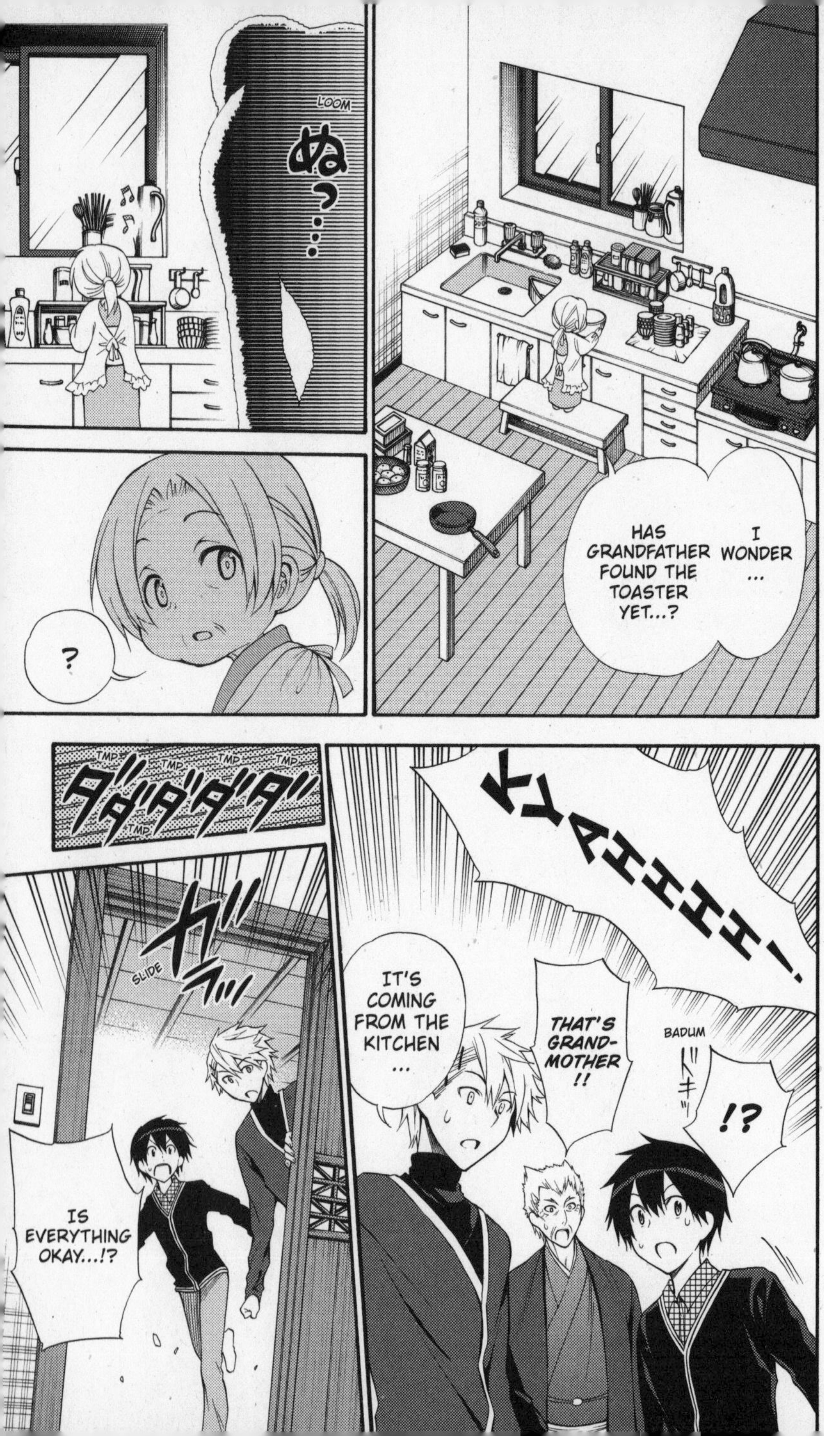
I WONDER ... HAS GRANDFATHER FOUND THE TOASTER YET...?
LOOM
ぬっ…
?
KYAIIIIII--!
BADUM
ドキッ
!?
THAT'S GRANDMOTHER!!
IT'S COMING FROM THE KITCHEN ...
TMP TMP TMP TMP TMP
ダダダダダ
SLIDE
ガラッ
IS EVERYTHING OKAY...!?

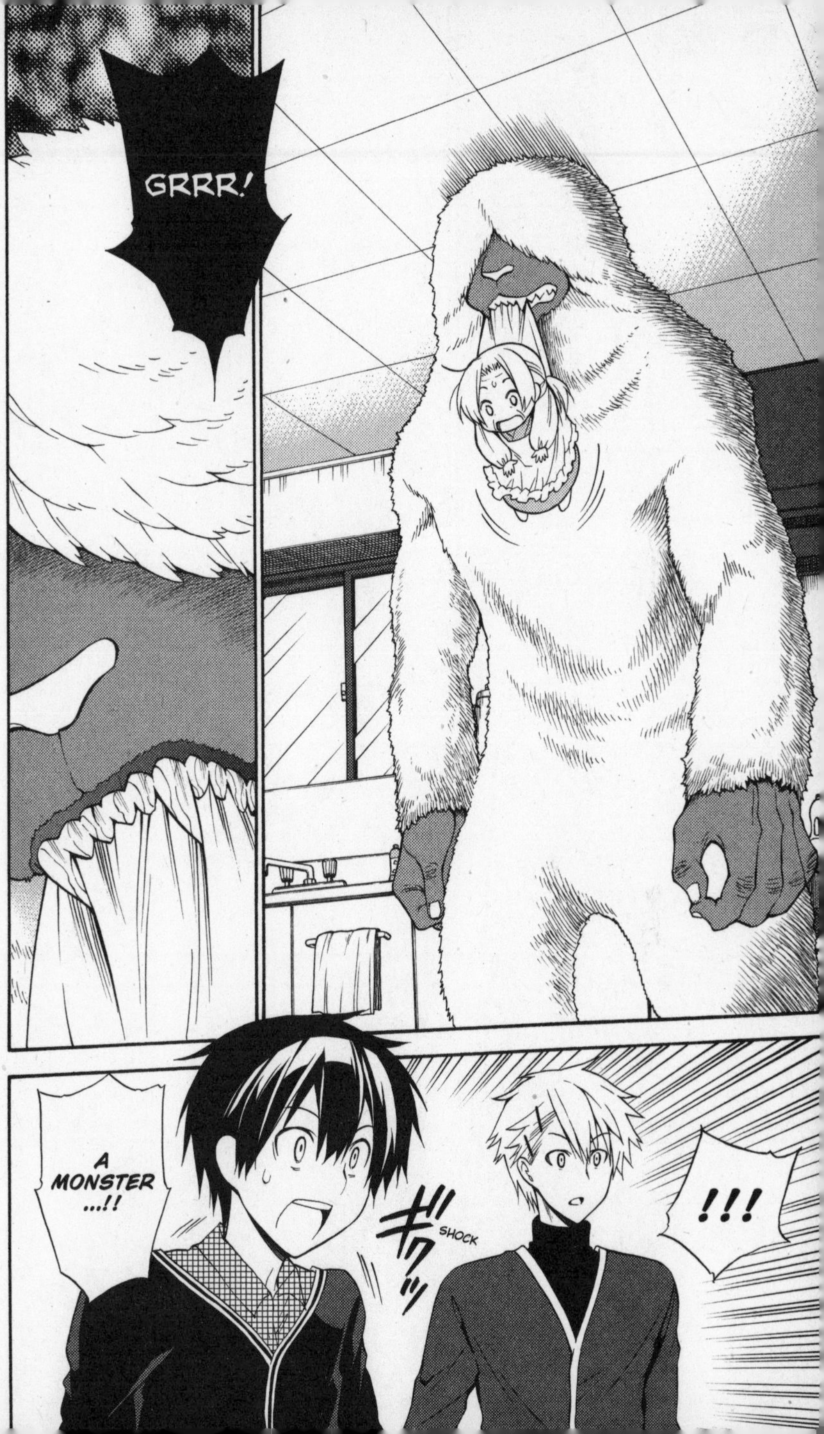
GRRR!
!!!
ギクッ
SHOCK
A MONSTER ...!!

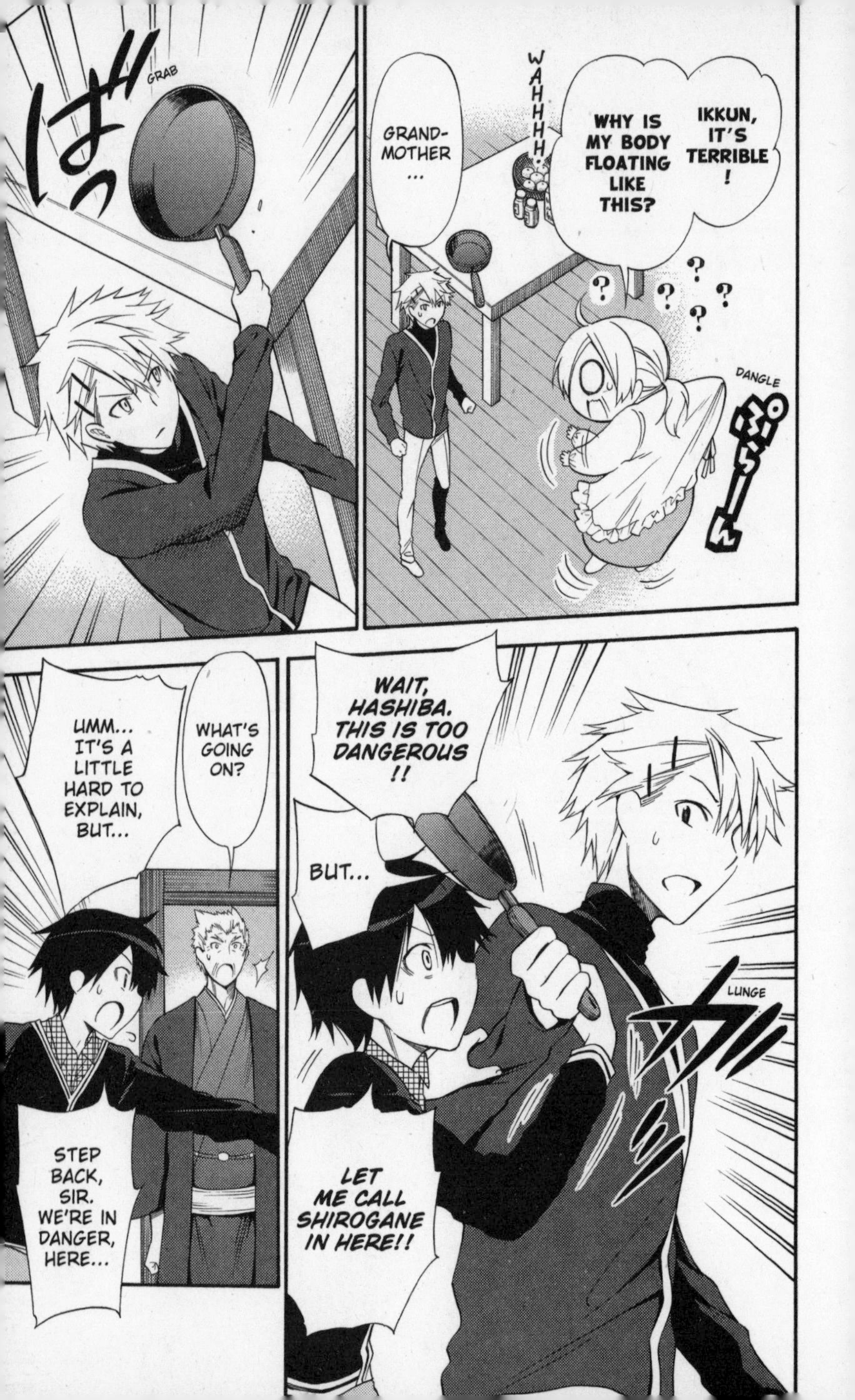

IKKUN, IT'S TERRIBLE!
WHY IS MY BODY FLOATING LIKE THIS?
WAHHHHH
GRAND-MOTHER...
DANGLE
GRAB
WAIT, HASHIBA. THIS IS TOO DANGEROUS!!
BUT...
LUNGE
LET ME CALL SHIROGANE IN HERE!!
WHAT'S GOING ON?
UMM... IT'S A LITTLE HARD TO EXPLAIN, BUT...
STEP BACK, SIR. WE'RE IN DANGER, HERE...

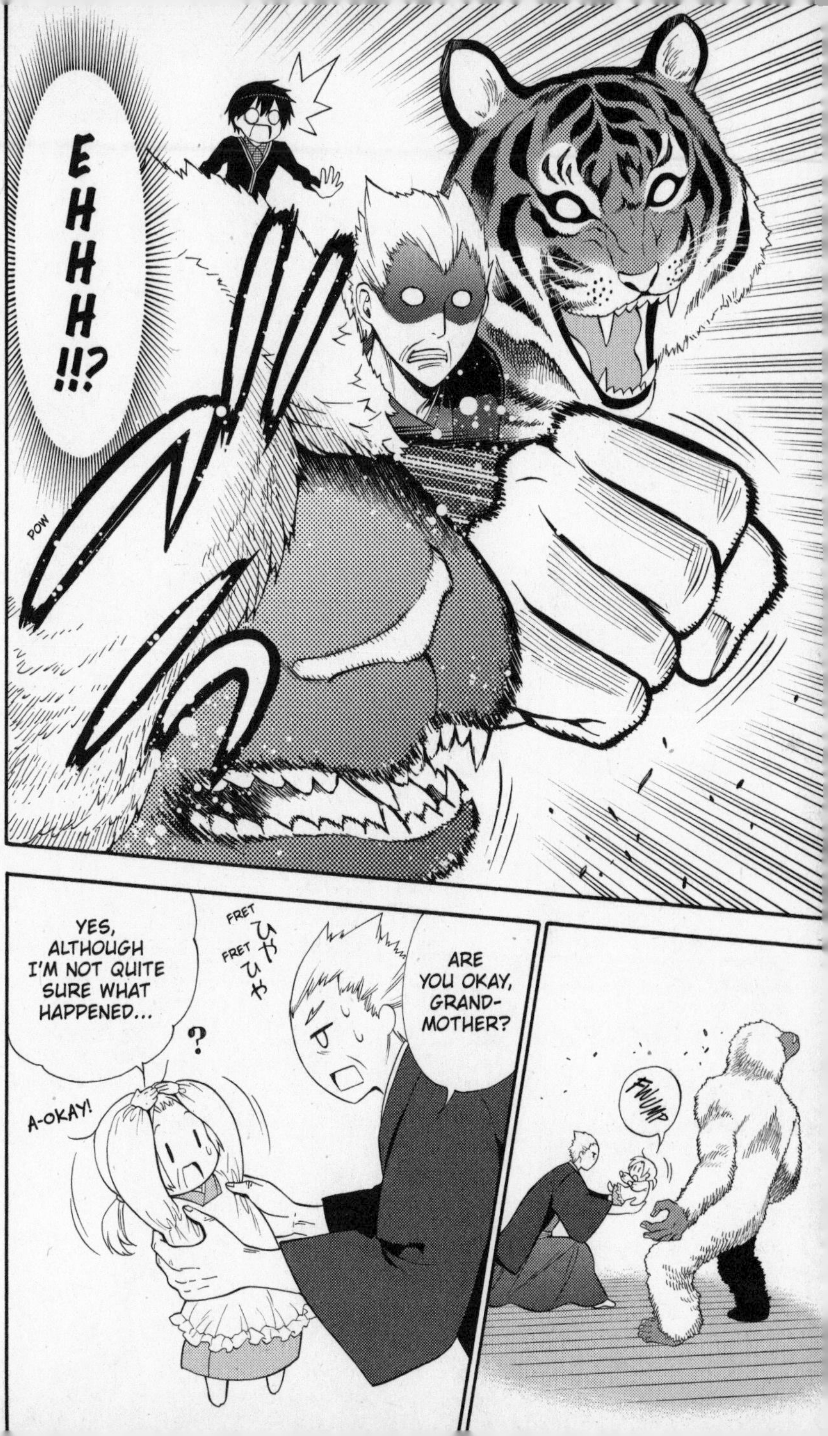

EHHHH!!?
POW
FWUMP
ARE YOU OKAY, GRANDMOTHER?
FRET ひや
FRET ひや
YES, ALTHOUGH I'M NOT QUITE SURE WHAT HAPPENED...
?
A-OKAY!

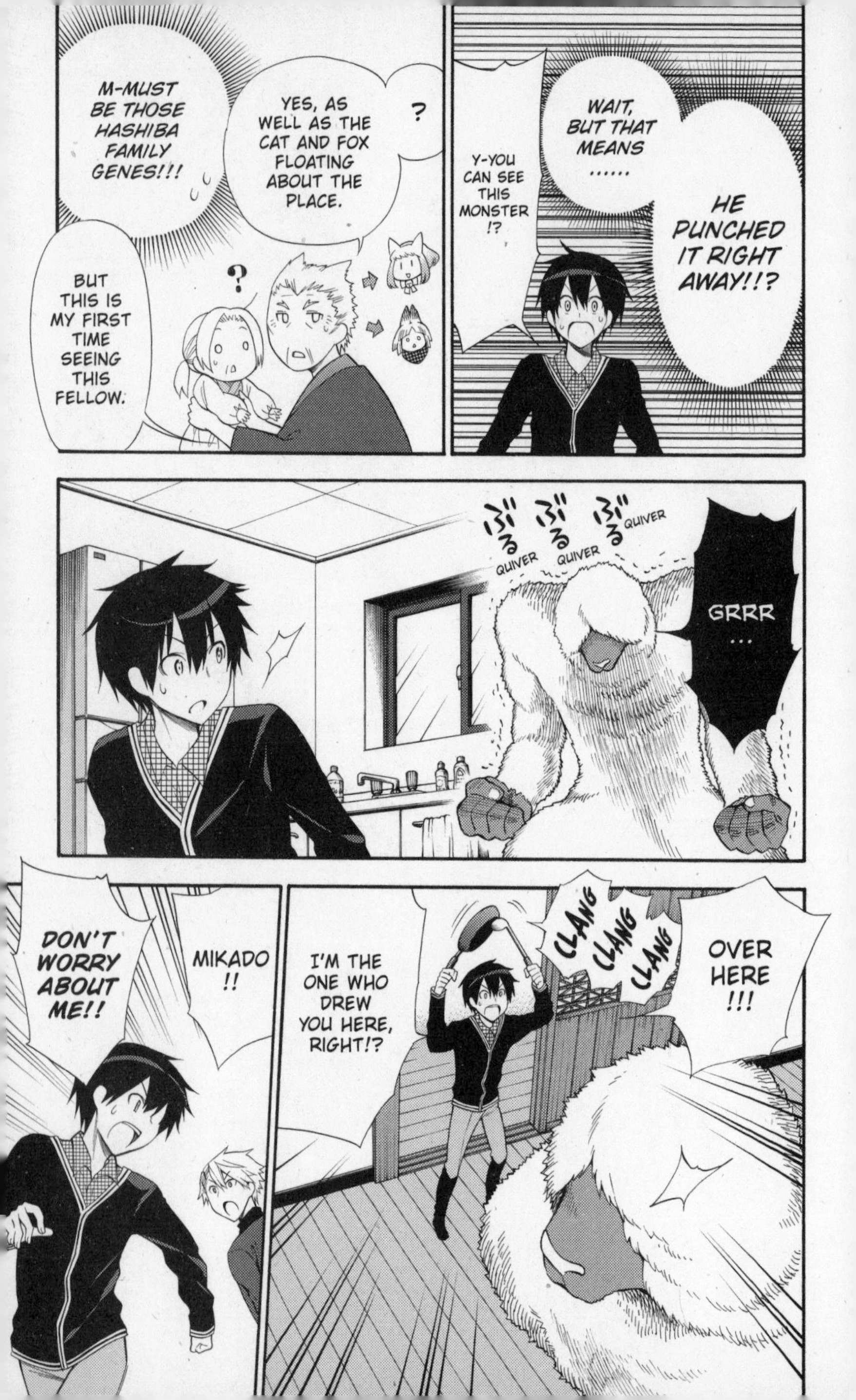
WAIT, BUT THAT MEANS ......
HE PUNCHED IT RIGHT AWAY!!?
Y-YOU CAN SEE THIS MONSTER !?
?
YES, AS WELL AS THE CAT AND FOX FLOATING ABOUT THE PLACE.
M-MUST BE THOSE HASHIBA FAMILY GENES!!!
?
BUT THIS IS MY FIRST TIME SEEING THIS FELLOW.
ぶる QUIVER
ぶる QUIVER
ぶる QUIVER
GRRR ...
OVER HERE !!!
CLANG CLANG CLANG
I'M THE ONE WHO DREW YOU HERE, RIGHT!?
MIKADO !!
DON'T WORRY ABOUT ME!!

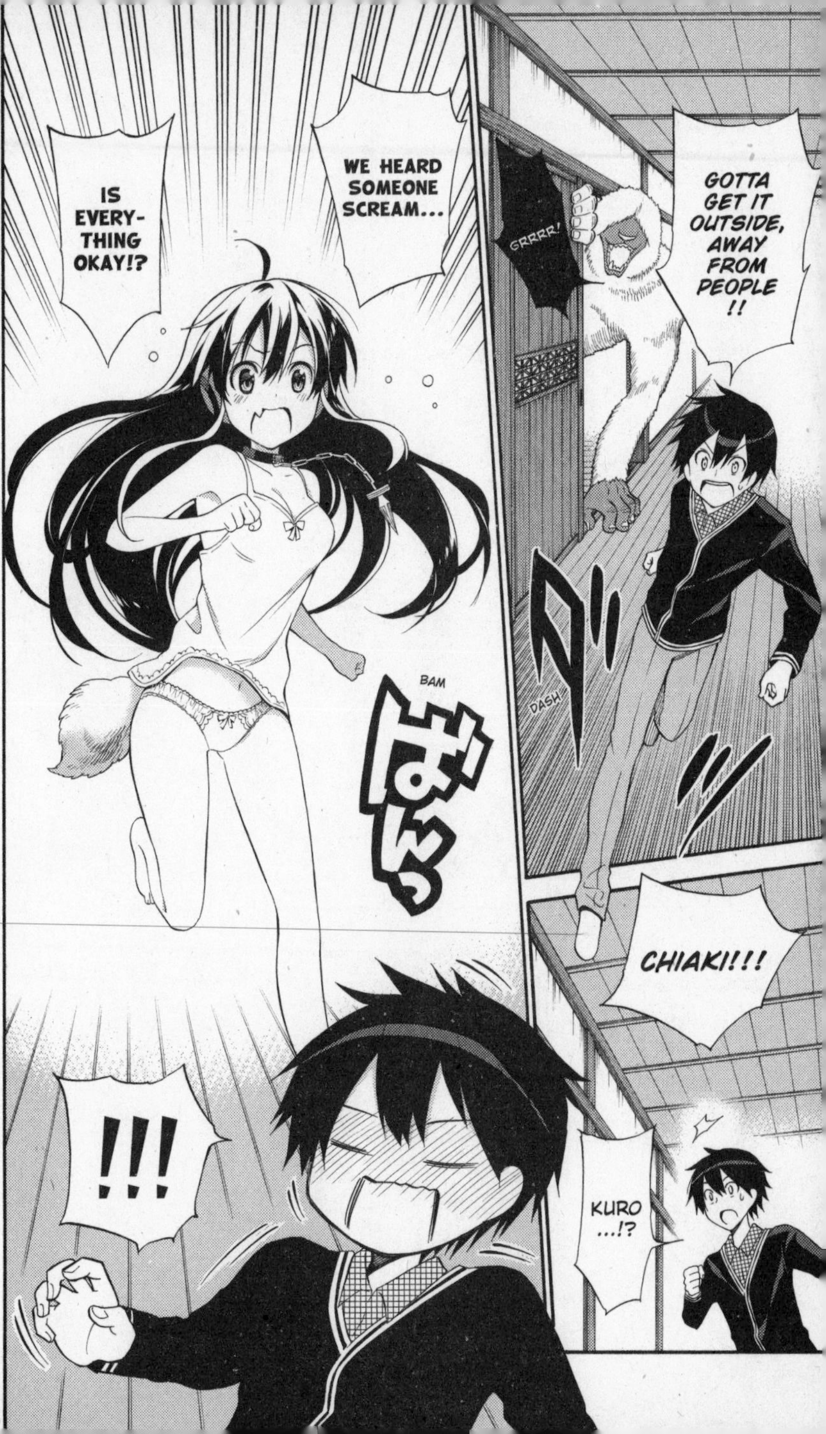
GRRRR!
GOTTA GET IT OUTSIDE, AWAY FROM PEOPLE!!
DASH
CHIAKI!!!
WE HEARD SOMEONE SCREAM...
IS EVERY-THING OKAY!?
BAM
KURO ...!?
!!!

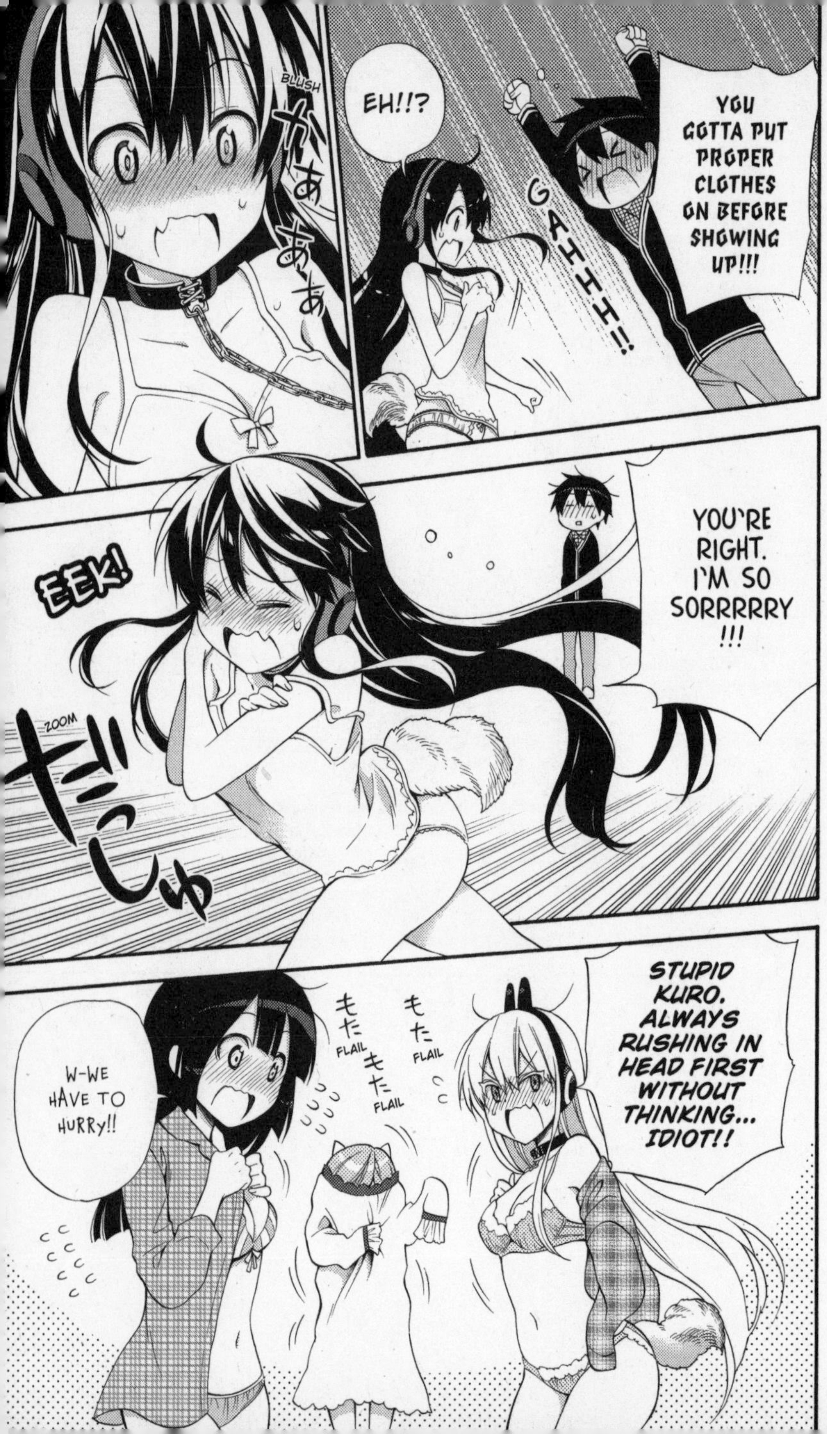

YOU GOTTA PUT PROPER CLOTHES ON BEFORE SHOWING UP!!!
GAHHHH!!
EH!!?
BLUSH
YOU'RE RIGHT. I'M SO SORRRRRY!!!
EEK!
ZOOM
STUPID KURO. ALWAYS RUSHING IN HEAD FIRST WITHOUT THINKING... IDIOT!!
FLAIL
FLAIL
FLAIL
W-WE HAVE TO HURRY!!

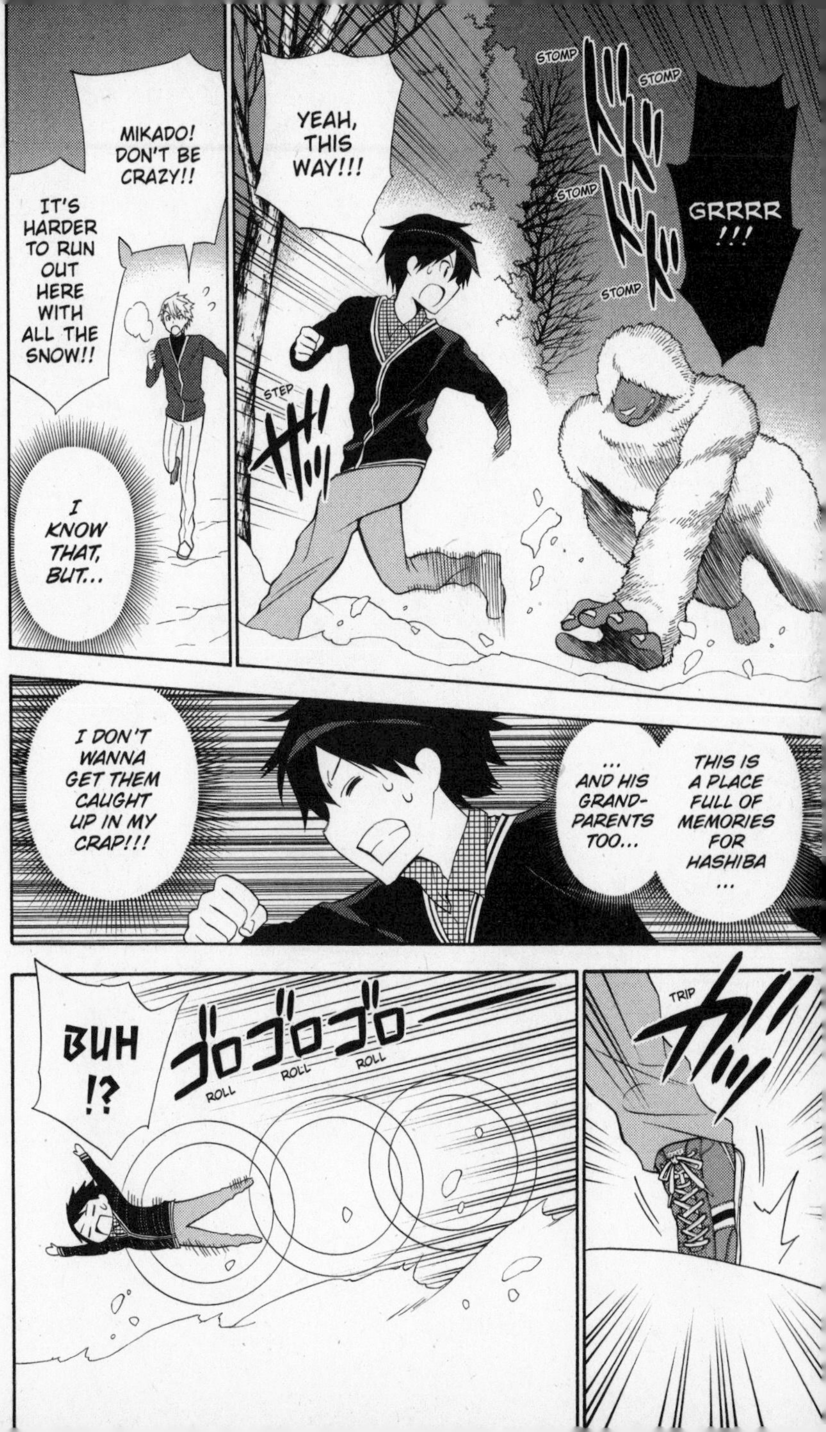
STOMP
STOMP
STOMP
STOMP
GRRRR !!!
YEAH, THIS WAY!!!
STEP
MIKADO! DON'T BE CRAZY!!
IT'S HARDER TO RUN OUT HERE WITH ALL THE SNOW!!
I KNOW THAT, BUT...
THIS IS A PLACE FULL OF MEMORIES FOR HASHIBA ...
... AND HIS GRAND-PARENTS TOO...
I DON'T WANNA GET THEM CAUGHT UP IN MY CRAP!!!
TRIP
BUH !?
ROLL
ROLL
ROLL

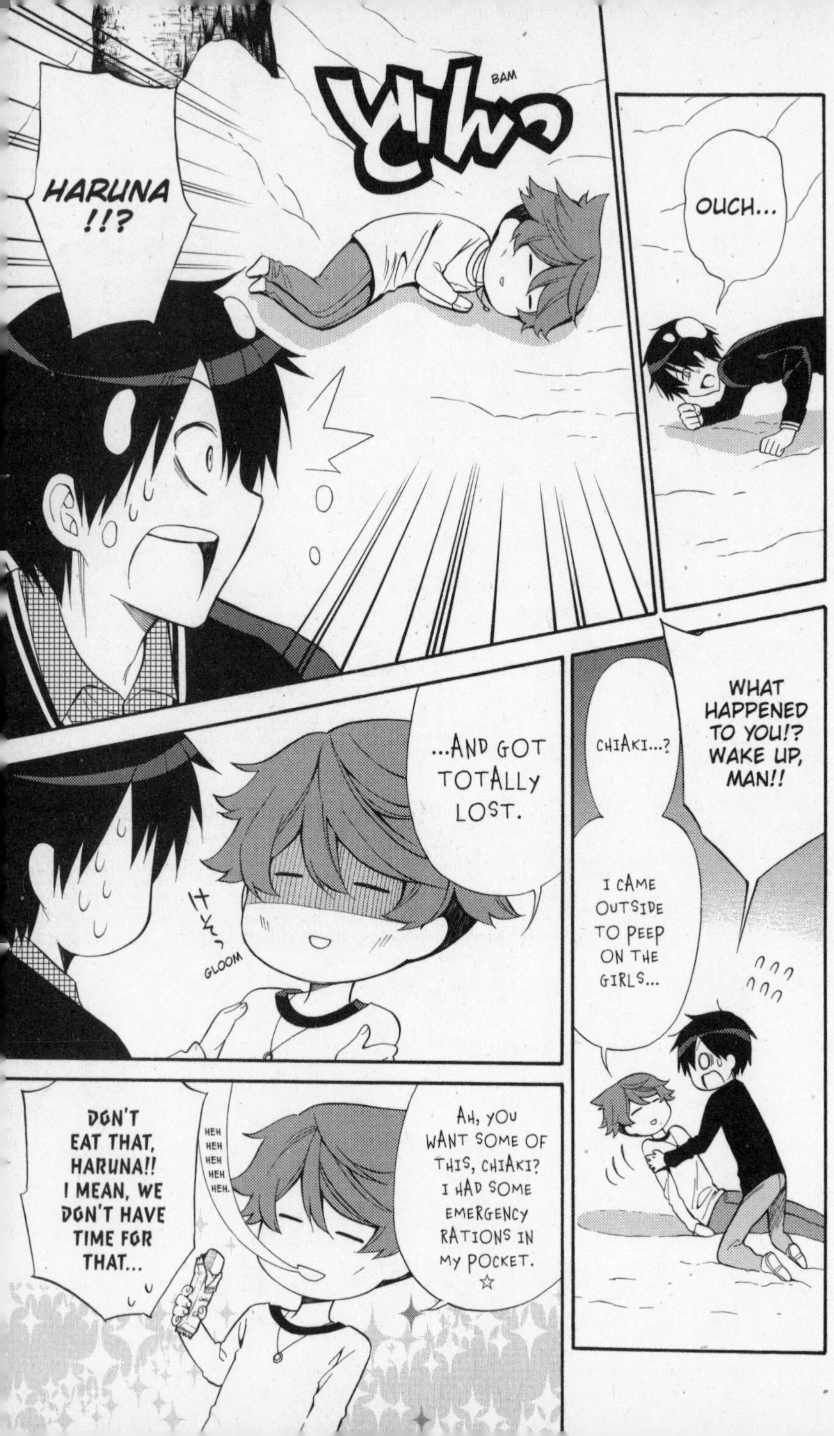
OUCH...
BAM
HARUNA!!?
WHAT HAPPENED TO YOU!? WAKE UP, MAN!!
CHIAKI...?
I CAME OUTSIDE TO PEEP ON THE GIRLS...
...AND GOT TOTALLY LOST.
GLOOM
AH, YOU WANT SOME OF THIS, CHIAKI? I HAD SOME EMERGENCY RATIONS IN MY POCKET. ☆
HEH HEH HEH HEH HEH.
DON'T EAT THAT, HARUNA!! I MEAN, WE DON'T HAVE TIME FOR THAT...

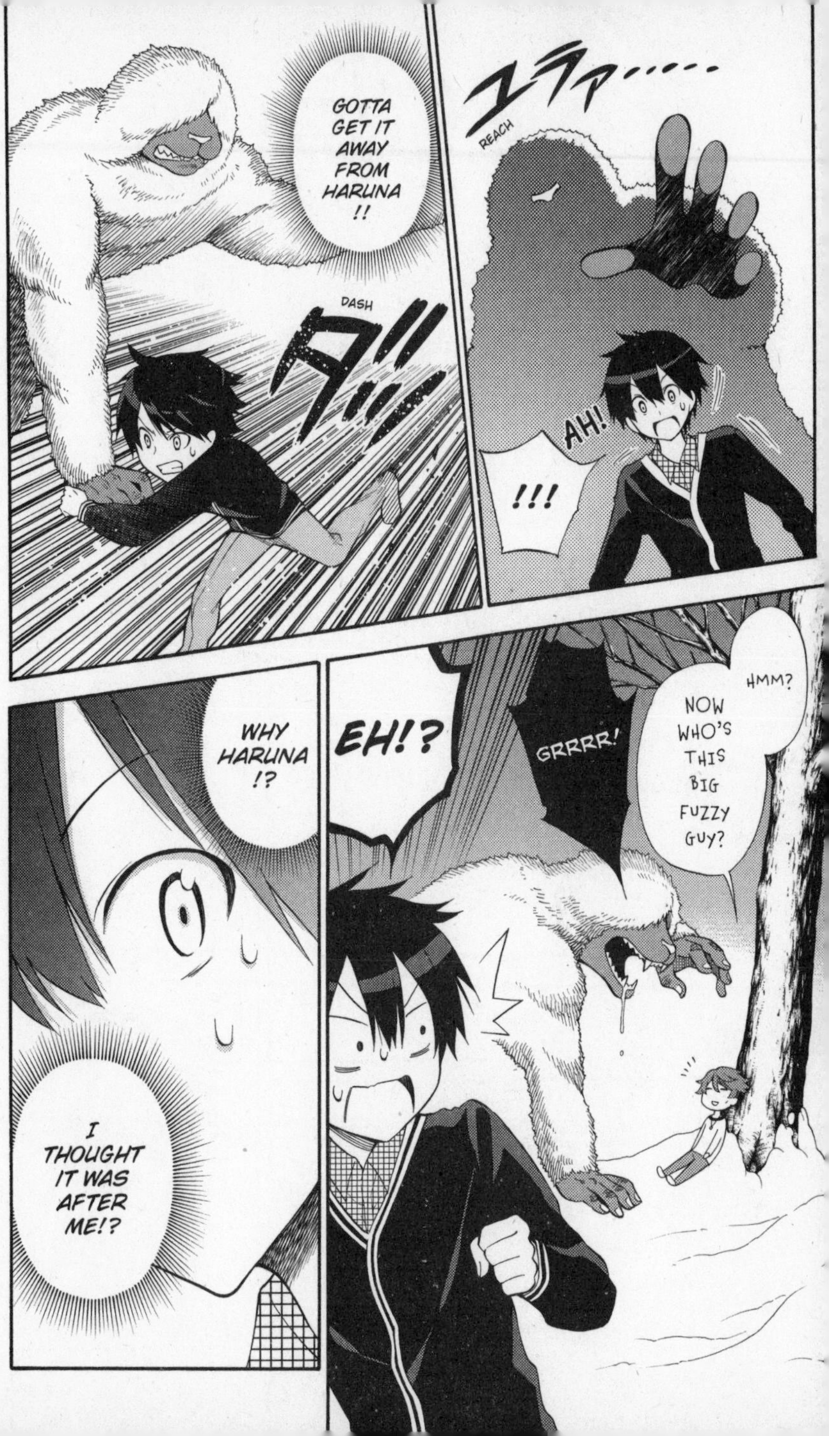

ユラァ……
REACH
AH!
!!!
GOTTA GET IT AWAY FROM HARUNA !!
DASH
タッ
HMM?
NOW WHO'S THIS BIG FUZZY GUY?
GRRRR!
EH!?
WHY HARUNA !?
I THOUGHT IT WAS AFTER ME!?

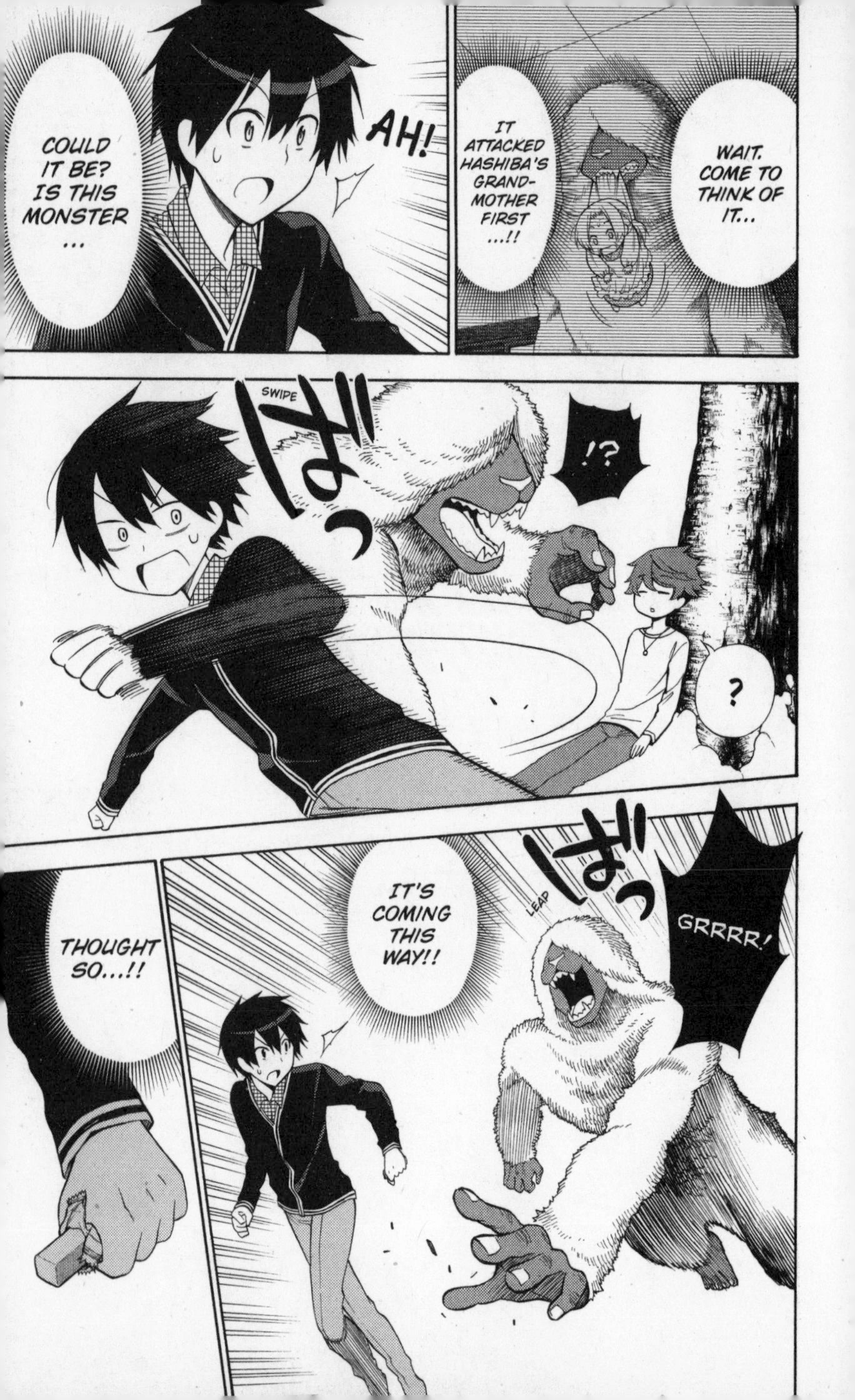
WAIT. COME TO THINK OF IT...
IT ATTACKED HASHIBA'S GRAND-MOTHER FIRST ...!!
AH!
COULD IT BE? IS THIS MONSTER ...
!?
ばっ
SWIPE
?
GRRRR!
ばっ
LEAP
IT'S COMING THIS WAY!!
THOUGHT SO...!!

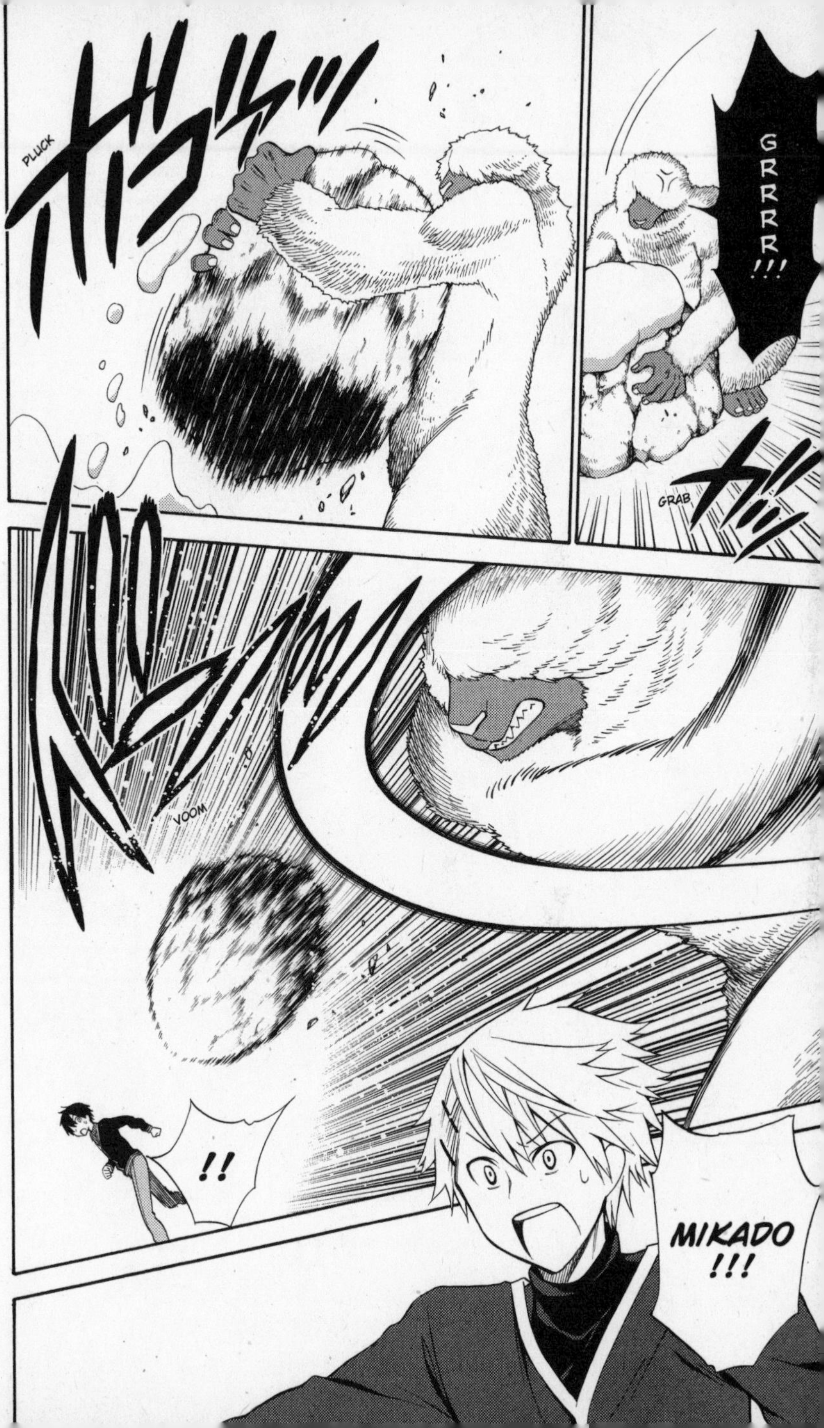
GRRRR!!!
GRAB
PLUCK
VOOM
MIKADO!!!
!!

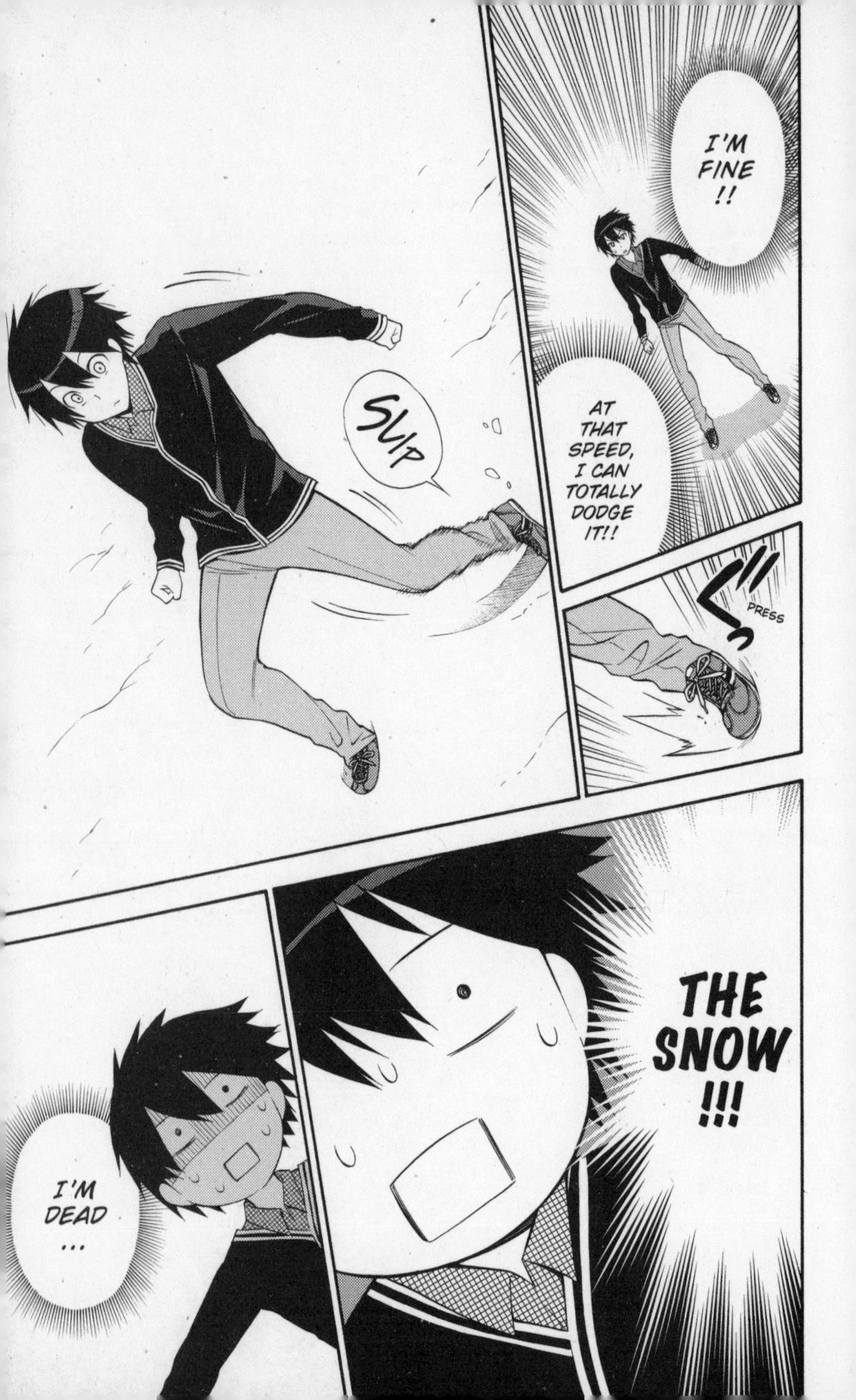

I'M FINE!!
AT THAT SPEED, I CAN TOTALLY DODGE IT!!
PRESS
SLIP
THE SNOW!!!
I'M DEAD...

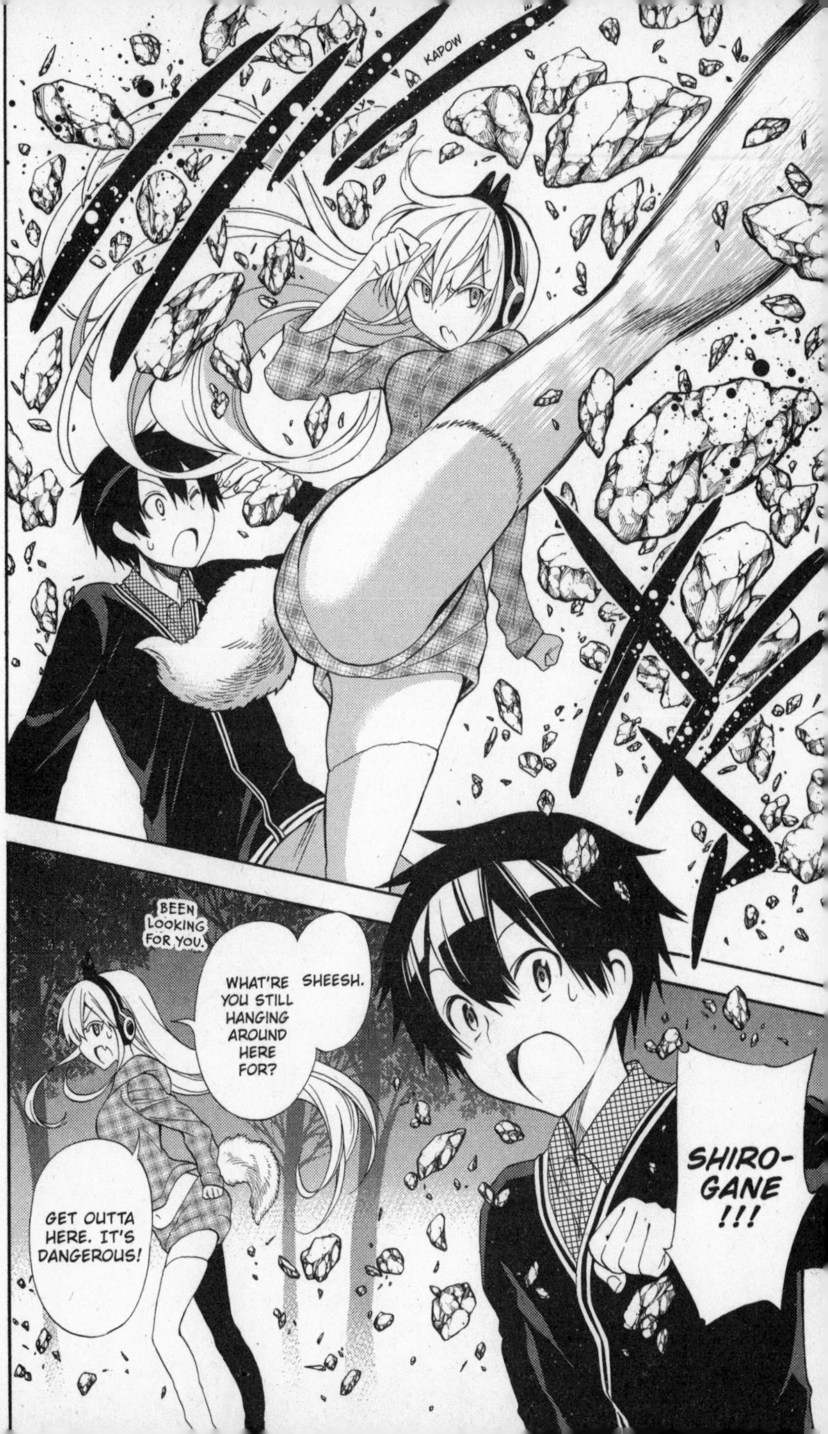
KAPOW
SHIRO-GANE!!!
SHEESH.
WHAT'RE YOU STILL HANGING AROUND HERE FOR?
BEEN LOOKING FOR YOU.
GET OUTTA HERE. IT'S DANGEROUS!

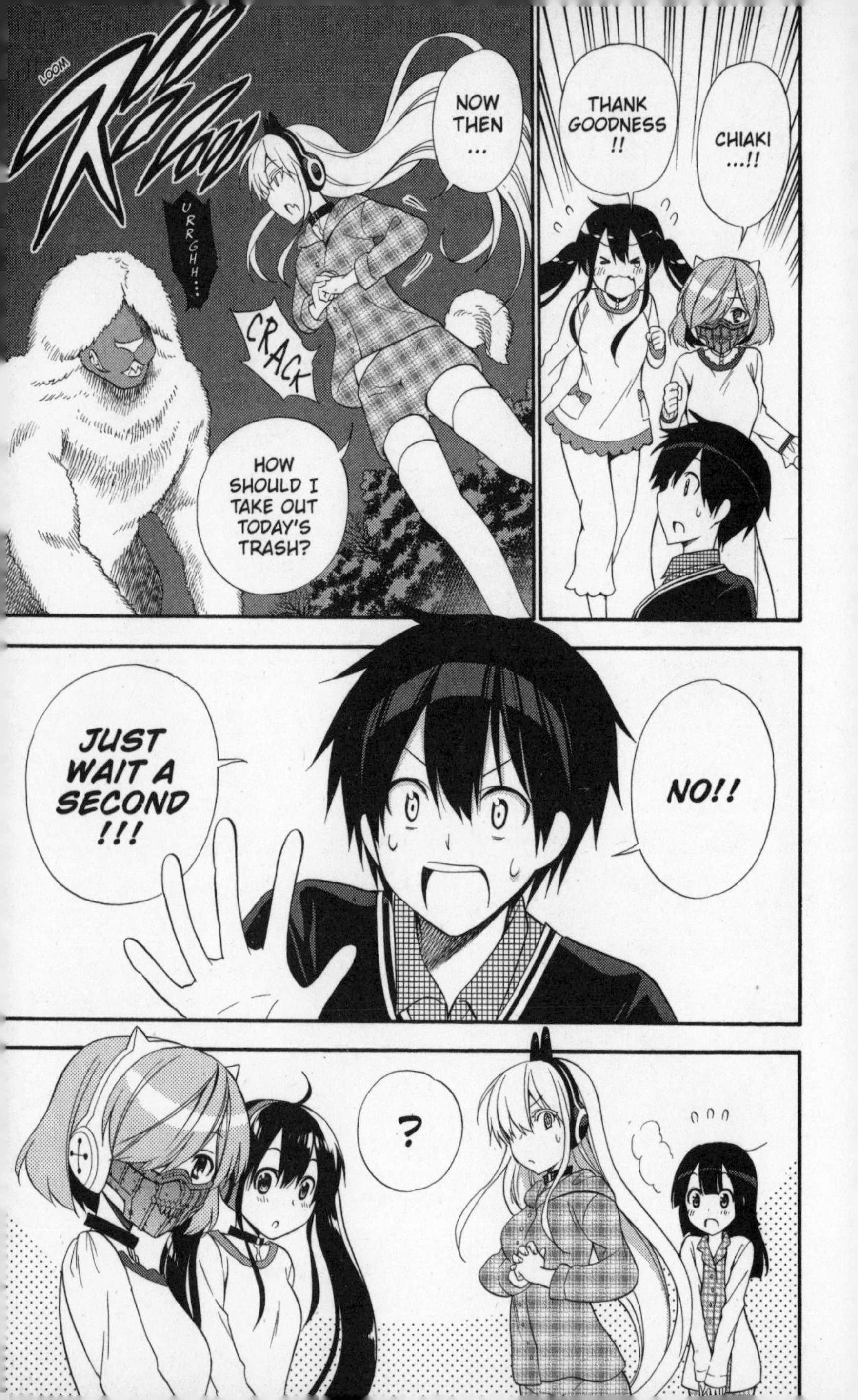
CHIAKI ...!!
THANK GOODNESS !!
NOW THEN ...
LOOM
URRGH...
CRACK
HOW SHOULD I TAKE OUT TODAY'S TRASH?
NO!!
JUST WAIT A SECOND !!!
?

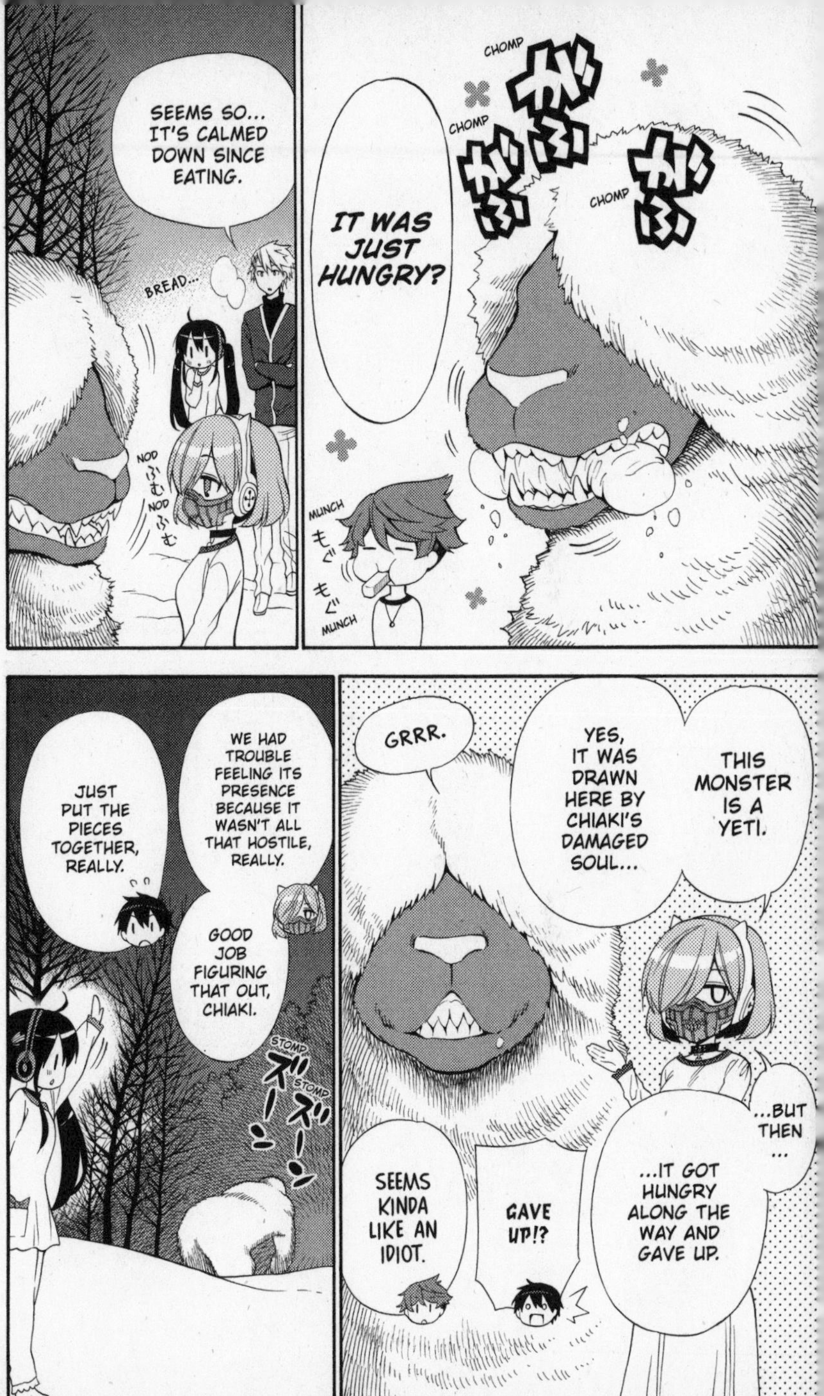
CHOMP
がぶ
CHOMP
がぶ
CHOMP
がぶ
IT WAS JUST HUNGRY?
MUNCH
もぐ
もぐ
MUNCH
SEEMS SO... IT'S CALMED DOWN SINCE EATING.
BREAD...
NOD
ふむ
NOD
ふむ
THIS MONSTER IS A YETI.
YES, IT WAS DRAWN HERE BY CHIAKI'S DAMAGED SOUL...
GRRR.
...BUT THEN...
...IT GOT HUNGRY ALONG THE WAY AND GAVE UP.
GAVE UP!?
SEEMS KINDA LIKE AN IDIOT.
WE HAD TROUBLE FEELING ITS PRESENCE BECAUSE IT WASN'T ALL THAT HOSTILE, REALLY.
JUST PUT THE PIECES TOGETHER, REALLY.
GOOD JOB FIGURING THAT OUT, CHIAKI.
STOMP
ズーン
STOMP
ズーン

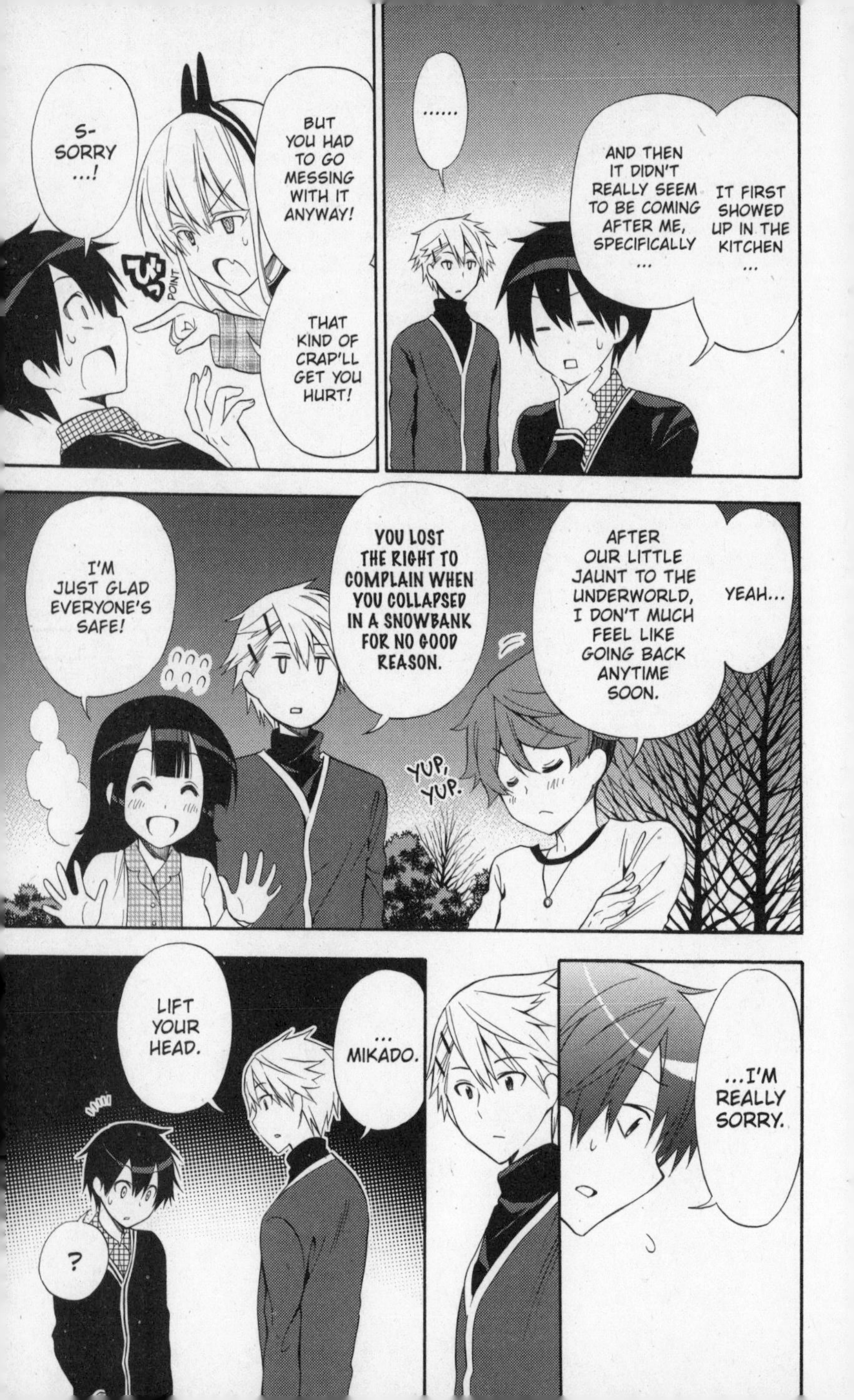
IT FIRST SHOWED UP IN THE KITCHEN ...
AND THEN IT DIDN'T REALLY SEEM TO BE COMING AFTER ME, SPECIFICALLY ...
......
BUT YOU HAD TO GO MESSING WITH IT ANYWAY!
THAT KIND OF CRAP'LL GET YOU HURT!
POINT
S-SORRY ...!
YEAH...
AFTER OUR LITTLE JAUNT TO THE UNDERWORLD, I DON'T MUCH FEEL LIKE GOING BACK ANYTIME SOON.
YUP, YUP.
YOU LOST THE RIGHT TO COMPLAIN WHEN YOU COLLAPSED IN A SNOWBANK FOR NO GOOD REASON.
I'M JUST GLAD EVERYONE'S SAFE!
...I'M REALLY SORRY.
... MIKADO.
LIFT YOUR HEAD.
?

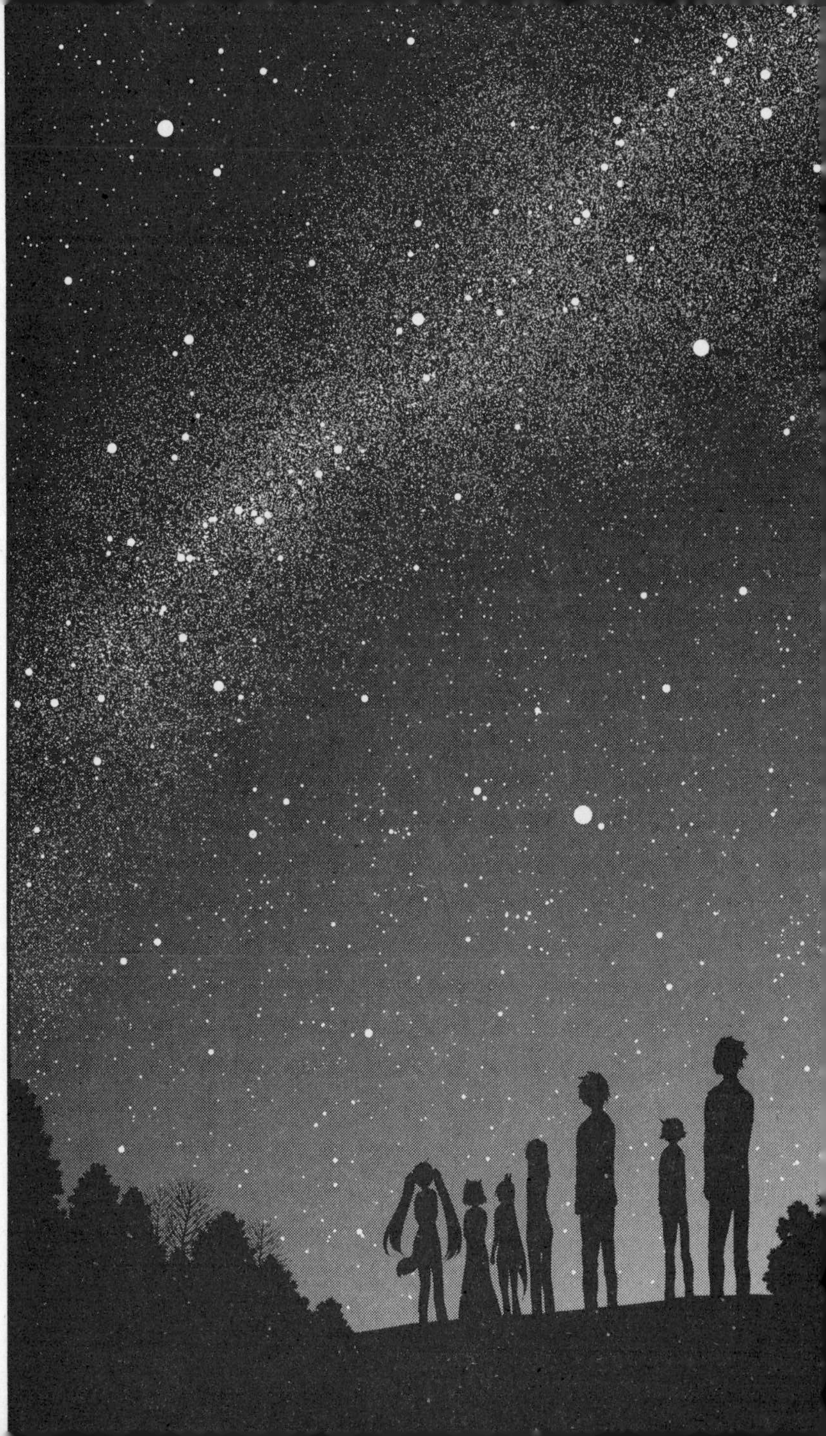

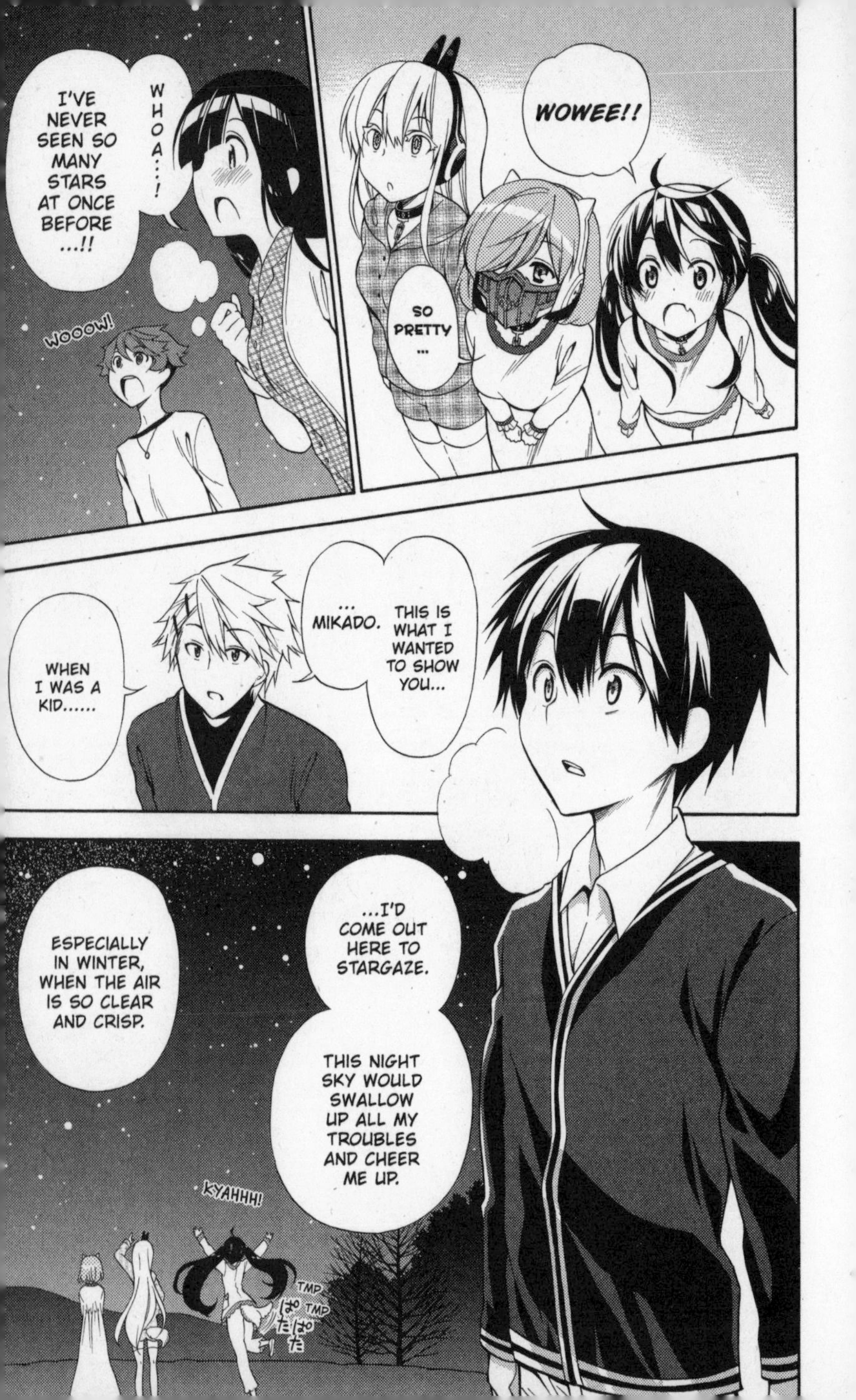
WOWEE!!
SO PRETTY ...
WHOA...!
I'VE NEVER SEEN SO MANY STARS AT ONCE BEFORE ...!!
WOOOW!
... MIKADO.
THIS IS WHAT I WANTED TO SHOW YOU...
WHEN I WAS A KID......
...I'D COME OUT HERE TO STARGAZE.
THIS NIGHT SKY WOULD SWALLOW UP ALL MY TROUBLES AND CHEER ME UP.
ESPECIALLY IN WINTER, WHEN THE AIR IS SO CLEAR AND CRISP.
KYAHHH!
TMP TMP
ぱたぱた

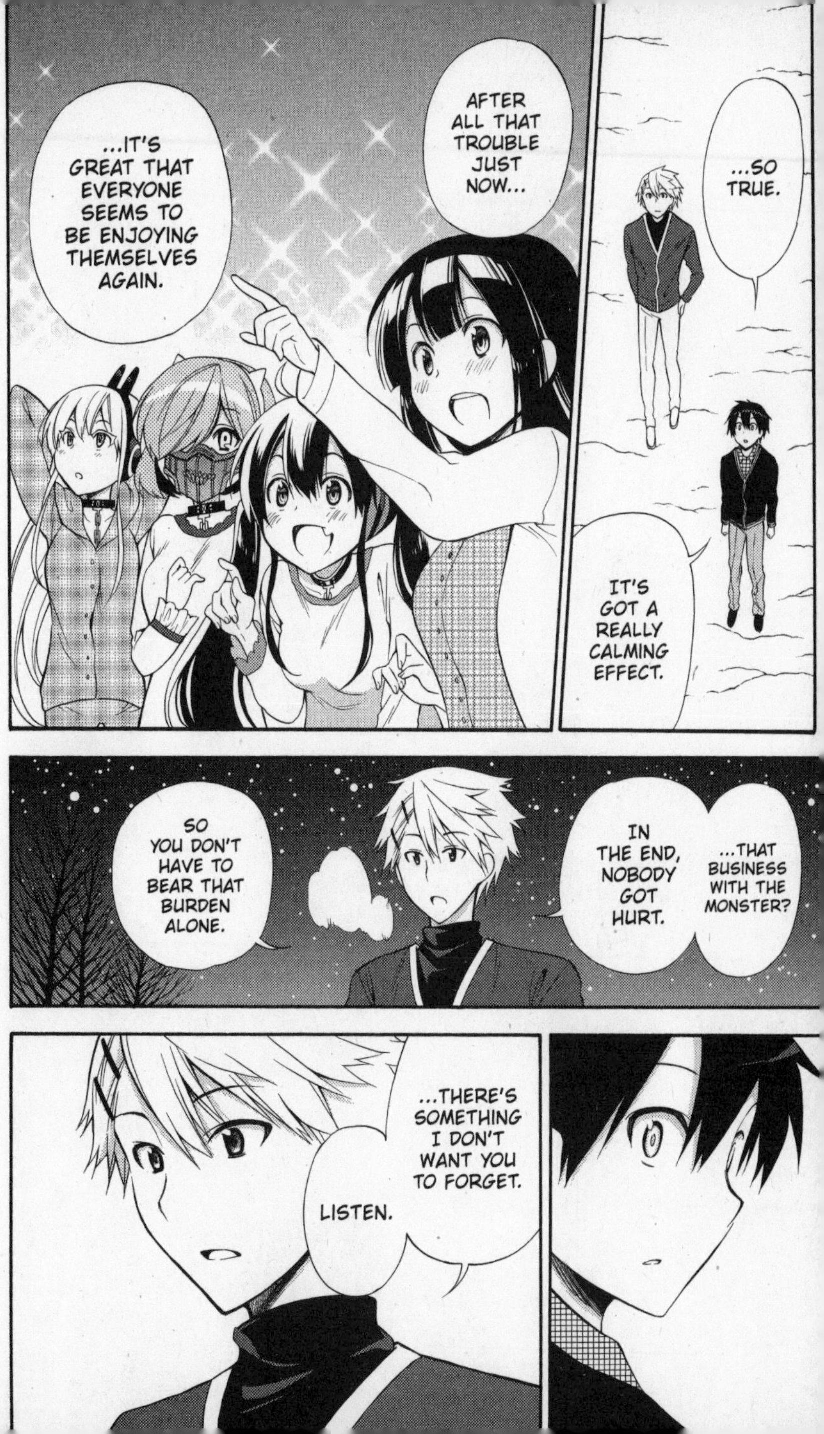
...SO TRUE.
IT'S GOT A REALLY CALMING EFFECT.
AFTER ALL THAT TROUBLE JUST NOW...
...IT'S GREAT THAT EVERYONE SEEMS TO BE ENJOYING THEMSELVES AGAIN.
...THAT BUSINESS WITH THE MONSTER?
IN THE END, NOBODY GOT HURT.
SO YOU DON'T HAVE TO BEAR THAT BURDEN ALONE.
...THERE'S SOMETHING I DON'T WANT YOU TO FORGET.
LISTEN.

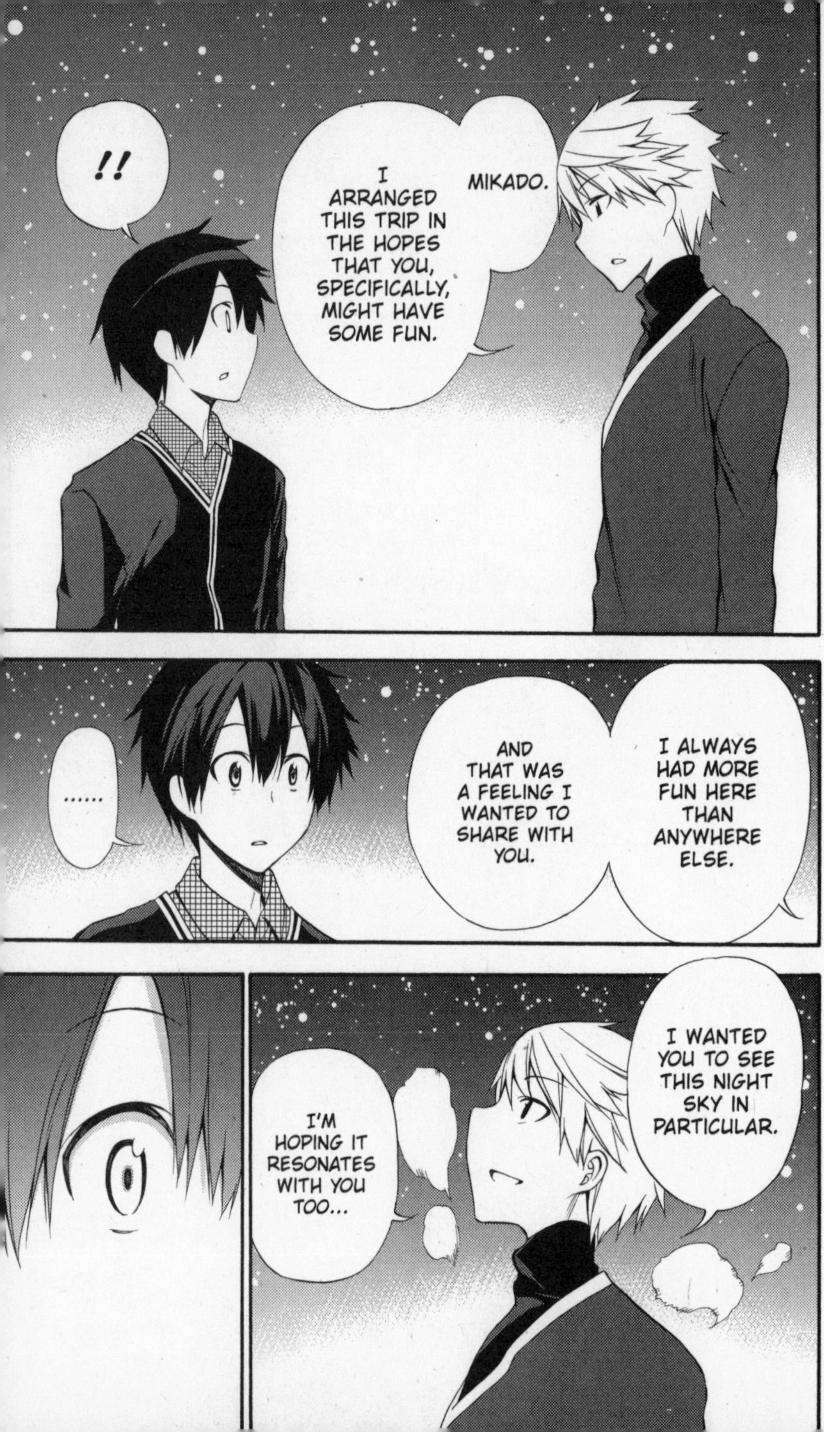
MIKADO.
I ARRANGED THIS TRIP IN THE HOPES THAT YOU, SPECIFICALLY, MIGHT HAVE SOME FUN.
!!
I ALWAYS HAD MORE FUN HERE THAN ANYWHERE ELSE.
AND THAT WAS A FEELING I WANTED TO SHARE WITH YOU.
......
I WANTED YOU TO SEE THIS NIGHT SKY IN PARTICULAR.
I'M HOPING IT RESONATES WITH YOU TOO...

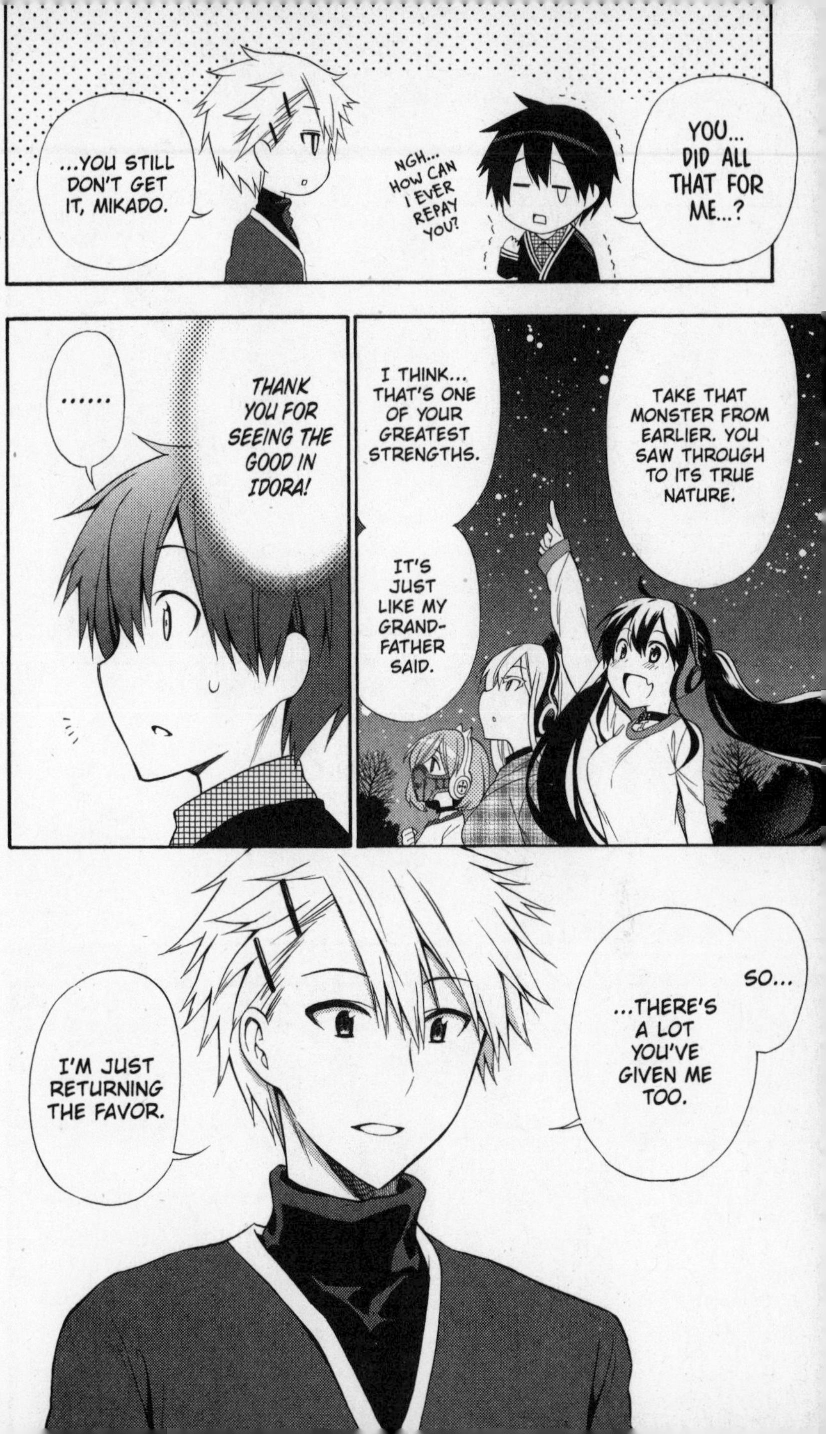
YOU... DID ALL THAT FOR ME...?
NGH... HOW CAN I EVER REPAY YOU?
...YOU STILL DON'T GET IT, MIKADO.
TAKE THAT MONSTER FROM EARLIER. YOU SAW THROUGH TO ITS TRUE NATURE.
I THINK... THAT'S ONE OF YOUR GREATEST STRENGTHS.
IT'S JUST LIKE MY GRAND-FATHER SAID.
THANK YOU FOR SEEING THE GOOD IN IDORA!
......
SO...
...THERE'S A LOT YOU'VE GIVEN ME TOO.
I'M JUST RETURNING THE FAVOR.

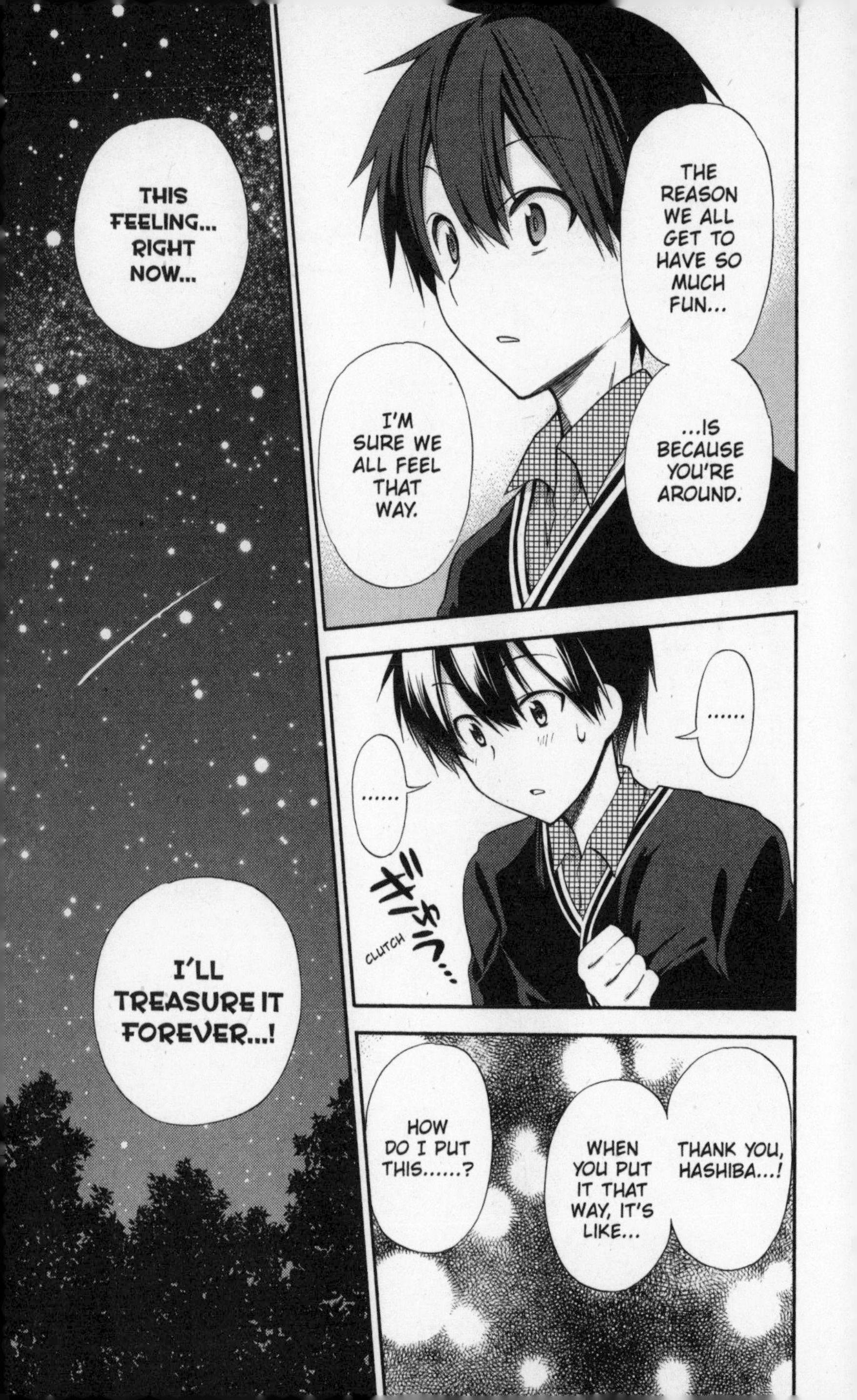
THE REASON WE ALL GET TO HAVE SO MUCH FUN...
...IS BECAUSE YOU'RE AROUND.
I'M SURE WE ALL FEEL THAT WAY.
......
......
CLUTCH
THANK YOU, HASHIBA...!
WHEN YOU PUT IT THAT WAY, IT'S LIKE...
HOW DO I PUT THIS......?
THIS FEELING... RIGHT NOW...
I'LL TREASURE IT FOREVER...!

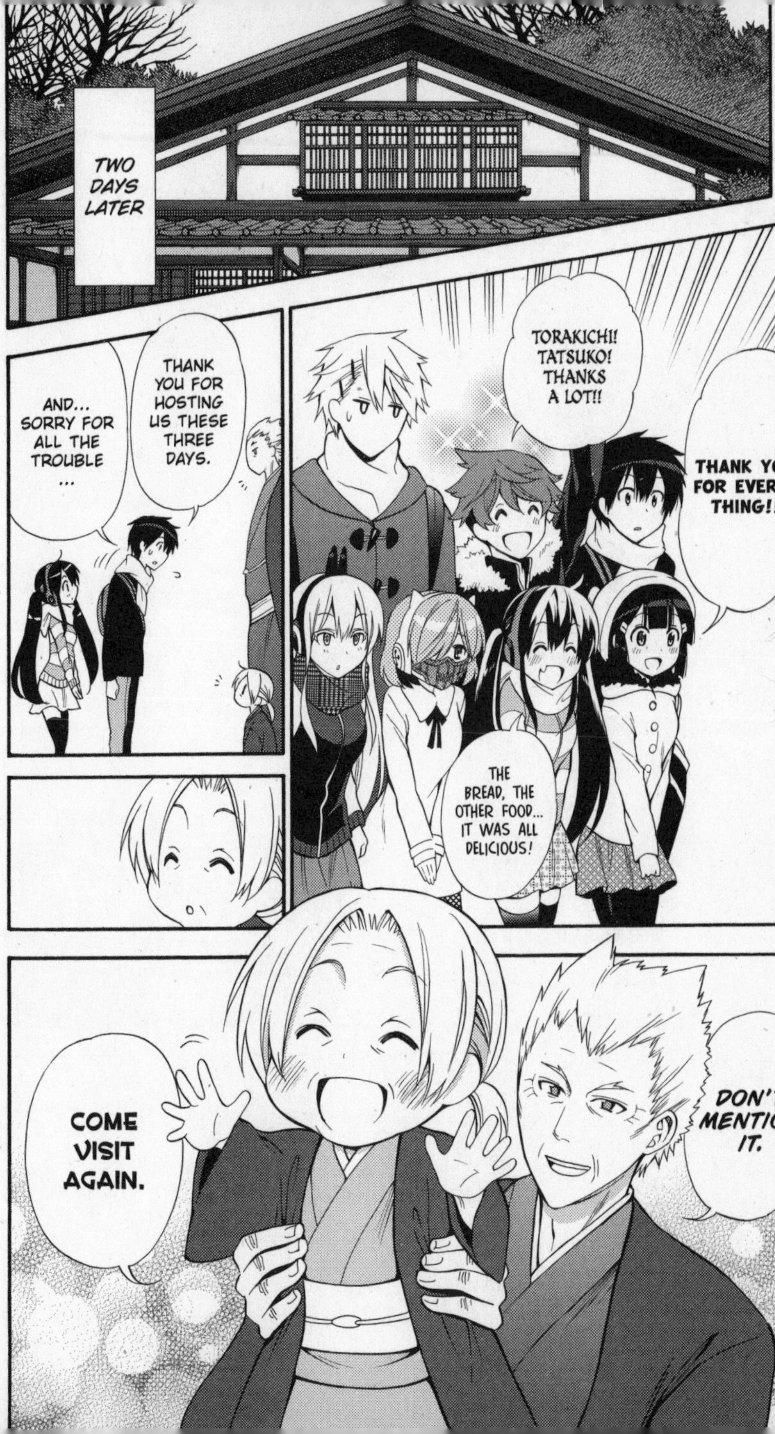
TWO DAYS LATER
TORAKICHI! TATSUKO! THANKS A LOT!!
THANK YOU FOR EVERY-THING!!
THE BREAD, THE OTHER FOOD... IT WAS ALL DELICIOUS!
THANK YOU FOR HOSTING US THESE THREE DAYS.
AND... SORRY FOR ALL THE TROUBLE...
DON'T MENTION IT.
COME VISIT AGAIN.

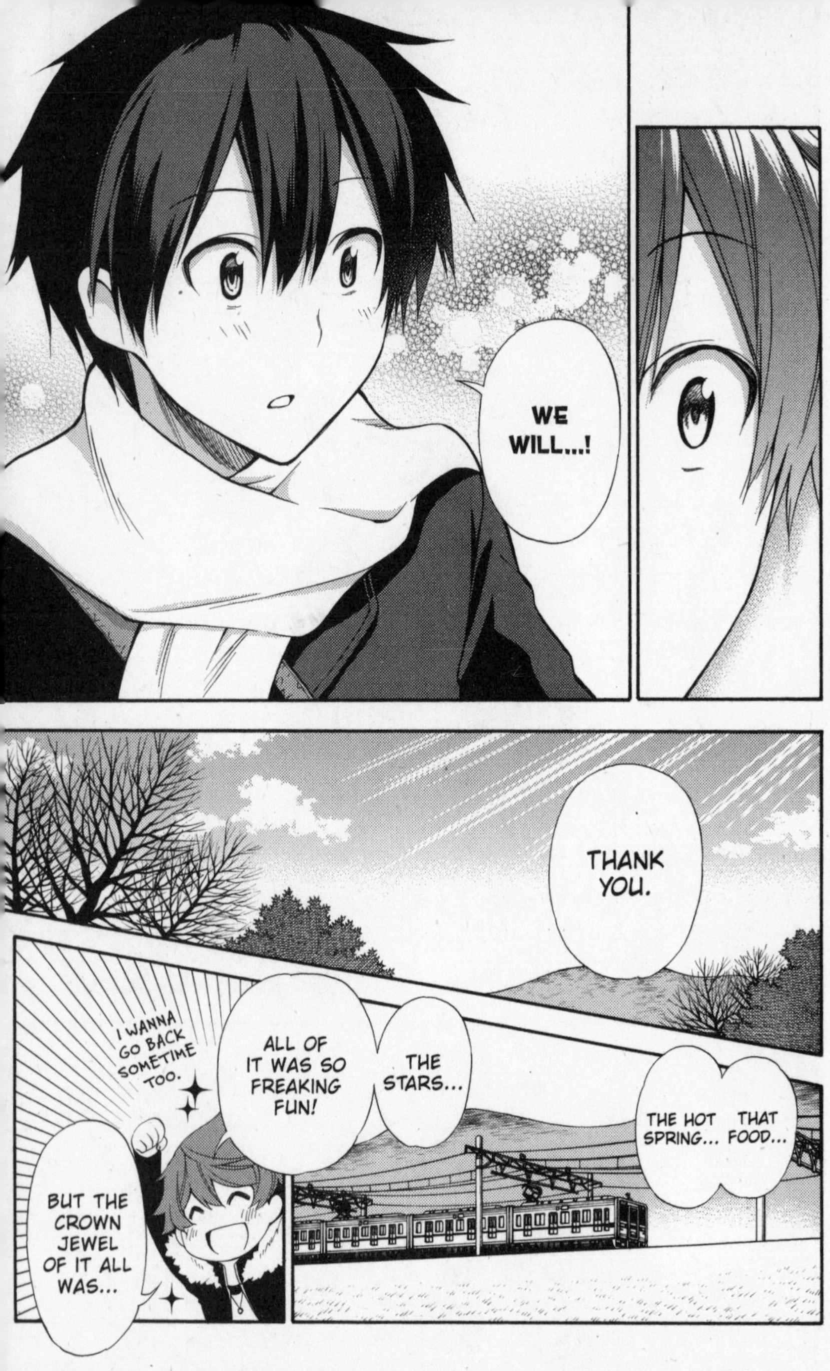
WE WILL...!
THANK YOU.
THAT FOOD...
THE HOT SPRING...
THE STARS...
ALL OF IT WAS SO FREAKING FUN!
I WANNA GO BACK SOMETIME TOO.
BUT THE CROWN JEWEL OF IT ALL WAS...

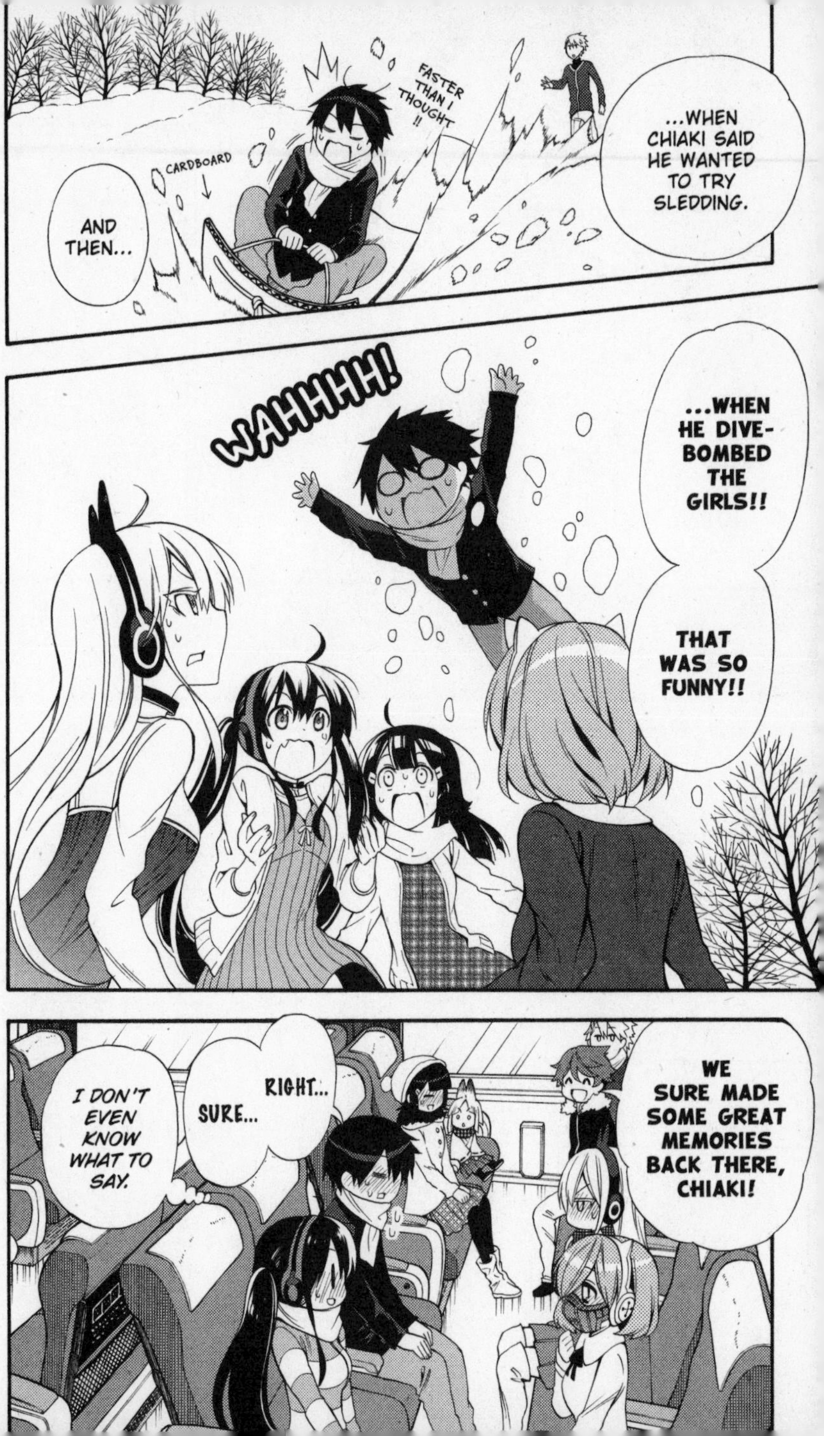
...WHEN CHIAKI SAID HE WANTED TO TRY SLEDDING.
FASTER THAN I THOUGHT!!
CARDBOARD
AND THEN...
...WHEN HE DIVE-BOMBED THE GIRLS!!
THAT WAS SO FUNNY!!
WAHHHH!
WE SURE MADE SOME GREAT MEMORIES BACK THERE, CHIAKI!
RIGHT... SURE...
I DON'T EVEN KNOW WHAT TO SAY.

TODAY'S CERBERUS

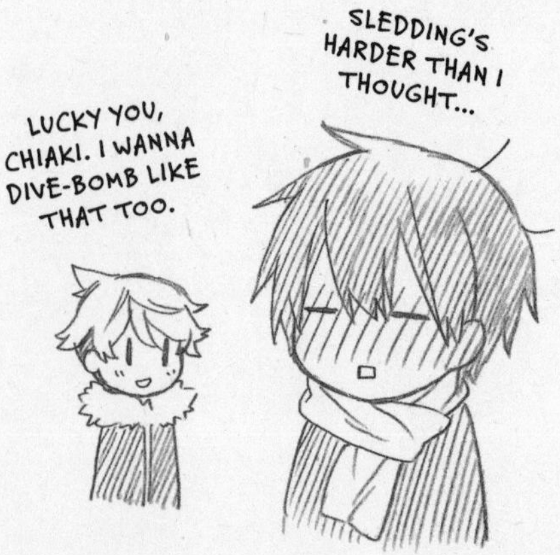
SLEDDING'S HARDER THAN I THOUGHT...
LUCKY YOU, CHIAKI. I WANNA DIVE-BOMB LIKE THAT TOO.

NOTES

PAGE 88
Haruna is referencing Kintaro, a figure from Japanese folklore. Supposedly based on real-life historical figure Sakata Kintoki, Kintaro is commonly depicted as an ax-wielding mountain child. Idora's skill with an ax must have reminded Haruna of the fairytale.

PAGE 161
Ifrit are fire-based demons or spirits found in Arabic folklore.

PAGE 180
"Koro" is one of the most common names for dogs in Japan, akin to "Spot" in the United States.

TODAY'S CERBERUS

SO NERVOUS ABOUT SO MANY THINGS.

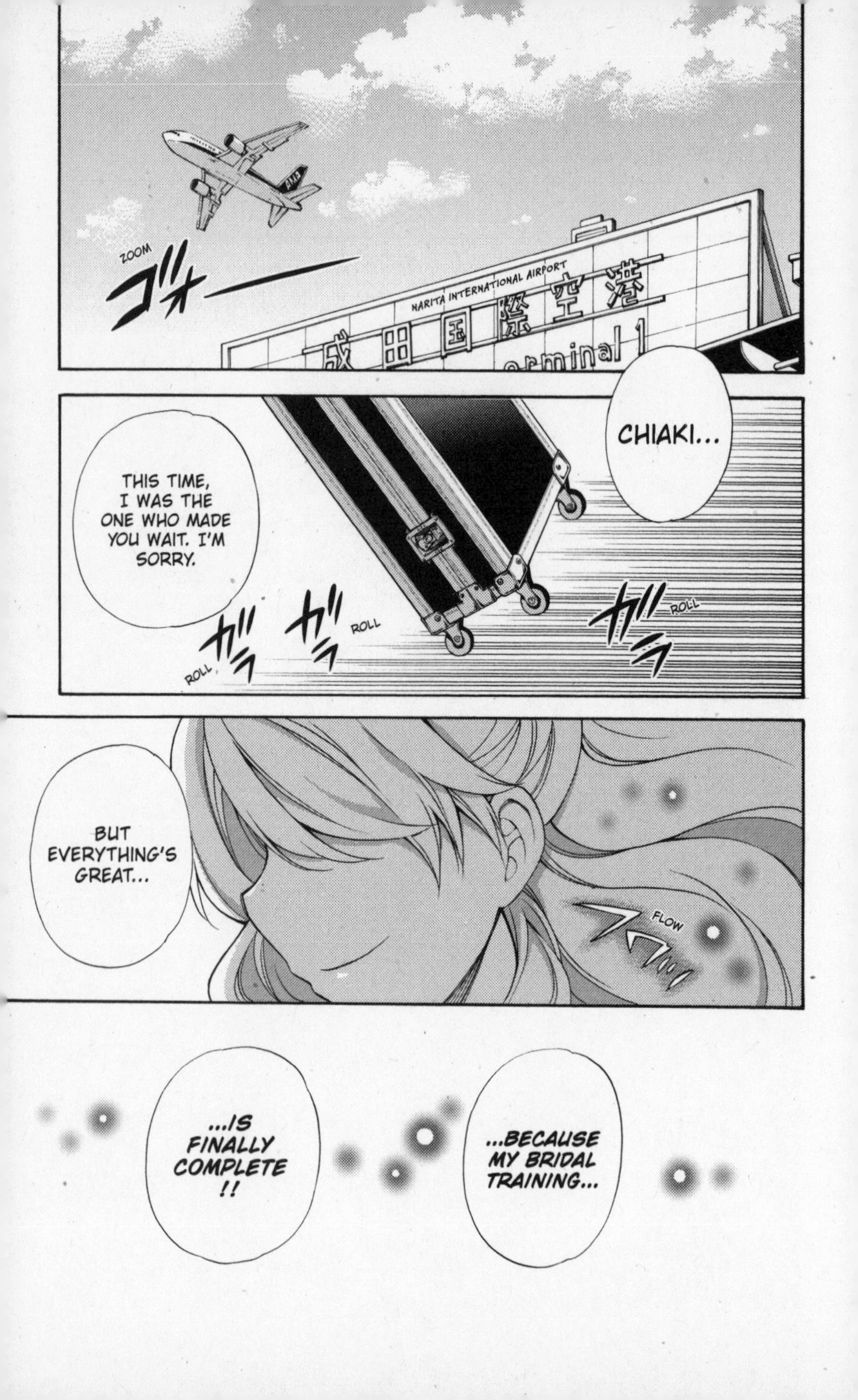
ZOOM
NARITA INTERNATIONAL AIRPORT
成田国際空港
CHIAKI...
ROLL
ROLL
THIS TIME, I WAS THE ONE WHO MADE YOU WAIT. I'M SORRY.
ROLL
FLOW
BUT EVERYTHING'S GREAT...
...BECAUSE MY BRIDAL TRAINING...
...IS FINALLY COMPLETE!!

CHAPTER 39
ONCE AGAIN

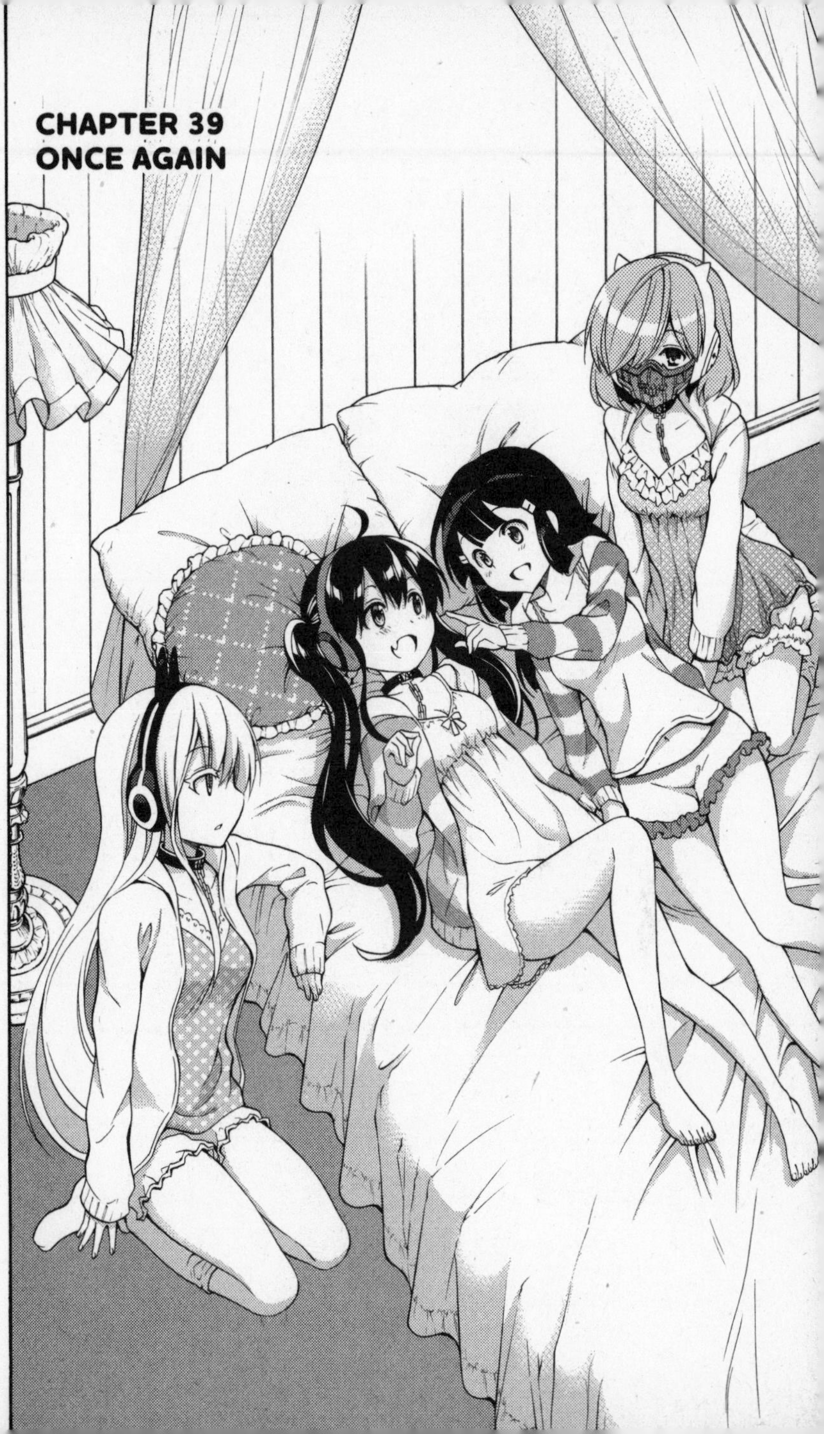

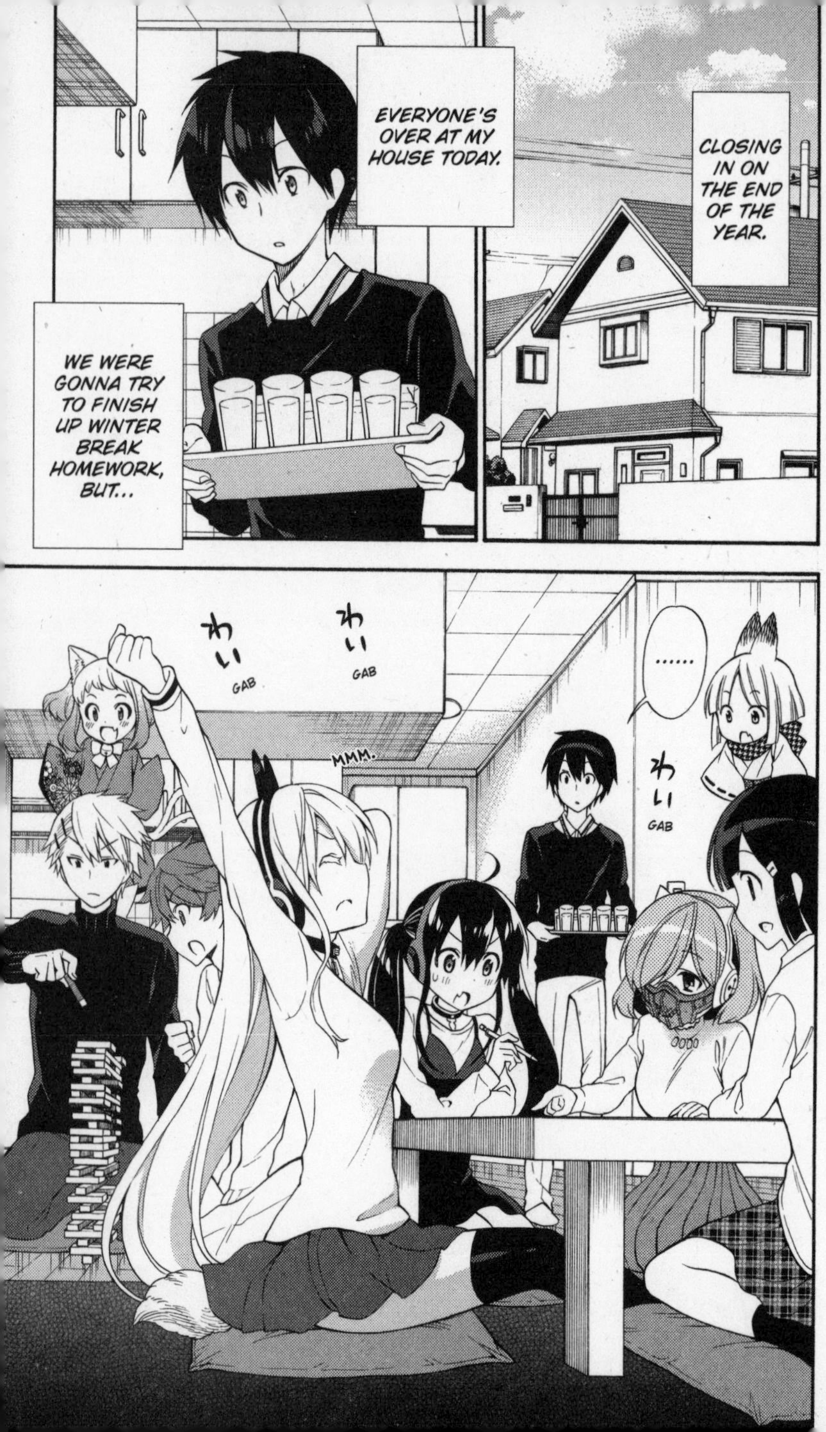
CLOSING IN ON THE END OF THE YEAR.
EVERYONE'S OVER AT MY HOUSE TODAY.
WE WERE GONNA TRY TO FINISH UP WINTER BREAK HOMEWORK, BUT...
......
わい
GAB
わい
GAB
わい
GAB
MMM.

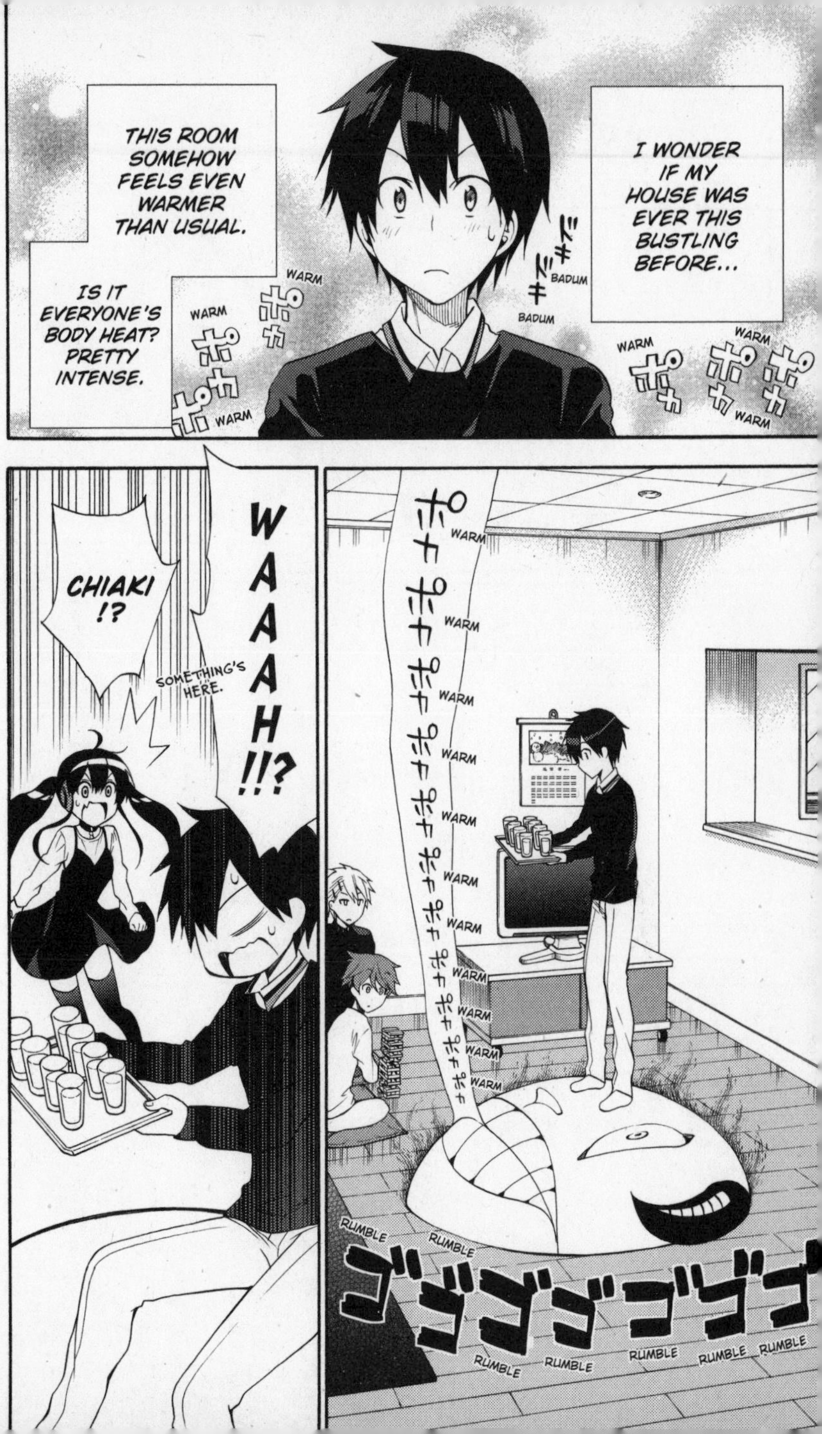
I WONDER IF MY HOUSE WAS EVER THIS BUSTLING BEFORE...
BADUM
BADUM
THIS ROOM SOMEHOW FEELS EVEN WARMER THAN USUAL.
IS IT EVERYONE'S BODY HEAT? PRETTY INTENSE.
WARM
WARM
WARM
WARM
WARM
WARM
WARM
WARM
WARM
WARM
WARM
WARM
WARM
WARM
WARM
WARM
RUMBLE
RUMBLE
RUMBLE
RUMBLE
RUMBLE
RUMBLE
RUMBLE
WAAAAH!!?
CHIAKI!?
SOMETHING'S HERE.

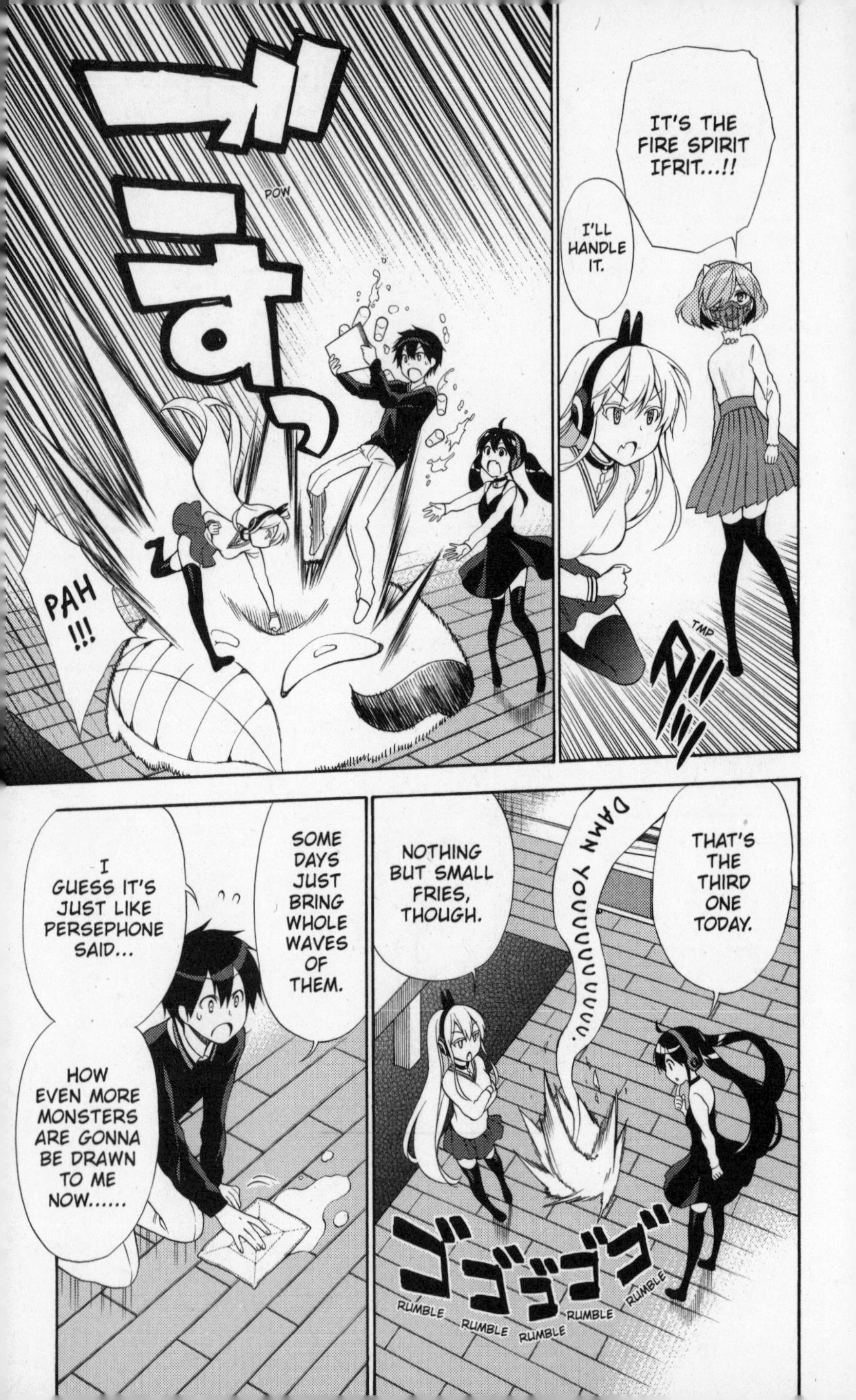
IT'S THE FIRE SPIRIT IFRIT...!!
I'LL HANDLE IT.
TMP
POW
PAH !!!
THAT'S THE THIRD ONE TODAY.
DAMN YOUUUUUUUUU.
NOTHING BUT SMALL FRIES, THOUGH.
RUMBLE RUMBLE RUMBLE RUMBLE RUMBLE
SOME DAYS JUST BRING WHOLE WAVES OF THEM.
I GUESS IT'S JUST LIKE PERSEPHONE SAID...
HOW EVEN MORE MONSTERS ARE GONNA BE DRAWN TO ME NOW......

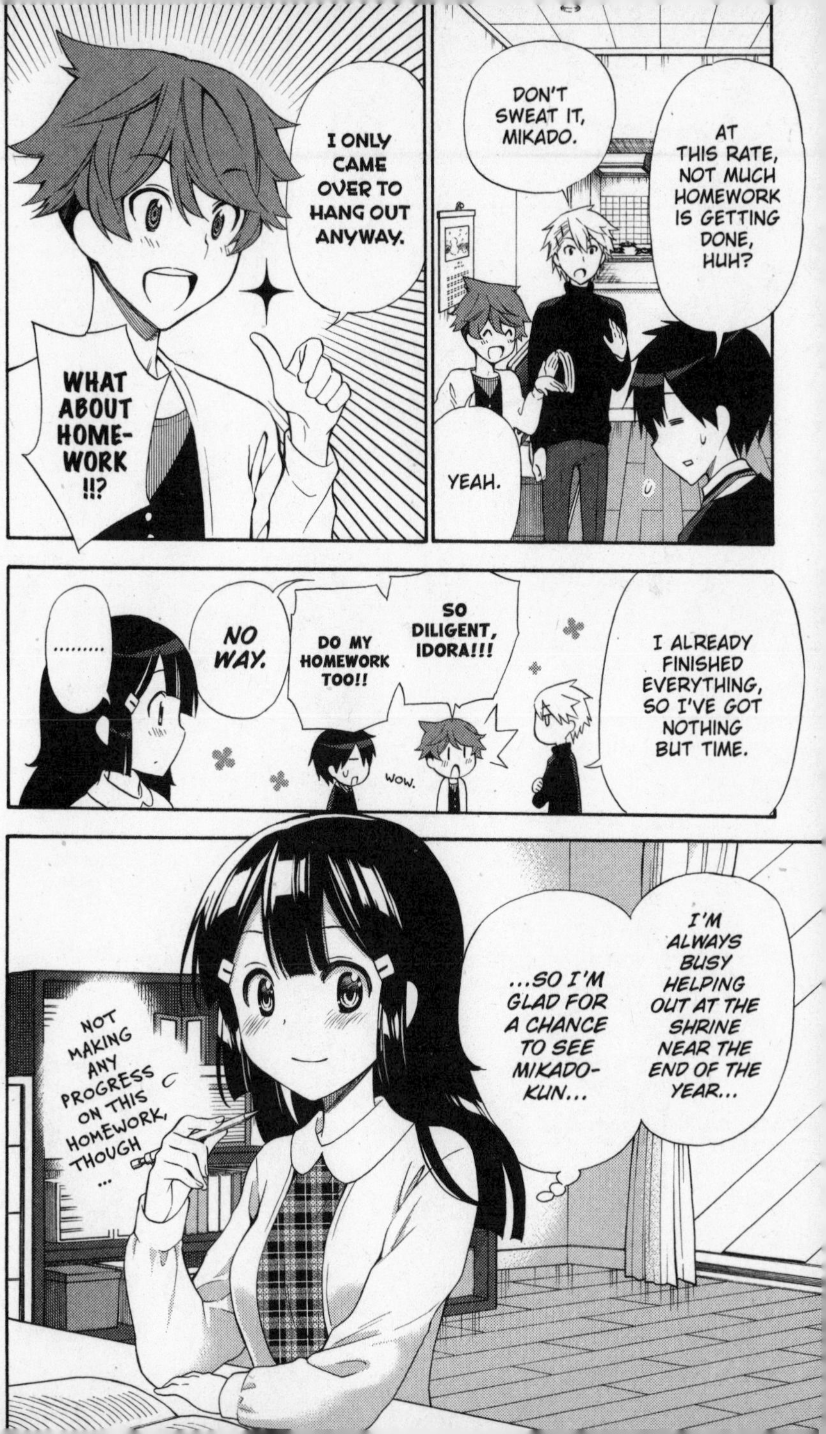
AT THIS RATE, NOT MUCH HOMEWORK IS GETTING DONE, HUH?
DON'T SWEAT IT, MIKADO.
YEAH.
I ONLY CAME OVER TO HANG OUT ANYWAY.
WHAT ABOUT HOME-WORK!!?
I ALREADY FINISHED EVERYTHING, SO I'VE GOT NOTHING BUT TIME.
SO DILIGENT, IDORA!!!
DO MY HOMEWORK TOO!!
WOW.
NO WAY.
....
I'M ALWAYS BUSY HELPING OUT AT THE SHRINE NEAR THE END OF THE YEAR...
...SO I'M GLAD FOR A CHANCE TO SEE MIKADO-KUN...
NOT MAKING ANY PROGRESS ON THIS HOMEWORK, THOUGH ...

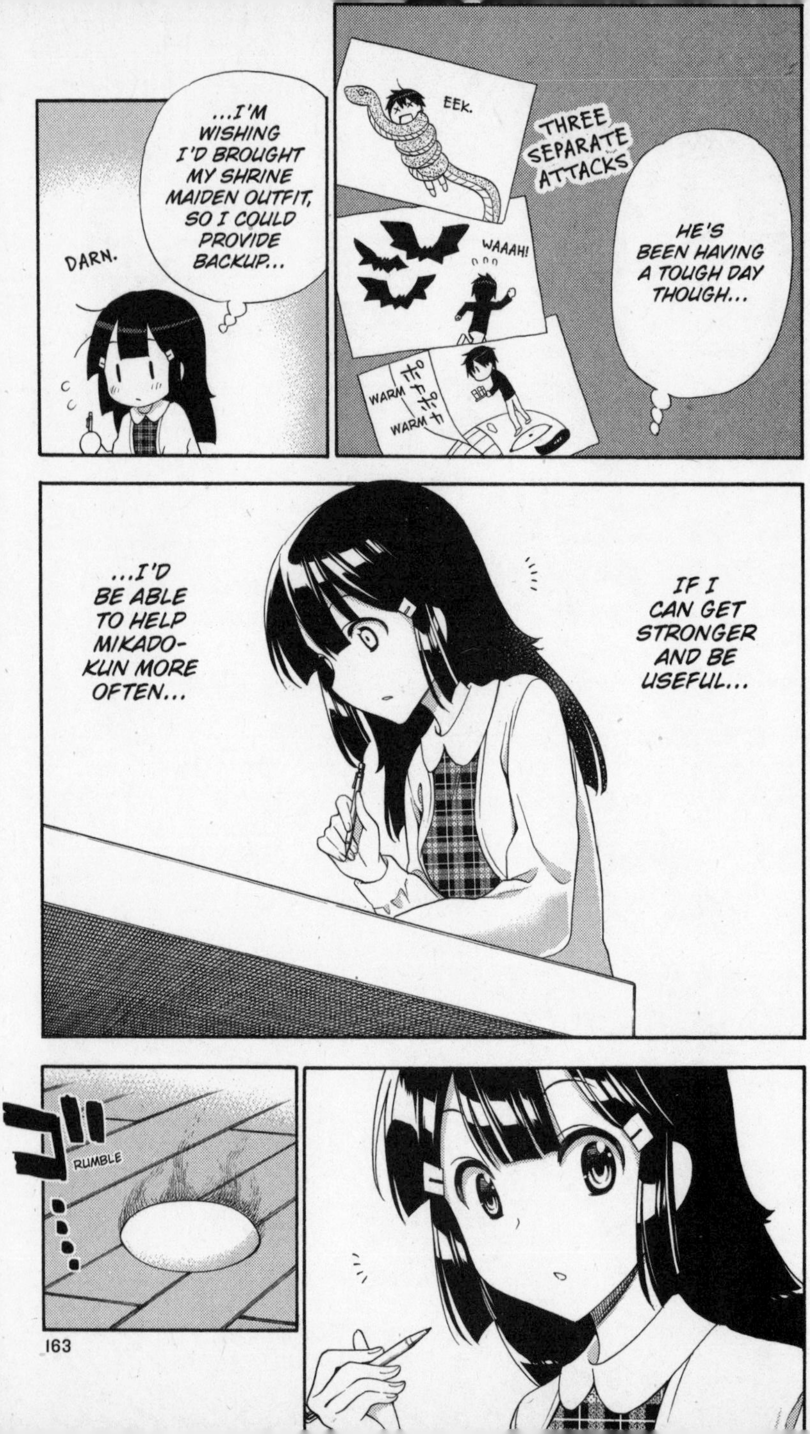
THREE SEPARATE ATTACKS
EEK.
WAAAH!
WARM
WARM
HE'S BEEN HAVING A TOUGH DAY THOUGH...
...I'M WISHING I'D BROUGHT MY SHRINE MAIDEN OUTFIT, SO I COULD PROVIDE BACKUP...
DARN.
IF I CAN GET STRONGER AND BE USEFUL...
...I'D BE ABLE TO HELP MIKADO-KUN MORE OFTEN...
ゴ
RUMBLE
...

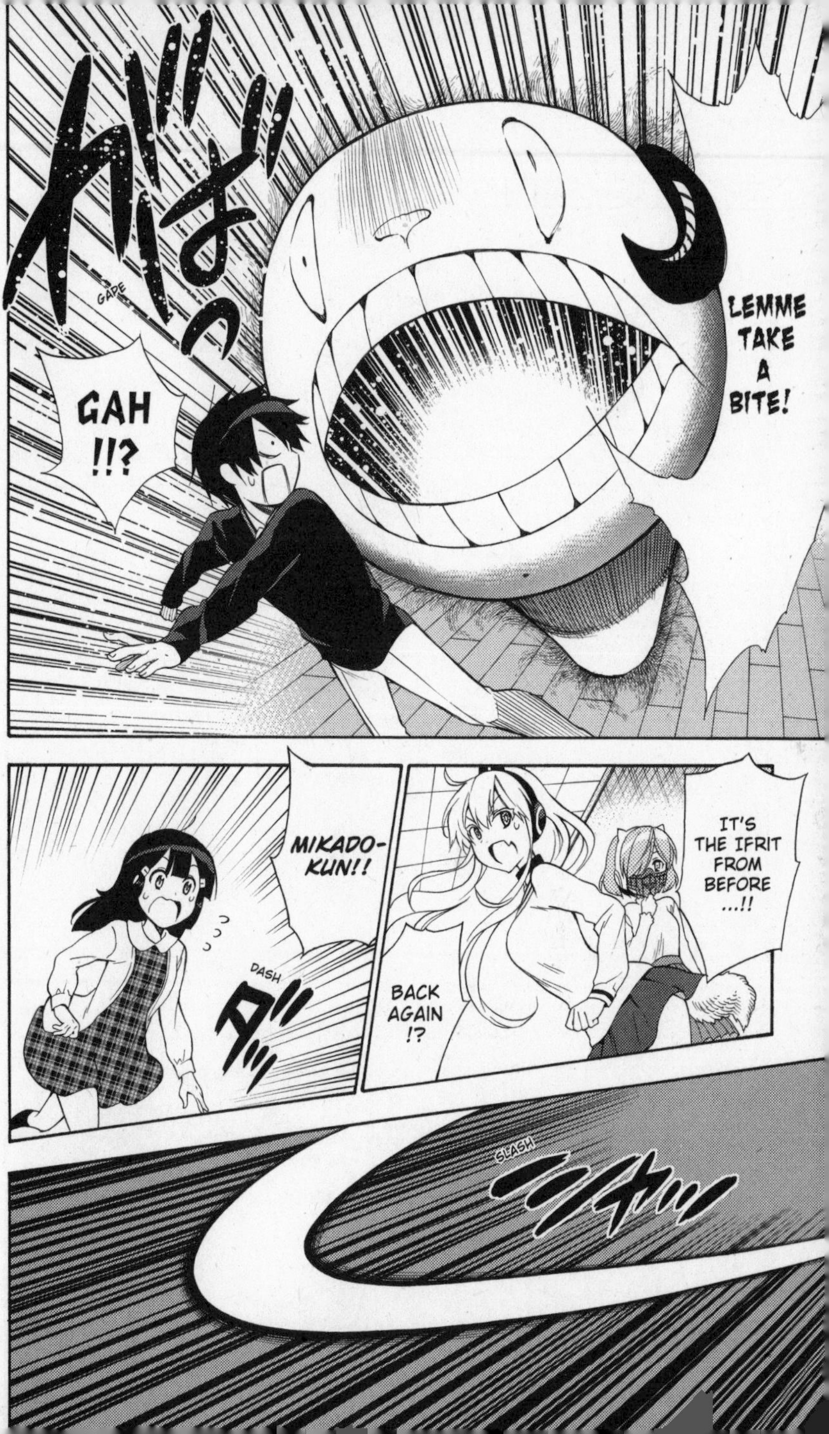
LEMME TAKE A BITE!
GAPE
GAH !!?
IT'S THE IFRIT FROM BEFORE ...!!
BACK AGAIN !?
MIKADO-KUN!!
DASH
SLASH

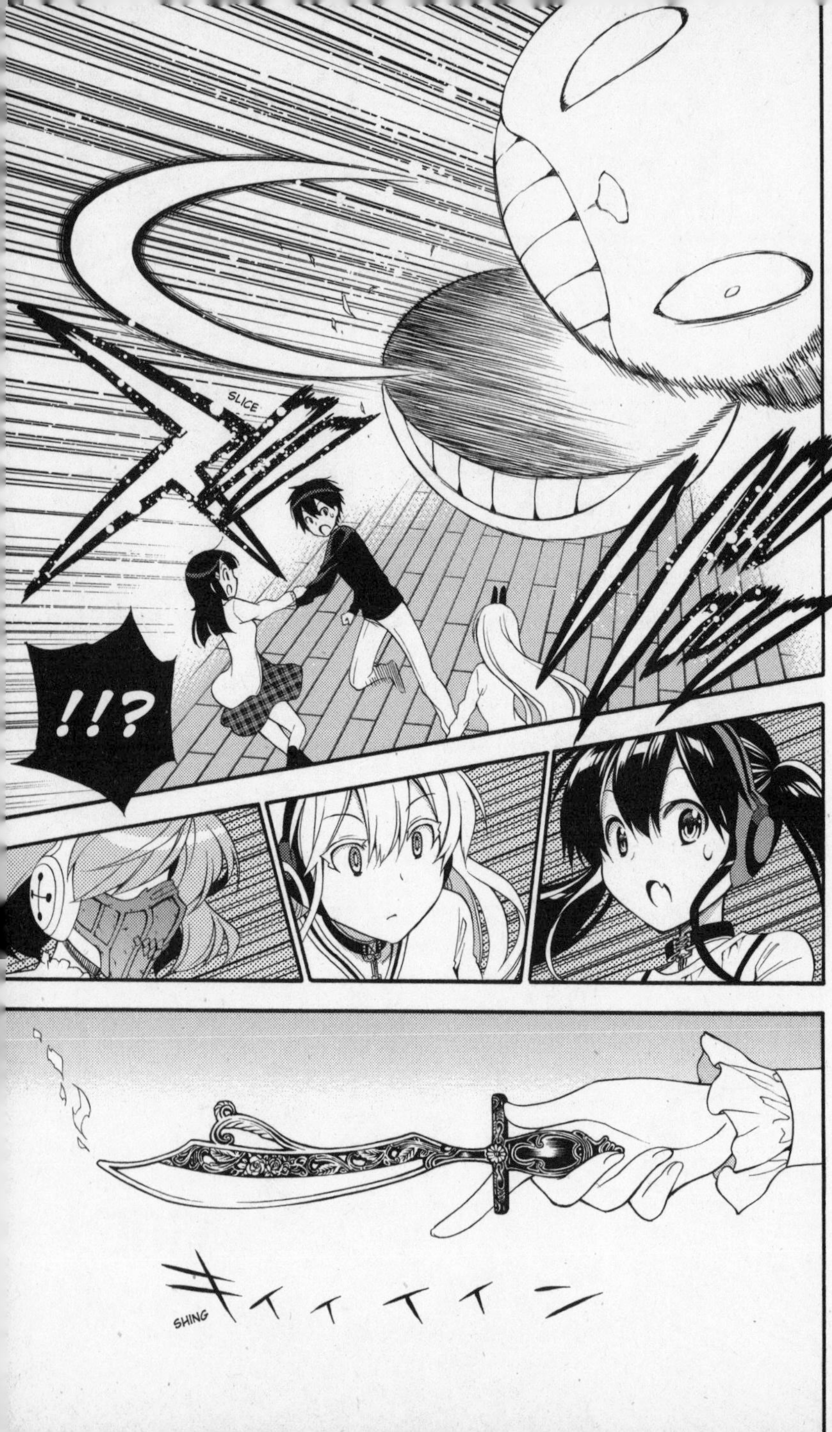
SLICE
!!?
SHING

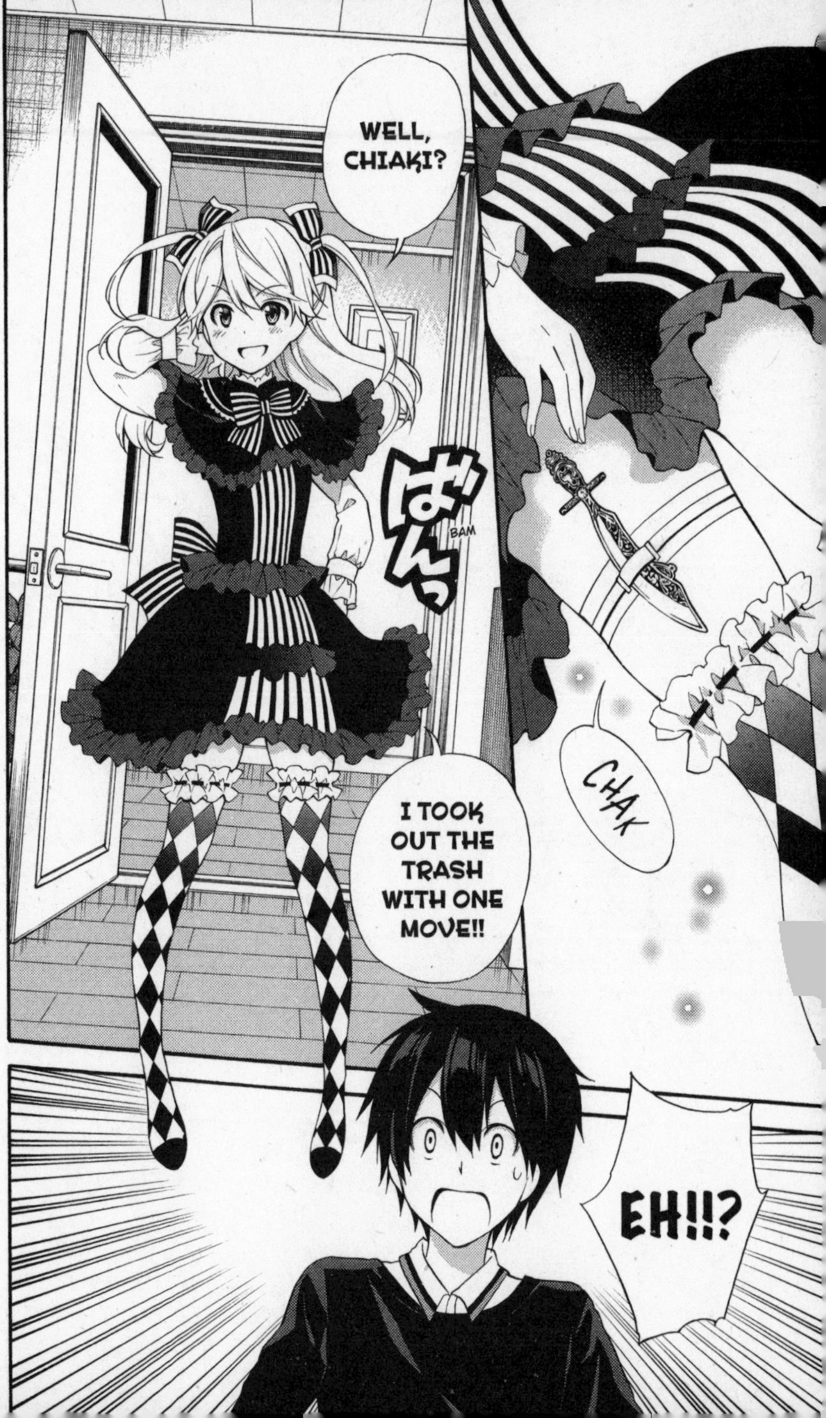
WELL, CHIAKI?
ばんっ
BAM
CHAK
I TOOK OUT THE TRASH WITH ONE MOVE!!
EH!!?

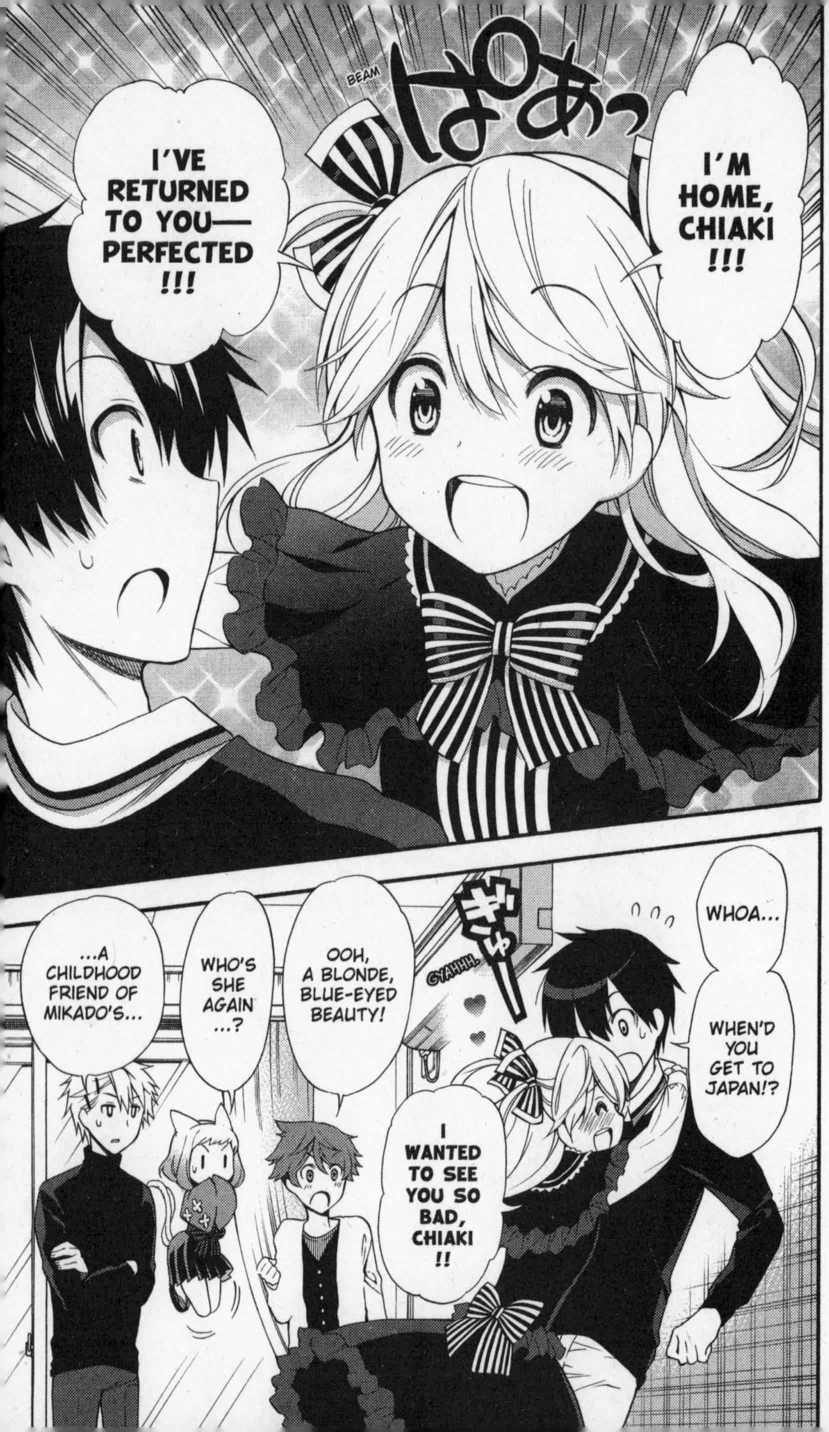
I'M HOME, CHIAKI!!!
ぱあっ
BEAM
I'VE RETURNED TO YOU—PERFECTED!!!
WHOA...
WHEN'D YOU GET TO JAPAN!?
ぎゅー
GYAHHH
I WANTED TO SEE YOU SO BAD, CHIAKI!!
OOH, A BLONDE, BLUE-EYED BEAUTY!
WHO'S SHE AGAIN...?
...A CHILDHOOD FRIEND OF MIKADO'S...

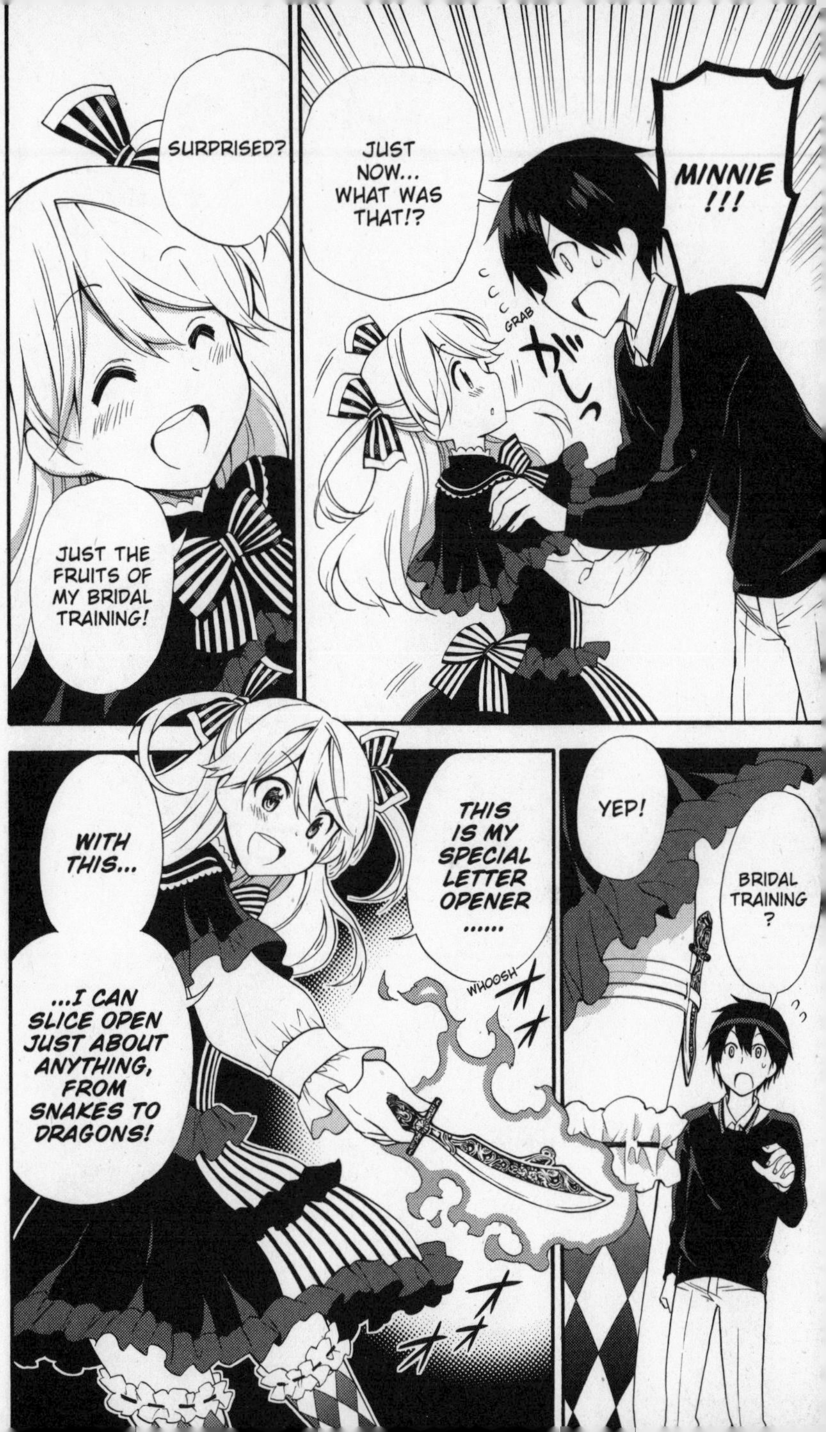
MINNIE!!!
JUST NOW... WHAT WAS THAT!?
GRAB
がしっ
SURPRISED?
JUST THE FRUITS OF MY BRIDAL TRAINING!
BRIDAL TRAINING?
YEP!
THIS IS MY SPECIAL LETTER OPENER......
WHOOSH
WITH THIS...
...I CAN SLICE OPEN JUST ABOUT ANYTHING, FROM SNAKES TO DRAGONS!

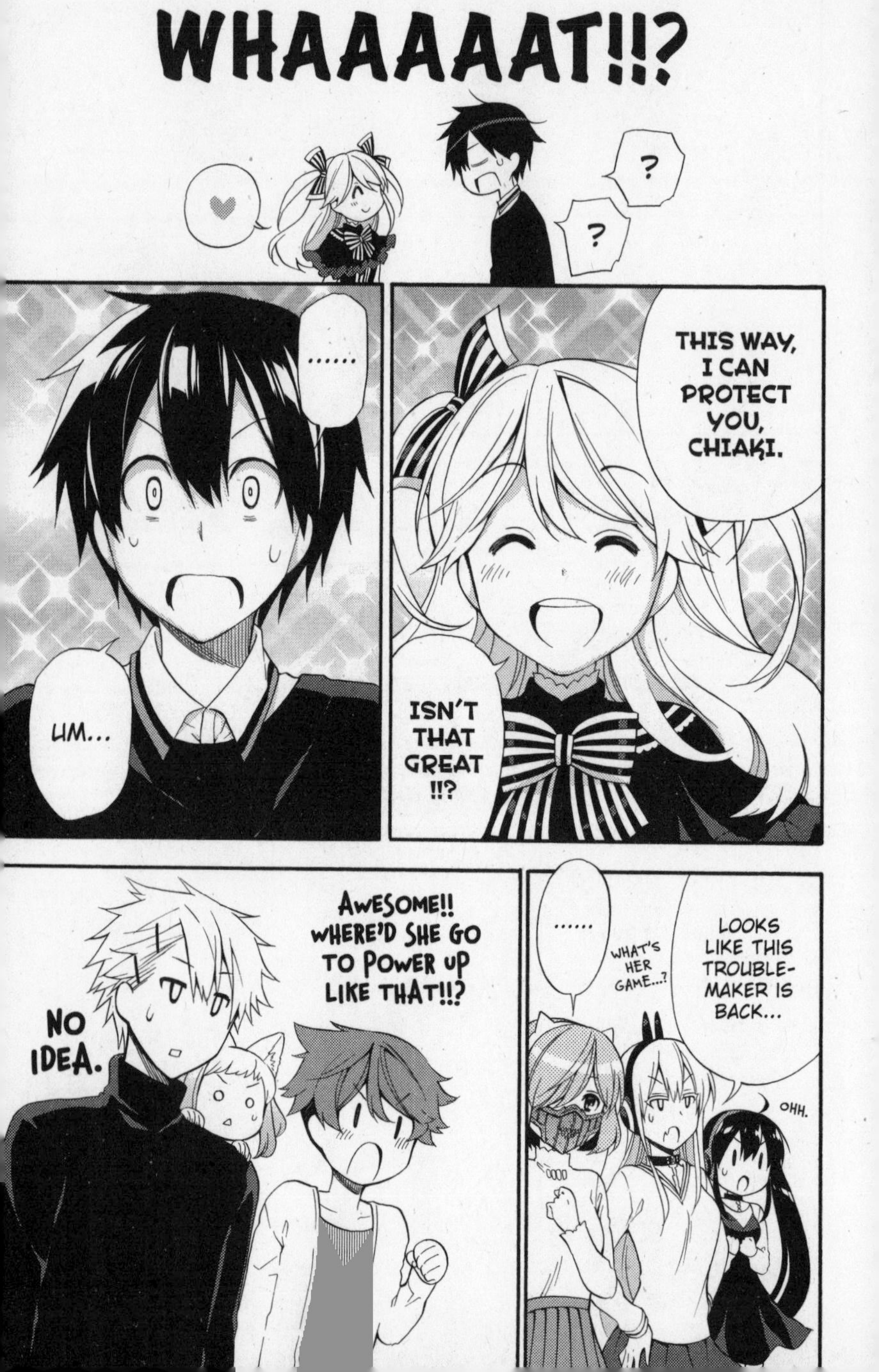
WHAAAAAT!!?
?
?
THIS WAY, I CAN PROTECT YOU, CHIAKI.
ISN'T THAT GREAT!!?
......
UM...
LOOKS LIKE THIS TROUBLE-MAKER IS BACK...
......
WHAT'S HER GAME...?
OHH.
AWESOME!! WHERE'D SHE GO TO POWER UP LIKE THAT!!?
NO IDEA.

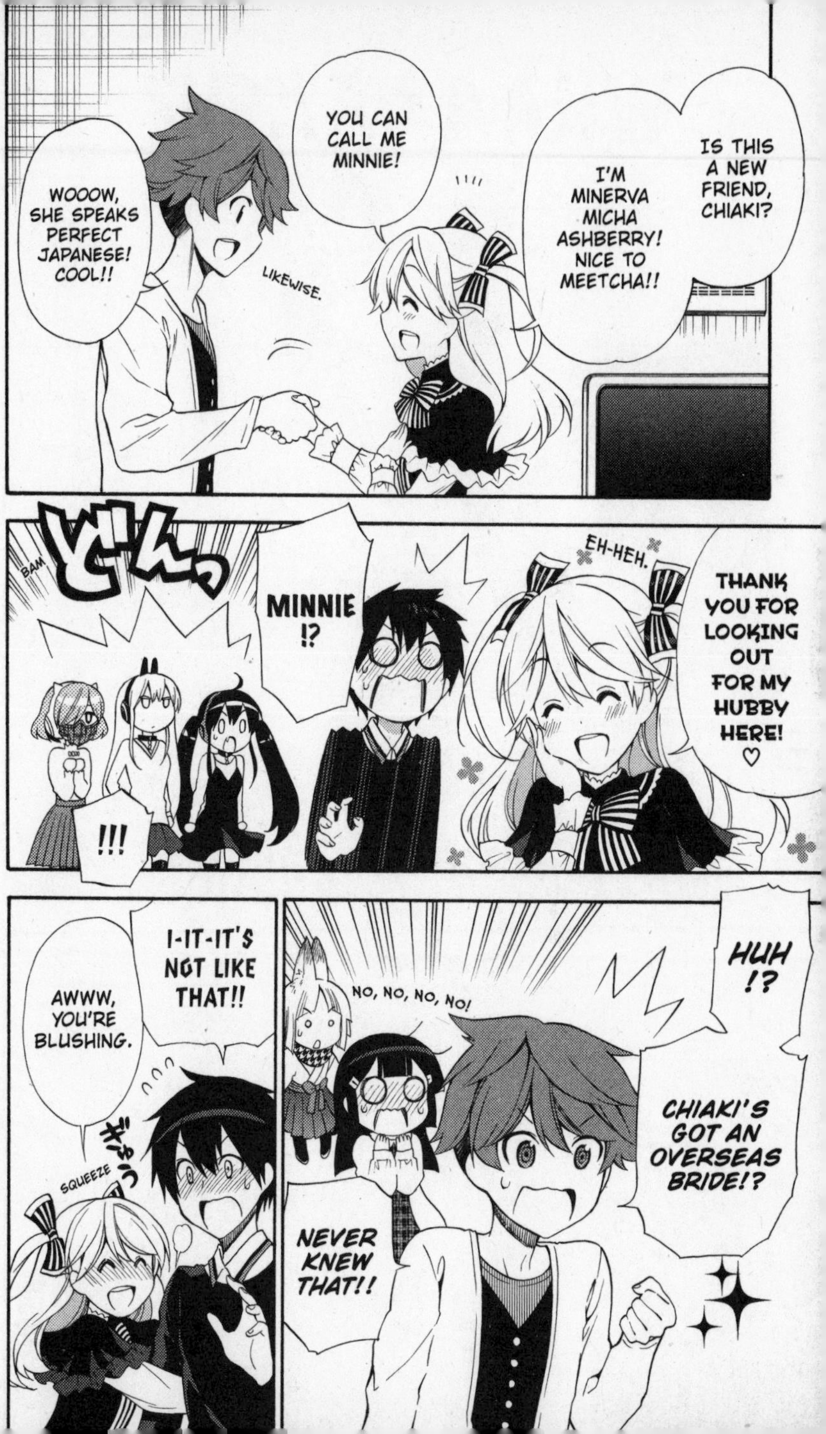
IS THIS A NEW FRIEND, CHIAKI?
I'M MINERVA MICHA ASHBERRY! NICE TO MEETCHA!!
YOU CAN CALL ME MINNIE!
LIKEWISE.
WOOOW, SHE SPEAKS PERFECT JAPANESE! COOL!!
THANK YOU FOR LOOKING OUT FOR MY HUBBY HERE! ♡
EH-HEH.
MINNIE !?
どんっ
BAM
!!!
HUH !?
CHIAKI'S GOT AN OVERSEAS BRIDE!?
NO, NO, NO, NO!
NEVER KNEW THAT!!
I-IT-IT'S NOT LIKE THAT!!
AWWW, YOU'RE BLUSHING.
ぎゅう
SQUEEZE

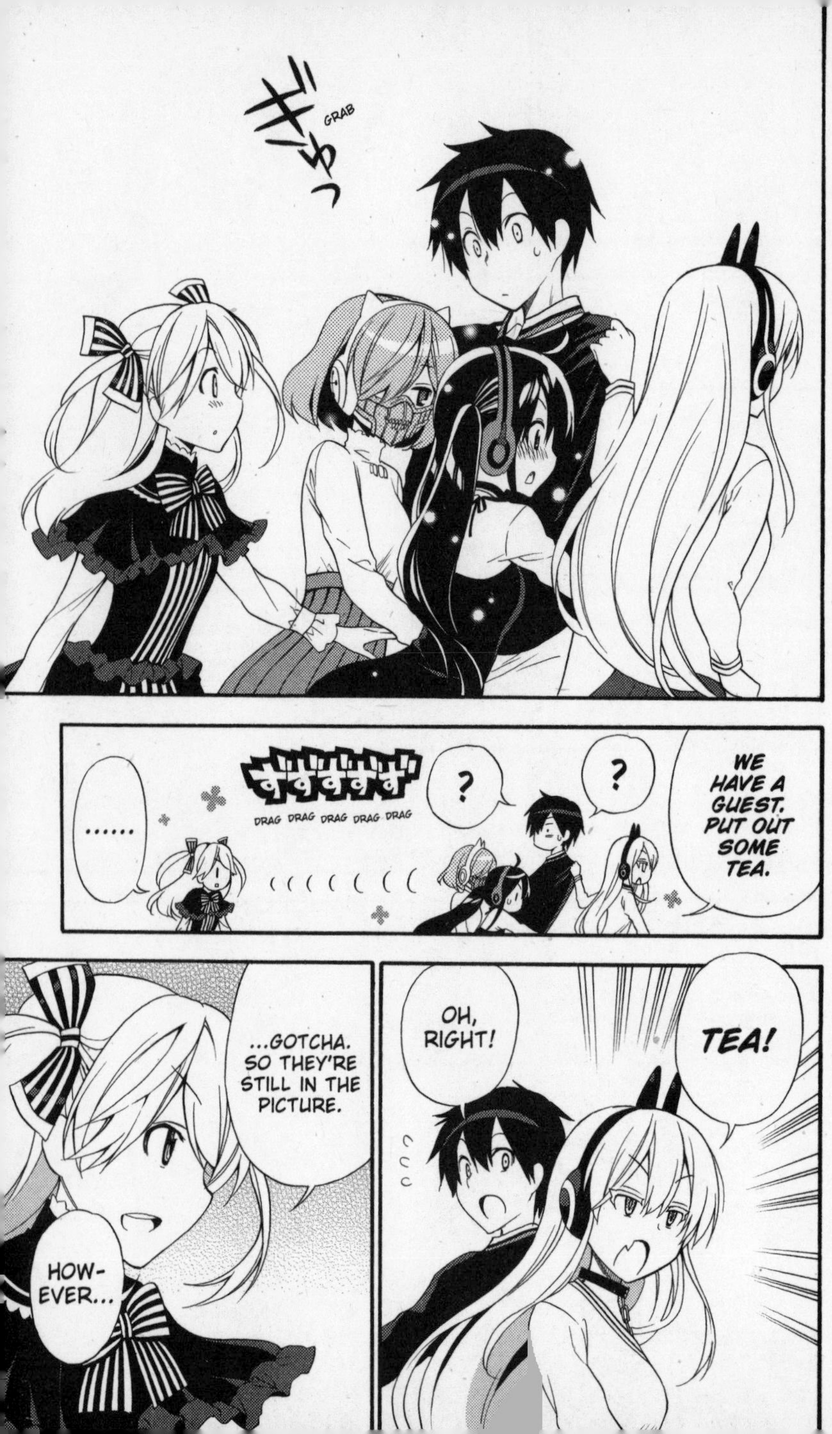
ぎゅっ
GRAB
WE HAVE A GUEST. PUT OUT SOME TEA.
?
?
ずずずずず
DRAG DRAG DRAG DRAG DRAG
......
TEA!
OH, RIGHT!
...GOTCHA. SO THEY'RE STILL IN THE PICTURE.
HOW-EVER...

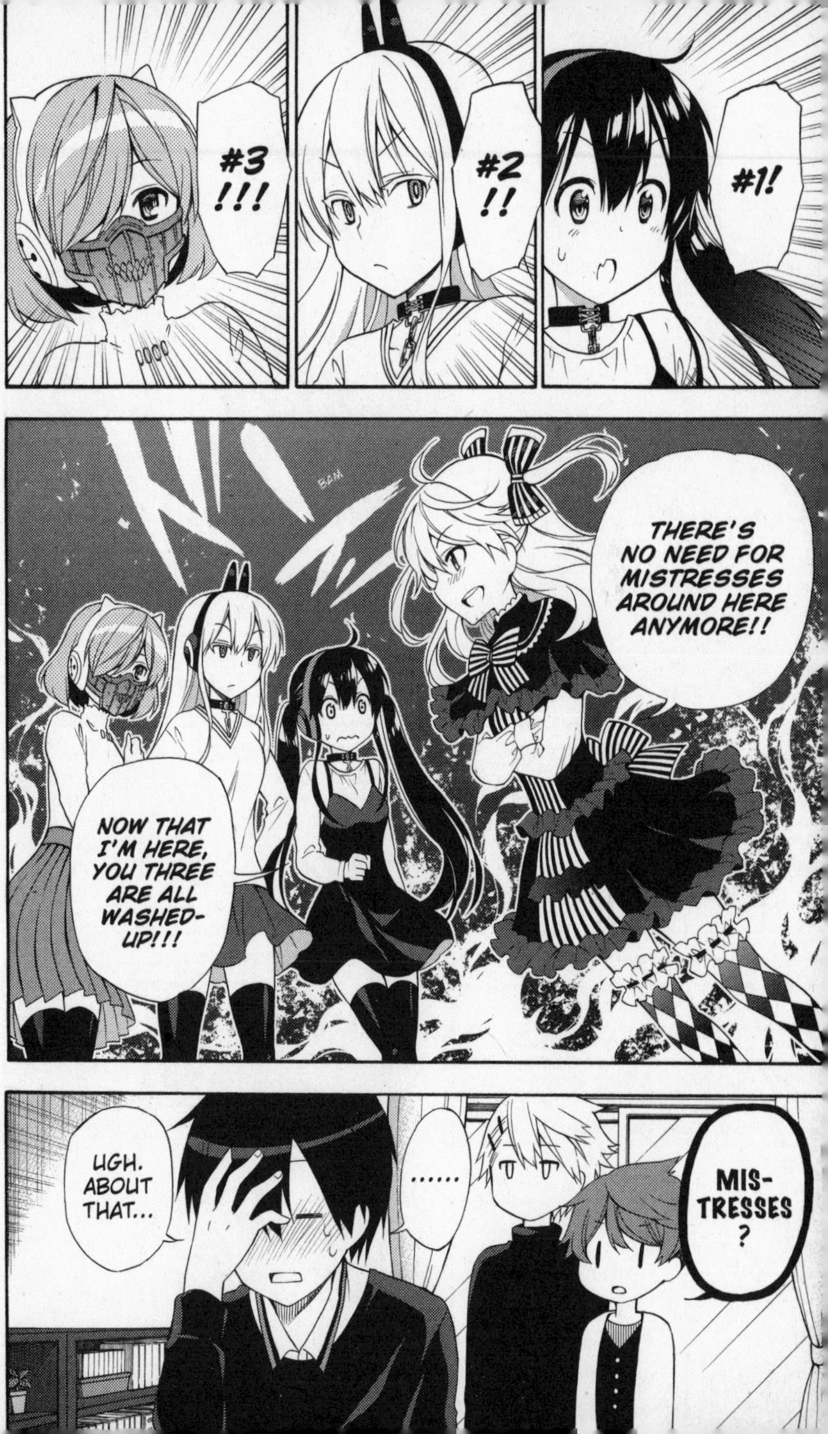
#1!
#2 !!
#3 !!!
BAM
THERE'S NO NEED FOR MISTRESSES AROUND HERE ANYMORE!!
NOW THAT I'M HERE, YOU THREE ARE ALL WASHED-UP!!!
MIS-TRESSES?
......
UGH. ABOUT THAT...

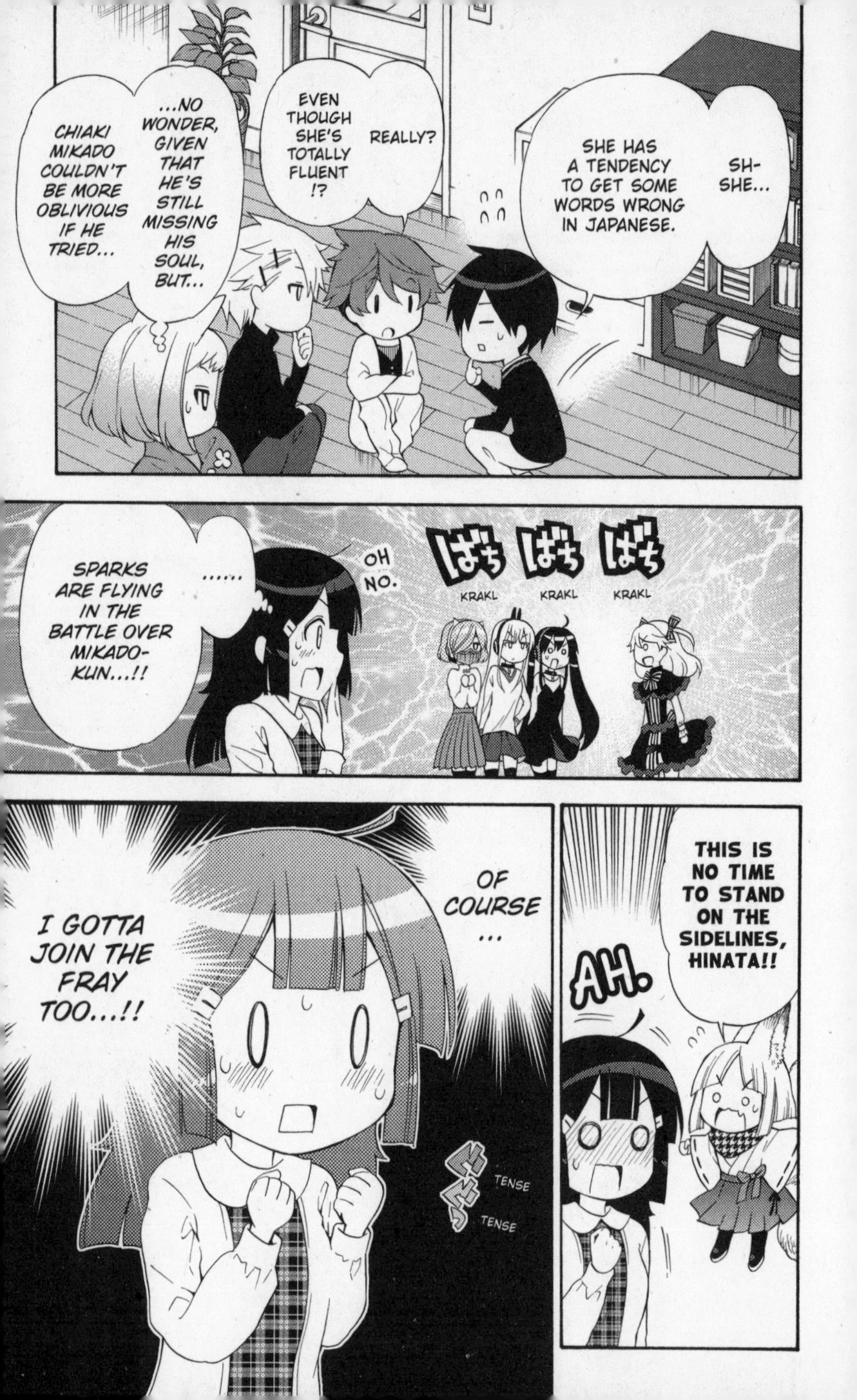
SH- SHE...
SHE HAS A TENDENCY TO GET SOME WORDS WRONG IN JAPANESE.
REALLY?
EVEN THOUGH SHE'S TOTALLY FLUENT!?
...NO WONDER, GIVEN THAT HE'S STILL MISSING HIS SOUL, BUT...
CHIAKI MIKADO COULDN'T BE MORE OBLIVIOUS IF HE TRIED...
ばち ばち ばち
KRAKL KRAKL KRAKL
OH NO.
......
SPARKS ARE FLYING IN THE BATTLE OVER MIKADO-KUN...!!
THIS IS NO TIME TO STAND ON THE SIDELINES, HINATA!!
AH.
OF COURSE...
TENSE
TENSE
I GOTTA JOIN THE FRAY TOO...!!

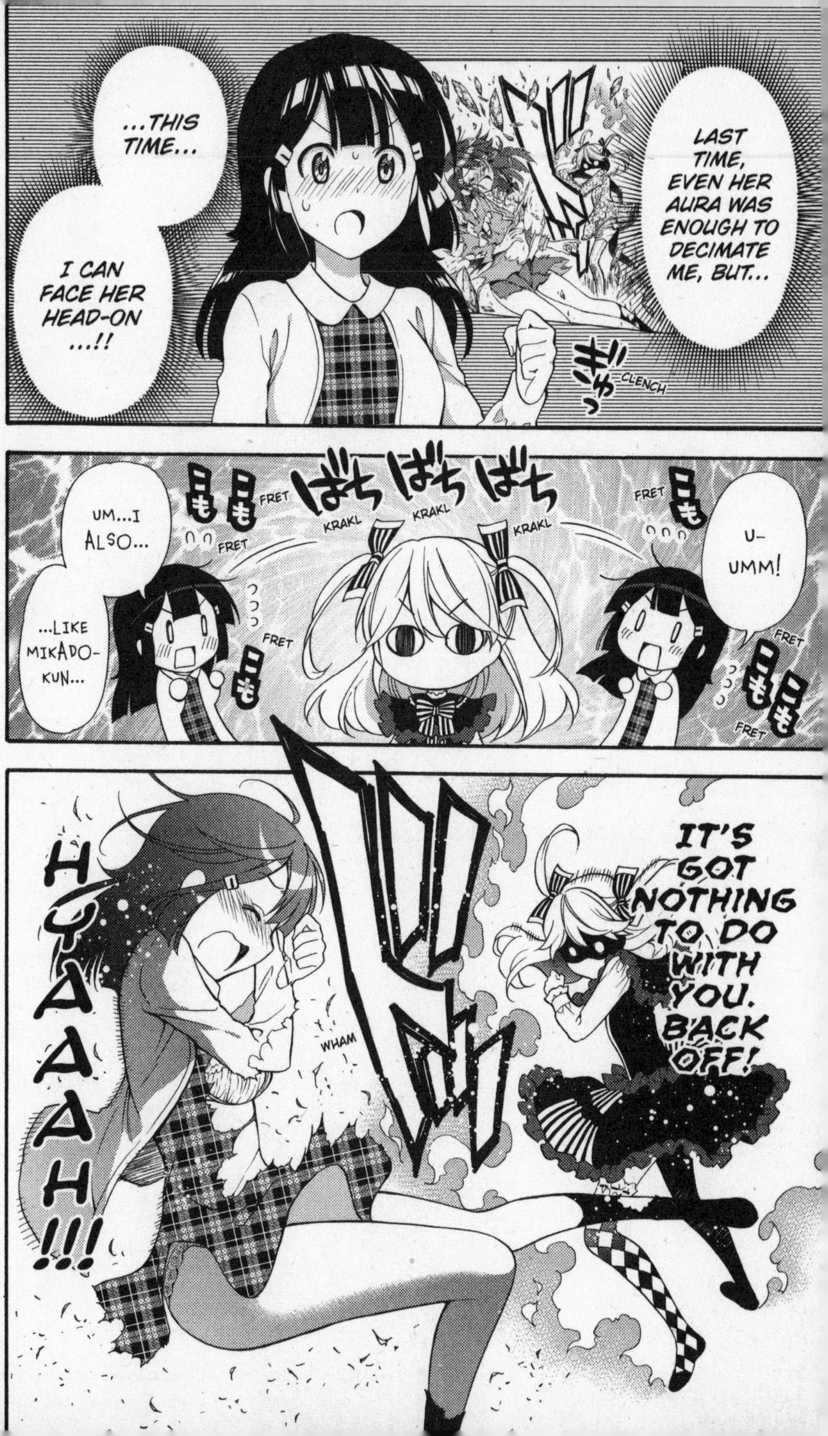
LAST TIME, EVEN HER AURA WAS ENOUGH TO DECIMATE ME, BUT...
...THIS TIME...
I CAN FACE HER HEAD-ON ...!!
CLENCH
U-UMM!
FRET
FRET
KRAKL
KRAKL
KRAKL
FRET
FRET
UM...I ALSO...
...LIKE MIKADO-KUN...
FRET
IT'S GOT NOTHING TO DO WITH YOU. BACK OFF!
WHAM
HYAAAAH!!!

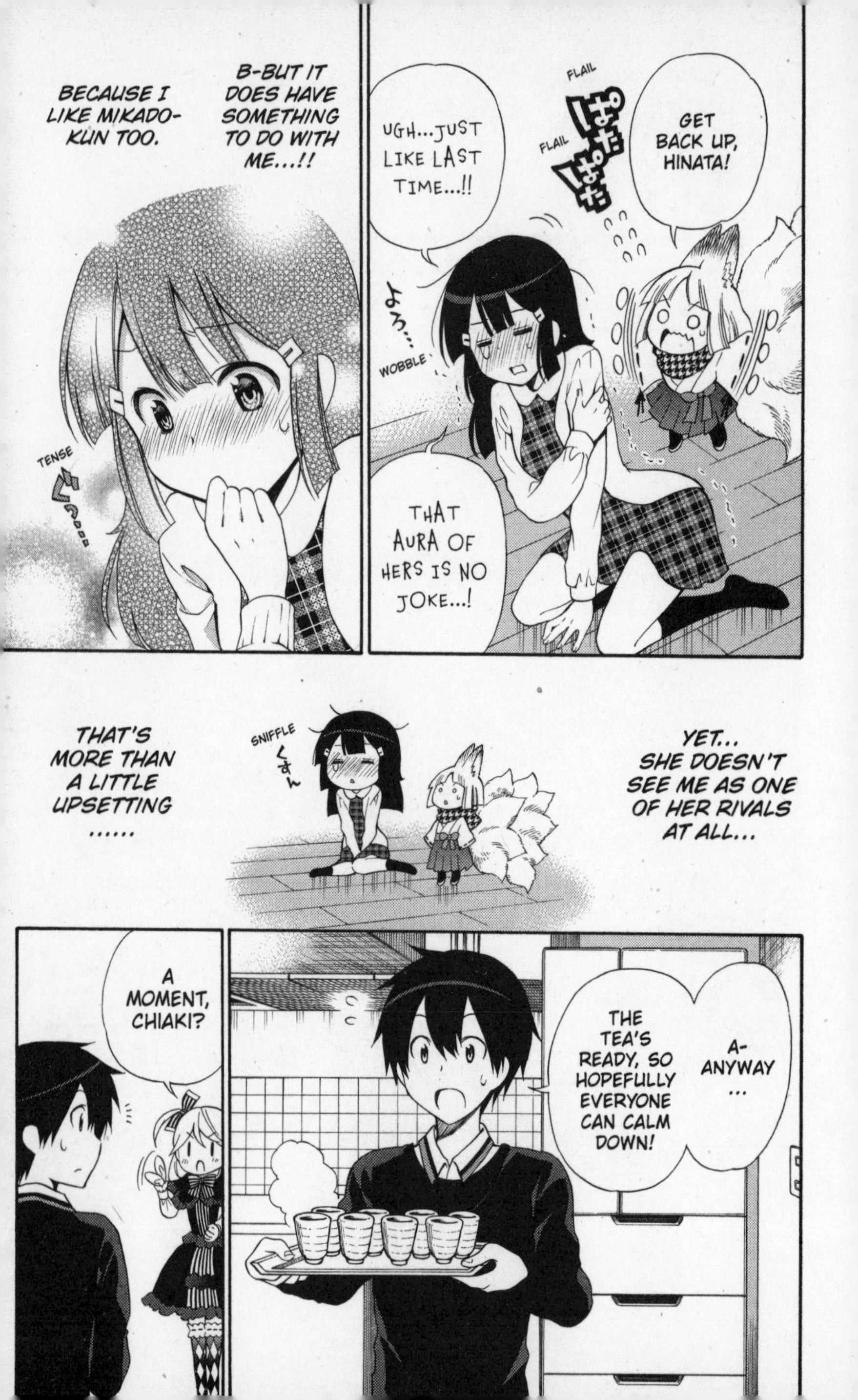
GET BACK UP, HINATA!
FLAIL
FLAIL
ぱたぱた
UGH...JUST LIKE LAST TIME...!!
よろ...
WOBBLE
THAT AURA OF HERS IS NO JOKE...!
B-BUT IT DOES HAVE SOMETHING TO DO WITH ME...!!
BECAUSE I LIKE MIKADO-KUN TOO.
TENSE
YET... SHE DOESN'T SEE ME AS ONE OF HER RIVALS AT ALL...
SNIFFLE
くすん
THAT'S MORE THAN A LITTLE UPSETTING......
A-ANYWAY...
THE TEA'S READY, SO HOPEFULLY EVERYONE CAN CALM DOWN!
A MOMENT, CHIAKI?

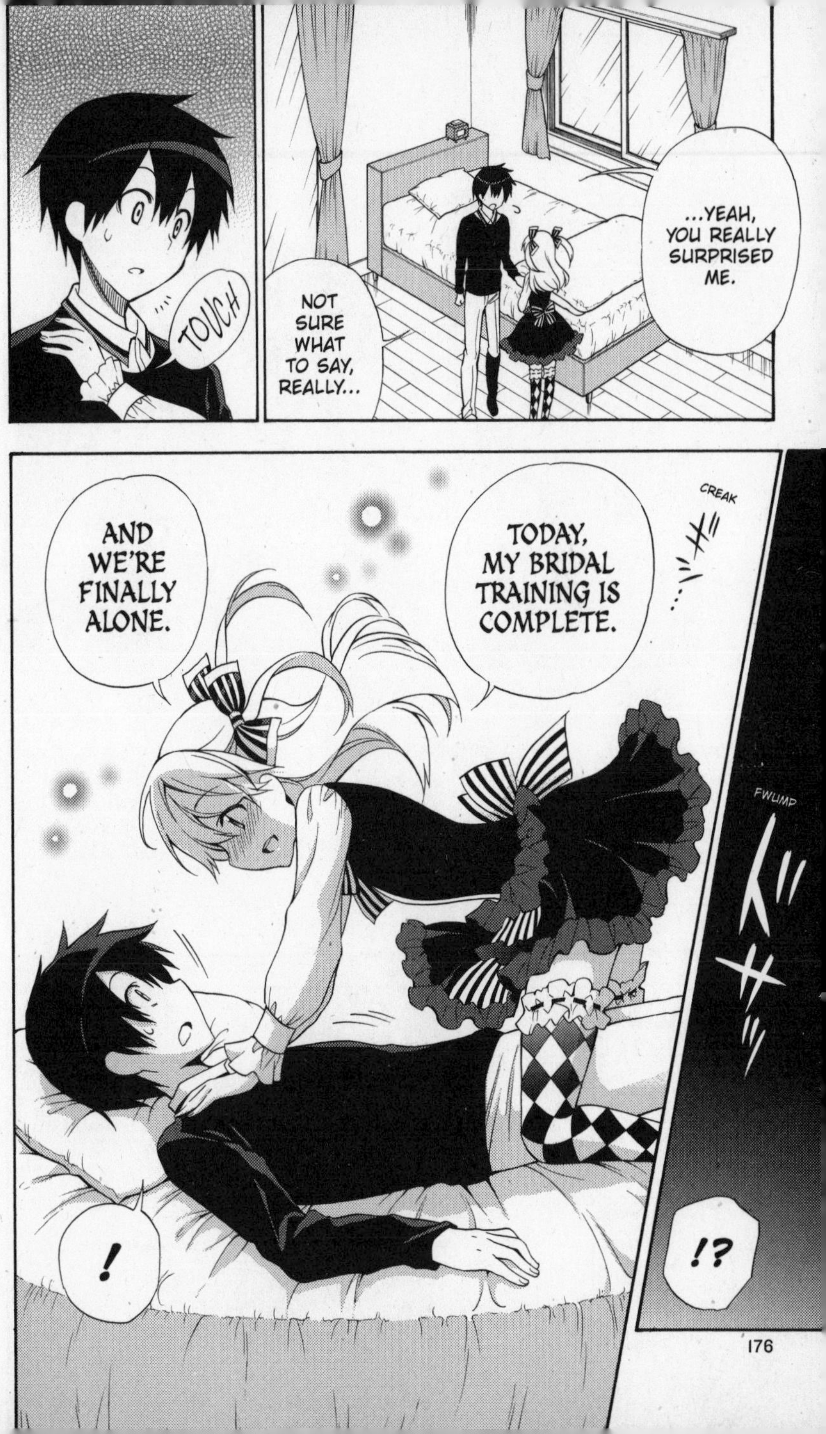
...YEAH, YOU REALLY SURPRISED ME.
NOT SURE WHAT TO SAY, REALLY...
TOUCH
CREAK
TODAY, MY BRIDAL TRAINING IS COMPLETE.
AND WE'RE FINALLY ALONE.
FWUMP
!?
!

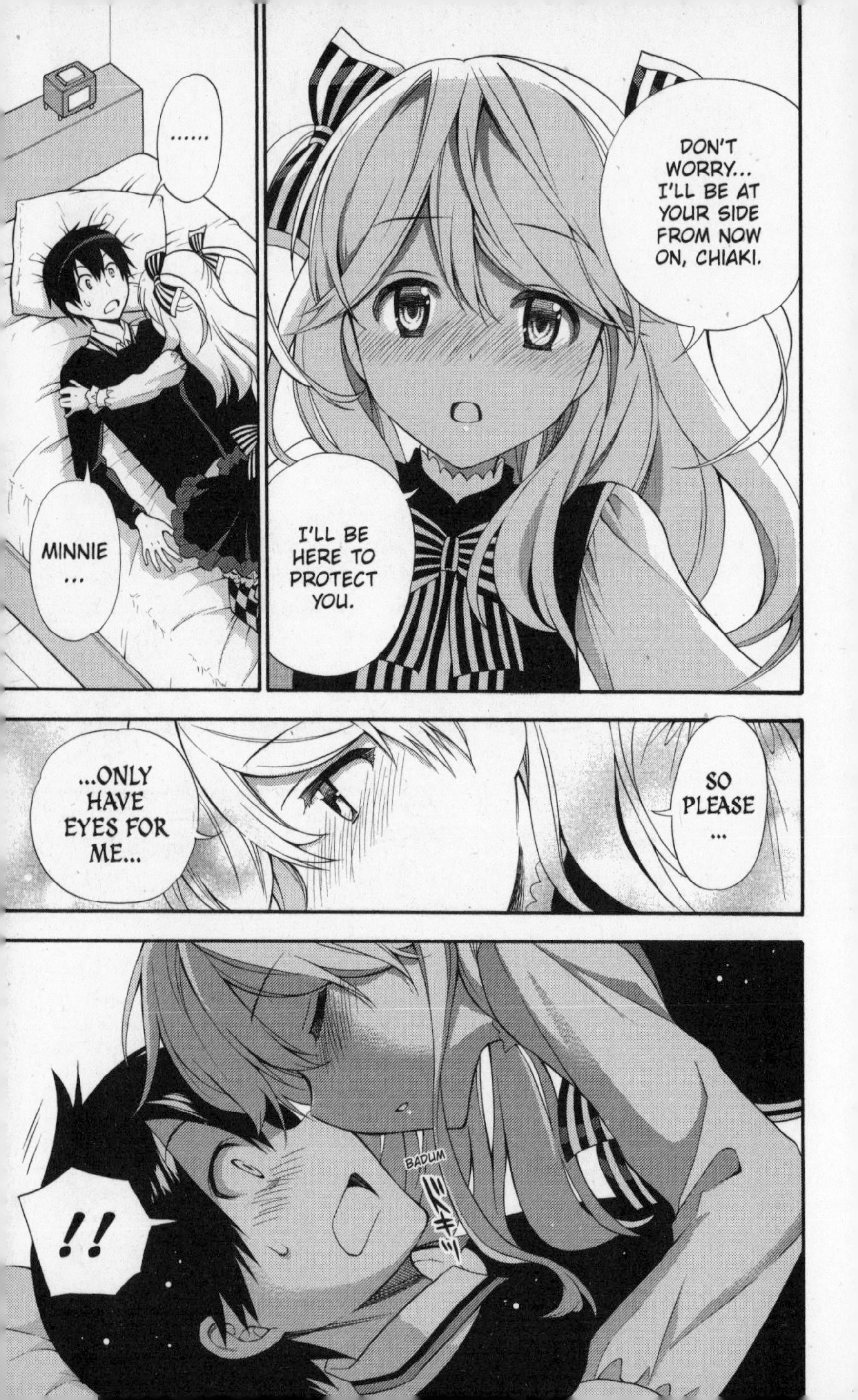
DON'T WORRY... I'LL BE AT YOUR SIDE FROM NOW ON, CHIAKI.
I'LL BE HERE TO PROTECT YOU.
......
MINNIE ...
SO PLEASE ...
...ONLY HAVE EYES FOR ME...
BADUM
!!

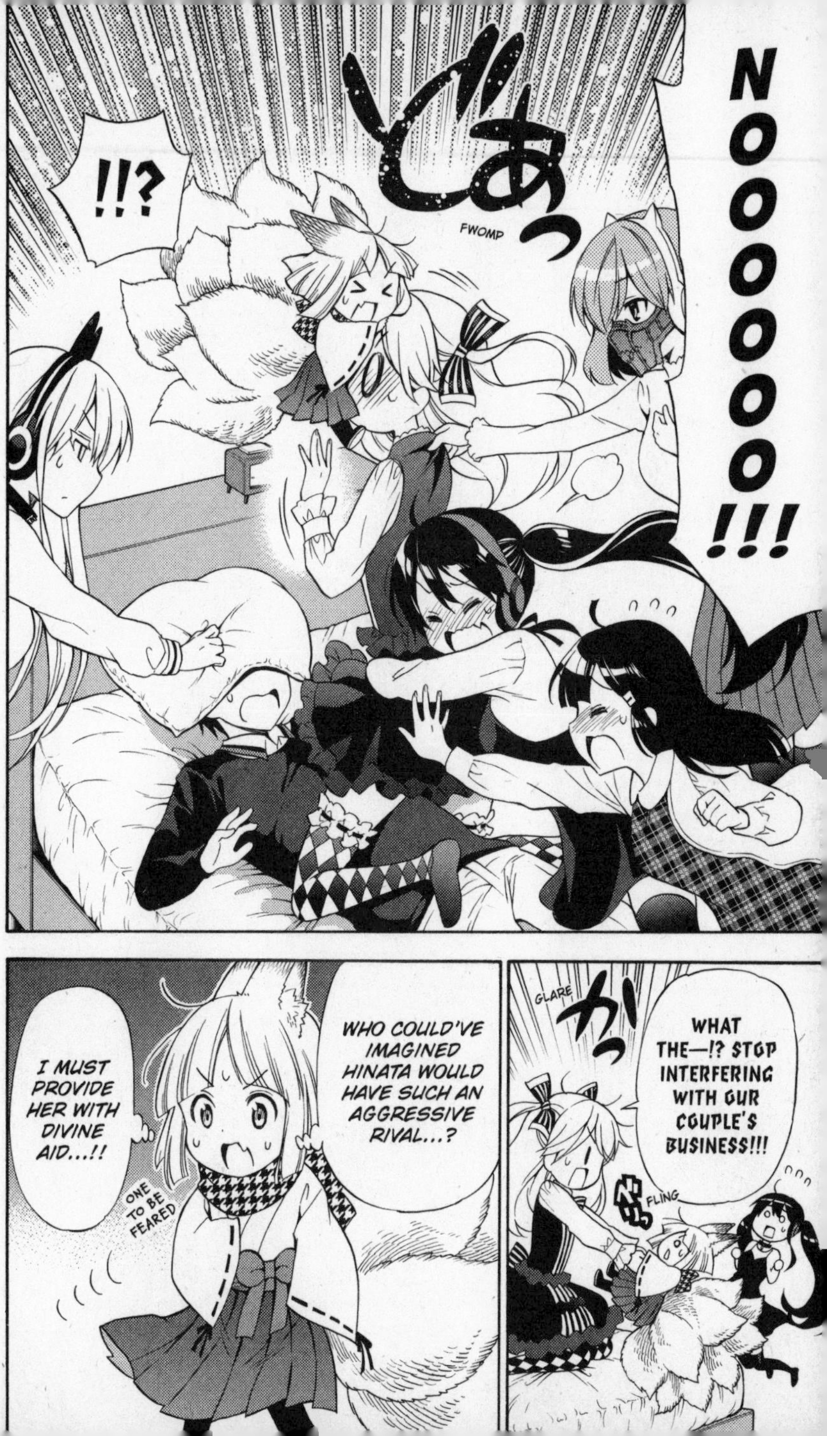
NOOOOOOO!!!
どあっ
FWOMP
!!?
GLARE
かっ
WHAT THE—!? STOP INTERFERING WITH OUR COUPLE'S BUSINESS!!!
FLING
WHO COULD'VE IMAGINED HINATA WOULD HAVE SUCH AN AGGRESSIVE RIVAL...?
I MUST PROVIDE HER WITH DIVINE AID...!!
ONE TO BE FEARED

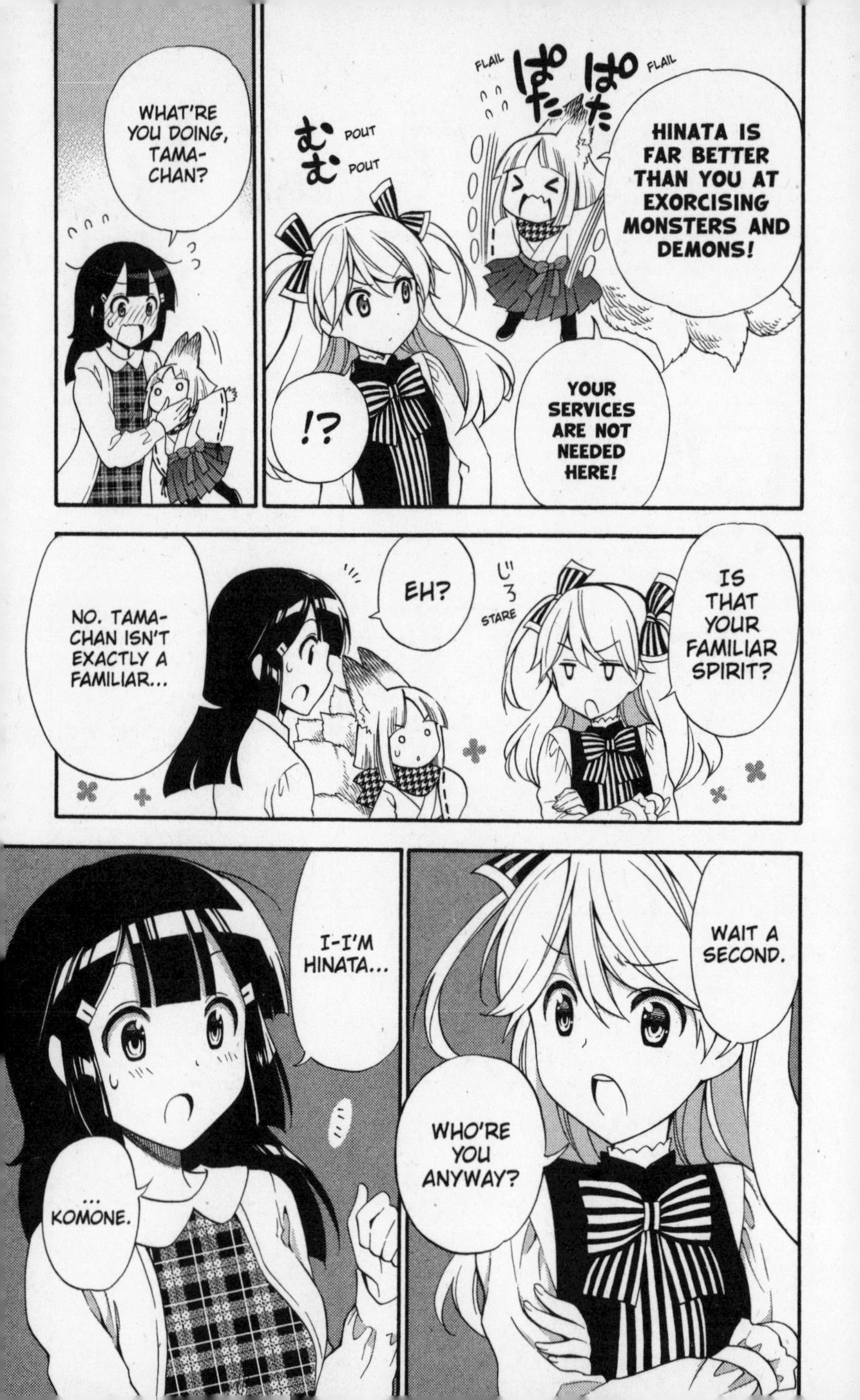
FLAIL
ぱた ぱた
FLAIL
HINATA IS FAR BETTER THAN YOU AT EXORCISING MONSTERS AND DEMONS!
むむ
POUT POUT
YOUR SERVICES ARE NOT NEEDED HERE!
!?
WHAT'RE YOU DOING, TAMA-CHAN?
IS THAT YOUR FAMILIAR SPIRIT?
じろ
STARE
EH?
NO. TAMA-CHAN ISN'T EXACTLY A FAMILIAR...
WAIT A SECOND.
WHO'RE YOU ANYWAY?
I-I'M HINATA...
...KOMONE.

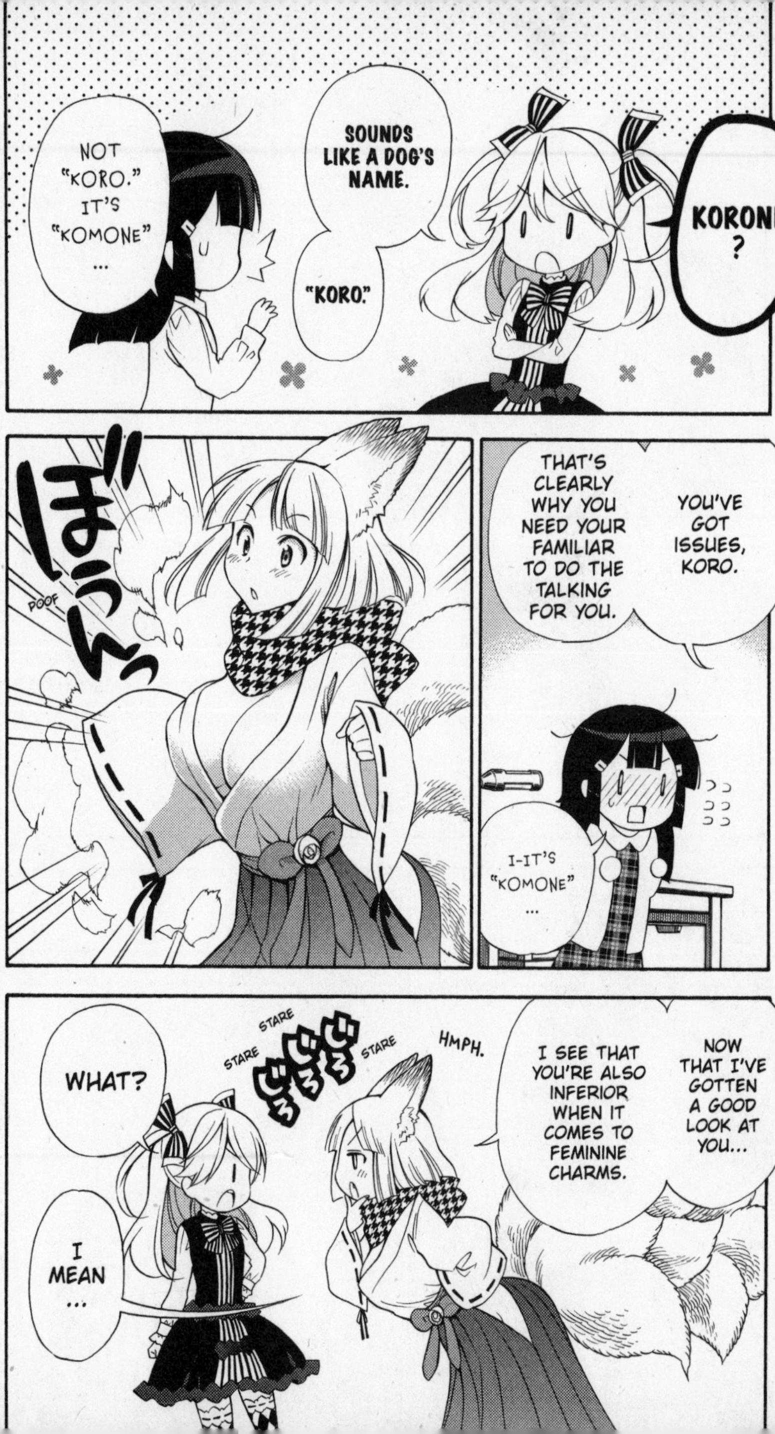
KORONE?
SOUNDS LIKE A DOG'S NAME.
"KORO."
NOT "KORO." IT'S "KOMONE"...
YOU'VE GOT ISSUES, KORO.
THAT'S CLEARLY WHY YOU NEED YOUR FAMILIAR TO DO THE TALKING FOR YOU.
I-IT'S "KOMONE"...
ぼうんっ
POOF
NOW THAT I'VE GOTTEN A GOOD LOOK AT YOU...
I SEE THAT YOU'RE ALSO INFERIOR WHEN IT COMES TO FEMININE CHARMS.
HMPH.
じろじろじろ
STARE
STARE
STARE
WHAT?
I MEAN...

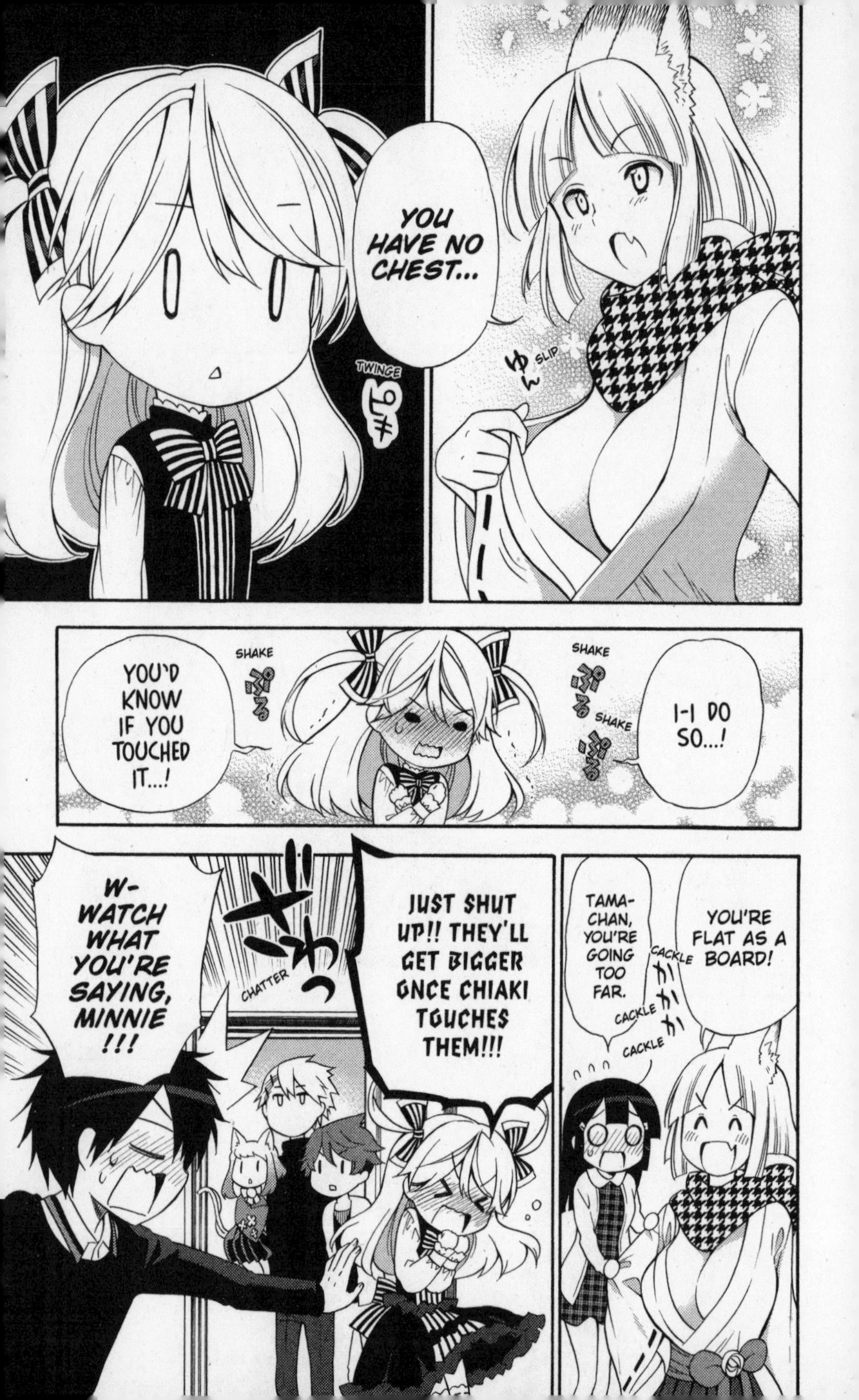
YOU HAVE NO CHEST...
SLIP
ゆん
TWINGE
ピキ
I-I DO SO...!
SHAKE
SHAKE
SHAKE
YOU'D KNOW IF YOU TOUCHED IT...!
YOU'RE FLAT AS A BOARD!
TAMA-CHAN, YOU'RE GOING TOO FAR.
CACKLE
か
CACKLE
か
CACKLE
か
JUST SHUT UP!! THEY'LL GET BIGGER ONCE CHIAKI TOUCHES THEM!!!
CHATTER
ざわっ
W-WATCH WHAT YOU'RE SAYING, MINNIE!!!

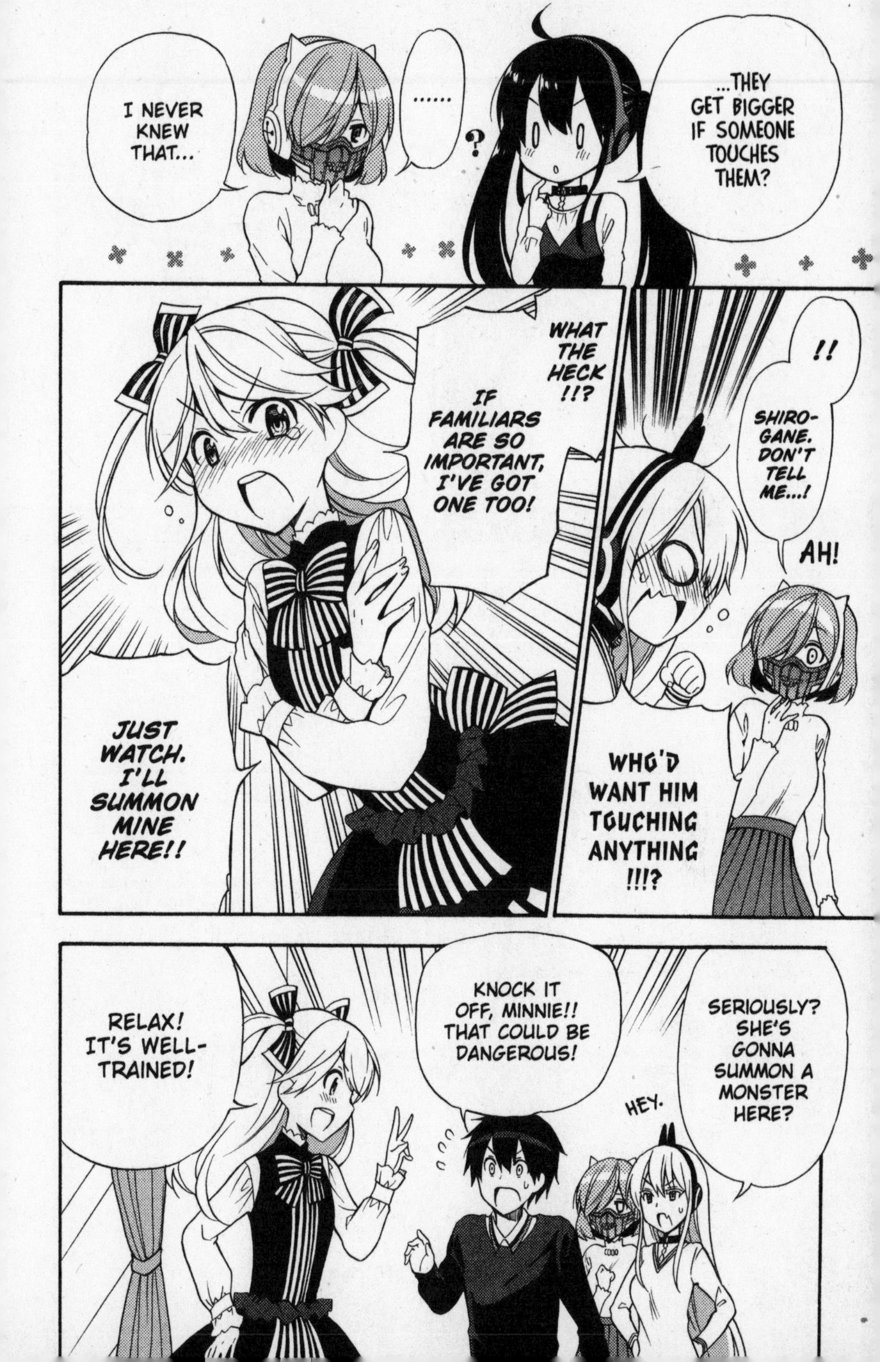
...THEY GET BIGGER IF SOMEONE TOUCHES THEM?
......
I NEVER KNEW THAT...
!!
SHIRO-GANE. DON'T TELL ME...!
AH!
WHO'D WANT HIM TOUCHING ANYTHING!!!?
WHAT THE HECK!!?
IF FAMILIARS ARE SO IMPORTANT, I'VE GOT ONE TOO!
JUST WATCH. I'LL SUMMON MINE HERE!!
SERIOUSLY? SHE'S GONNA SUMMON A MONSTER HERE?
HEY.
KNOCK IT OFF, MINNIE!! THAT COULD BE DANGEROUS!
RELAX! IT'S WELL-TRAINED!

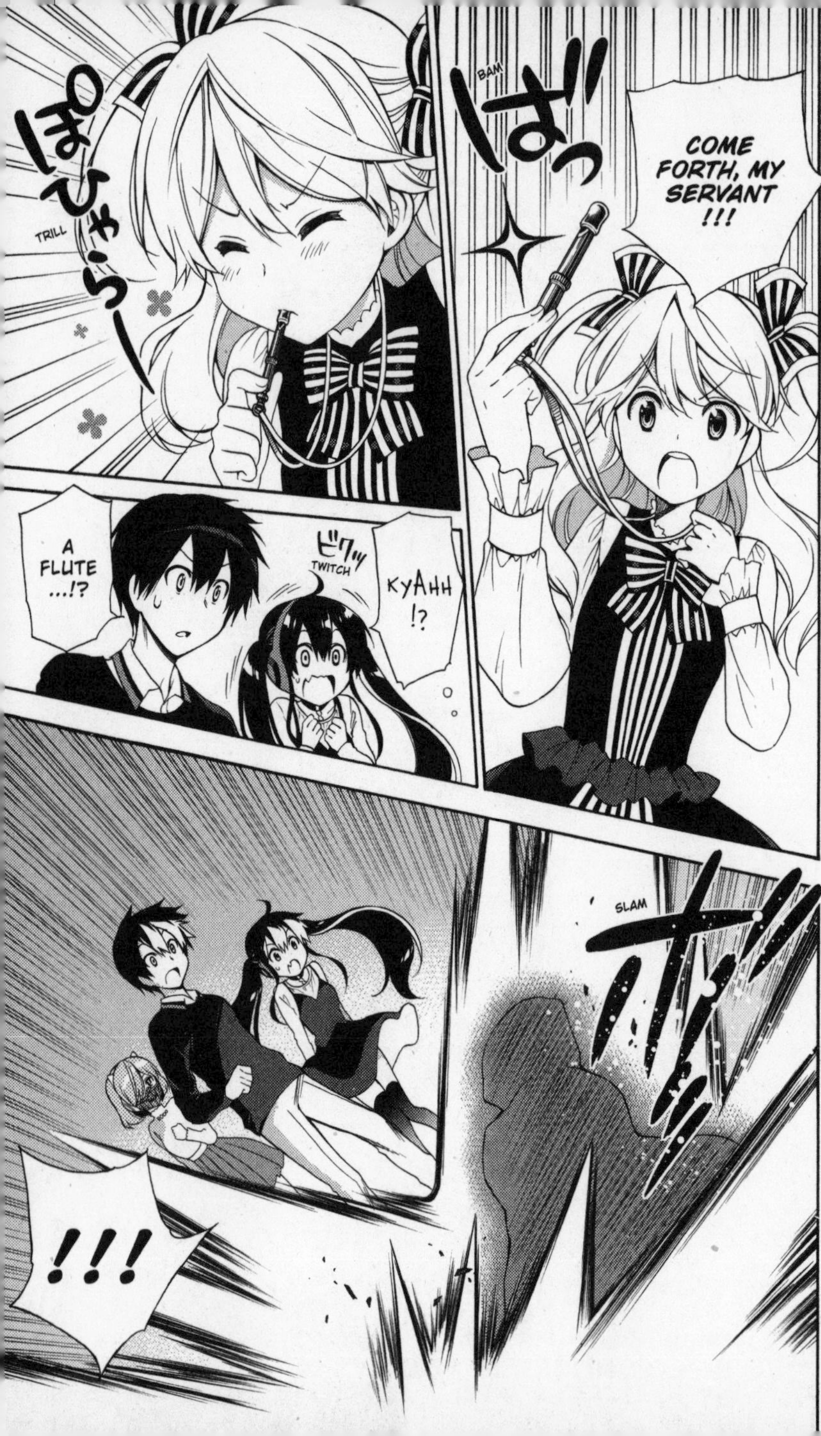

ばっ
BAM
COME FORTH, MY SERVANT!!!
ぽひゃら〜
TRILL
KYAHH!?
ビクッ
TWITCH
A FLUTE...!?
SLAM
!!!

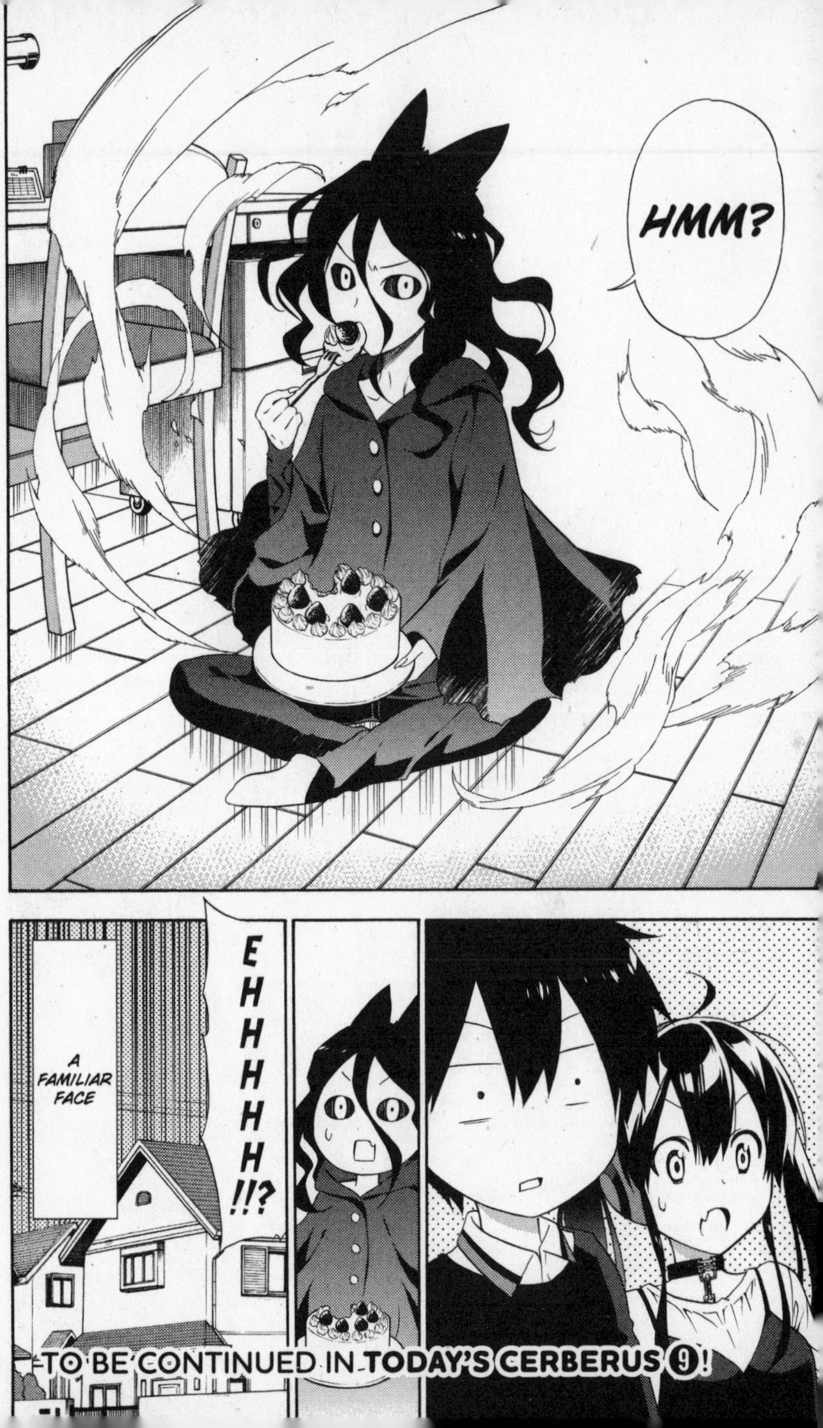
HMM?
EHHHHH!!?
A FAMILIAR FACE
TO BE CONTINUED IN TODAY'S CERBERUS 9!

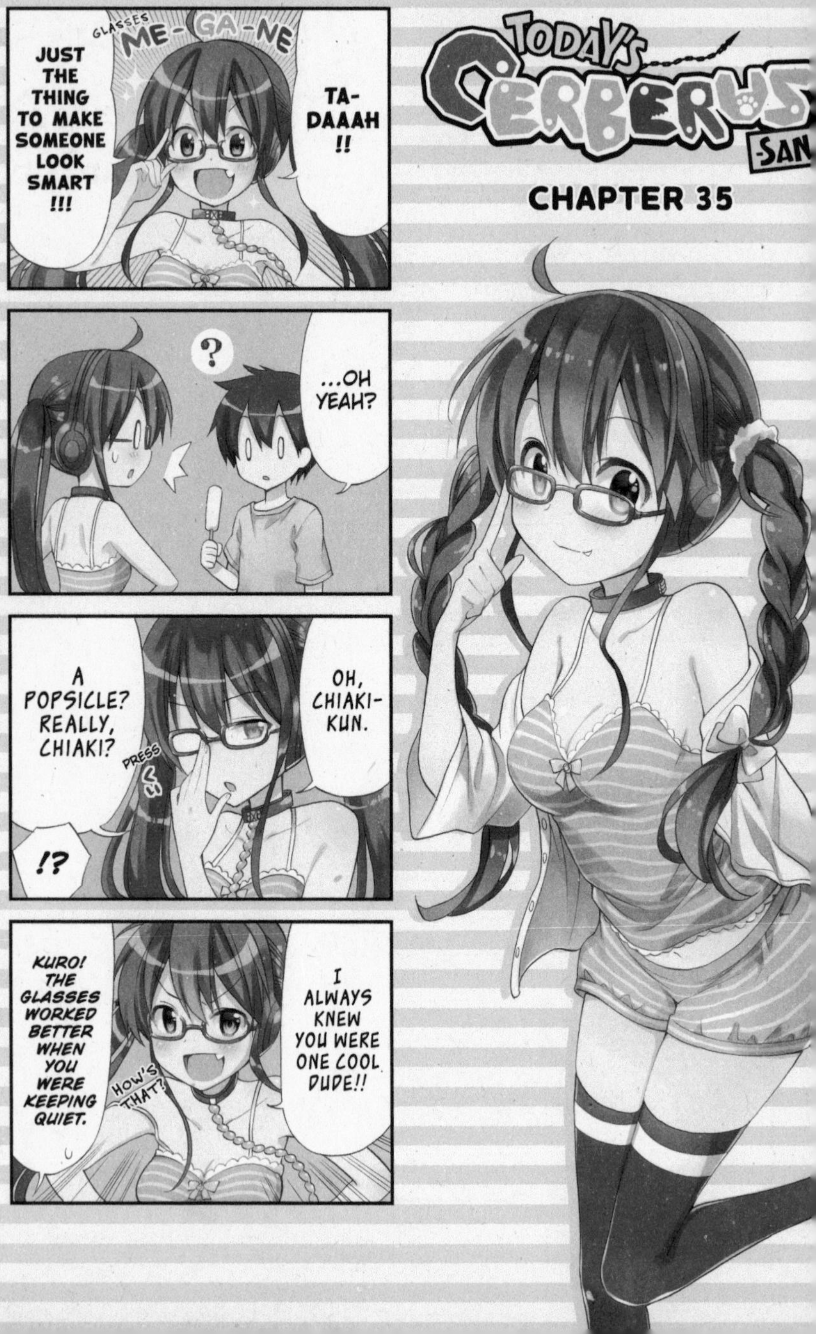
TODAY'S CERBERUS-SAN
CHAPTER 35
TA-DAAAH!!
GLASSES
ME-GA-NE
JUST THE THING TO MAKE SOMEONE LOOK SMART!!!
...OH YEAH?
?
OH, CHIAKI-KUN.
A POPSICLE? REALLY, CHIAKI?
PRESS
!?
I ALWAYS KNEW YOU WERE ONE COOL DUDE!!
HOW'S THAT?
KURO! THE GLASSES WORKED BETTER WHEN YOU WERE KEEPING QUIET.

TODAY'S CERBERUS-SAN

CHAPTER 36

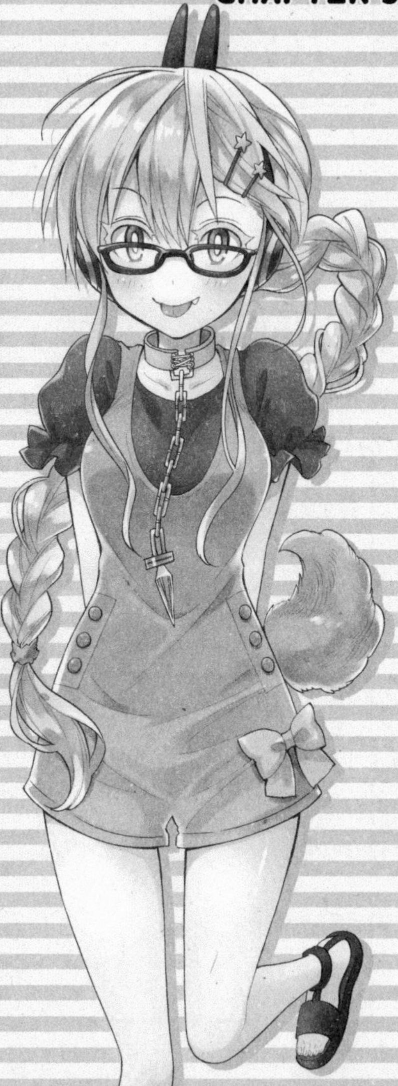

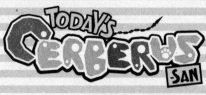

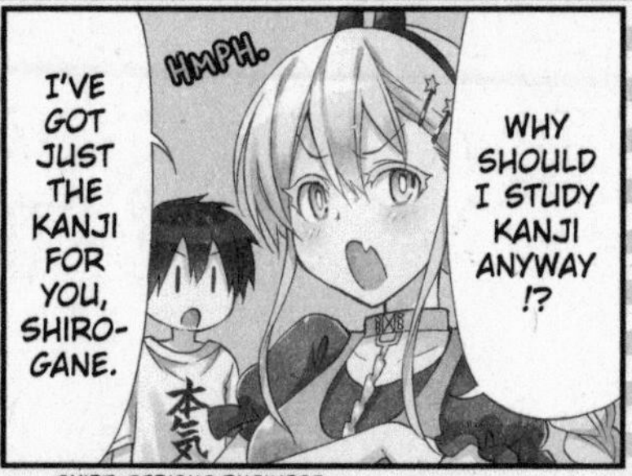
WHY SHOULD I STUDY KANJI ANYWAY!?
HMPH.
I'VE GOT JUST THE KANJI FOR YOU, SHIROGANE.
本気

SHIRT: SERIOUS BUSINESS

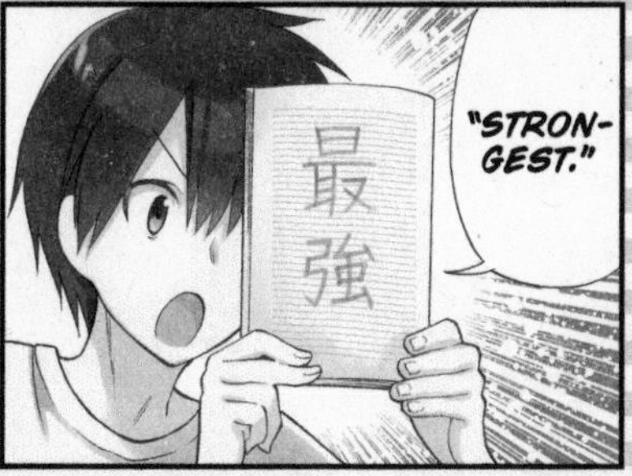
"STRONGEST."
最強

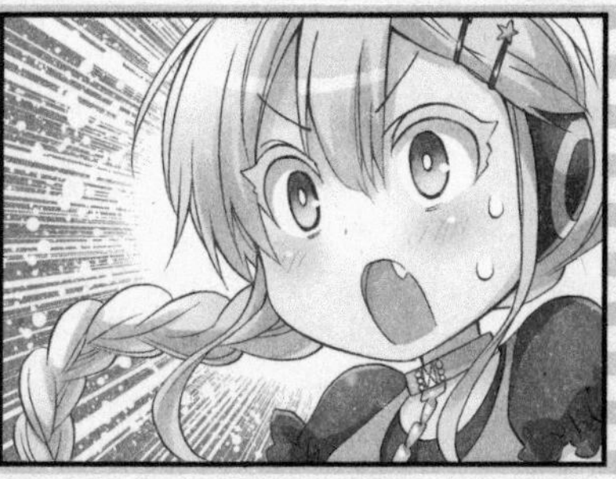

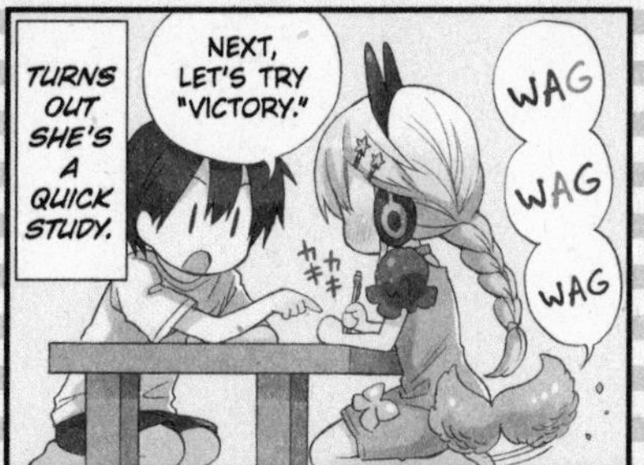
WAG
WAG
WAG
NEXT, LET'S TRY "VICTORY."
TURNS OUT SHE'S A QUICK STUDY.
カキカキ

SFX: SKRITCH SKRITCH

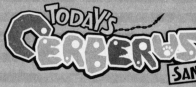

TODAY'S CERBERUS -SAN

CHAPTER 37

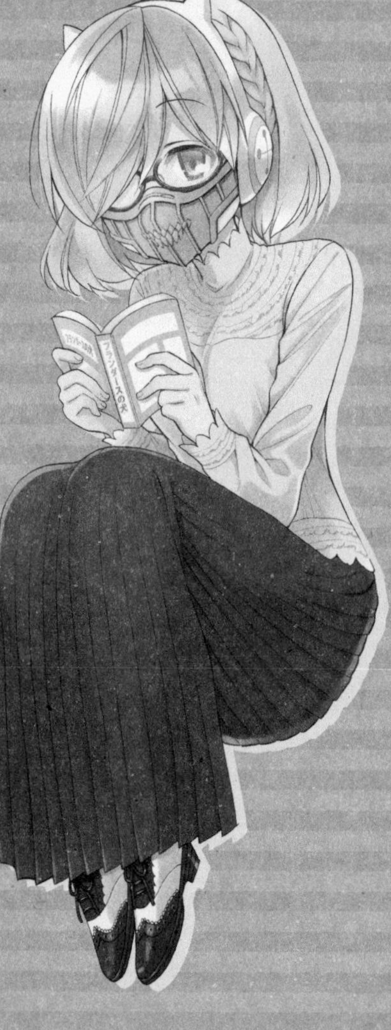
フランダースの犬

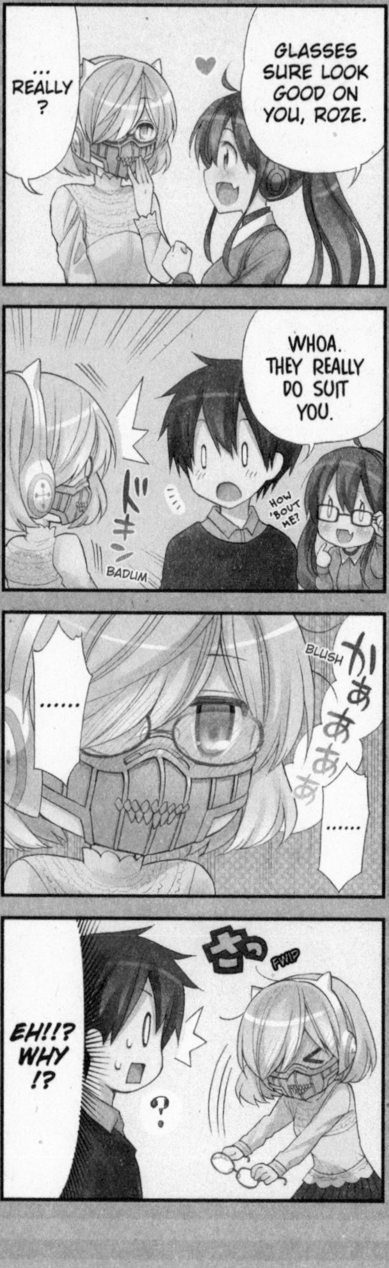
GLASSES SURE LOOK GOOD ON YOU, ROZE.
... REALLY ?
WHOA. THEY REALLY DO SUIT YOU.
ドキン
BADUM
...
HOW 'BOUT ME?
かぁあああ
BLUSH
......
......
さっ
FWIP
EH!!? WHY !?

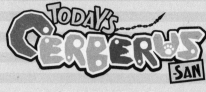

TODAY'S CERBERUS -SAN

CHAPTER 38

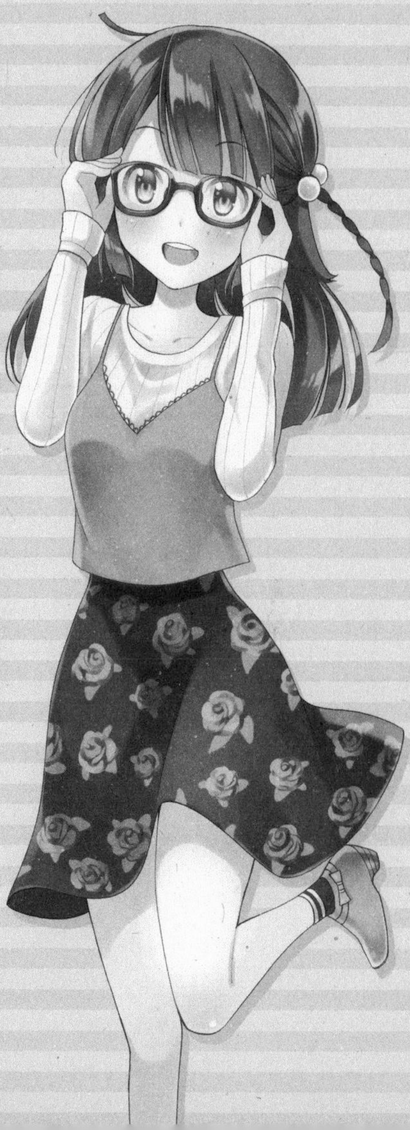

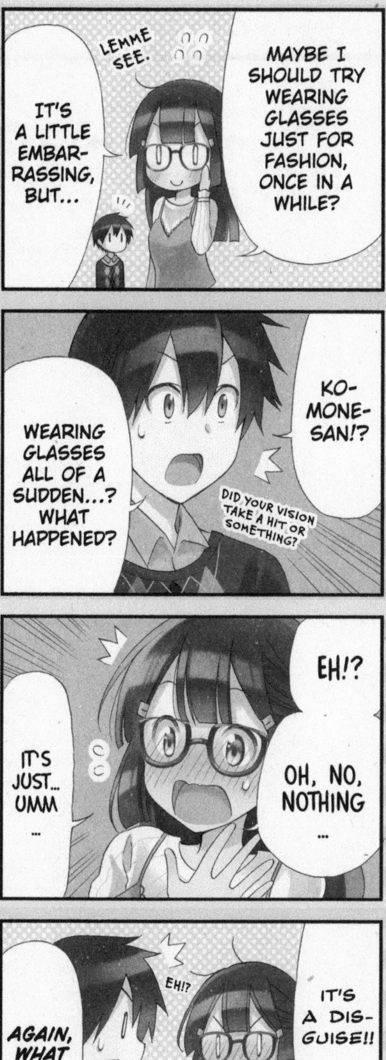
MAYBE I SHOULD TRY WEARING GLASSES JUST FOR FASHION, ONCE IN A WHILE?
LEMME SEE.
IT'S A LITTLE EMBARRASSING, BUT...
KO-MONE-SAN!?
DID YOUR VISION TAKE A HIT OR SOMETHING?
WEARING GLASSES ALL OF A SUDDEN...? WHAT HAPPENED?
EH!?
OH, NO, NOTHING...
IT'S JUST... UMM...
IT'S A DISGUISE!!
EH!?
AGAIN, WHAT HAPPENED!!?

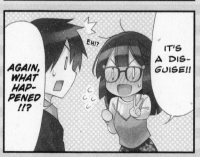

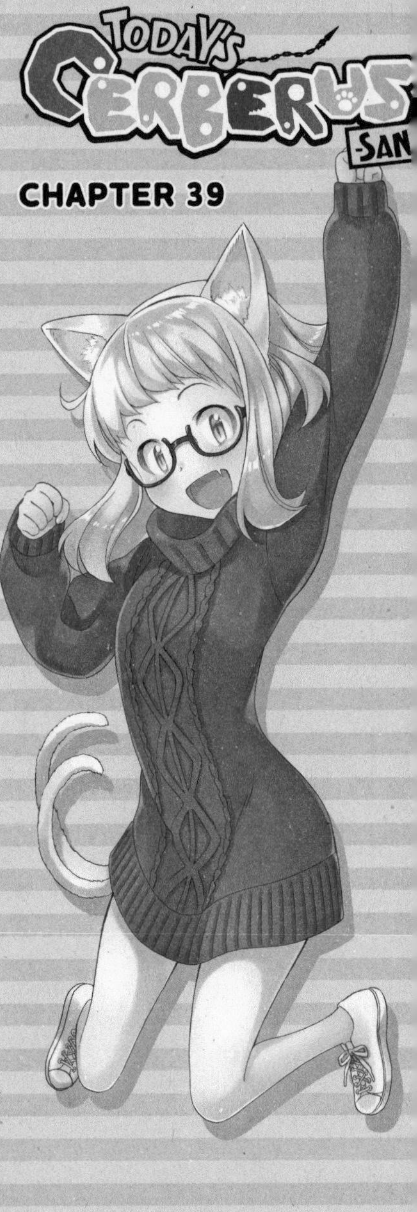
TODAY'S CERBERUS-SAN
CHAPTER 39

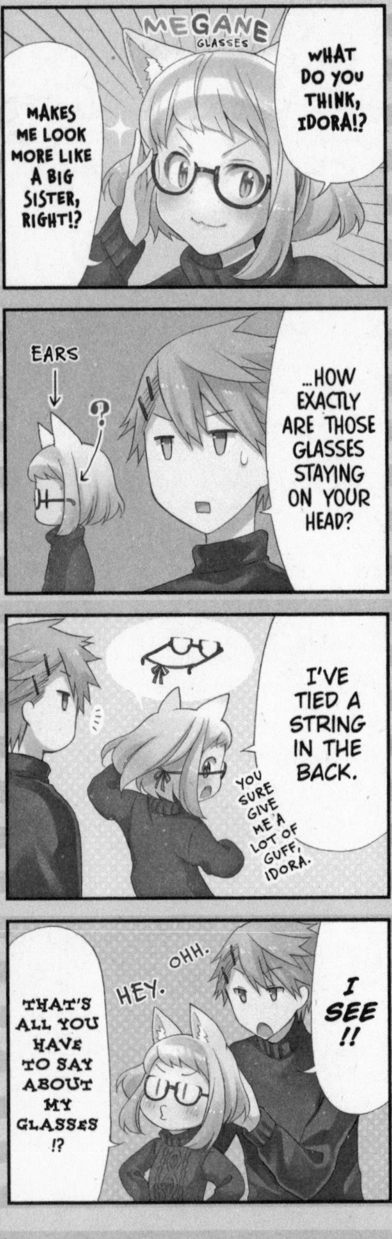
MEGANE
GLASSES
WHAT DO YOU THINK, IDORA!?
MAKES ME LOOK MORE LIKE A BIG SISTER, RIGHT!?
...HOW EXACTLY ARE THOSE GLASSES STAYING ON YOUR HEAD?
EARS
?
I'VE TIED A STRING IN THE BACK.
YOU SURE GIVE ME A LOT OF GUFF, IDORA.
I SEE!!
OHH.
HEY.
THAT'S ALL YOU HAVE TO SAY ABOUT MY GLASSES!?

TODAY'S CERBERUS -SAN

CHAPTER 39.5

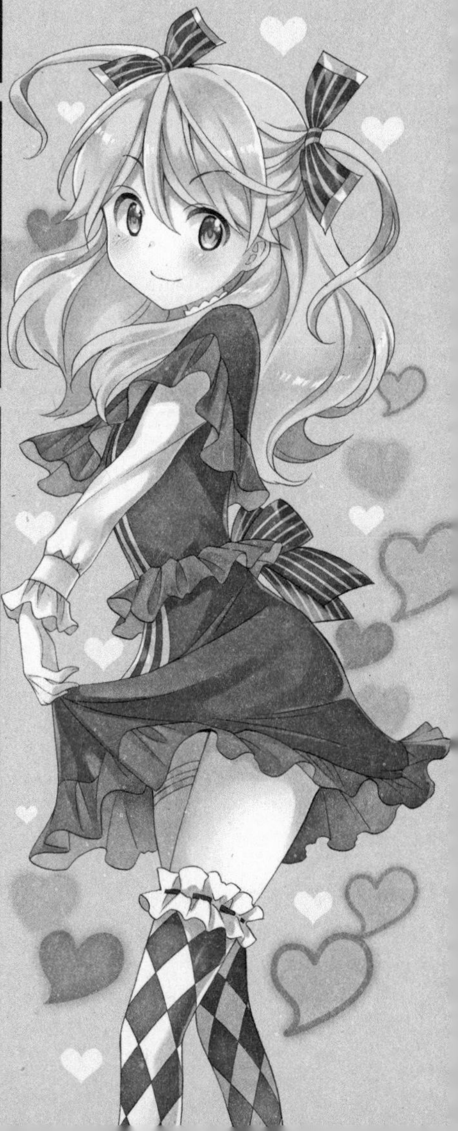

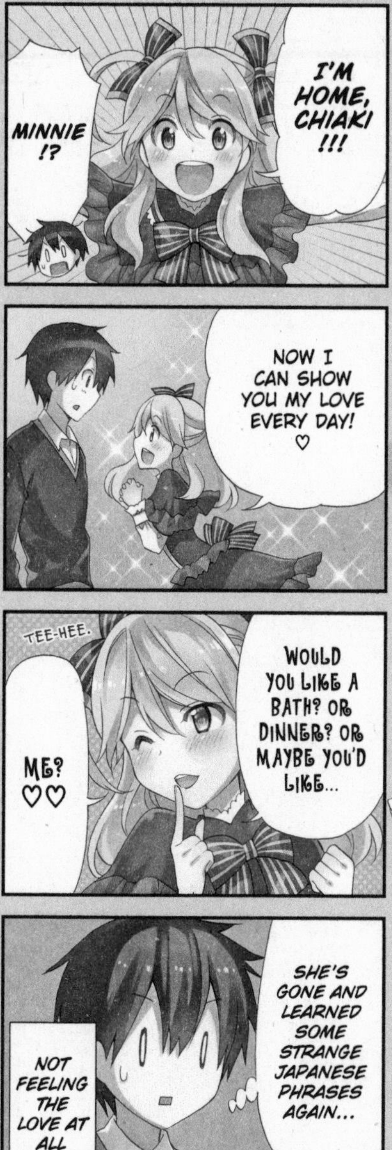
I'M HOME, CHIAKI!!!
MINNIE!?
NOW I CAN SHOW YOU MY LOVE EVERY DAY! ♡
WOULD YOU LIKE A BATH? OR DINNER? OR MAYBE YOU'D LIKE...
TEE-HEE.
ME? ♡♡
SHE'S GONE AND LEARNED SOME STRANGE JAPANESE PHRASES AGAIN...
NOT FEELING THE LOVE AT ALL

MASK

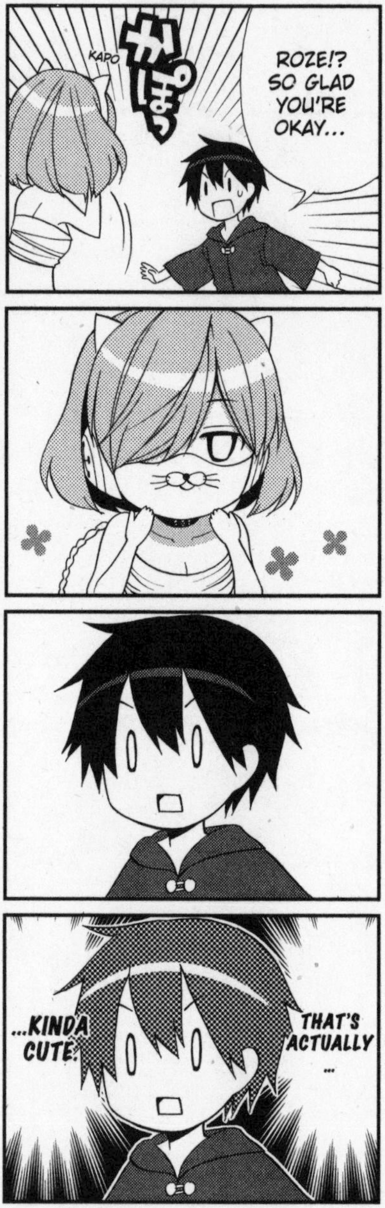
ROZE!? SO GLAD YOU'RE OKAY...
かぽっ
KAPO
THAT'S ACTUALLY ...
...KINDA CUTE.

INSENSITIVE

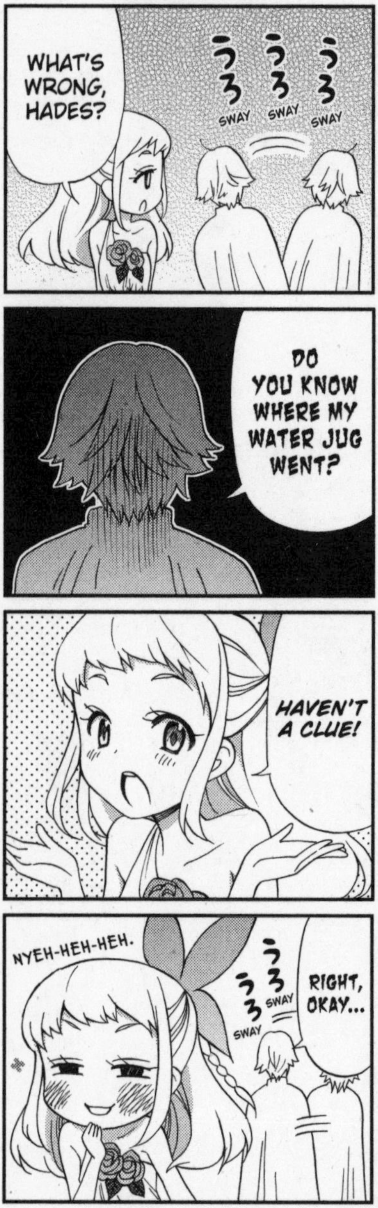
うろ
SWAY
うろ
SWAY
うろ
SWAY
WHAT'S WRONG, HADES?
DO YOU KNOW WHERE MY WATER JUG WENT?
HAVEN'T A CLUE!
RIGHT, OKAY...
うろ
SWAY
うろ
SWAY
NYEH-HEH-HEH.

THE SECOND NIGHT

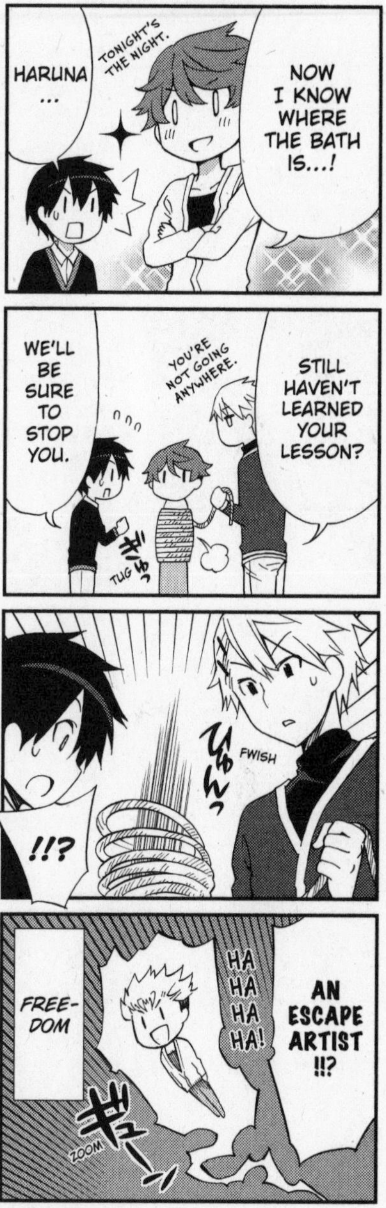
NOW I KNOW WHERE THE BATH IS...!
TONIGHT'S THE NIGHT.
HARUNA ...
STILL HAVEN'T LEARNED YOUR LESSON?
YOU'RE NOT GOING ANYWHERE.
WE'LL BE SURE TO STOP YOU.
TUG
FWISH
!!?
AN ESCAPE ARTIST !!?
HA HA HA HA!
FREE-DOM
ZOOM

CONSEQUENCES

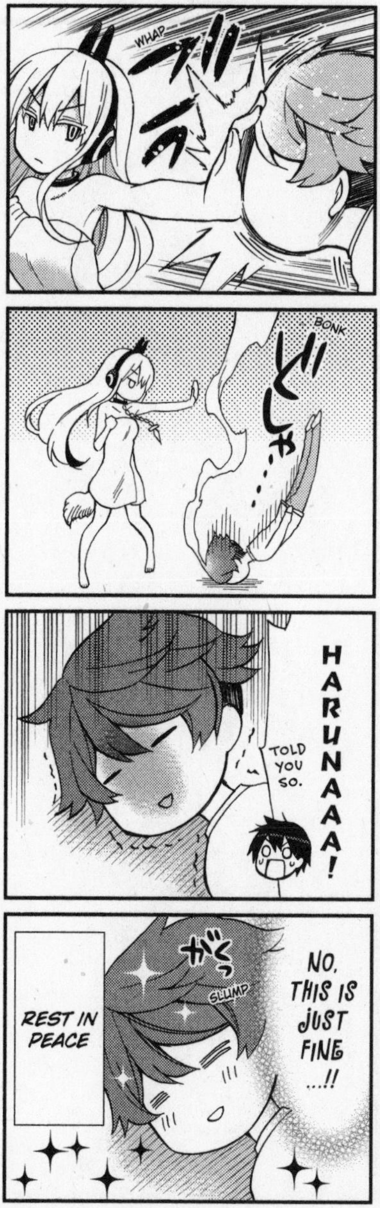
WHAP
BONK
HARUNAAAA!
TOLD YOU SO.
NO, THIS IS JUST FINE ...!!
SLUMP
REST IN PEACE

GROWING UP?

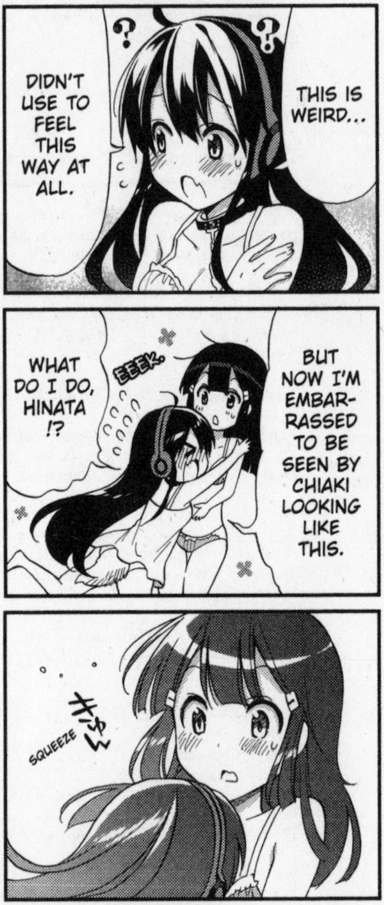
THIS IS WEIRD...
DIDN'T USE TO FEEL THIS WAY AT ALL.
BUT NOW I'M EMBARRASSED TO BE SEEN BY CHIAKI LOOKING LIKE THIS.
EEEK.
WHAT DO I DO, HINATA!?
SQUEEZE
KURO-CHAN... YOU'RE FINALLY LIKE A REAL GIRL. HOW CUTE ...!!
GYAAAH!
?

GIRLISH TROUBLES

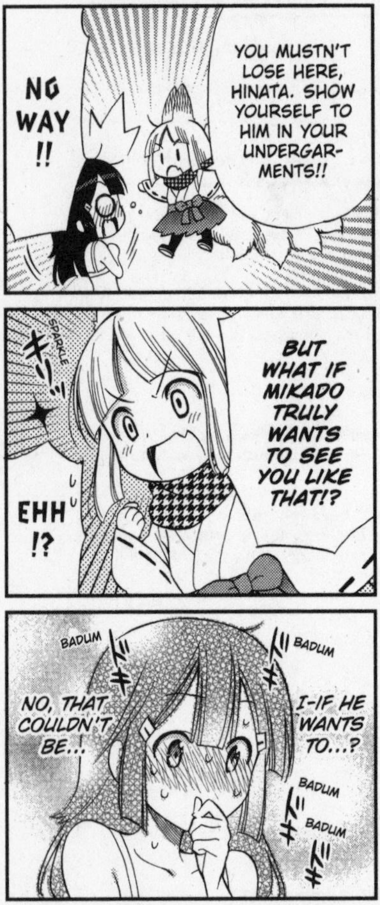
YOU MUSTN'T LOSE HERE, HINATA. SHOW YOURSELF TO HIM IN YOUR UNDERGARMENTS!!
NO WAY !!
BUT WHAT IF MIKADO TRULY WANTS TO SEE YOU LIKE THAT!?
SPARKLE
EHH !?
BADUM
I-IF HE WANTS TO...?
BADUM
BADUM
BADUM
NO, THAT COULDN'T BE...
JUST GIVE HIM A TASTE!!
TUG
NO, WAIT. I CAN'T DO IT AFTER ALL!!

STAFF ANALOG-> MORI, YUU JUNA, MASAYA
DIGITAL-> WATARI NI FUNE
COLOR LAYERING-> TSUBASA FUKUCHI

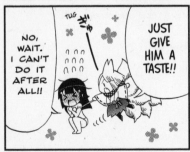

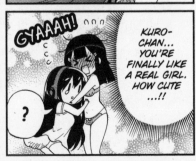

TODAY'S CERBEROS 8

Ato Sakurai

Translation: Caleb Cook • **Lettering: Bianca Pistillo**

TODAY'S KERBEROS Vol. 8 ©2016 Ato Sakurai/SQUARE ENIX CO., LTD. First published in Japan in 2016 by SQUARE ENIX CO., LTD. English translation rights arranged with SQUARE ENIX CO., LTD. and Yen Press, LLC through Tuttle-Mori Agency, Inc.

English translation ©2018 by SQUARE ENIX CO., LTD.

Yen Press
1290 Avenue of the Americas
New York, NY 10104

Visit us at yenpress.com
facebook.com/yenpress
twitter.com/yenpress
yenpress.tumblr.com
instagram.com/yenpress

First Yen Press Edition: April 2018
The chapters in this volume were originally published as ebooks by Yen Press.

Yen Press is an imprint of Yen Press, LLC.
The Yen Press name and logo are trademarks of Yen Press, LLC.

Library of Congress Control Number: 2016946072

ISBNs: 978-1-9753-0023-4 (paperback)
       978-1-9753-0024-1 (ebook)

10 9 8 7 6 5 4 3 2 1

WOR

Printed in the United States of America